Lecture Notes in Computer Science 10725

Commenced Publication in 1973
Founding and Former Series Editors:
Gerhard Goos, Juris Hartmanis, and Jan van Leeuwen

Editorial Board

More information about this series at http://www.springer.com/series/7407

Marian Gheorghe · Grzegorz Rozenberg
Arto Salomaa · Claudio Zandron (Eds.)

Membrane Computing

18th International Conference, CMC 2017
Bradford, UK, July 25–28, 2017
Revised Selected Papers

 Springer

Editors
Marian Gheorghe
University of Bradford
Bradford
UK

Grzegorz Rozenberg
Leiden University
Leiden
The Netherlands

Arto Salomaa
Turku Centre for Computer Science
Turku
Finland

Claudio Zandron
University of Milan-Bicocca
Milan
Italy

ISSN 0302-9743   ISSN 1611-3349   (electronic)
Lecture Notes in Computer Science
ISBN 978-3-319-73358-6   ISBN 978-3-319-73359-3   (eBook)
https://doi.org/10.1007/978-3-319-73359-3

Library of Congress Control Number: 2017962884

LNCS Sublibrary: SL1 – Theoretical Computer Science and General Issues

Printed on acid-free paper

This Springer imprint is published by Springer Nature
The registered company is Springer International Publishing AG
The registered company address is: Gewerbestrasse 11, 6330 Cham, Switzerland

Preface

This volume contains the invited contributions and a selection of papers presented at the 18th International Conference on Membrane Computing (CMC 18), which was held in Bradford, UK, during July 25–28, 2017 (further information can be found on the website at the following address: http://computing.brad.ac.uk/cmc18/), as well as one selected paper from the Asian Conference on Membrane Computing (ACMC 2017), which was held in Chengdu, China, during September 21–25, 2017 (website address: http://2017.asiancmc.org/).

The CMC series started with three workshops that were organized in Curtea de Argeş, Romania, in 2000, 2001 and 2002. The workshops were then held in Tarragona, Spain (2003), Milan, Italy (2004), Vienna, Austria (2005), Leiden, The Netherlands (2006), Thessaloniki, Greece (2007), and in Edinburgh, UK (2008).

The 10th edition was organized again in Curtea de Argeş, in August 2009, where it was decided to continue the series as the Conference on Membrane Computing (CMC). The following editions were held in Jena, Germany (2010), Fontainebleau, France (2011), Budapest, Hungary (2012), Chişinău, Moldova (2013), Prague, Czech Republic (2014), Valencia, Spain (2015), and Milan, Italy (2016).

A regional version of CMC, the Asian Conference on Membrane Computing, ACMC, started in 2012 in Wuhan (China), and continued in Chengdu, China (2013), Coimbatore, India (2014), Hefei, Anhui, China (2015), and Bangi, Selangor, Malaysia (2016).

CMC 18 was organized under the auspices of the International Membrane Computing Society and by the Modelling, Testing and Verification Research Group, School of Electrical Engineering and Computer Science, the University of Bradford, UK.

CMC 18 consisted of two parts: standard sessions, held from Tuesday to Thursday, and an interaction day between participants, held on Friday. Monday was the arrival day for most of the participants. The standard sessions included invited lectures given by Erzsébet Csuhaj-Varjú (Budapest, Hungary), Harold Fellermann (Newcastle, UK), Michael Fessing (Bradford, UK), and Maciej Koutny (Newcastle, UK).

The Best Student Paper Award, sponsored by Springer, was given to the paper "Generalized P Colony Automata and Their Relation to P automata," by Kristóf Kántor and György Vaszil.

The editors express their gratitude to the Program Committee, the invited speakers, the authors of the papers, the reviewers, and all the participants for their contributions to the success of CMC 18. The support of the School of Electrical Engineering and Computer Science of the University of Bradford and the Prize for the Best Student Paper award granted by Springer are gratefully acknowledged.

November 2017

Marian Gheorghe
Grzegorz Rozenberg
Arto Salomaa
Claudio Zandron

Organization

CMC and ACMC Steering Committee

Henry Adorna	Quezon City, Philippines
Artiom Alhazov	Chişinău, Moldova
Bogdan Aman	Iaşi, Romania
Matteo Cavaliere	Edinburgh, UK
Erzsébet Csuhaj-Varjú	Budapest, Hungary
Rudolf Freund	Vienna, Austria
Marian Gheorghe (Honorary Member)	Bradford, UK
Thomas Hinze	Jena, Germany
Florentin Ipate	Bucharest, Romania
Shankara N. Krishna	Bombay, India
Alberto Leporati	Milan, Italy
Taishin Y. Nishida	Toyama, Japan
Linqiang Pan (Co-chair)	Wuhan, China
Gheorghe Păun (Honorary Member)	Bucharest, Romania
Mario J. Pérez-Jiménez	Seville, Spain
Agustín Riscos-Núñez	Seville, Spain
Petr Sosík	Opava, Czech Republic
Kumbakonam Govindarajan Subramanian	Penang, Malaysia
György Vaszil	Debrecen, Hungary
Sergey Verlan	Paris, France
Claudio Zandron (Co-chair)	Milan, Italy
Gexiang Zhang	Chengdu, China

CMC 18 Organizing Committee

Marian Gheorghe (Co-chair)	Bradford, UK
Savas Konur (Co-chair)	Bradford, UK
Raluca Lefticaru (Communication Chair)	Bradford, UK
Daniel Neagu (Publicity Chair)	Bradford, UK

CMC 18 Program Committee

Henry Adorna	Quezon City, Philippines
Artiom Alhazov	Chişinău, Moldova
Bogdan Aman	Iaşi, Romania

Lucie Ciencialová	Opava, Czech Republic
Erzsébet Csuhaj-Varjú	Budapest, Hungary
Giuditta Franco	Verona, Italy
Rudolf Freund	Vienna, Austria
Marian Gheorghe (Co-chair)	Bradford, UK
Thomas Hinze	Jena, Germany
Florentin Ipate	Bucharest, Romania
Shankara N. Krishna	Bombay, India
Alberto Leporati	Milan, Italy
Vincenzo Manca	Verona, Italy
Giancarlo Mauri	Milan, Italy
Radu Nicolescu	Auckland, New Zealand
Linqiang Pan	Wuhan, China
Gheorghe Păun	Bucharest, Romania
Mario J. Pérez–Jiménez	Seville, Spain
Antonio E. Porreca	Milan, Italy
Agustín Riscos-Núñez	Seville, Spain
José M. Sempere	Valencia, Spain
Petr Sosík	Opava, Czech Republic
György Vaszil	Debrecen, Hungary
Sergey Verlan	Paris, France
Claudio Zandron (Co-chair)	Milan, Italy
Gexiang Zhang	Chengdu, China

Additional Reviewer

Luca Manzoni	Milan, Italy

Invited Talks

Simple and Small: On Two Concepts in P Systems Theory (Extended Abstract)

Erzsébet Csuhaj-Varjú

Department of Algorithms and Their Applications,
Faculty of Informatics, ELTE Eötvös Loránd University,
Pázmány Péter sétány 1/c, Budapest, 1117, Hungary
csuhaj@inf.elte.hu

In membrane computing, a lot of research has been devoted to the computational power of different variants of P systems, with special emphasis put on models with restricted size. It has been shown that several types of membrane systems even with limited size are very powerful, in some cases as powerful as Turing machines. Usually, the considered size parameters were the number of cells (compartments or nodes), the size and the number of rules in the component cells, the number of (distinguished) symbols of the P system or that of its components, even the size of the P system as a whole, represented by a word: all of them are standard static size complexity parameters of computing devices. Investigations in some well-known variants of P systems like standard symbol-object P systems, symport/antiport P systems, generalized communicating P systems, P colonies exemplify these approaches and results (see [3, 6, 8]).

Although mainly static size complexity parameters have been in the focus of interest, dynamic parameters, i.e. size parameters under functioning are important characteristics as well since they provide information on the use of the static structure of the P system. That is, the change of (maximum, minimum) number of cells, the (maximum, minimum) number of executed rules or rule types, the (maximal, minimal) number of (distinguished) symbols under functioning describe properties of the behaviour of the membrane system. This problem area still has a lot of open questions.

P systems can also be considered as models of biological complex systems and modeling tools for biological phenomena at the cell and tissue level. From this aspect, the concept small may obtain new interpretation. Can we state that small as a notion has biological relevance? Is a cell small? Can a tissue be considered small? These questions motivate us to define the concept of a small P system that also incorporates the relation of the P system and its environment. From this point of view, those parameters are particularly interesting which describe the relation of the size (some size parameter) of the P system and that of the environment available or observable for its components. (Notice that in case of certain P system variants the environment is generated or will be available step by step; see, for example [1, 2].)

Simple as a term can also play important role in P systems theory. Several approaches to this concept can be considered, starting from syntactic simplicity to simplicity in functioning. Structural simplicity, among others, may refer to the mutual relations of the constituents of the membrane system. Can a P system be obtained from some basic P systems by some elementary operations? If this is the case, what can we say about the minimal (optimal) number of these operations? We may consider operations like merge, separation, release, division; see for other operations [8]. Composition and transmission are also important: we may generate P system classes from a finite set of very simple P systems [7]. In the literature, we find several examples for P systems obtained from some basic types of P systems by some operations or mappings (for example, kernel P systems [5], networks of cells [4]). One other approach to simplicity is the so-called functional simplicity, i.e., cases where the P systems or their components are able to perform only one type of functional activities (for example, P colonies, see [3]). Determining P systems which consist of functionally simple components (ingredients) would imply useful conclusions on the computational process and also on the efficiency of these P systems in problem solving.

In our talk, we analyzed some important P system models from the point of view of being small and attempted to provide some general conditions that a P system should satisfy to be called simple. We also discussed the limits of using such simple P systems as computing devices. We concluded that simple and small are important general concepts in P systems theory, investigations in descriptional complexity of membrane systems are essential research directions. However, to define proper concepts and measures, in addition to aspects of computability, biological relevance should also be considered.

This work was supported by the National Research, Development, and Innovation Office - NKFIH, Hungary, Grant no. K 120558.

References

1. Balaskó, Á., Csuhaj-Varjú, E., Vaszil, G.: Dynamically changing environment for generalized communicating p systems. In: Rozenberg, G., et al. (eds.) CMC 2016. LNCS, vol. 9504, pp. 92–105. Springer, Switzerland (2015)
2. Ciencialová, L., Cienciala, L., Sosk, P.: P colonies with evolving environment. In: Leporati, A., et al. (eds.) CMC 2017. LNCS, vol. 1015, pp. 105–118. Springer, Switzerland (2016)
3. Ciencialová, L., Csuhaj-Varjú, E., Cienciala, L., Sosík, P.: P colonies. Bull. Int. Membrane Comput. Soc. **2**, 129–156 (2016)
4. Freund, R., Verlan, S.: A formal framework for static (tissue) p systems. In: Eleftherakis, G., et al. (eds.) WMC 2008. LNCS, vol. 4860, pp. 271–284. Springer, Berlin (2007)
5. Gheorghe, M., Ipate, F.: A kernel p systems survey. In: Alhazov, A., et al. (eds.) CMC 2013. LNCS, vol. 8340, pp. 1–9. Springer, Berlin (2014)
6. Gheorghe, M., Păun, G., Pérez-Jiménez, M.-J., Rozenberg, G.: Research frontiers of membrane computing: open problems and research topics. Int. J. Found. Comp. Sci. **24**(5), 547–624 (2013)
7. Long, H., Fu, Y.: A general approach for building combinational p automata. Int. J. Comput. Math. **84**(12), 1715–1730 (2007)
8. Păun, G., Rozenberg, G., Salomaa, A.: The Oxford Handbook of Membrane Computing. Oxford University Press, Inc., New York (2010)

Petri Net Based Synthesis of Tissue Systems

Maciej Koutny

School of Computing, Newcastle University,
1 Science Square, Newcastle upon Tyne, NE4 5TG, UK

Tissue systems, generalising membrane systems, are a computational model inspired by the functioning of living cells. In particular, they reflect the way in which chemical reactions take place in cells and molecules move from one compartment to another [4, 14]. Reactions are represented by evolution rules that specify which and how many molecules can be produced from given molecules of a certain kind and quantity. Membrane systems model the computational and communication processes within a single cell divided by membranes into compartments; rules belong to compartments and the molecules that are produced either remain in the compartment or can be delivered to a neighbouring (i.e., enclosed or surrounding) compartment. Hence a membrane system has an associated tree-like structure describing the connections that can be used for the transport of molecules. This is generalised in tissue structures to arbitrary graphs allowing communication along all edges. The nodes of the graph associated with a tissue system represent, e.g., cells in a tissue, and the edges are the channels along which molecules are passed. Both membrane and tissue systems are essentially multiset rewriting systems with their dynamic aspects including potential behaviour (computations), deriving from their evolution rules. Consequently, they are similar to Petri nets. In particular, there is a canonical way of translating membrane systems into Petri nets with transitions corresponding to evolution rules [10]. This translation is faithful in the sense that it relates computation steps at the lowest level and induces in a natural way extensions and interpretations of Petri net structure and behaviour. The membrane structure is translated into *localities* associated with transitions. The locality of a transition represents the compartment to which the corresponding evolution rule belongs. The localities of transitions make it possible to define a *locally maximal* step semantics in addition to the more common sequential semantics and (maximal) step semantics. Locally maximal steps model localised synchronised pulses with maximal concurrency restricted to compartments.

Petri nets are a well-established general model for distributed computation [5, 6, 15] with an extensive range of tools and methods for construction, analysis, and verification of concurrent systems. The strong semantical link between the two models invites to extend existing Petri net techniques, bringing them to the domain of membrane systems. An example is the process semantics of Petri nets that can help to understand the dynamics and causality in the biological evolutions represented by membrane systems [8, 10]. More details on the relationship between Petri nets and membrane systems can be found in, e.g., [7, 11].

This talk will focus on the synthesis problem understood as the problem of the algorithmic construction of a system from a specification of its observed or desired behaviour. Automated synthesis from behavioural specifications is an attractive and powerful way of constructing correct concurrent systems [1–3, 13]. The paper [9] considered the synthesis of membrane systems from (step) transition systems, and the paper [12] discussed the same problem for membrane systems. Both papers demonstrated how a solution to the synthesis problem of Petri nets, based on the notion of regions of a transition system, leads to a method for the automated synthesis of membrane systems. The talk will show how the synthesis problem for tissue systems (with locally maximal concurrency) can be solved when the tissue structure of the system to be constructed is given together with the step transition system. Following this, a method for extending the basic solution to cope with situations when the structure of the target tissue system has to be constructed will be presented.

Acknowledgement. This talk is based on research conducted in collaboration with Jetty Kleijn, Marta Pietkiewicz-Koutny, and Grzegorz Rozenberg.

References

1. Badouel, E., Darondeau, P.: Theory of regions. In: Part I of [15], pp. 529–586
2. Darondeau, P., Koutny, M., Pietkiewicz-Koutny, M., Yakovlev, A.: Synthesis of nets with step firing policies. Fundamenta Informaticae. **94**, 275–303 (2009)
3. Ehrenfeucht, A., Rozenberg, G.: Partial (set) 2-structures. Acta Informatica **27**, 315–368 (1989)
4. Păun, G., Rozenberg, G., Salomaa A. (eds.): The Oxford Handbook of Membrane Computing. Oxford University Press (2010)
5. Koch, I., Reisig, W., Schreiber F. (eds.): Modeling in Systems Biology — The Petri Net Approach. Springer, London (2010)
6. Jensen, K., van der Aalst, W.M.P., Balbo, G., Koutny, M., Wolf, K. (eds.): Transactions on Petri Nets and Other Models of Concurrency VII (2013)
7. Kleijn, J., Koutny, M.: Petri nets and membrane computing. In: [4], pp. 389–412
8. Kleijn, J., Koutny, M.: Processes of membrane systems with promoters and inhibitors. Theoret. Comput. Sci. **404**, 112–126 (2008)
9. Kleijn, J., Koutny, M., Pietkiewicz-Koutny, M., Rozenberg, G.: Membrane systems and petri net synthesis. MeCBIC. EPTCS **100**, 1–13 (2012)
10. Kleijn, J., Koutny, M., Rozenberg, G.: Process semantics for membrane systems. J. Automata, Lang. Comb. **11**, 321–340 (2006)
11. Kleijn, J., Koutny, M., Rozenberg, G.: Petri nets for biologically motivated computing. Sci. Ann. Comput. Sci. **21**, 199–225 (2011)
12. Kleijn, J., Koutny, M., Pietkiewicz-Koutny, M.: Tissue systems and Petri net synthesis. In: Transactions on Petri Nets and Other Models of Concurrency IX, pp. 124–146 (2014)
13. Kleijn, J., Koutny, M., Pietkiewicz-Koutny, M., Rozenberg, G.: Applying regions. Theoret. Comput. Sci. **658**, 205–215 (2017)
14. Păun, G.: Membrane Computing, An Introduction. Springer, Berlin (2002)
15. Reisig, W., Rozenberg, G. (eds.): Lectures on Petri Nets I & II. LNCS, vol. 1491 & 1492. Springer, Berlin (1998)

Contents

Simulating Evolutional Symport/Antiport by Evolution-Communication
and vice versa in Tissue P Systems with Parallel Communication   1
   Henry Adorna, Artiom Alhazov, Linqiang Pan, and Bosheng Song

Hierarchical P Systems with Randomized Right-Hand Sides of Rules   15
   Artiom Alhazov, Rudolf Freund, and Sergiu Ivanov

Controlled Reversibility in Reaction Systems   40
   Bogdan Aman and Gabriel Ciobanu

Multiset Patterns and Their Application to Dynamic Causalities
in Membrane Systems   54
   Roberto Barbuti, Roberta Gori, and Paolo Milazzo

Counting Membrane Systems   74
   Luis Valencia-Cabrera, David Orellana-Martín,
   Agustín Riscos-Núñez, and Mario J. Pérez-Jiménez

APCol Systems with Teams   88
   Lucie Ciencialová, Luděk Cienciala, and Erzsébet Csuhaj-Varjú

Bi-simulation Between P Colonies and P Systems
with Multi-stable Catalysts   105
   Erzsébet Csuhaj-Varjú and Sergey Verlan

Computationally Complete Generalized Communicating P Systems
with Three Cells   118
   Erzsébet Csuhaj-Varjú and Sergey Verlan

Event-Based Life in a Nutshell: How Evaluation of Individual Life Cycles
Can Reveal Statistical Inferences Using Action-Accumulating P Systems   129
   Thomas Hinze and Benjamin Förster

On Evolution-Communication P Systems with Energy Having Bounded
and Unbounded Communication   151
   Richelle Ann B. Juayong, Nestine Hope S. Hernandez,
   Francis George C. Cabarle, Kelvin C. Buño, and Henry N. Adorna

Generalized P Colony Automata and Their Relation to P Automata   167
   Kristóf Kántor and György Vaszil

Modelling and Validating an Engineering Application
in Kernel P Systems   183
   Raluca Lefticaru, Mehmet Emin Bakir, Savas Konur,
   Mike Stannett, and Florentin Ipate

Solving a Special Case of the P Conjecture Using Dependency Graphs
with Dissolution   196
   Alberto Leporati, Luca Manzoni, Giancarlo Mauri,
   Antonio E. Porreca, and Claudio Zandron

Most Common Words – A cP Systems Solution   214
   Radu Nicolescu

Tissue P Systems with Rule Production/Removal   230
   Linqiang Pan, Bosheng Song, and Gexiang Zhang

Reversing Steps in Membrane Systems Computations   245
   G. Michele Pinna

Families of Languages Encoded by SN P Systems   262
   José M. Sempere

On the Robust Power of Morphogenetic Systems for Time
Bounded Computation   270
   Petr Sosík, Vladimír Smolka, Jan Drastík, Jaroslav Bradík,
   and Max Garzon

Author Index   293

Simulating Evolutional Symport/Antiport by Evolution-Communication and vice versa in Tissue P Systems with Parallel Communication

Henry Adorna[1,2], Artiom Alhazov[1,3(✉)], Linqiang Pan[1,4], and Bosheng Song[1]

[1] Key Laboratory of Image Information Processing and Intelligent Control
of Education Ministry of China, School of Automation,
Huazhong University of Science and Technology, Wuhan 430074, China
lqpan@mail.hust.edu.cn, boshengsong@hust.edu.cn
[2] Department of Computer Science (Algorithm and Complexity),
University of the Philippines Diliman, 1101 Quezon City, Philippines
hnadorna@dcs.upd.edu.ph
[3] Institute of Mathematics and Computer Science Academy of Science of Moldova,
Academiei 5, 2028 Chişinău, Moldova
artiom@math.md
[4] School of Electric and Information Engineering,
Zhengzhou University of Light Industry, Zhengzhou 450002, China

Abstract. We aim to compare functionality of symport/antiport with embedded rewriting to that of symport/antiport accompanied by rewriting, by two-way simulation, in case of tissue P systems with parallel communication. A simulation in both directions with constant slowdown is constructed.

Keywords: Membrane computing · Evolution-communication
Evolutional symport/antiport · Simulation

1 Introduction

Membrane systems with symbol-objects are a theoretical framework of parallel distributed multiset processing. Its two essential features are rewriting (also sometimes called evolution) and communication. One extreme case is using rewriting alone, then in the non-cooperative case the computational power is rather weak, while cooperation of two symbols already leads to the computational completeness. To use distributivity, some mechanism of passing information between regions is necessary, and moving objects is most natural choice.

The second extreme case is using communication alone: moving objects without creating, destroying or modifying them. In one of the most studied models the rules are called symport/antiport rules, respectively if objects are moved across a membrane or channel in one/both directions. Clearly, without creating objects, for being able to use more symbols in the computation and/or result

© Springer International Publishing AG 2018
M. Gheorghe et al. (Eds.): CMC 2017, LNCS 10725, pp. 1–14, 2018.
https://doi.org/10.1007/978-3-319-73359-3_1

than there are initially in the system, some unbounded source of them is needed, e.g. the environment. Note that communication rules across the skin membrane can do the same work as rewriting rules do. It follows that already with a single membrane, communication rules involving up to three objects is already enough for computational completeness, while further restricting rules makes the second membrane necessary, and the proof become much more complicated.

The historically first model of membrane computing is the transitional one: communication is embedded into rewriting by target indications for objects in the right hand side of rules. While not increasing the computational power, it brings additional benefits from the structure, for example, generating languages is considered.

A different approach is to allow both rewriting (which may be restricted to be non-cooperative) and communication rules (no longer needing unbounded object supply in the environment). The model is called evolution-communication. It allows computational completeness constructions already with communication rules of up to two objects, and the proofs are simpler than in pure symport/antiport case.

Finally, a model embedding rewriting into communication rule has been recently introduced in [9], called evolutional symport/antiport. It has been shown to either reach the computational completeness or efficiency (i.e., solving intractable problems in polynomial number of steps) with smaller bounds on the size of rules, or improve existing symport/antiport results due to a more refined complexity measure, accounting for both the number of reactants and number of products.

Overall in the literature on membrane computing, a huge number of results are those establishing computational completeness of some model or variant by simulating another model, which is usually sequential. However, simulating P systems (except the classes P systems having considerably less power than the computational completeness) by something (significantly different P systems or completely different models of computation) are much more rare, and one of the reasons for it is immediate: implementing maximal parallelism itself is considerably more tedious than establishing the computational completeness. We can mention two example appearing in the literature: simulating a two-membrane proton pumping system (a special particular case of evolution-communication P system) with one proton by a P system with one bi-stable catalyst [1] and simulating spiking neural P systems with delays by those without delays [2]. However, the first one is a one-way simulation, and the latter is a simulation staying within the same model. Imagine that requiring the slowdown to be bounded by a constant would pose a significant additional difficulty. Yet, this is the kind of question to be addressed in this paper.

There was a discussion about how evolution-communication relates with evolutional symport/antiport; even though both models are known to be computationally complete, the proofs are rather different. Hence, it presents an interest to simulate by one model the **process** of computation in the other model and vice versa. To keep simulation transparent and "nice," we impose a condition that the simulation slowdown must be (limited by a) constant, and the configurations of the simulated system should be obtainable from the configurations of the simulating system in some easy way, e.g., a morphism. Note that we allow the simulation to be incorrect, as long as the corresponding computation of the simulating system is not halting. As it will be clear later, it is easily decidable which steps of simulation are incorrect, e.g., by checking for appearance of the special symbol #.

We should note that due to the nature of the problem, we assume two features of the models: tissue structure and parallel communication; we now explain the reasons for that. First, in evolution-communication model objects may be massively renamed in parallel; to be able to simulate this with a constant slowdown, communication rules must also be applicable in a massively parallel way. Second, without the tissue structure it would be very difficult to synchronize evolution with communication. Indeed, in pure symport systems the information is propagated such that the signal would return to the same region in even number of steps, while it could reach the neighboring region in odd number of steps. Using antiport, circumventing this problem does not seem easy either, since we assume the rules my be simulated in massively parallel way.

This paper is organized as follows: the necessary definitions are given, then some easy cases of the problem formulation are solved. Next, evolution-communication P systems are simulated by evolutional symport/antiport. The converse direction in general is more involved. After some preliminary arguments, the solution is incrementally constructed. First, the case of simulating one rule without idle objects is solved, also handling incorrect assignment of objects to rules. Second, idle objects are handled, also verifying the maximality of parallelism. Third, halting is approached within the same model. Finally, a complete solution is given in tables in the end of the paper. Having accomplished the goal and formulated the results, we give concluding remarks.

2   Definitions

This paper will be dealing with simulating evolution, and communication rules within the framework of tissue P systems with parallel communication. In particular, the well known evolution-communication rules are compared to the so-called evolutional symport/antiport rule introduced in [9]. We provide here only essential definitions that would be needed in the development of the result.

The basic P system structure that we will consider in doing simulations in both direction is the so-called tissue P systems, first considered in [8]. We now recall their definition, keeping in mind that we do not use states of cells, that the membrane channels can be easily deduced from the rules, and that the set of symport/antiport rules (evolutional or not) is global.

We denote k-th symbol of string u, $1 \leq k \leq |u|$, by $u[k]$.

Definition 1. Tissue P Systems [8] *A tissue P system or tP system, of degree* $m \geq 1$, *is a construct*

$$\Pi = (O, w_1, w_1, \ldots, w_m, R, i_{out}),$$

where:

1. O is a finite non-empty alphabet (of objects);
2. $i_{out} \in \{1, 2, \ldots, m\}$ indicates the output cell;
3. w_i specifies the initial multiset of objects in cell i, $1 \le i \le m$;
4. R is a finite set of rules.

Before proceeding with formal definition of rules, we would like to recall some notations existing in the literature. First of all, the most general case of distributed rewriting was introduced in the model called *network of cells*, [4]. Omitting permitting and forbidden conditions (not needed for the scope of this paper) and interchanging region and multiset for better readability, we obtain form

$$(1, u_1) \cdots (n, u_n) \;\rightarrow\; (1, v_1) \cdots (n, v_n),$$

meaning for every region i, multiset u_i is consumed, and for every region i, multiset v_i is produced.

Traditionally in membrane computing, rewriting rules were defined for every region i as a set R_i of rules of form $u \rightarrow v$, corresponding to $(i, u) \rightarrow (i, v)$ in the network of cells model. Here, we prefer to have a single set of rules, and use a short notation $(i, u \rightarrow v)$; we may still write $u \rightarrow v$ if there is a single working region in a membrane system.

For symport/antiport rules in the evolution–communication model [3], the following notations were used: (u, in), (v, out), $(v, out; u, in)$, and such rules were grouped in sets R_i' corresponding to moving across membrane i. When considering symport/antiport rules for the tissue structure, a single set of rules is defined, and rules have forms (i, u, j) and $(i, u/v, j)$, corresponding to $(i, u) \rightarrow (j, u)$ and $(i, u)(j, v) \rightarrow (i, v)(j/u)$ in the network of cells model, respectively. We recall that by (i, u, j) we mean from cell i a multiset of objects represented by u is sent to cell j; and $(i, u/v, j)$ means that cell i brings u to cell j, while cell j brings v to cell i at the same time.

Finally, evolutional symport/antiport is a generalization of symport/antiport where the multisets that are moved between cells may also be modified: $[u]_i[\,]_j \rightarrow [\,]_i[u']_j$ corresponds to $(i, u) \rightarrow (j, u')$ in the network of cells model, and $[u]_i[v]_j \rightarrow [v']_i[u']_j$ corresponds to $(i, u)(j, v) \rightarrow (i, v')(j, u')$ in the network of cells model. In the rest of the paper we use the network of cells notation for these rules. We now continue with definitions.

Definition 2. Evolution-Communication Rules

1. **Evolution rule:** $r : (i, a \rightarrow u)$, where $a \in O$ and $u \in O^*$. Rule r is non-cooperative.
2. **Symport rule:** (i, u, j), where u represents a multiset of symbols from O. The **length** of a symport rule is equal to $|u|$.
3. **Antiport rule:** $(i, u/v, j)$, where u and v represent multisets of symbols from O. The **length** of an antiport rule is equal to $|u| + |v|$.

The following definition is a system with rules introduced in [9] via the following P system variant, excluding cell division:

Definition 3 [9]. *A* **tissue** *P* *system (of degree $q \geq 1$) with* **evolutional symport/antiport** *rules is a tuple*

$$\Pi = (\Gamma, E, M_1, M_2, \ldots, M_q, R, i_{out}),$$

where

1. *Γ is an alphabet of objects.*
2. *$E \subseteq \Gamma$ is a set of objects initially located in the environment in unboundedly many copies.*
3. *M_i, $1 \leq i \leq q$, is a finite multiset over Γ.*
4. *R is a finite set of evolutional communication rules.*
5. *$i_{out} \in \{1, 2, \ldots, q\}$.*

In our purposes, we explicitly state the evolutional symport/antiport rules as follows:

Definition 4. Evolutional Symport/Antiport Rules [9]

1. **Evolutional symport rules:** $(i, u) \rightarrow (j, u')$, *where* $1 < i \leq q$, $0 < j \leq q$, $i \neq j$; $u \in \Gamma^+$, $u' \in \Gamma^*$ *or* $i = 0$, $1 < j \leq q$; $u \in \Gamma^+$, $u' \in \Gamma^*$, *and if* $i = 0$, *then u contains at least one object $a \in \Gamma \setminus E$;*
2. **Evolutional antiport rules:** $(i, u)(j, v) \rightarrow (i, v')(j, u')$, *where* $0 \leq i \leq q$, $0 \leq j \leq q$, $i \neq j$, $u, v \in \Gamma^+$, $u', v' \in \Gamma^*$.

It is straightforward to see that with evolution (either present besides communication, or embedded into it), the unbounded supply of objects is no longer needed (unlike in pure symport/antiport model), so the environment does not need to be treated as a special reasons. In what follows we do not use the environment; if it is needed for some reason, it can be regarded as a usual cell, and we enumerate cells from 1 to m.

We recall that either model operates in the usual maximally parallel mode: at each step, a non-extendable multiset of rules is chosen and applied. We call an object *idle* if no rule has been assigned to it, and it is carried over to the next configuration unchanged. Clearly, no rule may be applicable to all idle objects.

The typical assumption for tissue P systems is that at most one communication rule may be applied for each channel (i.e., for any unordered pair (i, j) of cells). Throughout this paper we consider tissue P systems *with parallel communication*, meaning that each channel works in the maximally parallel way, similarly to the typical functioning of symport/antiport in cell-like P systems.

Definition 5. Simulation
We say that a rule A is **simulated by** *a set of rules B, if there exists an injective morphism h from configurations of a simulated system into configurations of a simulating system such that for any configuration x, if $A(x)$ denotes the output of applying rule A on x, there exist applications of rules in B, possible taking multiple steps, such that their output $B(h(x))$ on input $h(x)$ equals $h(A(x))$. Moreover, any halting computation of the simulating system starting with $h(x)$ should correspond, in the manner described above, to a halting computation of the simulated system starting with x.*

3   Unrestricted Cases are Easy

It is not hard to see that if rewriting in the evolution-communication model is not required to be non-cooperative, then evolutional symport/antiport can be simulated by rewriting alone. This is a particular case of evolution-communication. The rule of the form $(i, u)(j, v) \rightarrow (i, v')(j, u')$ could be converted into rule of the form $h_i(u)h_j(v) \rightarrow h_i(v')h_j(u')$, where $h_k(a) = a_k$ for $a \in O$, $1 \leq k \leq m$; this procedure appears many times in the literature, and usually referred to as "*flattening*".

Moreover, if we allow the underlying structure of tissue P systems to allow self-loops (note that throughout this paper, we assume that all cells have different labels), then the converse simulation is trivial. Indeed, standard symport/antiport is a particular case of evolutional symport/antiport, while evolution rule $(i, a \rightarrow u)$ would correspond to an evolutional symport rule on a loop: $(i, a) \rightarrow (i, u)$.

In the rest of the paper, we follow standard assumptions: rewriting is restricted to the non-cooperative case, and self-loops are not allowed.

4   Evolution-Communication via Evolutional Symport/Antiport

Theorem 1. *Let Π be a tissue P system with non-cooperative evolution and parallel communication rules. Let $r : (i, a \rightarrow u)$ be a rewriting/evolution rule in Π. Then there exist two evolutional symport/antiport rules that simulate r in two steps.*

Moreover, the simulation needs rules of size at most $1 + |u|$, for a rewriting rule of size $1 + |u|$.

Proof. We use the following two evolutional symport/antiport rules and two cells, namely, i and i' in the simulation. The application of the rules is sequential.

$$(i, a) \rightarrow (i', r), \ (i', r) \rightarrow (i, u).$$

Note that the size of $(i, a \rightarrow u)$ is $1 + |u|$. Clearly, the maximal size of our evolutional symport rules is $|u| + |a| = |u| + 1$.

In the non-trivial case (at least two cells) we may take as i' the first cell different from i, only in the trivial case we need an additional cell.

Although symport/antiport rules are already a particular case of evolutional symport/antiport rules, our goal is a synchronized simulation.

Theorem 2. *Let Π be a tissue P system with non-cooperative evolution and parallel communication rules. Let $r : (i, u, j)$ be a symport rule in Π. Then there exist two evolutional symport rules that simulate r in two steps.*

Moreover, the simulation needs rule of size at most $|u| + 1$ for an antiport rule of size $|u| + 1$.

Proof. The following two evolutional symport/antiport rules simulate r : (i, u, j) :

$$(i, a) \rightarrow (i', r), \ (i', r) \rightarrow (j, u).$$

In the non-trivial case (at least three cells) we may take as i' the first cell different from i and j, only in the trivial case we need an additional cell.

The simulation is done in two steps using two appropriate rules of the simulating system. Also, the simulation needs rule of size at most $|u| + |v| + 2$ for an antiport rule of size $|u| + |v|$.

Theorem 3. *Let Π be a tissue P system with non-cooperative evolution and parallel communication rules. Let $r : (i, u/v, j)$ be an antiport rule in Π. Then there exist two evolutional antiport rules that simulate r in two steps.*

Moreover, the simulation needs rule of size at most $|u| + |v| + 2$ for an antiport rule of size $|u| + |v|$.

Proof. The following two evolutional symport/antiport rules simulate r : $(i, u/v, j)$:

$$(i, u)(j, v) \rightarrow (i, r')(j, r''), \ (i, r')(j, r'') \rightarrow (i, v)(j, u).$$

The simulation is done in two steps using two appropriate rules of the simulating system. Also, the simulation needs rule of size at most $|u| + |v| + 2$ for an antiport rule of size $|u| + |v|$.

5 Evolutional Symport/Antiport via Evolution-Communication

First, we look at the following example, before providing the results of this section:

Example 1. *Consider the following evolutional symport/antiport rules of a particular P system Π below.*

$$(1, ab) \rightarrow (2, x), \ (1, ac) \rightarrow (2, y), \ (1, bc) \rightarrow (2, z),$$

where $a, b, c, x, y, z \in O$.

Let $a^2 b^2 c^2$ be found in cell 1 of Π. Then in a single step, objects $a^2 b^2 c^2$ can be transformed into xyz in cell 2.

Let us try simulating these rules in a P system with evolution-communication rules where evolution rules are restricted to be non-cooperative.

Observation 1. *If we first do communications, then we would have moved $a^2 b^2 c^2$. Since rewriting is non-cooperative, we end up with an even number of copies of all objects. Thus, we fail.*

Observation 2. *Rewriting is also needed after the communication. In the case, when the right hand side of the rule is shorter than that of the left hand side of the rule, before some symbols are removed, the communication rules must verify their correspondence to the other objects of the rule.*

Hence, at least three steps are necessary for the simulation. Since evolution is non-cooperative, non-determinism seems to be unavoidable.

5.1 Simulating a Rule with No Idle Objects

Now consider each rule $r : (i, u)(j, v) \rightarrow (i, v')(j, u')$ of the simulated system.

Assume that the objects at the left hand side of each rule are ordered, that is, given by strings. Then we provide the simulating system with rules $(i, u[k] \rightarrow r_k)$. These rules rewrite objects represented by $u[k]$, for each position k, $1 \leq k \leq |u|$ of string u. Similarly, we provide the simulating system with the same kind of rules, that is, $(j, v[k] \rightarrow r'_k)$, for each k, $1 \leq k \leq |v|$.

In the next step, the simulating system performs the following antiport (communication) rule $(i, r_1 \cdots r_{|u|}/r'_1 \cdots r'_{|v|}, j)$. This rule allows objects $r_1 \cdots r_{|u|}$ and $r'_1 \cdots r'_{|v|}$ to be sent to regions j and i, respectively, in one step.

Finally, the simulating system will do the final rewriting rules in regions i and j to complete the simulation. In particular, we will have $(i, r'_1 \rightarrow v')$ and $(i, r'_k \rightarrow \lambda)$, $2 \leq k \leq |v|$, as well as $(j, r_1 \rightarrow u')$ and $(j, r_k \rightarrow \lambda)$, $2 \leq k \leq |u|$, respectively.

Note that the above construction suffices alone only if the objects are correctly assigned to the rules and no object remains idle.

We summarize this construction as follows:

Proposition 1. *Let Π be a tissue P system with evolutional symport/antiport rules without idle objects appearing in reachable configurations. An evolutional antiport rule can be simulated with evolution-communication (antiport) rules.*

Clearly, evolutional symport can be simulated as a degenerate case of evolutional antiport. We let one of the u or v be empty (string). Thus we have

Corollary 1. *Let Π be some tissue-like P system with evolutional symport/antiport without any object remaining idle.*

Remark 1. To handle objects that are incorrectly assigned to the rules, we add the following trap rules: $(i, r_k \rightarrow \#)$, $(i, \# \rightarrow \#)$ for $1 \leq k \leq |u|$ and $(j, r'_k \rightarrow \#)$, $(j, \# \rightarrow \#)$ for $1 \leq k \leq |v|$.

5.2 Simulations with Idle Objects

Idle objects are those objects in a region or cell that are not supposed to be evolved or communicated yet in a particular moment. These objects must wait until they are allowed to evolve or be communicated by the system, or until the system halts.

Observation 3. *We conclude that in the first simulation step, each object nondeterministically decides between evolving and staying idle. This adds the following rules: $(i, a \rightarrow a_0)$, (i, a_0, i'), $(i', a_0 \rightarrow a)$, (i', a, i), $a \in O$, $1 \leq i \leq m$, where m is the number of cells in the system being simulated and O is its alphabet.*

But the simulated system is not asynchronous, rather it is maximally parallel.

We proceed with the construction that would also verify that the parallelism of applied rule is maximal.

In order to consider maximality of parallelism during the simulation, we use a technique we call *technique of pairs of objects*. In this technique, one of the objects would be used to test the needed condition (such as absence of something), while the other one is for verifying that the first object passed the test. Thus, the rules we had for the idle objects would now be: $(i, a \rightarrow a^{(i)}a_0)$, $(i, a_0 \rightarrow a_1)$, $(i, a^{(i)}a_1, i')$, $(i', a_1 \rightarrow a)$, (i', a, i), $a \in O$, $1 \leq i \leq m$. Note that we could have a rule erasing $a^{(i)}$ in region i', but it is not necessary.

After applying these rules, objects $a^{(i)}$ wait for one step. We use this time to test that no rule should be applicable to the objects that are chosen to be idle: $(i, h^{(i)}(u)/h^{(j)}(v), j)$, where $h^{(k)}(a) = a^{(k)}$, $a \in O$, $1 \leq k \leq m$ define the corresponding morphism.

In the case that there was any applicable rule which was not chosen, we could force to disregard such computation by the following rules: $(j, h^{(i)}(a) \rightarrow \#)$ and $(i, h^{(j)}(a) \rightarrow \#)$.

Note that the simulation of one step for the idle objects takes five steps. To synchronize the simulation of rule applications we add two more steps. Hence, rules $(j, r_1 \rightarrow u')$, $(i, r'_1 \rightarrow v')$ are replaced by $(j, r_1 \rightarrow (u', 2))$, $(i, r'_1 \rightarrow (v', 2))$ where $(\cdot, 2)$ is a morphism naturally defined on O. Also, we add rules $(k, (a, 2) \rightarrow (a, 1))$, $(k, (a, 1) \rightarrow a)$ for $1 \leq k \leq m$, $a \in O$. This ends process of simulation and we summarize it in the following statement:

Theorem 4. *Let Π be a tissue-like P system with evolutional symport/antiport rules with no objects remaining idle. There exist evolution–communication system that handles such idle objects in maximally parallel manner.*

Corollary 2. *There is an evolution-communication system that handles idle objects of a tissue-like P system with evolutional symport/antiport rules.*

Proof. We replace the rules for the idle objects with the following rules: $(i, a \rightarrow a^{(i)}a_0)$, (i, a_0, i'), $(i', a_0 \rightarrow a^{(i)})$, $(1, a^{(i)}/a_1, i')$, $(i, a_1 \rightarrow a)$.

Note that unless the simulated system halts with all the regions being empty, the simulating system never halts.

At this point we would like to mention two "cheating" possibilities to avoid further complexity. The first one is to define for the simulated system, in case of no applicable rules the next configuration to be the same as the current one, and redefine halting as repeating the configuration after a specified number of steps, replacing $(i, \# \rightarrow \#)$ by $(i, \# \rightarrow \#\#)$. The second possibility is to globally produce specific additional objects in simulating the application of rules, erased after one step, and use them as promoters to continue the computation. However, we are interested in staying within the same model: classical definition of maximal parallelism and halting and no additional features.

5.3   To Halt or Not to Halt

So far, in the first step of the simulation, each object had two alternatives; to be used in some rule (possibly having choice between multiple rules), or to stay idle;

with verification that no rule is further applicable to the idle objects and that the rule assignment is correct. Now, these objects should have a third alternative: **to halt.** Indeed, recall that our goal is a simulation with a slowdown by a factor of constant, and the population of objects in unbounded.

On objects choosing between these three alternatives, we need to verify the following additional conditions. First, either all objects choose halting, or none. Second, no rule should be applicable to the "halting" objects. Third, none of the objects should choose to be "idle, but not halting" if no rule is applicable in the whole system.

Observation 4. *The second condition is similar to that for the idle objects. The first one could be implemented by the pairs technique. The third condition is the most difficult. We verify it with the help of one additional control object in the system.*

We proceed by listing the following rules for the simulating system:

Applying a rule:
We replace $(i, u[k] \rightarrow r_k)$ by $(i, u[k] \rightarrow r_k e e_0)$ if $i \neq 1$, and by $(1, u[k] \rightarrow r_k(e, 1))$ if $i = 1$.
Producing witnesses of rule applications throughout the system:
Add rules $(1, (e, 1) \rightarrow e e_0), (i, e, 1), (i, e_0, 1), (1, e_0 \rightarrow e_1), (1, e e_1, 1')$.
Control object:
(will halt)

$$(1, I_0 \rightarrow I_1), (1, I_1 \rightarrow I_2 I), (1, I_2 \rightarrow I_3), (1, I_3 I, 1').$$

(continue the computation)

$$(2, I \rightarrow I_4), (2, I_4, 1), (1, I_3 I_4, 1'), (1', I_4 \rightarrow (I_0, 2)),$$

$$(1', (I_0, 2), 1), (1, (I_0, 2) \rightarrow (I_0, 1)), (1, (I_0, 1) \rightarrow I_0).$$

Notice that object e returns to region 1 from region 2 and moves with an extra object e_1 to region $1'$ by the previous rule.
Checking for absence of "idle but not halting objects."

$$(1, I \rightarrow f^{(1)} f_0^{(1)} \cdots f^{(m)} f_0^{(m)}), (1', f^{(i)}, i), (1', f_0^{(i)}, i),$$

$$(i, f_0^{(i)} \rightarrow f_1^{(i)}, (i, f^{(i)} f_1^{(i)}, 2)$$

will be done in the seventh step of the simulation, in each region i by the idle object $f^{(i)}$.
Idle objects:
Replace $(i, a \rightarrow a^{(i)} a_0)$ by $(i, a \rightarrow a^{(i)} a_{-5})$, adding rules $(i, a_k \rightarrow a_{k+1}, -5 \leq k \leq -1$.
Add rules $(i, a^{(i)} f^{(i)}, 2'), (i, f_1^{(i)} \rightarrow \#)$.
Halting objects:
Add rules $(i, a \rightarrow a_h^{(i)})$.

Checking inapplicability:

$$(i, H^{(i)}(u)/H^{(j)}(v), j), \text{ where } H^{(k)}(a) = a^{(k)}, a \in O, 1 \leq k \leq m,$$

define the corresponding morphisms.

In case there was any additionally applicable rule which was not chosen, rules $(j, H^{(i)}(a) \to \#)$ and $(i, H^{(j)}(a) \to \#)$ will force such computations to be disregarded.

Table 1. Simulation Synchronization Table, $F = f^{(1)}f_0^{(1)} \cdots f^{(m)}f_0^{(m)}$, $G = g^{(1)}g_0^{(1)} \cdots g^{(m)}g_0^{(m)}$

N	Evolve	Idle, not halt	Halting	Control	G	ee_0
1	$(u[k] \to r_k ee_0 G)$ $(i', u[k] \to r_k(e,1)G)$ $(j, v[k] \to r'_k ee_0 G)$ $(j', v[k] \to r'_k(e,1)G)$ $i' = 1 = j', i \neq 1 \neq j$	$(i, a \to a^{(i)}a_{-5}G)$	$(i, a \to a_h^{(i)})$	$(1, I_0 \to I_1)$		
2	$(i, r_1 \cdots r_{|u|}$ $/r'_1 \cdots r'_{|v|}, j)$ $(i, r_k \to \#)$ $(j, r'_k \to \#)$	$(i, a_{-5} \to a_{-4})$ $(i, h^{(i)}(u)$ $/h^{(j)}(v), j)$	$(i, H^{(i)}(u)$ $/H^{(j)}(v), j)$	$(1, I_1$ $\to I_2 I)$	$(i, g^{(k)}, k)$ $(i, g_0^{(k)}, k)$ may be skipped if $i = k$	$(i, e, 1),$ $(i, e_0, 1),$ $i \neq 1$ $(1, (e, 1)$ $\to ee_0)$
3	$(j, r_1 \to (u', 7))$ $(j, r_k \to \lambda),$ $2 \leq k \leq |u|$ $(i, r'_1 \to (v', 7)),$ $(i, r'_k \to \lambda)$ $2 \leq k \leq |v|$ $(k, \# \to \#), k \in \{i, j\}$	$(i, a_{-4} \to a_{-3})$ $(j, a^{(i)} \to \#),$ $i \neq j$	$(j, a_h^{(i)} \to \#)$ $(i, a_h^{(j)} \to \#)$ $i \neq j$	$(1, I_2 \to I_3)$ $(1, eI, 2)$	$(i, g_0^{(i)}$ $\to g_1^{(i)})$ $(i, g^{(i)}a_h^{(i)}, 2')$ may be done 1 step before	$(1, e_0$ $\to e_1)$
4	$(k, (a, 7) \to (a, 6))$ $k \in \{i, j\}$	$(i, a_{-3} \to a_{-2})$		$(1, I_3 I, 1')$ $(2, I \to I_4)$	$(i, g^{(i)}g_1^{(i)}, 2')$ $(i, g_1^{(i)} \to \#)$	$(1, ee_1, 1')$ $(2, e, 1)$
5	$(k, (a, 6) \to (a, 5))$ $k \in \{i, j\}$	$(i, a_{-2} \to a_{-1})$		$(2, I_4, 1)$ $(1', I \to F)$		$(1, ee_1, 1')$

N	Evolve	Idle, not halting	Control	$F = f^{(1)}f_0^{(1)} \cdots f^{(m)}f_0^{(m)}$
6	$(k, (a, 5) \to (a, 4))$ $k \in \{i, j\}$	$(i, a_{-1} \to a_0)$	$(1, I_3 I_4, 1')$	$(1', f^{(i)}, i)$ $(1', f_0^{(i)}, i)$
7	$(k, (a, 4) \to (a, 3))$ $k \in \{i, j\}$	$(i, a_0 \to a_1)$	$(1', I_4 \to (I_0, 2))$	$(i, f_0^{(i)} \to f_1^{(i)})$ $(i, a^{(i)}f^{(i)}, 2')$
8	$(k, (a, 3) \to (a, 2))$ $k \in \{i, j\}$	$(i, a^{(i)}a_1, i')$	$(1', (I_0, 2), 1)$	$(i, f^{(i)}f_1^{(i)}, 2')$ $(i, f_1^{(i)} \to \#)$
9	$(k, (a, 2) \to (a, 1))$ $k \in \{i, j\}$	$(i', a_1 \to a)$	$(1, (I_0, 2) \to (I_0, 1))$	
10	$(k, (a, 1) \to a)$ $k \in \{i, j\}$	(i', a, i)	$(1, (I_0, 1) \to I_0)$	
Res	a	a	I_0	

Checking absence of $a_h^{(i)}$ in regions i by both rule applications and by "idle but not halting" objects:
Add $g^{(1)}g_0^{(1)} \cdots g^{(m)}g_0^{(m)}$ to the right sides of the rules

$$(i, a \rightarrow a^{(i)}a_{-5}), i \neq 1, (i, u[k] \rightarrow r_k ee_0), i \neq 1 \text{ and } (1, u[k] \rightarrow r_k(e, 1)).$$

Add rules

$$(i, g^{(k)}, k), (i, g_0^{(k)}, k), (i, g_0^{(i)} \rightarrow g_1^{(i)}),$$
$$(i, g^{(i)}g_1^{(i)}, 2'), (i, g^{(i)}a_h^{(i)}, 2), (i, g_1^{(i)} \rightarrow \#).$$

Now, if we put together all these rules that we listed for the systems simulating evolutional symport/antiport, see also the simulation synchronization tables, we would have the following results (Table 1):

Theorem 5. *An evolutional symport/antiport rule on a tissue-like P system with parallel communication could be simulated by evolution-communication symport/antiport rule with constant slowdown.*

Finally, we give our main result:

Theorem 6. (Main Results)
In a tissue P system with parallel communication and non-cooperative evolution rules, we have.

1. *An evolutional symport/antiport rule simulates evolution–communication symport/antiport rule.*
2. *An evolutional symport/antiport rule could be simulated by evolution–communication symport/antiport rule.*

   Moreover, the simulation in both directions is with a constant slowdown.

6   Concluding Remarks

We have constructed a simulation of evolutional symport/antiport rule by evolution-communication rules and also, evolution-communication rule being simulated by a system with evolutional symport/antiport rules. We restricted our systems to be tissue P systems with non-cooperative evolution rules and performing parallel communications. The construction is rather challenging and involved, if not very difficult in one direction, but fairly easy in the other direction. Additionally, we presented simulations in both directions with constant slowdown.

We have recalled previous results that provided results relating some model of P systems to another one; transition P systems in evolution–communication P systems with energy [5,6], and transition P Systems in weighted SN P Systems [7], among others. As we have commented earlier, these are mostly one-way simulation of one model by another. These one-way simulations suggests that there is some homomorphism between these P systems involved. And that under this homomorphism, one could investigate the capability of the simulated system with respect to the properties of the simulating systems under such homomorphism.

In this paper, we somehow suggest that we could have a stronger relation with respect to some homomorphism between these systems. However, we focused on simulating rules of the system itself. It may not be hard to notice that corollary to some simulation results reported in the literature, same analysis as we did in this paper, could be obtained from their construction, say in [1,2,5–7], among others.

Our result could spring board some ideas for further investigations:

1. Since we could somehow establish a two-way simulations of rules from different P systems, it might be nice to ask: how could we define the idea of isomorphic P systems?
2. Since we introduce a two-way simulations of rules that allow constant slow-down, could we suggest to have created an idea of a *"reasonable"* reduction scheme for P systems.
3. Since, we have somehow suggested an idea to define "reducibility" in P systems, we might want to realize some complete problems in P systems, also.

Acknowledgments. The work is supported by the National Natural Science Foundation of China (61320106005, 61033003, 61772214, and 61602192), the Innovation Scientists and Technicians Troop Construction Projects of Henan Province (154200510012), and the China Postdoctoral Science Foundation (2016M600592, 2017T100554).

References

1. Alhazov, A.: Number of protons/bi-stable catalysts and membranes in P systems. time-freeness. In: Freund, R., Păun, G., Rozenberg, G., Salomaa, A. (eds.) WMC 2005. LNCS, vol. 3850, pp. 79–95. Springer, Heidelberg (2006). https://doi.org/10.1007/11603047_6
2. Cabarle, F.G.C., Buño, K.C., Adorna, H.N.: Time after time: notes on delays in spiking neural P systems. In: Nishizaki, S., Numao, M., Caro, J., Suarez, M.T. (eds.) PICT 2013, vol. 7. Springer, Tokyo (2013). https://doi.org/10.1007/978-4-431-54436-4_6
3. Cavaliere, M.: Evolution–communication P systems. In: Păun, G., Rozenberg, G., Salomaa, A., Zandron, C. (eds.) WMC 2002. LNCS, vol. 2597, pp. 134–145. Springer, Heidelberg (2003). https://doi.org/10.1007/3-540-36490-0_10
4. Freund, R., Verlan, S.: A formal framework for static (tissue) P systems. In: Eleftherakis, G., Kefalas, P., Păun, G., Rozenberg, G., Salomaa, A. (eds.) WMC 2007. LNCS, vol. 4860, pp. 271–284. Springer, Heidelberg (2007). https://doi.org/10.1007/978-3-540-77312-2_17
5. Juayong, R.A.B, Adorna, H.N.: On simulating cooperative transition P system-sin evolution–communication P systems with energy. Nat. Comput. 1–11 (2016). https://doi.org/10.1007/s11047-016-9589-7

6. Juayong, R.A.B., Adorna, H.N.: Relating computations in non-cooperative transition P systems and evolution-communication P systems with energy. Fundamenta Informaticae **136**(3), 209–217 (2015). https://doi.org/10.3233/FI-2015-1152
7. Juayong, R.A.B., Hernandez, N.H.S., Cabarle, F.G.C., Adorna, H.N.: A simulation of transition P systems in weighted spiking neural P systems. In: Nishizaki, S., et al. (eds.) Proceedings of Workshop on Computation: Theory and Practice 2013, WCTP 2013, pp. 62–78. World Scientific (2014)
8. Martín-Vide, C., Păun, G., Pazos, J., Rodriguez-Patón, A.: Tissue P systems. Theor. Comput. Sci. **296**, 295–326 (2003). https://doi.org/10.1016/S0304-3975(02)00659-X
9. Song, B., Zhang, C., Pan, L.: Tissue-like P systems with evolutional symport/antiport rules. Inf. Sci. **378**, 177–193 (2017). https://doi.org/10.1016/j.ins.2016.10.046

Hierarchical P Systems with Randomized Right-Hand Sides of Rules

Artiom Alhazov[1,2], Rudolf Freund[3], and Sergiu Ivanov[4,5(✉)]

[1] Institute of Mathematics and Computer Science, Academy of Sciences of Moldova,
Academiei 5, 2028 Chişinău, Moldova
artiom@math.md

[2] Key Laboratory of Image Information Processing and Intelligent Control
of Education Ministry of China, School of Automation,
Huazhong University of Science and Technology, Wuhan 430074, China

[3] Faculty of Informatics, TU Wien, Favoritenstraße 9–11, 1040 Vienna, Austria
rudi@emcc.at

[4] LACL, Université Paris Est – Créteil Val de Marne, 61, av. Général de Gaulle,
94010 Créteil, France
sergiu.ivanov@u-pec.fr

[5] TIMC-IMAG/DyCTiM, Faculty of Medicine of Grenoble,
5 avenue du Grand Sablon, 38700 La Tronche, France
sergiu.ivanov@univ-grenoble-alpes.fr

Abstract. P systems are a model of hierarchically compartmentalized multiset rewriting. We introduce a novel kind of P systems in which rules are dynamically constructed in each step by non-deterministic pairing of left-hand and right-hand sides. We define three variants of right-hand side randomization and compare each of them with the power of conventional P systems. It turns out that all three variants enable non-cooperative P systems to generate exponential (and thus non-semi-linear) number languages. We also give a binary normal form for one of the variants of P systems with randomized rule right-hand sides.

1 Introduction

Membrane computing is a research field originally founded by Păun in 1998, see [13]. Membrane systems (also known as P systems) are a model of computing based on the abstract notion of a membrane. Formally, a membrane is treated as a container delimiting a region; a region may contain objects which are acted upon by the rewriting rules associated with the membranes. Quite often, the objects are plain symbols coming from a finite alphabet, but P systems operating on more complex objects (e.g., strings, arrays) are often considered, too, e.g., see [10].

A. Alhazov—The work is supported by National Natural Science Foundation of China (61320106005, 61033003, and 61772214) and the Innovation Scientists and Technicians Troop Construction Projects of Henan Province (154200510012).

© Springer International Publishing AG 2018
M. Gheorghe et al. (Eds.): CMC 2017, LNCS 10725, pp. 15–39, 2018.
https://doi.org/10.1007/978-3-319-73359-3_2

A comprehensive overview of different flavors of membrane systems and their expressive power is given in the handbook which appeared in 2010, see [14]. For a state of the art snapshot of the domain, we refer the reader to the P systems website [17], as well as to the bulletin series of the International Membrane Computing Society [16].

Dynamic evolution of the set of available rules has been considered from the very beginning of membrane computing. Already in 1999, generalized P systems were introduced in [9]; in these systems the membranes, alongside the objects, contain *operators* which act on these objects, while the P system itself acts on the operators, thereby modifying the transformations which will be carried out on the objects in the subsequent steps. Among further ideas on dynamic rules, one may list rule creation [5], activators [1], inhibiting/deinhibiting rules [8], and symport/antiport of rules [7]. One of the more recent developments in this direction are *polymorphic P systems* [3,4,12], in which rules are defined by pairs of membranes, whose contents may be modified by moving objects in or out.

We remark that the previous studies on dynamic rule sets either treated the rules as atomic entities (symport/antiport of rules, operators in generalized P systems), or allowed virtually unlimited possibilities of tampering with their shape (polymorphic P systems). In the present work, we propose a yet different approach which can be seen as an intermediate one.

In *hierarchical P systems with randomized rule-right-hand sides* (or with randomized RHS, for short), the available left-hand sides and right-hand sides of rules are fixed, but the associations between them are *re-evaluated in every step*: a left-hand side may pick a right-hand side arbitrarily (randomly). In Sect. 3, we present three different formal definitions of this intuitive idea of randomized RHS:

1. rules *exchange* their RHS,
2. each rule randomly picks an RHS from a *common* collection of RHS, *shared* between the rules,
3. each rule randomly picks an RHS from a possible collection of *RHS associated with the rule itself.*

P systems with randomized RHS may have a real-world (possibly biological) application for representing systems in a hostile environment. The modifications such P systems effect on their rules may be used to represent perturbations caused by the environment (mutations), somewhat in the spirit of faulty Turing machines (e.g., see [6]).

In this article, we will focus on the expressive power of P systems with randomized RHS, as well as on comparing them to the classical model with or without cooperative rules. One of the central conclusions of the present work is that non-cooperative P systems with randomized RHS can generate *exponential* number languages, thus (partially) surpassing the power of conventional P systems.

This paper is structured as follows. Section 2 recalls some preliminaries about multisets, strings, permutations, as well as conventional P systems. Section 3 defines the three variants of RHS randomization. Section 4 discusses the computational power of the three variants of P systems with randomized RHS. Section 5 shows a binary normal form for one of the variants of P systems with randomized RHS. Finally, Sect. 6 summarizes the results of the article and gives some directions for future work.

2   Preliminaries

In this paper, the set of positive natural numbers $\{1, 2, \dots\}$ is denoted by $\mathbb{N}^+$, the set of natural numbers also containing 0, i.e., $\{0, 1, 2, \dots\}$, is denoted by $\mathbb{N}$. Given $k \in \mathbb{N}^+$, we will call the set $\mathbb{N}^+_k = \{x \in \mathbb{N}^+ \mid 1 \le x \le k\}$ an *initial segment* of $\mathbb{N}^+$.

An *alphabet* V is a finite set. The families of recursively enumerable, context-free, linear, and regular languages, and of languages generated by tabled Lindenmayer systems are denoted by RE, CF, LIN, REG, and $ET0L$, respectively. The families of sets of Parikh vectors as well as of sets of natural numbers (multiset languages over one-symbol alphabets) obtained from a language family F are denoted by PsF and NF, respectively.

For further introduction to the theory of formal languages and computability, we refer the reader to [14, 15].

2.1   Linear Sets over $\mathbb{N}$

A *linear* set over $\mathbb{N}$ generated by a set of vectors $A = \{\mathbf{a}_i \mid 1 \le i \le d\} \subset_{fin} \mathbb{N}^n$ (here $A \subset_{fin} B$ indicates that A is a finite subset of B) and an offset $\mathbf{a}_0 \in \mathbb{N}^n$ is defined as follows:

$$\langle A, \mathbf{a}_0 \rangle_{\mathbb{N}} = \left\{ \mathbf{a}_0 + \sum_{i=1}^{d} k_i \mathbf{a}_i \;\middle|\; k_i \in \mathbb{N},\; 1 \le i \le d \right\}.$$

If the offset $\mathbf{a}_0$ is the zero vector $\mathbf{0}$, we call the corresponding linear set *homogeneous*; we also use the short notation $\langle A \rangle_{\mathbb{N}} = \langle A, \mathbf{0} \rangle_{\mathbb{N}}$.

We use the notation $\mathbb{N}^n LIN_{\mathbb{N}} = \{\langle A, \mathbf{a}_0 \rangle_{\mathbb{N}} \mid A \subset_{fin} \mathbb{N}^n, \; \mathbf{a}_0 \in \mathbb{N}^n\}$, to refer to the class of all linear sets of n-dimensional vectors over $\mathbb{N}$. Semi-linear sets are defined as finite unions of linear sets. We use the notation $\mathbb{N}^n SLIN_{\mathbb{N}}$ to refer to the classes of semi-linear sets of n-dimensional vectors. In case no restriction is imposed on the dimension, n is replaced by $*$. We may omit n if $n = 1$. A finite union of linear sets which only differ in the starting vectors is called *uniform semilinear*:

$$\mathbb{N}^n SLIN_{\mathbb{N}}^{U} = \left\{ \bigcup_{\mathbf{b} \in B} \langle A, \mathbf{b} \rangle_{\mathbb{N}} \mid A \subset_{fin} \mathbb{N}^n, \; B \subset_{fin} \mathbb{N}^n \right\}$$

Let us denote such a set by $\langle A, B \rangle_{\mathbb{N}}$.

Note that a uniform semilinear set $\langle A, B \rangle_{\mathbb{N}}$ can be seen as a pairwise sum of the finite set B and the homogeneous linear set $\langle A \rangle_{\mathbb{N}}$:

$$\langle A, B \rangle_{\mathbb{N}} = \{\mathbf{a} + \mathbf{b} \mid \mathbf{a} \in \langle A \rangle_{\mathbb{N}}, \mathbf{b} \in B\}.$$

This observation immediately yields the conclusion that the sum of two uniform semilinear sets $\langle A_1, B_1 \rangle_\mathbb{N}$ and $\langle A_2, B_2 \rangle_\mathbb{N}$ is uniform semilinear as well and can be computed in the following way:

$$\langle A_1, B_1 \rangle_\mathbb{N} + \langle A_2, B_2 \rangle_\mathbb{N} = \{\mathbf{a} + \mathbf{b} \mid \mathbf{a} \in \langle A_1 \cup A_2 \rangle_\mathbb{N}, \mathbf{b} \in B_1 + B_2\}.$$

As is folklore,

$$PsCF = PsLIN = PsREG = \mathbb{N}^* SLIN_\mathbb{N}.$$

2.2   Multisets

A *multiset* over V is any function $w : V \to \mathbb{N}$; $w(a)$ is the *multiplicity* of a in w. A multiset w is often represented by one of the strings containing exactly $w(a)$ copies of each symbol $a \in V$. The set of all multisets over the alphabet V is denoted by V°. By abusing string notation, the empty multiset is denoted by λ. The *projection* (restriction) of w over a sub-alphabet $V' \subseteq V$ is the multiset $w|_{V'}$ defined as follows:

$$w|_{V'}(a) = \begin{cases} w(a), & a \in V'; \\ 0, & a \in V \setminus V'. \end{cases}$$

Example 1. The string aab can represent the multiset $w : \{a, b\} \to \mathbb{N}$ with $w(a) = 2$ and $w(b) = 1$. The projection $w|_{\{a\}} = w'$ is defined as $w'(a) = w(a) = 2$ and $w'(b) = 0$.

We will (ab)use the symbol $\in$ to denote the relation "is a member of" for multisets. Therefore, for a multiset w, $a \in w$ will stand for $w(a) > 0$.

2.3   Strings and Permutations

A (non-empty) *string* s over an alphabet V traditionally is defined as a finite ordered sequence of elements of V. Equivalently, we can define a string of length k as a function assigning symbols to positions: $s : \mathbb{N}^+{}_k \to V$. Thus, the string $s = aab$ can be equivalently defined as the function $s : \mathbb{N}^+{}_3 \to \{a, b\}$ with $s(1) = a, s(2) = a$, and $s(3) = b$. We will use the traditional notation $|s|$ to refer to the length of the string s (i.e., the size k of the initial segment $\mathbb{N}^+{}_k$ it is defined on). In addition, the size of the empty string λ is 0.

A string $s : \mathbb{N}^+{}_k \to V$ is not necessarily surjective (there may be symbols from V that do not appear in s). We will use the notation $set(s)$ to refer to the set of symbols appearing in s (the image of s):

$$set(s) = \left\{a \in V \mid a = s(i) \text{ for some } i \in \mathbb{N}^+{}_{|s|}\right\}.$$

Given a string $s : \mathbb{N}^+{}_k \to V$, a *prefix* of length $k' \leq k$ of s is the restriction of s to $\mathbb{N}^+{}_{k'} \subseteq \mathbb{N}^+{}_k$. For example, aa is a prefix of length 2 of the string aab. We will use the notation $\mathrm{pref}_{k'}(s)$ to denote the prefix of length k' of s.

Given a finite set A, a *permutation* of A is any bijection $\rho : A \to A$. Given a permutation $\sigma : \mathbb{N}^+{}_k \to \mathbb{N}^+{}_k$ and a string $s : \mathbb{N}^+{}_k \to V$ of length k, *applying σ to s* is defined as $\sigma(s) = s \circ \sigma$ (where $\circ$ is the function composition operator).

Example 2. Following the widespread tradition, we will write permutations in Cauchy's two-line notation. The permutation σ_{rev} of $\mathbb{N}^+{}_3$ which "reverses the order" of the numbers, can be written as follows:

$$\sigma_{rev} = \begin{pmatrix} 1 & 2 & 3 \\ 3 & 2 & 1 \end{pmatrix}.$$

Applying σ_{rev} to a string reverses it:

$$\sigma_{rev}(aab) = baa.$$

Any finite set B trivially can be represented by one of the strings listing all of its elements exactly once. All such strings are equivalent modulo permutations. Given a fixed enumeration $B = \{b_1, \ldots, b_n\}$, we define the *canonical string representation* of B to be the string $\delta(B) = b_1 \ldots b_n$.

2.4 Rule Sides

We consider arbitrary labeled multiset rules $r : u \to v$ over an alphabet V, where r is the rule label we attach for convenience, and u and v are strings over V representing multisets. As usual, the application of such a rule means replacing the multiset represented by u by the multiset represented by v.

For a given rule $r : u \to v$, we define the left-hand-side and the right-hand-side functions as follows:

$$lhs(u \to v) = lhs(r) = (u),$$
$$rhs(u \to v) = rhs(r) = (v).$$

Using the brackets (and), for a given string w, the notation (w) is used to describe the multiset represented by w. As usual, we will extend the notations for these functions lhs and rhs lifted to sets of rules: given a set of rules R, $lhs(R) = \{lhs(r) \mid r \in R\}$ and $rhs(R) = \{rhs(r) \mid r \in R\}$. Furthermore, for any *string* (finite ordered sequence) of rules $\rho : \mathbb{N}^+{}_k \to R$ we define the strings of left-hand sides $lhs(\rho) = lhs \circ \rho$ and of right-hand sides $rhs(\rho) = rhs \circ \rho$.

Example 3. Take $R = \{r_1 : aa \to ab, r_2 : cc \to cd\}$ and consider the string of rules $\rho = r_1 r_1 r_2$. Then $lhs(\rho) = (aa)(aa)(cc)$ and $rhs(\rho) = (ab)(ab)(cd)$. Thus, $lhs(\rho)$ and $rhs(\rho)$ can be considered as *strings of multisets*.

We will (ab)use the symbol $\to$ for *combining* two strings of multisets $\alpha, \beta :$ $\mathbb{N}^+{}_k \to V^\circ$ of the same length k. The string $\alpha \to \beta$ will be defined as follows, for any $i \in \mathbb{N}^+{}_k$:

$$(\alpha \to \beta)(i) = \alpha(i) \to \beta(i).$$

Example 4. Consider the following two strings of multisets: $\alpha = (aa)(aa)(cc)$ and $\beta = (ab)(ab)(cd)$. $\alpha \to \beta$ is simply the string of rules that can be obtained by taking the multisets from α as left-hand sides and β as right-hand sides, in the given order: $\alpha \to \beta = (aa) \to (ab)(aa) \to (ab)(cc) \to (cd)$ (which exactly corresponds with ρ from Example 3).

2.5   (Hierarchical) P Systems

A (hierarchical) *P system* is a construct

$$\Pi = (O, T, \mu, w_1, \ldots, w_n, R_1, \ldots R_n, h_i, h_o),$$

where O is the alphabet of objects, $T \subseteq O$ is the alphabet of terminal objects, μ is the membrane structure injectively labeled by the numbers from $\{1, \ldots, n\}$ and usually given by a sequence of correctly nested brackets, w_i are the multisets giving the initial contents of each membrane i $(1 \leq i \leq n)$, R_i is the finite set of rules associated with membrane i $(1 \leq i \leq n)$, and h_i and h_o are the labels of the input and the output membranes, respectively $(1 \leq h_i \leq n, 1 \leq h_o \leq n)$.

In the present work, we will mostly consider the *generative case*, in which Π will be used as a multiset language-generating device. We therefore will systematically omit specifying the input membrane h_i.

Quite often the rules associated with membranes are multiset rewriting rules (or special cases of such rules). Multiset rewriting rules have the form $u \to v$, with $u \in O^\circ \setminus \{\lambda\}$ and $v \in O^\circ$. If $|u| = 1$, the rule $u \to v$ is called *non-cooperative*; otherwise it is called *cooperative*. Rules may additionally be allowed to send symbols to the neighboring membranes. In this case, for rules in $R_i, v \in O \times Tar_i$, where Tar_i contains the targets *out* (corresponding to sending the symbol to the parent membrane), *here* (indicating that the symbol should be kept in membrane i), and in_h (indicating that the symbol should be sent into the child membrane h of membrane i). Note that all variants of the function rhs, as well as the operator $\to$ from the previous section can be naturally extended to rules having right-hand sides with target indications (from $O \times Tar_i$).

In P systems, rules are often applied in the maximally parallel way: in any derivation step, a non-extendable multiset of rules has to be applied. The rules are not allowed to consume the same instance of a symbol twice, which creates competition for objects and may lead to the P system choosing non-deterministically between the maximal collections of rules applicable in one step.

A computation of a P system is traditionally considered to be a sequence of configurations it can successively pass through, stopping at the halting configuration. A halting configuration is a configuration in which no rule can be applied any more, in any membrane. The result of a computation of a P system Π as defined above is the contents of the output membrane h_o projected over the terminal alphabet T.

Example 5. For readability, we will often prefer a graphical representation of P systems. For example, the P system $\Pi_1 = (\{a, b\}, \{b\}, [_1 \ ]_1, a, R, 1)$ with the rule set $R = \{a \to aa, a \to b\}$ may be depicted as in Fig. 1.

Due to maximal parallelism, at every step Π_1 may double some of the symbols a, while rewriting some other instances into b.

Note that, even though Π_1 might express the intention of generating the set of numbers of the powers of two, it will actually generate the whole of $\mathbb{N}^+$ (due to halting). Indeed, for any $n \in \mathbb{N}^+, a^n$ can be generated in n steps by choosing to apply, in the first $n - 1$ steps, $a \to aa$ to exactly one instance of a and $a \to b$

Fig. 1. The example P system Π_1

to all the other instances, and by applying $a \to b$ to every a in the last step (in fact, for $n > 1$, in each step except the last one, in which $a \to b$ is applied twice, both rules are applied exactly once, as exactly two symbols a are present, whereas all other symbols are copies of b).

While maximal parallelism and halting by inapplicability are staple ingredients, various other derivation modes and halting conditions have been considered for P systems, e.g., see [14].

We will use the notation $OP_n(coo)$ to denote the family of P systems with at most n membranes, with cooperative rules. To denote the family of such P systems with *non-cooperative* rules, we replace coo by $ncoo$. To denote the family of languages of multisets generated by these P systems, we prepend Ps to the notation, and to denote the family of the generated number languages, we prepend N.

3   P Systems with Randomized RHS

In this section we consider three different variants of defining P systems with randomized RHS. We immediately point out that, despite the common intuitive background, the details of the resulting semantics vary quite a lot.

3.1   Variant 1: Random RHS Exchange

In this variant of P systems, rules randomly exchange right-hand sides at the beginning of every evolution step. This variant was the first to be conceived and is the closest to the classical definition.

A *P system with random RHS exchange* is a construct

$$\Pi = (O, T, \mu, w_1, \ldots, w_n, R_1, \ldots R_n, h_o),$$

where the components of the tuple are defined as in the classical model (Sect. 2.5).

As different from conventional P systems, Π does not apply the rules from R_i directly. Instead, for each membrane $1 \leq i \leq n$, we take the canonical representation of R_i, i.e., $\delta(R_i)$, and non-deterministically (randomly) choose a permutation $\sigma : \mathbb{N}^+{}_{|R_i|} \to \mathbb{N}^+{}_{|R_i|}$ to compute the canonical representation of R_i^σ from $\delta(R_i)$ as follows:

$$\delta(R_i^\sigma) = lhs(\delta(R_i)) \to \sigma(rhs(\delta(R_i))).$$

We now extract the set of rules $R_i^\sigma = set(\delta(R_i^\sigma))$ described by the string $\delta(R_i^\sigma)$ as constructed above. Π will then apply the rules from R_i^σ according to the usual maximally parallel semantics in membrane i.

In other words, Π *non-deterministically permutes* the right-hand sides of rules in each membrane i, and then applies the obtained rules according to the maximally parallel semantics.

Note that we first have to transform the set R_i into its canonical string representation $\delta(R_i)$ in order to be able to obtain a correct representation of the $|R_i|$ rules and from that a correct representation of the $|R_i|$ rules in R_i^σ, even if the number of different left-hand sides and/or different right-hand sides of rules does not equal $|R_i|$.

Example 6. Consider the P system $\Pi_2 = (\{a, b\}, \{b\}, [_1 \ ]_1, a, R, 1)$ with the rule set $R = \{a \to aa, c \to b\}$. Π_2 is graphically represented in Fig. 2.

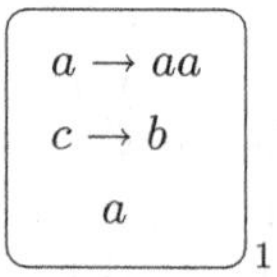

$$
\boxed{
\begin{array}{c}
a \to aa \\
c \to b \\
a
\end{array}
}_1
$$

Fig. 2. The P system Π_2 with random RHS exchange generating the number language $\{2^n \mid n \in \mathbb{N}\}$.

The number language generated by Π_2 (the set of numbers of instances of b that may appear in the skin after Π_2 has halted) is exactly $\{2^n \mid n \in \mathbb{N}^+\}$. Indeed, while Π_2 applies the identity permutation on the right-hand sides, $a \to aa$ will double the number of symbols a, while the rule $c \to b$ will never be applicable. When Π_2 exchanges the right-hand sides of the rules, the rule $a \to b$ will rewrite every symbol a into a symbol b. After this has happened, no rule will ever be applicable any more and Π_2 will halt with 2^n symbols b in the skin, where $n + 1$ is the number of computation steps taken.

We will use the notation

$$OP_n(rhsExchange, coo)$$

to denote the family of P systems with random RHS exchange, with at most n membranes, with cooperative rules. To denote the family of such P systems with *non-cooperative* rules, we replace *coo* by *ncoo*. To denote the family of languages of multisets generated by these P systems, we prepend Ps to the notation, and to denote the family of the generated number languages, we prepend N.

3.2   Variant 2: Randomized Pools of RHS

In this variant of P systems, every membrane has some fixed left-hand sides and a *pool* of available right-hand sides to build rules from. An RHS from the pool can only be used once.

A *P system with randomized pools of RHS* is a construct

$$\Pi = (O, T, \mu, w_1, \ldots, w_n, H_1, \ldots H_n, h_o),$$

where H_i defines the left- and right-hand sides available in membrane i and the other components of the tuple are defined as in the classical model (Sect. 2.5).

For $1 \leq i \leq n, H_i = (l_i, r_i)$ is a pair of strings of multisets over O. The string r_i may contain target indications (i.e., be a string of multisets over $O \times Tar_i$). The strings l_i and r_i are not necessarily of the same length. The length of the shortest of the two strings l_i and r_i is denoted by

$$k_i = \min(|l_i|, |r_i|).$$

At the beginning of every computation step in Π, for every membrane i, we construct the set of rules it will apply in the following way:

1. non-deterministically choose two (random) permutations

$$\sigma_l : \mathbb{N}^+{}_{|l_i|} \rightarrow \mathbb{N}^+{}_{|l_i|}, \quad \sigma_r : \mathbb{N}^+{}_{|r_i|} \rightarrow \mathbb{N}^+{}_{|r_i|};$$

2. take the first k_i elements out of $\sigma_l(l_i)$ and $\sigma_r(r_i)$:

$$l'_i = \mathrm{pref}_{k_i}(\sigma_l(l_i)), \quad r'_i = \mathrm{pref}_{k_i}(\sigma_r(r_i));$$

3. construct the set of rules R_i to be applied in membrane i by combining the left- and right-hand sides from l'_i and r'_i:

$$R_i = set(l'_i \rightarrow r'_i).$$

In step (3), we combine the strings l'_i and r'_i using the operator $\rightarrow$ defined in Subsect. 2.4 and then apply the operator *set* to obtain the corresponding set of rules from the string representation.

After having constructed the set R_i for each membrane i, Π will proceed to applying the obtained rules according to the usual maximally parallel semantics.

When computing the strings l'_i and r'_i, we apply *two* different permutations σ_l and σ_r to l_i and r_i, in order to ensure fairness for the participation of left-hand and right-hand sides when $|l_i| \neq |r_i|$. For example, if we only permuted r_i in the case in which $|l_i| > |r_i|$, the left-hand sides located at positions $k > |r_i|$ in l_i would never be used.

We do not explicitly prohibit repetitions in l_i or in r_i, but we avoid repeated rules by constructing R_i using the *set* function.

Example 7. Consider the following P system with randomized pools of RHS: $\Pi_3 = (\{a, b\}, \{b\}, [_1 \ ]_1, a, H, 1)$, with $H = ((a), (aa)(b))$; (a) stands for the multiset containing an instance of a, while $(aa)(b)$ is the string denoting the two multisets (aa) and (b). The graphical representation of Π_3 is given in Fig. 3.

The pair $H = (l, r)$ of strings of multisets is represented by listing the multisets of l and r in two columns and by drawing a vertical line between the two columns.

Fig. 3. The P system Π_3 with randomized pools of RHS generating the number language $\{2^n \mid n \in \mathbb{N}\}$.

Π_3 follows exactly the same pattern as Π_2 from Example 6: while the identity permutation is applied to r, Π_3 keeps doubling the symbols a in the skin. Once the multisets (aa) and (b) are permuted in r, and thus the rule $a \to b$ is formed, all symbols a are rewritten into symbols b in one step and Π_3 must halt. Note that randomly taking the right-hand sides from a given pool avoids having the extra dummy rule $c \to b$ in Π_2.

We will use the notation

$$OP_n(rhsPools, coo)$$

to denote the family of P systems with randomized pools of RHS, with at most n membranes, with cooperative rules. To denote the family of such P systems with *non-cooperative* rules, we replace coo by $ncoo$. To denote the family of languages of multisets generated by these P systems, we prepend Ps to the notation, and to denote the family of the generated number languages, we prepend N.

3.3   Variant 3: Individual Randomized RHS

In this variant of P systems, each rule is constructed from a left-hand side and a set of possible right-hand sides.

A *P system with individual randomized RHS* is a construct

$$\Pi = (O, T, \mu, w_1, \ldots, w_n, P_1, \ldots P_n, h_o),$$

where P_i is the set of *productions* associated with the membrane i and the other components of the tuple are defined as in the classical model (Sect. 2.5).

A production is a pair $u \to R$, where $u \in O^\circ$ is the left-hand side and $R \subseteq O^\circ$ is a finite set of right-hand sides. The right-hand sides in R may have target indications, i.e., for a production in membrane i, we may consider $R \subseteq (O \times Tar_i)^\circ$. At the beginning of each computation step, for every membrane i, for each production $u \to R \in R_i$, Π will non-deterministically (randomly) pick a right-hand side v from R and will construct the rule $u \to v$ (this happens once per production). Π will then apply the rules thus constructed according to the maximally parallel semantics.

Example 8. Generating the language of the powers of two is the easiest compared with Variants 1 and 2. Indeed, consider the P system with individual randomized RHS $\Pi_4 = (\{a, b\}, \{b\}, [_1 \ ]_1, a, P, 1)$ with only one production: $P = \{a \to \{aa, b\})\}$. Its graphical representation is given in Fig. 4.

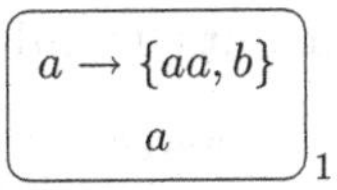

$$\boxed{\begin{array}{c} a \to \{aa, b\} \\ a \end{array}}_1$$

Fig. 4. The P system Π_4 with individual randomized RHS generating the number language $\{2^n \mid n \in \mathbb{N}\}$.

Π_4 works exactly like Π_2 and Π_3 from Examples 6 and 7: it doubles the number of symbols a and halts by rewriting them to b in the last step.

We will use the notation

$$OP_n(rndRhs, coo)$$

to denote the family of P systems with individual randomized RHS, with at most n membranes, with cooperative rules. To denote the family of such P systems with *non-cooperative* rules, we replace *coo* by *ncoo*. To denote the family of languages of multisets generated by these P systems, we prepend Ps to the notation, and to denote the family of the generated number languages, we prepend N.

We will sometimes want to set an upper bound k on the number of right-hand sides per production. To refer to the family of P systems with individual randomized RHS with such an upper bound, we will replace *rndRhs* by $rndRhs^k$ in the notation above.

3.4 Halting with Randomized RHS

The conventional (total) halting condition for P systems can be naturally lifted to randomized RHS: a P system Π with randomized RHS (Variant 1, 2, or 3) halts on a configuration C if, however it permutes rule right-hand sides in Variant 1, or however it builds rules out of the available rule sides in Variants 2 and 3, no rule can be applied in C, in any membrane.

Note that, for Variants 1 and 3, the permutations chosen do *not* affect the applicability of rules, because applicability only depends on left-hand sides, which are always the same in any membrane. The situation is different for Variant 2, because the number of available left-hand sides in a membrane of Π may be bigger than the number of available right-hand sides. Therefore, if Π is a P system with randomized pools of RHS, the way rule sides are permuted may affect the number of rules applicable in a given configuration. This is why, for Π to halt on C, we require no rule to be applicable for any permutation.

In this paper, we will mainly consider P systems with randomized pools of RHS in which, in every membrane, there are at least as many right-hand sides as there are left-hand sides. To refer to P systems with this restriction, we will use the notation $rhsPools'$. In these systems, the problem with the applicability of rules as described above can be avoided.

3.5   Equivalence Between Variants 1 and 2

Before discussing the computational power of the P systems with randomized RHS in general, we will briefly point out a strong relationship between P systems with random RHS exchange and P systems with randomized pools of RHS, *with the restriction that every membrane contains at least as many right-hand sides as it has left-hand sides, i.e., for P systems with randomized RHS of type rhsPools'.*

Theorem 1. *For any $k \in \{coo, ncoo\}$, the following holds:*

$$PsOP_n(rhsExchange, k) = PsOP_n(rhsPools', k).$$

Proof. Any membrane with random RHS exchange trivially can be transformed into a membrane with randomized pools of RHS by listing the left-hand sides of the rules in the pool of LHS and the right-hand sides of the rules in the pool of RHS.

Conversely, consider a membrane i with randomized pools of RHS, with the string l_i of LHS and the string r_i of RHS, $|l_i| \leq |r_i|$. We can transform it into a membrane with random RHS exchange as follows. For every LHS u from l_i, pick (and remove) an RHS v from r_i, and construct the rule $u \to v$. According to our supposition, we will exhaust the LHS before (or at the same time as) the RHS. For every RHS v' which is left, we add a new (dummy) symbol z' to the alphabet, and add the rule $z' \to v'$. Since the symbol z' is new and does not appear in any RHS, it will never be produced and the rule $z' \to v'$ will essentially serve as a stash for the RHS v'.   □

3.6   Flattening

The folklore flattening construction (see [14] for several examples as well as [11] for a general construction) is quite directly applicable to P systems with individual randomized RHS.

Proposition 1 (flattening). *For any $k \in \{coo, ncoo\}$, the following is true:*

$$PsOP_1(rndRhs, k) = PsOP_n(rndRhs, k).$$

Proof (sketch). Since in the case of individual randomized RHS, randomization has per rule granularity (whereas in the other two variants randomization occurs at the level of membranes), we can simulate multiple membranes by attaching membrane labels to symbols. For example, a production $ab \to \{cd, f\}$ in membrane h becomes $a_h b_h \to \{c_h d_h, f_h\}$, while the send-in production $a \to \{(b, in_i), (b, in_j)\}$ becomes $a_h \to \{b_i, b_j\}$.   □

On the other hand, for Variants 1 and 2 similar results cannot be proved in such a way, a situation which happens very seldom in the area of P systems, especially in the case of variants of the standard model. Yet intuitively, it is easy to understand why this happens, as in both Variants 1 and 2 the right-hand sides in just one membrane can randomly be chosen for any left-hand side, whereas different membranes can separate the possible combinations of left-hand sides and right-hand sides of rules. A formal proof showing that flattening is impossible for the types *rhsExchange* and *rhsPools'* will be given in the succeeding section by constructing a suitable example.

4   Computational Power of Randomized RHS

In this section, we look into the computational power of the three different versions of P systems with randomized right-hand sides. We first shortly consider the case of cooperative rules and then focus on the case of non-cooperative rules.

4.1   Cooperative Rules

The following result concerning the relationship between P systems with individual randomized RHS and conventional P systems holds for both cooperative and non-cooperative rules:

Proposition 2. *For any $n \in \mathbb{N}^+$ and $\alpha \in \{ncoo, coo\}, PsOP_n(rndRhs, \alpha) \supseteq PsOP_n(\alpha)$.*

Proof. Any conventional P system can be trivially seen as a P system with individual randomized RHS in which every production has exactly one right-hand side. □

Now, the computational completeness of *cooperative* P systems trivially implies the computational completeness of P systems with individual randomized RHS.

Corollary 1. *For any $n \in \mathbb{N}^+$, $PsOP_n(rndRhs, coo) = PsRE$.*

4.2   Non-cooperative Rules

First we mention an upper bound for the families $PsOP_n(\rho, ncoo)$, for any variant $\rho \in \{rhsExchange, rhsPools', rndRhs\}$:

Proposition 3. *For any $n \in \mathbb{N}^+$ and $\rho \in \{rhsExchange, rhsPools', rndRhs\}$,*

$$PsOP_n(\rho, ncoo) \subseteq PsET0L.$$

Proof. No matter how the rule sets are constructed in the three different variants, we always get a finite set of different sets of rules – *tables* – corresponding to tables in *ET0L*-systems, which can also mimic the contents of different membranes in the usual way by using symbols marked with the corresponding membrane label. □

Next we show one of the central results of this paper: randomized rule right-hand sides allow for generating *non-semilinear languages* already in the non-cooperative case.

Theorem 2. *The following is true for $\rho \in \{rhsExchange, rhsPools', rndRhs\}$:*

$$\{2^m \mid m \in \mathbb{N}\} \in NOP_n(\rho, ncoo) \setminus NOP_n(ncoo).$$

Proof. The statement follows (for $n \geq 1$) from the constructions given in Examples 6, 7, and 8 and from the well-known fact that non-cooperative P systems operating under the total halting condition cannot generate non-semilinear number languages (for example, see [14]).   □

This result is somewhat surprising at a first glance, but becomes less so when one remarks that the constructions from all three examples only effectively use *one rule* to do the multiplication, which is non-deterministically changed to a "halting" rule. Since there is only one rule acting at any time, randomized right-hand sides allow for clearly delimiting different *derivation phases*.

It turns out that this approach of synchronization by randomization can be exploited to generate even more complex non-semilinear languages.

Theorem 3. *Given a fixed subset of natural factors $\{f_1, \ldots, f_k\} \subseteq \mathbb{N}$, the following is true for any $\rho \in \{rhsExchange, rhsPools', rndRhs\}$:*

$$L = \{f_1^{n_1} \cdot \ldots \cdot f_k^{n_k} \mid n_1, \ldots, n_k \in \mathbb{N}\} \in NOP_1(\rho, ncoo).$$

Proof. First consider the P system with randomized pools of RHS $\Pi_5 = (\{a, b\}, \{b\}, [_1]_1, a, H, 1)$ with $H = (l, r), l = (a)$ and $r = (a^{f_1}) \ldots (a^{f_k})(b)$. This P system is graphically represented in Fig. 5.

Similarly to the P systems from Examples 6, 7, and 8, Π_5 halts by choosing to pick the right-hand side b and constructing the rule $a \to b$. If Π_5 picks a different right-hand side, it will multiply the contents of the skin membrane (membrane 1) by one of the factors $f_i, 1 \leq i \leq k$. This proves that $L \in NOP_1(rhsPools', ncoo)$, and, according to Theorem 1, $L \in NOP_1(rhsExchange, ncoo)$ as well: take the P system with the rules $\{a \to a^{f_1}, z_2 \to a^{f_2}, \ldots, z_k \to a^{f_k}, z_{k+1} \to b\}$ (the rules with z_j in their left-hand sides are dummy rules).

To show that $L \in NOP_1(rndRhs, ncoo)$, just construct a P system with the only production $a \to \{a^{f_1}, \ldots, a^{f_k}, b\}$.   □

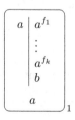

Fig. 5. The P system Π_5 with randomized pools of RHS generating the number language $\{f_1^{n_1} \cdot \ldots \cdot f_k^{n_k} \mid n_1, \ldots, n_k \in \mathbb{N}\}$.

Therefore, randomizing the right-hand sides of rules in non-cooperative P systems allows for generating non-semilinear languages which cannot be generated without randomization. A natural question to ask is whether randomizing the RHS leads to a *strict increase* in the computational power. The answer is trivially positive for P systems with individual randomized RHS (Variant 3).

Proposition 4. *For any $n \in \mathbb{N}^+$, $PsOP_n(rndRhs, ncoo) \supsetneq PsOP_n(ncoo)$.*

Proof. The inclusion follows from Proposition 2, as any conventional P system can be trivially seen as a P system with individual randomized RHS in which every production has exactly one right-hand side. Theorem 3 proves the strictness of the inclusion. □

On the other hand, the other two variants of randomizing right-hand sides— random RHS exchange (Variant 1) and randomized pools of RHS (Variant 2)— actually *prevent* one-membrane P systems with non-cooperative rules from generating some semilinear languages, which result also shows that flattening is not possible for these two variants.

In what follows, we will use the expression "only one rule is applied" to refer to the fact that only one given rule $u \to v$ is applied in a certain configuration, possibly in multiple copies. Dually, by saying "at least two rules are applied", we mean that at least two different rules, $u \to v$ and $u' \to v'$, are applied, possibly in multiple copies each.

Theorem 4. *For $\rho \in \{rhsExchange, rhsPools'\}$, the following holds:*

$$L_{ab} = \{a^n \mid n \in \mathbb{N}\} \cup \{b^n \mid n \in \mathbb{N}\} \notin PsOP_1(\rho, ncoo).$$

Proof. Consider a P system Π with randomized RHS of the variant given by ρ and with non-cooperative rules. We immediately remark that no left-hand side in Π may be a or b, because in this case Π will never be able to halt with its only (skin) membrane containing either the multiset a^n or b^n. Furthermore, any RHS of Π contains combinations of symbols a, b, or LHS symbols. Indeed, if an RHS contained a symbol not belonging to these three classes, instances of this symbol would pollute the halting configuration. Finally, Π contains no RHS v such that $a \in v$ and $b \in v$. If Π did contain such an RHS, then any computation could be hijacked to produce a mixture of symbols a and b.

With these remarks in mind, the statement of the theorem follows from the contradicting Lemmas 1 and 2, which are shown immediately after this proof. □

Lemma 1. *Take a $\Pi \in OP_1(\rho, ncoo), \rho \in \{rhsExchange, rhsPools'\}$, such that it generates the number language $Ps(\Pi) = L_{ab}$. Then it must have a computation in which more than one rule is applied (two different left-hand sides are employed) in at least one step.*

Proof. Suppose that Π applies exactly one rule in every step of every computation. We make the following two remarks:

1. Since the words in L_{ab} are of unbounded length, Π must have an LHS t and an RHS v such that $t \in v$, otherwise all computations of Π would have one step and would only produce words of bounded length.
2. Every such RHS v must contain at most one kind of LHS, i.e., if t_1 and t_2 are two LHS of Π then $t_1 \in v$ and $t_2 \in v$ implies $t_1 = t_2$. If this were not the case, after using v, Π would *have* to apply two different rules (assuming that Π has at least as many RHS as LHS).

According to these observations, as well as to those from the proof of Theorem 4, any RHS v of Π is the of the form $v = \alpha\beta$, where $\alpha \in \{a^k, b^k \mid k \in \mathbb{N}\}, \beta \in \{t^k \mid k \in \mathbb{N}\}$, and t is an LHS of Π. Note that both α and β may be empty. According to observation (1), Π must have at least an RHS for which $\beta \neq \lambda$ and there exists such an RHS which must be applied an unbounded number of times.

In what follows, we will separately treat the cases in which Π contains or does not contain mixed RHS, i.e., RHS for which both $\alpha \neq \lambda$ and $\beta \neq \lambda$.

No mixed RHS: Suppose that any RHS of Π which contains a left-hand side is of the form t_2^k. Then, according to our previous observations on the possible forms of the RHS of Π, all RHS containing a are of the form a^i and all RHS containing b are of the form b^j. According to the remarks from the proof of Theorem 4, a and b must not be LHS of Π. Therefore, in any computation of Π, all of a's and b's are produced in the last step. But then, the number of terminal symbols Π produces in a computation can be calculated as a product of the sizes of the RHS of the rules it has applied, which implies that there exists such a $p \in \mathbb{N}$ such that $a^p \notin Ps(\Pi)$ and therefore $Ps(\Pi) \neq L_{ab}$. (p may be picked to be the smallest prime number greater than the length of the longest RHS of Π.)

Mixed RHS: It follows from the previous paragraph that, in order to generate the number language L_{ab}, Π should contain and apply at least one RHS of the form $a^i t_1^{k_1}$ and at least one RHS of the form $b^j t_2^{k_2}$. Take a computation C of Π producing a and applying the rule $t \to a^i t_1^{k_1}$ at a certain step. Instead of this rule, apply $t \to b^j t_2^{k_2}$, and, in the following step, the rule $t_2 \to a^i t_1^{k_1}$. (We can do so because Π is allowed to pick any permutation of RHS.) Now, Π may continue applying the same rules as in C and eventually halt with a configuration containing *both* a and b. This implies that $Ps(\Pi) \neq L_{ab}$.

It follows from our reasoning that, if Π applies exactly one rule in any step of any computation, it cannot produce L_{ab}, which proves the lemma. □

Lemma 2. *Take a $\Pi \in OP_1(\rho, ncoo), \rho \in \{rhsExchange, rhsPools'\}$, such that it generates the number language $Ps(\Pi) = L_{ab}$. Then, in every computation of Π, exactly one rule is applied (one left-hand side is employed) in every step.*

Proof. Suppose that, in every computation of Π, there exists a step at which at least two different rules are applied. This immediately implies that Π has no RHS of the form a^i or b^j, for $i, j \geq 0$. Indeed, consider a computation producing the multiset a^n and a step in it at which more than one rule is applied. Then

Π can replace one of the RHS introduced into the system at this step by b^j and thus end up with a mix of a's and b's in the halting configuration. Therefore, all RHS of Π containing a have the form $a^i v_a$ and all RHS containing b have the form $b^j v_b$, where v_a and v_b are non-empty multisets which only contain LHS symbols (which are neither a nor b).

Now, consider a computation C_a of Π halting on the multiset a^n, and take the *last* step s_a at which at least two different rules are applied. We will consider three different cases, based on whether a and an LHS t appear in the configurations of C_a *after* step s_a.

Both a and t are present: Suppose both a and an LHS t are present at step $s_a + 1$ in computation C_a. Then t is the only LHS present, because, by our hypothesis, only one rule is applied (maybe in multiple instances) at step $s_a + 1$. In this case, replace the rule applied at step $s_a + 1$ in C_a by $t \to b^j v_b$, where $b^j v_b$ is a right-hand side of Π used in a computation C_b producing b's. From step $s_a + 2$ on in the modified computation, just apply the same rules as applied to the symbols of v_b (and to those derived from v_b) in C_b. The modified computation will reach a halting configuration containing a mix of a's and b's.

Only a is present: Suppose only a is present at step $s_a + 1$ in computation C_a. Then all of the RHS used at step s_a are λ, because Π has no RHS of the form a^i. Then, replace one of these empty RHS by $b^j v_b$, where $b^j v_b$ is a right-hand side of Π used in a computation C_b producing b's. As before, just apply the same rules as in C_b in the modified computation to get a mix of a's and b's in the halting configuration.

No symbols a are present: Suppose now that there are no instances of a present at step $s_a + 1$ in computation C_a. Recall that Π has no RHS of the form a^i. Since we suppose that s_a is the last step at which at least two different rules are applied, this means that, in order to produce any a's in C_a, Π must have and use an RHS of the form $a^i t^k$. This RHS contains (multiple copies of) exactly one kind of LHS symbol: t.

Consider a computation C_b halting on the multiset b^n. We pick n sufficiently big to ensure that C_b uses at least two RHS containing b: $b^j v_b$ and $b^{j'} v_b'$ (possibly the same). Without losing generality, we may suppose that these two RHS are either used at the same step in C_b or that $b^{j'} v_b'$ is used at a later step than $b^j v_b$. Then, replace $b^{j'} v_b'$ by $a^i t^k$, pick one of the LHS symbols $t' \in v_b'$ and apply the same rules to t (and to the symbols derived from t) in the modified derivation as were applied to t' (and to the symbols derived from t') in C_b. The modified derivation will therefore contain a mix of a's and b's in the halting configuration.

It follows from our reasoning that, if in any derivation of Π there is a step at which at least two different rules are applied, then $Ps(\Pi) \neq L_{ab}$, which proves the lemma. $\square$

The previous two lemmas are contradicting each other, which means that there exist no one-membrane P systems with random RHS exchange or with random pools of RHS which generate the union language $L_{ab} = \{a^n \mid n \in \mathbb{N}\} \cup \{b^n \mid n \in \mathbb{N}\}$ (this is the statement of Theorem 4). Together with Theorem 3, this leads us to the curious conclusion that one-membrane non-cooperative P systems with random RHS exchange or with randomized pools of RHS are *incomparable* in power to the conventional P systems.

Corollary 2. *For $\rho \in \{rhsExchange, rhsPools'\}$, the following two statements are true:*

$$PsOP_1(\rho, ncoo) \setminus PsOP_1(ncoo) \neq \emptyset, \tag{1}$$

$$PsOP_1(ncoo) \setminus PsOP_1(\rho, ncoo) \neq \emptyset. \tag{2}$$

Proof. Statement (1) follows from Theorem 3. Statement (2) follows from Theorem 4. □

Theorem 4 also allows us to draw a negative conclusion as to the computational completeness of one-membrane non-cooperative P systems with random RHS exchange (Variant 1) and non-cooperative P systems with randomized pools of RHS (Variant 2).

Corollary 3. *For $\rho \in \{rhsExchange, rhsPools'\}$, the following is true:*

$$PsOP_1(\rho, ncoo) \subsetneq PsRE.$$

It turns out that allowing multiple membranes strictly increases the expressive power of Variants 1 and 2 and allows for easily generating *all semilinear* languages, as shown by the following theorem.

Theorem 5. *For $\rho \in \{rhsExchange, rhsPools'\}$, the following holds:*

$$\mathbb{N}^* SLIN_\mathbb{N} \in PsOP_*(\rho, ncoo).$$

Proof. Consider the following semilinear language of d-dimensional vectors $L = \bigcup_{1 \leq i \leq n} \langle A_i, \mathbf{b}_i \rangle_\mathbb{N}$, where $A_i \subset_{fin} \mathbb{N}^d$ and $\mathbf{b}_i \in \mathbb{N}^d$. We construct the corresponding P system with randomised pools of RHS:

$$\Pi_6 = \left(O, T, [\, [\,]_2 \cdots [\,]_{n+1}]_1, w_0, \lambda, \ldots, \lambda, H_1, \ldots H_{n+1}, 1\right),$$

with the alphabet and the initial contents of the skin defined as follows:

- $O = \{a_1, \ldots, a_d, t\}$ contains a symbol per each dimension of the vectors, plus the special symbol t,
- $T = \{a_1, \ldots, a_d\}$ contains exactly one symbol per dimension of vectors,
- $w_0 = t$.

The pools of LHS and RHS $H_1 = (l_1, r_1)$ associated with the skin membrane 1 of Π_6 are:

$$l_1 = (t), \quad r_1 = \left(u_1(t, in_2)\right) \ldots \left(u_n(t, in_{n+1})\right),$$

where the multiset u_i corresponds to the offset $\mathbf{b}_i$: $Ps(u_i) = \mathbf{b}_i, 1 \leq i \leq n$. Finally, the pools of rule sides $H_{i+1} = (l_{i+1}, r_{i+1})$ associated with inner membrane $i+1$ are defined as follows:

$$l_{i+1} = (t), \quad r_{i+1} = \left(t(v_{i1}, out)\right) \ldots \left(t(v_{ik_i}, out)\right)(\lambda),$$

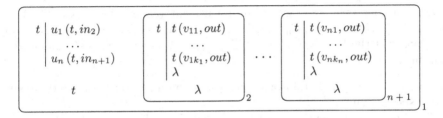

Fig. 6. The P system Π_6 with randomized pools of RHS generating the semilinear language $L = \bigcup_{1 \leq i \leq n} \langle A_i, \mathbf{b}_i \rangle_{\mathbb{N}}$.

where the multisets $v_{ij}, 1 \leq j \leq k_i$, correspond to the vectors of the set $A_i = \{\mathbf{a}_{i1}, \ldots, \mathbf{a}_{ik_i}\}$: $Ps(v_{ij}) = \mathbf{a}_{ij}, 1 \leq j \leq k_i$. By abuse of notation, we write (w, out) to mean that every symbol instance in w gets the target indication out. Π_6 is graphically represented in Fig. 6.

Π_6 starts by non-deterministically building one of the rules $t \to u_i (t, in_{i+1})$ in the skin membrane. An application of this rule adds the multiset corresponding to the offset $\mathbf{b}_i$ to the skin membrane and puts t into inner membrane $i + 1$. In the following steps only rules in membrane $i + 1$ may become applicable. In this membrane, Π_6 may build rules of the form $t \to t(v_{ij}, out), 1 \leq j \leq k_i$, which will sustain t while also sending the multiset v_{ij} corresponding to the vector $\mathbf{a}_{ij} \in A_i$ out into the skin. Alternatively, Π_6 may choose to build the rule $t \to \lambda$, an application of which will erase t and halt the system. In such a computation, Π_6 generates the multiset language corresponding to $\langle A_i, \mathbf{b}_i \rangle_{\mathbb{N}}$. Since Π_6 can choose to send t into any one of its inner membranes in the first step and since the computations of said membranes cannot interfere, we conclude that $Ps(\Pi_6) = L$.

To complete the proof, we evoke Theorem 1 to show that there exists a P system with random RHS exchange (Variant 1) generating the same language L.

This theorem allows us to draw a definitive conclusion about the impossibility of flattening for non-cooperative Variants 1 and 2, in contrast to Proposition 1 showing the opposite result for Variant 3.

Corollary 4. *For $\rho \in \{rhsExchange, rhsPools'\}$ and any $k \geq 2$, the following holds:*

$$PsOP_1(\rho, ncoo) \subsetneq PsOP_k(\rho, ncoo).$$

We conclude this section with two more observations regarding the computational power of the Variants 1 and 2. We have seen that, with a single membrane and without cooperation, such P systems cannot generate all semilinear languages; yet it turns out they can generate all *uniform semilinear* languages.

Theorem 6. *For $\rho \in \{rhsExchange, rhsPools'\}$, the following is true:*

$$\mathbb{N}^* SLIN_{\mathbb{N}}^U \subseteq PsOP_1(\rho, ncoo).$$

Proof. Consider two finite sets of d-dimensional vectors $A, B \subset_{fin} \mathbb{N}^d, A = \{\mathbf{x}_1, \ldots, \mathbf{x}_n\}, B = \{\mathbf{y}_1 \ldots, \mathbf{y}_m\}$, and the uniform semilinear set $\langle A, B \rangle_{\mathbb{N}}$. We will now construct the P system $\Pi = (O, T, [\ ]_1, w_0, H, 1)$ with pools of randomized RHS in the following way:

- $O = \{a_1, \ldots, a_d, t\}$ contains a symbol per each dimension of the vectors, plus the special symbol t,
- $T = \{a_1, \ldots, a_d\}$ contains exactly one symbol per dimension of vectors,
- $w_0 = t$,
- $H = (l, r)$, with $l = (t)$ and $r = (w_1' t) \ldots (w_n' t) (v_1') \ldots (v_m')$, such that $Ps(w_i') = \mathbf{x}_i, 1 \leq i \leq n$, and $Ps(v_j') = \mathbf{y}_j, 1 \leq j \leq m$.

In every step, Π either chooses one of the RHS $(w_i' t)$ which will enable it to reuse the left-hand side symbol t in the following step, or it constructs a rule of the form $t \to v_j'$, which erases the only instance of t and halts the system. Thus, Π performs arbitrary additions of vectors $\mathbf{x}_i \in A$ and then, in the last step of the computation, introduces one of the initial offsets $\mathbf{y}_j \in B$. Therefore, $Ps(\Pi) = \langle A, B \rangle_{\mathbb{N}}$. The fact that we can construct such a P system Π for any uniform semilinear set proves the statement of the theorem. □

Even though one-membrane non-cooperative P systems with random RHS exchange and with randomized pools of RHS cannot generate all unions of linear languages (Theorem 4), they can still generate some limited unions of exponential languages.

Theorem 7. *For $\rho \in \{rhsExchange, rhsPools'\}$, the following is true:*

$$L_{ab}' = \left\{a^{2^n} \mid n \in \mathbb{N}\right\} \cup \left\{b^{2^n} \mid n \in \mathbb{N}\right\} \in PsOP_1(\rho, ncoo).$$

Proof. A P system Π_7 generating the language L_{ab}' can be constructed as follows: $\Pi_7 = (\{a, b, t\}, \{a, b\}, [\ ]_1, t, H, 1)$, where $H = (l, r), l = (t)$ and $r = (tt)(a)(b)$. A graphical representation of Π_7 is given in Fig. 7.

Π_7 works by sequentially multiplying the number of symbols t by 2, until it decides to rewrite every instance of t to a or every instance of t to b. Therefore, $Ps(\Pi_7) = L_{ab}'$. According to Proposition 1, there also exists a P system with random RHS exchange generating L_{ab}', which completes the proof. □

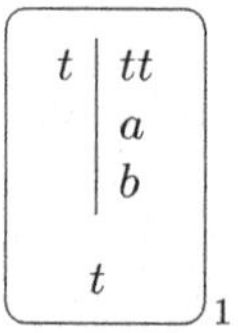

Fig. 7. The P system Π_7 with randomized pools of RHS generating the union language $L_{ab}' = \left\{a^{2^n} \mid n \in \mathbb{N}\right\} \cup \left\{b^{2^n} \mid n \in \mathbb{N}\right\}$

The construction from the previous proof can be clearly extended to any number of distinct terminal symbols and to any function of the number of steps $f(n)$ given by a product of exponentials (like in Theorem 3). That is, one can construct a P systems with random RHS exchange or with randomized pools of RHS generating the union language $\left\{ a_i^{f(n)} \mid n \in \mathbb{N}, 1 \le i \le m \right\}$, for some fixed number m. Note, however, that we cannot use the same approach to generate unions of two different exponential functions. We conjecture that generating such unions is entirely impossible with Variants 1 and 2 of randomized RHS.

5 Variant 3: A Binary Normal Form

In this section we present a binary normal form for P systems with individual randomized RHS: we prove that, for any such P system, there exists an equivalent one in which every production has at most two right-hand sides.

We now introduce a (rather common) construction: symbols with finite timers attached to them. Given an alphabet O, we define the following two functions:

$$timers_o(t, O) = \bigcup_{i=1}^{t} \{\langle a, i \rangle \mid a \in O\},$$
$$timers_r(t) = \{\langle a, i \rangle \to \langle a, i - 1 \rangle \mid 2 \le i \le t\}$$
$$\cup \{\langle a, 1 \rangle \to a \mid a \in O\}.$$

Informally, $timers_o(t, O)$ attaches a t-valued timer to every symbol in O, while $timers_r(t)$ contains the rules making this timer work.

We also define the following function setting a timer to the value $t > 0$ for each symbol in a given string $a_1 \ldots a_n$:

$$wait(t, a_1 \ldots a_n) = \langle a_1, t \rangle \ldots \langle a_n, t \rangle.$$

For $t = 0, wait$ is defined to be the identity function: $wait(0, a_1 \ldots a_n) = a_1 \ldots a_n$.

We can now show that, for any P system with individual randomized RHS there exists an equivalent one having at most two RHS per production.

Theorem 8 (normal form). *For any $\Pi \in OP_n(rndRhs, k), k \in \{coo, ncoo\}$, there exists a $\Pi' \in OP_n(rndRhs^2, k)$ such that $Ps(\Pi') = Ps(\Pi)$.*

Proof. Consider the following P system with individual randomized RHS $\Pi = (O, T, \mu, w_1, \ldots, w_n, P_1, \ldots P_n, h_o)$ that has at least one production with more than two RHS. We will construct another P system with individual randomized RHS $\Pi' = (O', T, \mu, w_1, \ldots, w_n, P_1', \ldots P_n', h_o)$ such that $Ps(\Pi') = Ps(\Pi)$. The new alphabet will be defined as

$$O' = O \cup timers_o(t, O) \cup \{p_1, \ldots, p_t \mid p \in V_p\},$$

where $t + 2$ is the number of right-hand sides in the productions of Π having the most of them, and V_p is an alphabet containing a symbol for each of the individual productions of Π. (If there are two identical productions in Π which belong to two different membranes, V_p will contain one different symbol for each of these two productions.)

For every membrane $1 \leq i \leq n$, the new set of productions P'_i is constructed by applying the following procedure to every production $p \in P_i$:

- If p has the form $u \to \{v\}$, we add the production $u \to \{wait(t, v)\}$ to P'_i.
- If p has the form $u \to \{v_1, v_2\}$, we add $u \to \{wait(t, v_1), wait(t, v_2)\}$ to P'_i.
- If p has the form $u \to \{v_1, \ldots, v_k\}$, with $k \geq 3$, we add the following productions to P_i:

$$\{u \to \{wait(t, v_1), p_1\}\}$$
$$\cup \{p_j \to \{wait(t - j, v_{j+1}), p_{j+1}\} \mid 1 \leq j < k - 2\}$$
$$\cup \{p_{k-2} \to \{wait(t - k + 2, v_{k-1}), wait(t - k + 2, v_k)\}\}.$$

These productions are graphically represented in Fig. 8, in which arrows go from LHS to the associated RHS.

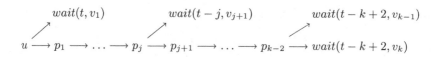

Fig. 8. Timers allow sequential choice between any number of right-hand sides.

Finally we add the rules from $timers_r(t)$, treated as one-RHS production, to every P'_i.

Instead of directly choosing between the right hand-sides of a production $p : u \to \{v_1, \ldots, v_k\}$ in one step, Π' chooses between v_1 and delaying the choice to the next step, by producing p_1. This choice between settling on an RHS or continuing the enumeration in the next step may be kept on until $k - 2$ RHS have been discarded. If p_{k-2} is reached, Π' must choose one of the two remaining RHS.

Thus, Π' evolves in "macro-steps", each consisting of exactly t steps. In the first step of a "macro-step", Π' acts on the symbols from O, producing some symbols with timers and delaying some of the choices by producing symbols p_j. All symbols with timers wait exactly until the t-th step of the "macro-step" to turn into the corresponding clean versions from O. Since $t + 2$ is the number of RHS in the biggest production of Π, Π' has the time to enumerate all of the RHS of this production.

Since every delayed choice of Π' is uniquely identified by a production-specific symbol p_j, and since only the productions from $timers_r(t)$ can act upon the symbols with timers in Π', the simulations of two different productions of Π cannot interfere. This concludes the proof of the normal form. $\qquad\square$

6   Conclusions and Open Problems

In this article, we introduced and partially studied P systems with randomized rule right-hand sides. This is a model of P systems with dynamic rules, in which the matching between left-hand and right-hand sides is non-deterministically changed during the evolution. In each step, such P systems first construct the rules from the available rule sides and then apply them, in a maximally parallel way.

We defined three different randomization semantics: random RHS exchange (Variant 1), randomized pools of RHS (Variant 2), and individual randomized RHS (Variant 3). We studied the computational power of the three variants and showed that Variant 3 is quite different in power from Variants 1 and 2. Indeed, P systems with individual randomized RHS (Variant 3) appear as a strict extension of conventional P systems, while random RHS exchange (Variant 1) and randomized pools of RHS (Variant 2) seem to increase the power when only one LHS is used, but to decrease the power when more LHS are present. Finally, we gave a binary normal form for P systems with individual randomized RHS (Variant 3).

6.1   Open Questions

The present work leaves open quite a number of open questions. We list the ones appearing important to us, in no particular order.

Full power of Variants 1 and 2: Are cooperative, multi-membrane P systems with random RHS exchange (Variant 1) or with randomized pools of RHS (Variant 2) computationally complete? If not, what would be the upper bound on their power? In this article, we showed that applying these two randomization semantics to the non-cooperative, one-membrane case, yields a family of multiset languages incomparable with the family of semi-linear vector sets. How much more can be achieved with cooperativity? We conjecture that, even with LHS containing more than one symbol, Variants 1 and 2 will *not* be computationally complete. However, we expect that considering systems with multiple membranes may actually bring a substantial boost in computational power, because, in both Variants 1 and 2, randomization happens over each single membrane, meaning that one might use a rich membrane structure to finely control its effects.

Compare the variants: How do the three variants of RHS randomization compare among one another when applied to non-cooperative rules? We saw that, in all three cases, exponential number languages can be generated. We also saw that individual randomized RHS (Variant 3) produce a strict superset of the semi-linear languages (Proposition 4). Does it imply that Variant 3 is strictly more powerful than Variants 1 and 2? We conjecture a positive answer to this question.

Excess of LHS: In the case of P systems with randomized pools of RHS (Variant 2), what is the consequence of having *more LHS* available in a membrane than there are RHS? The results in this paper concern a "restricted" version of

Variant 2, in which we require that LHS are never in excess. How strong is this restriction? Our conjecture is that allowing an excess of LHS does not increase the computational power.

Applications to vulnerable systems: As noted in the introduction to the present work, randomized RHS can be seen as a representation of systems mutating in a toxic environment. However, we did not give any concrete examples. It would be interesting to look up any such concrete cases and to evaluate the relevance of this unconventional modeling approach.

6.2 Further Variants

Forbidding identical rules: In any of the three variants, it may happen that identical rules are constructed, in any membrane. In the previous chapters, in this case this rule was simply taken into the set of rules. Yet we could also forbid such a situation to happen and in such a case completely abandon the whole rule set. Another solution can be to take out all rules having been constructed more than once from the constructed rule set.

The situation of getting identical rules can easily be avoided by avoiding identical RHS: the right-hand sides of rules can be made different by adding suitable powers of a dummy symbol d, which does not count for the final result (i.e., d is no terminal symbol). As d also does not appear on the left-hand side of a rule, the computational power of any of the P systems variant considered in this paper will not be changed by this changing of the set of RHS available for constructing the set of rules.

Identical RHS in Variant 3: In P systems with individual randomized RHS the computational power mainly arises from the possibility to specify different sets of RHS for the left-hand sides of rules. What happens if the set R of RHS must be the same for all left-hand sides?

Tissue P systems with randomized RHS: The idea of randomizing right-hand sides can be extended from hierarchical P systems, i.e., from P systems with a tree-like membrane structure, to tissue P systems, i.e., P systems with cells arranged in an arbitrary graph structure.

Several issues, especially the variants of tissue P systems with randomized RHS, are discussed together with some first results in a preliminary but extended version of this paper, see [2].

References

1. Alhazov, A.: A note on P systems with activators. In: Păun, G., Riscos-Núñez, A., Romero-Jiménez, A., Sancho-Caparrini, F. (eds.) Second Brainstorming Week on Membrane Computing, Sevilla, Spain, 2–7 February 2004, pp. 16–19 (2004)
2. Alhazov, A., Freund, R., Ivanov, S.: P systems with randomized right-hand sides of rules. In: 15th Brainstorming Week on Membrane Computing, Sevilla, Spain, 31 January–5 February 2017 (2017)

3. Alhazov, A., Freund, R., Ivanov, S., Oswald, M.: Observations on P systems with states. In: Gheorghe, M., Petre, I., Pérez-Jiménez, M.J., Rozenberg, G., Salomaa, A. (eds.) Multidisciplinary Creativity. Hommage to Gheorghe Păun on His 65th Birthday, Spandugino (2015)

4. Alhazov, A., Ivanov, S., Rogozhin, Y.: Polymorphic P systems. In: Gheorghe, M., Hinze, T., Păun, G., Rozenberg, G., Salomaa, A. (eds.) CMC 2010. LNCS, vol. 6501, pp. 81–94. Springer, Heidelberg (2010). https://doi.org/10.1007/978-3-642-18123-8_9

5. Arroyo, F., Baranda, A.V., Castellanos, J., Păun, G.: Membrane computing: the power of (rule) creation. J. Univers. Comput. Sci. **8**, 369–381 (2002)

6. Çapuni, I., Gács, P.: A turing machine resisting isolated bursts of faults. CoRR, abs/1203.1335 (2012)

7. Cavaliere, M., Genova, D.: P systems with symport/antiport of rules. In: Păun, G., Riscos-Núñez, A., Romero-Jiménez, A., Sancho-Caparrini, F. (eds.) Second Brainstorming Week on Membrane Computing, Sevilla, Spain, 2–7 February 2004, pp. 102–116 (2004)

8. Cavaliere, M., Ionescu, M., Ishdorj, T.-O.: Inhibiting/de-inhibiting rules in P systems. In: Mauri, G., Păun, G., Pérez-Jiménez, M.J., Rozenberg, G., Salomaa, A. (eds.) WMC 2004. LNCS, vol. 3365, pp. 224–238. Springer, Heidelberg (2005). https://doi.org/10.1007/978-3-540-31837-8_13

9. Freund, R.: Generalized P-systems. In: Ciobanu, G., Păun, G. (eds.) FCT 1999. LNCS, vol. 1684, pp. 281–292. Springer, Heidelberg (1999). https://doi.org/10.1007/3-540-48321-7_23

10. Freund, R.: P systems working in the sequential mode on arrays and strings. In: Calude, C.S., Calude, E., Dinneen, M.J. (eds.) DLT 2004. LNCS, vol. 3340, pp. 188–199. Springer, Heidelberg (2004). https://doi.org/10.1007/978-3-540-30550-7_16

11. Freund, R., Leporati, A., Mauri, G., Porreca, A.E., Verlan, S., Zandron, C.: Flattening in (tissue) P systems. In: Alhazov, A., Cojocaru, S., Gheorghe, M., Rogozhin, Y., Rozenberg, G., Salomaa, A. (eds.) CMC 2013. LNCS, vol. 8340, pp. 173–188. Springer, Heidelberg (2014). https://doi.org/10.1007/978-3-642-54239-8_13

12. Ivanov, S.: Polymorphic P systems with non-cooperative rules and no ingredients. In: Gheorghe, M., Rozenberg, G., Salomaa, A., Sosík, P., Zandron, C. (eds.) CMC 2014. LNCS, vol. 8961, pp. 258–273. Springer, Cham (2014). https://doi.org/10.1007/978-3-319-14370-5_16

13. Păun, G.: Computing with membranes. J. Comput. Syst. Sci. **61**, 108–143 (1998)

14. Păun, G., Rozenberg, G., Salomaa, A.: The Oxford Handbook of Membrane Computing. Oxford University Press Inc., New York (2010)

15. Rozenberg, G., Salomaa, A. (eds.): Handbook of Formal Languages, vol. 3. Springer, New York (1997). https://doi.org/10.1007/978-3-642-59126-6

16. Bulletin of the International Membrane Computing Society (IMCS). http://membranecomputing.net/IMCSBulletin/index.php

17. The P Systems Website. http://ppage.psystems.eu/

Controlled Reversibility in Reaction Systems

Bogdan Aman[✉] and Gabriel Ciobanu

Institute of Computer Science, Romanian Academy,
Blvd. Carol I no. 8, 700505 Iaşi, Romania
bogdan.aman@gmail.com, gabriel@info.uaic.ro

Abstract. We study the controlled reversibility in reaction systems, a bio-inspired formalism in which the reactions take place only if some inhibitors are not present. Forward reactions are exactly those of the reaction systems, while reverse reactions happen when a special symbol indicates a change in the environment. The reversible reaction systems are translated into rewriting systems which are executable on the Maude software platform. Given such an implementation, several properties of the reversible reaction systems could be verified.

1 Introduction

In this paper we investigate the reversibility of biochemical reactions in the framework of natural computing. Natural computing [16] is the field of research dealing with models and computational techniques inspired by nature, helping us to understand the biochemical world around us in terms of information processing. Two important theories of natural computing inspired by the functioning of living cells are membrane computing [22] and reaction systems [13].

Membrane computing deals with multisets of symbols processed in the compartments of a membrane structure according to some multiset rewriting rules. The symbols are present with their multiplicity within the regions delimited by membranes. Some of these symbols evolve in parallel according to the rules associated with their membranes, while the others remain unchanged and can be used in the subsequent steps. The situation is different in reaction systems. These systems represent a qualitative model, and they deal with sets rather than multisets. Two major assumptions set the reaction systems apart from the membrane systems: (i) *threshold assumption* claiming that if a resource is present in the system, then it is present in a "sufficient amount" such that several reactions needing such a resource will not be in conflict (this means that reaction systems have actually an infinite multiplicity for their resources); (ii) *no permanency assumption* claiming that an entity will vanish from the current state unless it is produced by one of the reactions enabled in that state.

Reversible computation is an emerging paradigm extending the standard forwards-only mode of computation with the ability to execute also reversely, such that a computation can run backwards as naturally as it can go forwards. It has been studied for Turing machines [9,21] and register machines [20] in

© Springer International Publishing AG 2018
M. Gheorghe et al. (Eds.): CMC 2017, LNCS 10725, pp. 40–53, 2018.
https://doi.org/10.1007/978-3-319-73359-3_3

which the reversible computation provides the possibility of returning to the initial state from any reachable state. It is worth pointing out that there exist both uncontrolled and controlled reversibility. Uncontrolled reversibility means that reversing a system is done without indicating exactly when backward steps are executed. Reversibility appears naturally in chemical and biological systems, and it is probably related to the fault tolerance and stability of these systems. However, some steps are reversed only when there exist a specific context, an environmental modification which activates the computation in a backward direction. Taking care of the systems in which backward and forward evolutions depend on specific physical conditions, in this paper we consider a controlled reversibility in reaction systems. In order to control the reversibility, a special rollback symbol ρ is used to activate the backward evolution. We use specific sequences including this special symbol coming from the environment; these sequences control the direction of the computation in order to recover from failures or to avoid deadlocks, for instance.

Rewrite theories and rewriting logic [19] has been used for more than two decades as computational frameworks able to express several paradigms. Computationally, rewriting logic represents a semantic framework in which various models are naturally formalized; for instance, membrane systems can be executed and analyzed as rewrite theories [2,6]. Logically, rewriting logic is a framework within which various logics can be represented. A list of calculi, logics, programming languages and models described as rewrite theory and rewriting logic is presented in [19]. We use rewriting logic and present an implementation of the reversible reaction systems in the rewriting engine Maude based on a correspondence between their operational semantics and their rewriting logic translation. This allows the automated verification of their properties.

2 Reaction Systems

Reaction systems (abbreviated as RS) are used for modelling processes driven by biochemical reactions; the fundamental idea in this framework is that the biochemical reactions are based on the mechanisms of facilitation and inhibition [10]. Thus a reaction is modelled as a triplet: a set of reactants, a set of inhibitors, and a set of products. A reaction can take place in a given state if all its reactants are present in that state, and none of its inhibitors are present; when triggered, the reaction creates its products. We recall in what follows some elementary notions and notations about reaction systems, as presented in [10].

Let S be an alphabet (its elements are called molecules, or simply symbols). A reaction over S is a triple $a = (R, I, P)$, where R, I, P are non-empty subsets of S such that $R \cap I = \emptyset$. R is the reactant set of a, I is the inhibitor set of a, and P is the product set of a; R, I, P are also denoted as R_a, I_a, P_a, respectively. We denote by $rac(S)$ the set of all reactions in S.

Given a configuration $T \subseteq S$ and a reaction $a \in rac(S)$, a is enabled by T (denoted by $a \ en \ T$) if $R_a \subseteq T$ and $I_a \cap T = \emptyset$. The result $res(a, T)$ of a on T is defined by $res(a, T) = P_a$. This reaction can be written as a rewrite of the form $T \xrightarrow{a} res(a, T)$. If a is not enabled by T, then $res(a, T) = \emptyset$; the fact that T cannot be rewritten by applying a is written as $T \not\xrightarrow{a}$.

If A is a finite set of reactions, then the result of A on T is defined by $res(A, T) = \bigcup_{a \in A} res(a, T)$. This can be written as $T \xrightarrow{A} res(A, T)$. The activity of a set of reactions A on a finite set T is defined by $en(A, T) = \{a \in A \mid a \text{ } en \text{ } T\}$. Thus, $en(A, T)$ is the set of all reactions from A that are enabled by T. Note that $res(A, T) = res(en(A, T), T)$; this means that only the reactions from A which are enabled on T contribute to the result of A on T.

A *reaction system* is an ordered pair $\mathcal{A} = (S, A)$, where S is an alphabet and $A \subseteq rac(S)$. The dynamic behaviour of the reaction systems is captured through the notion of an interactive process defined as follows.

Definition 1. *Let $\mathcal{A} = (S, A)$ be a reaction system. An interactive process in $\mathcal{A}$ is a pair $\pi = (\gamma, \delta)$ of finite sequences such that $\gamma = C_0, C_1, \ldots, C_{n-1}, \delta = D_1, \ldots, D_n$ with $n \geq 1$, where $C_0, \ldots, C_{n-1}, D_1, \ldots, D_n \subseteq S, D_1 = res(A, C_0)$, and $D_i = res(A, D_{i-1} \cup C_{i-1})$ for each $2 \leq i \leq n$.*

The sequences $C_0, \ldots, C_{n-1}$ and $D_1, \ldots, D_n$ are the context and result sequences of π, respectively. Context C_0 represents the initial state of π (the state in which the interactive process is initiated), and the contexts $C_1, \ldots, C_{n-1}$ represent the influence of the environment to the computation. It should be noticed that the context sequence $\gamma = C_0, C_1, \ldots, C_{n-1}$ is described by a regular expression over S. This sequence formalizes the fact that we work with an open system interacting with the environment, somehow similar to what happens in the spiking neural P systems with input neurons [14]. The sequence $sts(\pi) = W_0, \ldots, W_n$ denotes the state sequence of π, where $W_0 = C_0$ (the initial state), and $W_i = D_i \cup C_i$ for all $1 \leq i \leq n$. The sequence $act(\pi) = E_0, \ldots, E_{n-1}$ of subsets of A such that $E_i = en(A, W_i)$ for all $0 \leq i \leq n - 1$ represents the activity sequence of π. Thus, the evolution can be written as

$$W_0 \xrightarrow{E_0} W_1 \xrightarrow{E_1} \ldots \xrightarrow{E_{n-1}} W_n.$$

In the definition of the result of a set A of reactions on a set T of molecules, it is easy to note the two assumptions mentioned in the previous section: a molecule can evolve by means of several reactions (or can inhibit several reactions if it appears in inhibitor sets), hence the multiplicity of each molecule is unbounded, while all the molecules present at a given time "disappear" after the reactions are enabled and the computation continues with the set of molecules produced by the reactions.

Example 1. We describe the self-assembly of intermediate filaments from vimentin tetramers presented in [8] by using the reaction systems. Two tetramers (denoted by T) join to form an octamer (denoted by O), two octamers join to form a hexadecamer (denoted by H), while two hexadecamer join to form a unit length filament ULF. We consider the ULFs as elementary filaments (generically denoted by F). Two longer filaments join by end-to-end interactions, and form a longer complex. We present the molecular model of this basic representation and the corresponding reactions in the following reaction system $\mathcal{A} = (S, A)$ with $S = \{T, O, H, F, d_I\}$:

Reaction in the molecular model	Reaction in the reaction system
$2T \rightarrow O$	$(\{T\}, \{d_I\}, \{O\})$
$2O \rightarrow H$	$(\{O\}, \{d_I\}, \{H\})$
$2H \rightarrow F$	$(\{H\}, \{d_I\}, \{F\})$
$2F \rightarrow F$	$(\{F\}, \{d_I\}, \{F\})$

The dummy variable d_I is used only to respect the constraint that the set of inhibitors should be non-empty in each reaction.

A possible evolution of this system is into a loop after the third state, a loop from which every state W_i with $i \geq 3$ contains all the species of the system:

State	C_i	D_i	W_i
0	$\{T\}$	$\emptyset$	$\{T\}$
1	$\{T\}$	$\{O\}$	$\{T, O\}$
2	$\{T\}$	$\{O, H\}$	$\{T, O, H\}$
3	$\{T\}$	$\{O, H, F\}$	$\{T, O, H, F\}$
4	$\{T\}$	$\{O, H, F\}$	$\{T, O, H, F\}$

This evolution is obtained if the context sequence γ has the form $\gamma = T^n$, namely $C_i = \{T\}$ for all $0 \leq i \leq n - 1$.

Another possible evolution of the system is into a loop after the initial state from which every state W_i with $i \geq 1$ contains only the initial input:

State	C_i	D_i	W_i
0	$\{F\}$	$\emptyset$	$\{F\}$
1	$\emptyset$	$\{F\}$	$\{F\}$
2	$\emptyset$	$\{F\}$	$\{F\}$

This alternative evolution is obtained if the context sequence γ has the form $\gamma = T$, namely $C_0 = \{F\}$ and $C_i = \emptyset$ for all $1 \leq i \leq n - 1$. As C_0 represents the initial state, we have $C_0 \neq \emptyset$.

3   Reversible Reaction Systems

In order to have backward computations, we add to each state W_i a register T_i keeping track of the symbols that will disappear after step i as they were not created by the reactions of the current step (to assure the *no permanency assumption*). This is required by the fact that these symbols need to be recreated when we intend to reverse the computation. Thus, we work with register states $W_i' = (W_i, T_i)$, where $T_i \subseteq S \times \mathbb{N}$ is the set of objects disappearing during the evolution together with a number indicating how many steps ago this happened. We can see each state W_i as an equivalence relation of register states obtained by ignoring the sets T_i; namely, we define a relation $\equiv$ over register states given by $(W_i, T) \equiv (W_i, T')$ for all $T, T' \subseteq S \times \mathbb{N}$. Obviously, $\equiv$ is an equivalence relation.

Proposition 1. *The set $S \times (S \times \mathbb{N})/_{\equiv}$ of equivalence classes is isomorphic with the set S of states of the reaction system $\mathcal{A}$.*

Proof. We define $\phi : S \times (S \times \mathbb{N}) \to S$ inductively by $\phi((W, T)) = W$. This map induces a bijection $\overline{\phi} : S \times (S \times \mathbb{N})/_{\equiv} \to S$.

The evolution $W_0 \xrightarrow{E_0} W_1$ described in Sect. 2 becomes $(W_0, T_0) \xrightarrow{E_0} (W_1, T_1)$, where $T_0 = \emptyset$ and $T_1 = \bigcup_{t \in W_0 \setminus lhs(E_0)}(t, 0)$. In a similar manner, $W_i \xrightarrow{E_i} W_{i+1}$ for $i \geq 1$ becomes $(W_i, T_i) \xrightarrow{E_i} (W_{i+1}, T_{i+1})$, where $T_{i+1} = inc(T_i) \cup \bigcup_{t \in W_i \setminus lhs(E_i)}(t, 0)$ and $inc(T) = \bigcup_{(t,i) \in T}(t, i+1)$. The set $lhs(E) = \bigcup_{(R,I,P) \in E} R$ is the collection of all reactants from the set of enabled reactions E, while $W \setminus lhs(E)$ is used to compute the set of molecules that vanishes after the reactions from E are applied to W.

To reverse a computation, a natural approach is to reverse its reactions. Reversing a reaction $a = (R_a, I_a, P_a)$ means that its reverse $\tilde{a}$ is able to undo the effects of a. According to [2], if the rule does not contain inhibitors, then $(P, \emptyset, R)$ is the reverse of $(R, \emptyset, P)$; this means to switch the position of reactants and products. If in a step a reaction a is applied, then its inhibitors I_a are not present (and not modified by rules of A). This means that the set of inhibitors remains the same when we reverse the effect of such a reaction.

Definition 2. *The reverse of a reaction $a = (R_a, I_a, P_a)$ is given by the reaction $\tilde{a} = (P_a, I_a, R_a)$. Similarly, the reverse of a set A of reactions is the set $\tilde{A} = \{\tilde{a} \mid a \in A\}$.*

Since in Sect. 2 we imposed $R \cap I = \emptyset$ for a reaction $a = (R, I, P)$, the definition above has the problem that the reverse $\tilde{a} = (R', I', P')$ might not be a reaction because $R' \cap I' \neq \emptyset$. For example, let us consider the reaction $a = (b, c, c)$ and assume that $res(A, c) = \emptyset$. The resulting reverse reaction would be $\tilde{a} = (c, c, b)$, which is not a reaction because reactants and inhibitors have a non-empty intersection. To overcome this problem, we impose from now on that we work only with reactions $a = (R, I, P)$ satisfying that $R \cap I = P \cap I = \emptyset$. It should be noticed that the principle of double negation is valid when we use Definition 2, namely we have $\tilde{\tilde{a}} = a$.

To avoid going backward and forward between two states for an infinite number of times, we also impose that the reverse computation is realized only when a special object ρ is introduced from the environment (context). The control is therefore performed by an (active) environment that provides at certain steps the special rollback symbol ρ signalling the system that it has to reverse its computation. This ρ is an abstraction of a physical reality in which a system is informed that a certain change in the environment has an effect on its evolution, as happens in heat shock response modelled previously by using the reaction systems in [7]. We assume also that this special symbol cannot be created by any reaction of A.

In this general framework, the evolution can take place by applying one of the following two rules:

$$(fwd) \quad \frac{\rho \notin W_i \qquad E_i \neq \emptyset}{(W_i, T_i) \xrightarrow{E_i} (W_{i+1}, T_{i+1})}$$

where $T_{i+1} = inc(T_i) \cup \bigcup_{t \in W_i \setminus lhs(E_i)} (t, 0)$, $inc(T) = \bigcup_{(t,i) \in T} (t, i+1)$ and $W_{i+1} = res(E_i, W_i)$;

$$(rev) \quad \frac{\rho \in W_i \qquad \tilde{E}_i \neq \emptyset}{(W_{i+1}, T_{i+1}) \xrightarrow{\tilde{E}_i} (W_i, T_i)}$$

where $T_i = dec(T_{i+1})$, $dec(T_d) = \bigcup_{(t,i) \in T_d; i > 0} (t, i-1)$ and $W_i = res(\tilde{E}_i, W_{i+1})$ $\cup\, zero(T_{i+1})$ with $zero(T) = \bigcup_{(t,0) \in T} t$. Also, $\tilde{E}_i = en(\tilde{A}, W_{i+1})$.

This means that if $C_i \cap \{\rho\} = \emptyset$ then a forward computation takes place, while if $C_i \cap \{\rho\} \neq \emptyset$ then a backward computation takes place.

Example 2. To reverse a computation, we first construct the reversed reactions:

a	$\tilde{a}$
$(\{T\}, \{d_I\}, \{O\})$	$(\{O\}, \{d_I\}, \{T\})$
$(\{O\}, \{d_I\}, \{H\})$	$(\{H\}, \{d_I\}, \{O\})$
$(\{H\}, \{d_I\}, \{F\})$	$(\{F\}, \{d_I\}, \{H\})$
$(\{F\}, \{d_I\}, \{F\})$	$(\{F\}, \{d_I\}, \{F\})$

As d_I is a dummy variable, then it is kept also in the reversed reactions.

We present now a possible evolution of the reaction system describing the self-assembly of intermediate filaments from vimentin tetramers by using also the reversed reactions when the special symbol ρ appears:

State	C_i	D_i	W_i	T_i
0	$\{T\}$	$\emptyset$	$\{T\}$	$\emptyset$
1	$\{T\}$	$\{O\}$	$\{T, O\}$	$\emptyset$
2	$\{\rho\}$	$\{O, H\}$	$\{\rho, O, H\}$	$\emptyset$
3	$\{\emptyset\}$	$\{T, O\}$	$\{T, O\}$	$\emptyset$
4	$\{T\}$	$\{O, H\}$	$\{T, O, H\}$	$\emptyset$
5	$\{T\}$	$\{O, H, F\}$	$\{T, O, H, F\}$	$\emptyset$
6	$\{\rho\}$	$\{O, H, F\}$	$\{\rho, O, H, F\}$	$\emptyset$
7	$\emptyset$	$\{T, O, H, F\}$	$\{T, O, H, F\}$	$\emptyset$

It can be easily noticed that if the rollback symbol ρ is introduced from the environment, then the system reaches the previous state going backward.

Another possible evolution of the system is:

State	C_i	D_i	W_i	T_i
0	$\{F\}$	$\emptyset$	$\{F\}$	$\emptyset$
1	ρ	$\{F\}$	$\{\rho, F\}$	$\emptyset$
2	ρ	$\{H, F\}$	$\{\rho, H, F\}$	$\emptyset$
3	ρ	$\{O, H, F\}$	$\{\rho, O, H, F\}$	$\emptyset$
4	$\emptyset$	$\{T, O, H, F\}$	$\{T, O, H, F\}$	$\emptyset$
5	$\emptyset$	$\{O, H, F\}$	$\{O, H, F\}$	$\emptyset$
6	$\emptyset$	$\{H, F\}$	$\{H, F\}$	$\emptyset$
7	$\emptyset$	$\{F\}$	$\{F\}$	$\emptyset$

In this case it is worth noting that even if we start from a system containing only F, the forward evolution keeps the same state while the backward evolution reaches the state $\{T, O, H, F\}$ from which going forward we reach again the state F (whenever the environment does not offer other rollback symbols).

Remark 1. For the purpose of this paper it is enough to consider the controlled reversibility by using context sequences with symbols from $\{\emptyset; \rho\}$ for $C_i, i > 0$. The case of considering scenarios using symbols from an extended set represents further work.

Our reversible reaction systems (RRS) represent only a decoration of the reaction systems (RS) defined in the previous sections. In fact, as for the most of the existing reversible approaches, such decorations can be erased by a forgetful map $\phi : RRS \rightarrow RS$ defined as $\phi((W_i, T_i)) = W_i$. Conversely, one can lift any RS configuration to an RRS configuration by using the map $l : RS \rightarrow RRS$ defined by $l(W_i) = (W_i, \emptyset)$, namely by adding an empty register to a state.

It is enough to forget about backward rules by considering $C_i = \emptyset$ $(i > 0)$ in the reversible reaction systems. In this way, there is no object ρ coming from the environment to inhibit the forward rules. This is formally stated in what follows; the next result shows that a step in the initial reaction system can be modelled by a forward step in the reversible reaction system.

Proposition 2. $W \xrightarrow{E} W'$ *if and only if* $(W, T) \xrightarrow{E} (W', T')$.

Proof. $\Rightarrow$: If $W \xrightarrow{E} W'$, then $W' = res(E, W)$. According to our constructions, for each configuration W of a reaction system there exist a corresponding configuration of a reversible reaction system given by $l(W) = (W, \emptyset)$. By applying the rule *(fwd)* to (W, T) where $T = \emptyset$, we obtain the configuration (W'', T') where $W'' = res(E', W)$ and $T' = \bigcup_{t \in W \setminus lhs(E)}(t, 0)$. Due to the threshold assumption of the reaction systems, we got that $E = E'$; namely, there is an unique set of reactions applicable to W. This means that $W'' = W'$, and so $(W, T) \xrightarrow{E} (W', T')$ holds.

$\Leftarrow$: If $(W, T) \xrightarrow{E} (W', T')$, then $T' = \cup_{(t,i) \in T}(t, i+1) \cup \bigcup_{t \in W \setminus lhs(E)}(t, 0)$ and $W' = res(E, W)$. By applying the forgetful map ϕ to the configuration (W, T) of the reversible reaction systems, we obtain the configuration W of the reaction systems. By applying all the possible reactions to this configuration, we obtain $W \xrightarrow{E'} W''$, where $W'' = res(E', W)$. Due to the threshold assumption of the reaction systems, we got that $E = E'$; namely, there is a unique set of reactions applicable to W. This means that $W'' = W'$, and so $W \xrightarrow{E} W'$ holds. $\square$

Remark 2. Note that by using a reaction system, it is possible to reverse a computation beyond its initial state. This means that there are cases in which the construction provided before produces, by going backward from a certain state (W, T), a state (W', T') in which W' is not contained in the set of pre-images of W. Our approach is similar with the one presented in [17], where a process calculus for the out-of-causal order reversible computation was proposed. This approach is illustrated by the last case of Example 2, where starting from $\{F\}$ and going backward some steps without performing any forward step previously, we reach a new state $\{T, O, H, F\}$ which is not contained in the set of pre-images of $\{F\}$.

The following two theorems show that, in certain cases, if the current state is related to the new obtained one by certain relations, then the reversible reaction systems enjoy a standard property of reversible calculi described by so-called *loop lemma* in [12]: backward reductions are the inverse of the forward ones, and vice-versa. It is worth noting that the following two theorems specify the necessary conditions such that the reverse reactions defined as in Definition 2 are able to provide, together with the additional memory, a way of "going back" one step in the computation (i.e., a causal reversibility).

Theorem 1. *If* $W = res(\tilde{E}, W') \cup zero(T')$ *and* $\rho \in W'$, *then*

$$(W, T) \xrightarrow{E} (W', T') \text{ implies } (W', T') \overset{\tilde{E}}{\rightsquigarrow} (W, T).$$

Proof. If $(W, T) \xrightarrow{E} (W', T')$, then $T' = inc(T) \cup \bigcup_{t \in W \setminus lhs(E)}(t, 0), inc(T) = \bigcup_{(t,i) \in T}(t, i+1)$ and $W' = res(E, W)$. Since $\rho \in W'$, then a *(rev)* rule can be applied, and so $(W', T') \overset{\tilde{E}}{\rightsquigarrow} (W'', T'')$ with $T'' = dec(T')$ and $dec(T') = \bigcup_{(t,i) \in T'; i>0}(t, i-1)$, as well as $W'' = res(\tilde{E}, W') \cup zero(T')$ with $zero(T') = \bigcup_{(t,0) \in T'} t$. Notice that $T'' = dec(T') = dec(inc(T) \cup \bigcup_{t \in W \setminus lhs(E)}(t, 0)) = dec(inc(T)) \cup dec(\bigcup_{t \in W \setminus lhs(E)}(t, 0)) = T \cup \emptyset = T$, and also due to the hypothesis that $W'' = res(\tilde{E}, W') \cup zero(T') = W$. This means that we got $(W', T') \overset{\tilde{E}}{\rightsquigarrow} (W, T)$, as desired. $\square$

Theorem 2. *If $W' = res(E, W)$ and $\rho \notin W$, then*

$$(W', T') \overset{\tilde{E}}{\rightsquigarrow} (W, T) \text{ implies } (W, T) \overset{E}{\longrightarrow} (W', T').$$

Proof. If $(W', T') \overset{\tilde{E}}{\rightsquigarrow} (W, T)$, then $T = dec(T')$ where $dec(T') = \bigcup_{(t,i) \in T'; i > 0}$ $(t, i - 1)$ and $W = res(\tilde{E}, W') \cup zero(T')$ with $zero(T') = \bigcup_{(t,0) \in T'} t$. Since $\rho \notin W$, then a *(fwd)* rule can be applied, and so $(W, T) \overset{E}{\longrightarrow} (W'', T'')$ with $T'' = inc(T) \cup \bigcup_{t \in W \setminus lhs(E)} (t, 0)$, $inc(T) = \bigcup_{(t,i) \in T} (t, i+1)$ and $W'' = res(E, W)$. It should be noticed that $T'' = inc(T) \cup \bigcup_{t \in W \setminus lhs(E)} (t, 0)$

$= inc(dec(T')) \cup \bigcup_{t \in (res(\tilde{E}, W') \cup zero(T')) \setminus lhs(E)} (t, 0)$

$= (T' \setminus \bigcup_{t \in zero(T')} (t, 0)) \cup \bigcup_{t \in (rhs(\tilde{E}) \cup zero(T')) \setminus lhs(E)} (t, 0)$

$= (T' \setminus \bigcup_{t \in zero(T')} (t, 0)) \cup \bigcup_{t \in (lhs(E) \cup zero(T')) \setminus lhs(E)} (t, 0)$

$= (T' \setminus \bigcup_{t \in zero(T')} (t, 0)) \cup \bigcup_{t \in zero(T')} (t, 0) = T'$

and also due to the hypothesis that $W'' = res(E, W) = W'$. This means that we got $(W, T) \overset{E}{\longrightarrow} (W', T')$, as desired. □

Remark 3. The hypotheses of the above two theorems could appear too strong, and that these theorems are applicable indifferent of the reversibility for a reaction given in Definition 2. We present a counterexample for Theorem 1 to illustrate that this in not true.

Let us consider $A = \{r_1, r_2\}$, where $r_1 = (a, b, c)$ and $r_2 = (b, a, c)$. By applying Definition 2, we get the reverse rules $\tilde{r_1} = (c, b, a)$ and $\tilde{r_2} = (c, a, b)$. If $(W, T) = (a, \emptyset)$, it implies that $E = en(A, W) = r_1$ and $(W, T) \overset{E}{\longrightarrow} (W', T')$ with $W' = c$ and $T' = T = \emptyset$. By definition, $\tilde{E} = en(\tilde{A}, W') = \{\tilde{r_1}, \tilde{r_2}\}$; thus $(W', T') \overset{\tilde{E}}{\longrightarrow} (W'', T'')$ with $W'' = res(\tilde{E}, W') \cup zero(T') = ab$ and $T'' = T' = \emptyset$. This implies that $W'' \neq W$, and so the theorem is not applicable as the theorem holds only if the set of reversed rules $\tilde{E}$ is able to recreate the initial configuration W. This is why we have added the strong hypothesis stating that only in certain conditions the step of a system is truly reversible.

4   Implementation of Reversible Reaction Systems

Rewriting logic is a computational logic which combines equational logic with term rewriting. According to [11], a *rewrite theory* is a triple (Σ, E, R), where Σ is a signature of function symbols, E a set of (possibly conditional) Σ-equations, and R a set of (possibly conditional) Σ-rewrite rules. The conditions for a rewrite rule can involve both equations and rewrite rules. Generally, a typed setting is used in [18] under the form of an order-sorted equational logic (Σ, E) which has sorts, subsort inclusions and kinds (connected components of sorts). The notation $\mathcal{R} \vdash t \to t'$ is used to express that $t \to t'$ is provable in the theory $\mathcal{R}$ using the inference rules of the rewriting logic. For a kind k and a set of kinded variables $X, T_\Sigma(X)_k$ denotes the set of Σ-terms of kind k over the variables in X. If s is a sort in the kind $k, T_\Sigma(X)_s$ is the subset of $T_\Sigma(X)_k$ consisting of Σ-terms of sort s over X. Given a rewrite theory $\mathcal{R} = (\Sigma, E, R)$, the sentences which $\mathcal{R}$ proves are of form $(\forall X)t \to t'$, with $t, t' \in T_\Sigma(X)_k$ for some kind k. These sentences are obtained from the following inference rules:

Reflexivity. For each $t \in T_\Sigma(X)$, $\dfrac{}{\mathcal{R} \vdash t \to t}$

Equality. $\dfrac{(\forall X)u \to v, E \vdash u = u', E \vdash v = v'}{(\forall X)u' \to v'}$

Congruence. For each $f \in \Sigma_{s_1 \ldots s_n, s}, t_i \in T_\Sigma(X)_{s_i}$

$$\frac{(\forall X)t_j \to t'_j, j \in J \subseteq [n]}{(\forall X)f(t_1, \ldots, t_n) \to f(t'_1, \ldots, t'_n)}, \text{ where } t'_i := t_i \text{ whenever } i \notin J;$$

Replacement. For each $\theta : X \to T_\Sigma(Y)$ and for each rule in $\mathcal{R}$ of the form $(\forall X)t \to t'$ if $(\bigwedge_i u_i = u'_i) \wedge (\bigwedge w_j \to w'_j)$, we have

$$\frac{\bigwedge_x (\forall Y)\theta(x) \to \theta'(x)) \wedge (\bigwedge_i (\forall Y)\theta(u_i) = \theta(u'_i)) \wedge (\bigwedge_j (\forall Y)\theta(w_j) \to \theta(w'_j))}{(\forall Y)\theta(x) \to \theta(x')}$$

where θ' is the substitution obtained from θ by some rewritings $\theta(x) \to \theta'(x)$ for each $x \in X$;

Transitivity. $\dfrac{(\forall X)t_1 \to t_2, (\forall X)t_2 \to t_3}{(\forall X)t_1 \to t_3}.$

In what follows we use the rewriting engine Maude to describe a rewriting theory corresponding to the semantics of the reversible reaction systems. In order to translate the syntax of reversible reaction systems, we use several sorts with easy-to-understand names: e.g., `ESymbol` is used to represent symbols from the environment. Between the given sorts there exist some subsorting relations, from which we mention `subsorts ESymbol < ESymbols` illustrating the fact that an environment symbol is part of a set of environment symbols. The sort `TSymbol` is used to count the number of steps since a symbol was removed from the system.

```
sorts Symbol Symbols ESymbol ESymbols TSymbol TSymbols
      RState Reaction Reactions .
subsorts Symbol < ESymbol Symbols .
subsorts Symbols < ESymbols .
subsorts ESymbol < ESymbols .
subsorts TSymbol < TSymbols .
subsorts Reaction < Reactions .
```

To represent the symbols, reactions and states of the reaction systems, we use the constructors described below. The sets of symbols and reactions are described by using associative and commutative constructors.

```
op es : -> Symbol [ctor] .
op _ | _ : Symbols Symbols -> Symbols [assoc comm id: es] .
op rho : -> ESymbol [ctor] .
op fw : -> ESymbol [ctor] .
op _ ~ _ : ESymbols ESymbols -> ESymbols [assoc] .
op et : -> TSymbol [ctor] .
op _ || _ : TSymbols TSymbols -> TSymbols [assoc comm id: et] .
op [_ , _] : Symbols Nat -> TSymbols .
op {_ , _ , _} : Symbols Symbols Symbols -> Reaction .
op er : -> Reaction [ctor] .
op _ ; _ : Reactions Reactions -> Reactions [assoc comm id: er] .
op < _ $ _ $ _ $ _ > : ESymbols Symbols TSymbols Reactions -> RState .
```

The reactions are simulated as conditional rewrite rules:

```
crl [Fwd] : < fw ~ E $ X $ ts $ A > =>
                < E $ res(A, X) $ inc(ts) || addtime(rem(lhs(A), X)) $ A >
                  if en(A, X) =/= er.

crl [FwdFin] : < fw $ X $ ts $ A > =>
                < es $ res(A, X) $ inc(ts) || addtime(rem(lhs(A), X)) $ A >
                  if en(A, X) =/= er.

crl [Rev] : < rho ~ E $ X $ ts $ A > =>
                < E $ res(rev(A, A), X) | zero(ts) $ dec(ts) $ A >
                  if en(rev(A, A), X) =/= er.

crl [RevFin] : < rho $ X $ ts $ A > =>
                < es $ res(rev(A, A), X) | zero(ts) $ dec(ts) $ A >
                  if en(rev(A, A), X) =/= er.

crl [FwdStop] : < fw ~ E $ X $ ts $ A > =>
                < E $ es $ inc(ts) || addtime(X) $ A >
                  if en(A, X) == er /\ X =/= es.

crl [RevStop] : < rho ~ E $ X $ ts $ A > =>
                < E $ es $ inc(ts) || addtime(X) $ A >
                  if en(A, X) == er /\ X =/= es.
```

It should be noticed that there are three instances for both reactions *(fwd)* and *(rev)*. The need for these instances is due to the fact that either the input provided by the environment ends or the system cannot evolve anymore. The functions `res`, `addtime`, `rem`, `lhs`, `en`, `zero`, `inc` and `dec` are used to compute the next configurations and to test if rules are applicable. They are defined similarly to the ones used in the reactions *(fwd)* and *(rev)*.

The correspondence between the operational semantics of the reversible reaction systems on one hand and the rewrite theory on the other hand is given by a mapping ψ : RRS → RState defined inductively by

$$\psi((W_i, T_i), A) = <C_i \sim C_{i+1} \ldots \sim Cn \$ D_i \$ T_i \$ A>,$$

where $W_i = C_i \cup D_i$ and $C_{i+1} \sim \ldots \sim Cn$ represents the remaining of the external input. For simplification and a more straightforward translation, we could use a function that after using the current C_i provides the next input from the environment.

By $\mathcal{R}_{RRS}$ we denote the rewrite theory defined by the rewrite rules [Fwd], [FwdFin], [Rev], [RevFin], [FwdStop] and [RevStop] together with the operators and equations defining them. The next theorem proves the correspondence between the dynamics of a reversible reaction system and its rewrite theory.

Theorem 3. $(W, T) \xrightarrow{E} (W', T')$ iff $\mathcal{R}_{RRS} \vdash \psi((W, T), A) \Rightarrow \psi((W', T'), A)$.

Proof. By structural induction. The proof follows by using the mapping ψ and the definition of the rewrite theory $\mathcal{R}_{RRS}$ presented above.

Example 3. We provide a small example of a reversible reaction system, and then analyze it by using the Maude implementation. We can verify that the rules are applied properly, and the results are the desired ones.

Consider the following reversible reaction system:

```
< fw ~ fw ~ rho ~ fw  $ (c|d|f) $ et $ ({c,d1,d}; {f,d1,c}) >.
```

When using the rewrite command **rew** on the above system, Maude executes the specification by applying the previously presented rules and equations, and finally returns the output below. Since sometime we are not interested to display all the steps and states, the command **rew [n]** can be used to obtain systems reachable in *n* steps:

```
rewrite [1] in RS-EXAMPLE : < fw ~ fw ~ rho ~ fw $ c | d | f $ et $
        {c,d1,d}; {f,d1,c} >.
rewrites: 121 in 0ms cpu (0ms real) (~ rewrites/second)
result RState: < fw ~ rho ~ fw $ c | d $ [d,0] $
        {c,d1,d}; {f,d1,c} >
===============================================
rewrite [2] in RS-EXAMPLE : < fw ~ fw ~ rho ~ fw $ c | d | f $ et $
        {c,d1,d}; {f,d1,c} >.
rewrites: 304 in 0ms cpu (0ms real) (~ rewrites/second)
result RState: < rho ~ fw $ d $ [d,0] || [d,1] $
        {c,d1,d}; {f,d1,c} >
===============================================
rewrite [3] in RS-EXAMPLE : < fw ~ fw ~ rho ~ fw $ c | d | f $ et $
        {c,d1,d}; {f,d1,c} >.
rewrites: 569 in 4ms cpu (1ms real) (142250 rewrites/second)
result RState: < fw $ c | d $ [d,0] $  {c,d1,d} ; {f,d1,c} >
===============================================
rewrite [4] in RS-EXAMPLE : < fw ~ fw ~ rho ~ fw $ c | d | f $ et $
        {c,d1,d} ; {f,d1,c} >.
rewrites: 696 in 0ms cpu (1ms real) (~ rewrites/    second)
result RState: < es $ d $ [d,0] || [d,1] $ {c,d1,d} ; {f,d1,c} >
```

It is easy to notice that, ignoring the context symbols, the configurations after one and three rewrites and after two and four rewrites are equal, meaning that the reversing evolution works as desired.

5   Conclusion

Membrane computing [22] and reaction systems [13] are branches of natural computing aiming to define computing models from the structure and functioning of the living cell. Membrane systems represent a quantitative model of multiset rewriting, while reaction systems represent a qualitative model of set rewriting. Some research comparing them was done in [23], while in [4] are presented membrane systems with no-persistence assumption of reaction systems from the viewpoint of the computational power.

Reversible membrane systems were considered in [15], but the model does not uses maximal parallel rewriting; the main result is the simulation of the Fredkin gate, and so it actually studies the reversible circuits. The reversibility of membrane systems with maximal parallelism systems only from a computability point of view was studied in [5]. The dual P systems [1] present reversibility in membrane systems as duality (under the influence of category theory). A full description of this kind of reversibility in membrane systems is given in [3].

In this paper we presented a controlled reversibility in the context of reaction systems. An important aspect of this approach is given by considering additional reversing reactions to the initial set of reactions with inhibitors, as well as by adding an external control by means of a special symbol ρ informing the system that a rollback is needed. Specific results (including so-called *loop* results) are proved, as well as an operational correspondence between reaction systems and rewriting theory. This operational correspondence allows to translate the reversible reaction systems into rewriting systems which are executable in the rewriting engine Maude. Given such an implementation, several properties of the reversible reaction systems can be verified.

Acknowledgements. We thank the reviewers for their helpful comments and suggestions. This work was partially supported by the COST Action IC1405.

References

1. Agrigoroaiei, O., Ciobanu, G.: Dual P systems. In: Corne, D.W., Frisco, P., Păun, G., Rozenberg, G., Salomaa, A. (eds.) WMC 2008. LNCS, vol. 5391, pp. 95–107. Springer, Heidelberg (2009). https://doi.org/10.1007/978-3-540-95885-7_7
2. Agrigoroaiei, O., Ciobanu, G.: Rewriting logic specification of membrane systems with promoters and inhibitors. Electron. Notes Theor. Comput. Sci. **238**, 5–22 (2009)
3. Agrigoroaiei, O., Ciobanu, G.: Reversing computation in membrane systems. J. Logic Algebraic Program. **79**, 278–288 (2010)
4. Alhazov, A., Aman, B., Freund, R., Ivanov, S.: Simulating R systems by P systems. In: Leporati, A., Rozenberg, G., Salomaa, A., Zandron, C. (eds.) CMC 2016. LNCS, vol. 10105, pp. 51–66. Springer, Cham (2017). https://doi.org/10.1007/978-3-319-54072-6_4
5. Alhazov, A., Morita, K.: On reversibility and determinism in P systems. In: Păun, G., Pérez-Jiménez, M.J., Riscos-Núñez, A., Rozenberg, G., Salomaa, A. (eds.) WMC 2009. LNCS, vol. 5957, pp. 158–168. Springer, Heidelberg (2010). https://doi.org/10.1007/978-3-642-11467-0_12
6. Andrei, O., Ciobanu, G., Lucanu, D.: Executable specifications of P systems. In: Mauri, G., Păun, G., Pérez-Jiménez, M.J., Rozenberg, G., Salomaa, A. (eds.) WMC 2004. LNCS, vol. 3365, pp. 126–145. Springer, Heidelberg (2005). https://doi.org/10.1007/978-3-540-31837-8_7
7. Azimi, S., Iancu, B., Petre, I.: Reaction system models for the heat shock response. Fundamenta Informaticae **131**(3–4), 299–312 (2014)
8. Azimi, S., Panchal, C., Czeizler, E., Petre, I.: Reaction systems models for the self-assembly of intermediate filaments. Ann. Univ. Buchar. **LXII**(2), 9–24 (2015)
9. Bennett, C.H.: Logical reversibility of computation. IBM J. Res. Dev. **17**, 525–532 (1973)
10. Brijder, R., Ehrenfeucht, A., Main, M.G., Rozenberg, G.: A tour of reaction systems. Int. J. Found. Comput. Sci. **22**(7), 1499–1517 (2011)

11. Clavel, M., Durán, F., Eker, S., Lincoln, P., Martí-Oliet, N., Meseguer, J., Talcott, C.L.: All About Maude - A High Performance Logical Framework: How to Specify, Program, and Verify Systems in Rewriting Logic. Springer, Heidelberg (2007). https://doi.org/10.1007/978-3-540-71999-1
12. Danos, V., Krivine, J.: Reversible communicating systems. In: Gardner, P., Yoshida, N. (eds.) CONCUR 2004. LNCS, vol. 3170, pp. 292–307. Springer, Heidelberg (2004). https://doi.org/10.1007/978-3-540-28644-8_19
13. Ehrenfeucht, A., Rozenberg, G.: Reaction systems. Fundamenta Informaticae 75(1), 263–280 (2007)
14. Ionescu, M., Păun, G., Yokomori, T.: Spiking neural P systems. Fundamenta Informaticae 71(2), 279–308 (2006)
15. Leporati, A., Zandron, C., Mauri, G.: Reversible P systems to simulate Fredkin circuits. Fundamenta Informaticae 74(4), 529–548 (2006)
16. Kari, L., Rozenberg, G.: The many facets of natural computing. Commun. ACM 51, 72–83 (2008)
17. Kuhn, S., Ulidowski, I.: A calculus for local reversibility. In: Devitt, S., Lanese, I. (eds.) RC 2016. LNCS, vol. 9720, pp. 20–35. Springer, Cham (2016). https://doi.org/10.1007/978-3-319-40578-0_2
18. Meseguer, J.: Membership algebra as a logical framework for equational specification. In: Presicce, F.P. (ed.) WADT 1997. LNCS, vol. 1376, pp. 18–61. Springer, Heidelberg (1998). https://doi.org/10.1007/3-540-64299-4_26
19. Meseguer, J.: Twenty years of rewriting logic. J. Logic Algebraic Program. 81(7–8), 721–781 (2012)
20. Morita, K.: Universality of a reversible two-counter machine. Theor. Comput. Sci. 168, 303–320 (1996)
21. Morita, K., Yamaguchi, Y.: A universal reversible Turing machine. In: Durand-Lose, J., Margenstern, M. (eds.) MCU 2007. LNCS, vol. 4664, pp. 90–98. Springer, Heidelberg (2007). https://doi.org/10.1007/978-3-540-74593-8_8
22. Păun, G.: Computing with membranes. J. Comput. Syst. Sci. 61, 108–143 (1998)
23. Păun, G., Pérez-Jiménez, M.J.: Towards bridging two cell-inspired models: P systems and R systems. Theor. Comput. Sci. 429, 258–264 (2012)

Multiset Patterns and Their Application to Dynamic Causalities in Membrane Systems

Roberto Barbuti, Roberta Gori, and Paolo Milazzo$^{(\boxtimes)}$

Dipartimento di Informatica, Università di Pisa,
Largo Pontecorvo 3, 56127 Pisa, Italy
{barbuti,gori,milazzo}@di.unipi.it

Abstract. In this paper we investigate dynamic causalities in membrane systems by proposing the concept of "predictor", originally defined in the context of Ehrenfeucht and Rozemberg's reaction systems. The goal is to characterize sufficient conditions for the presence of a molecule of interest in the configuration of a P system after a given number of evolution steps (independently from the non-deterministic choices taken). Such conditions can be used to study causal relationships between molecules. To achieve our goal, we introduce the new concept of "multiset pattern" representing a logical formula on multisets. A predictor can be expressed as a pattern characterizing the initial multisets that will surely lead (sufficient condition) to the presence of the molecule of interest after the given number of evolution steps. We define also an operator that computes such a predictor.

1   Introduction

The understanding of causal relationships among the events happening in a biological (or bio-inspired) system is an issue investigated in the context both of systems biology (see e.g. [6,7,12]) and of natural computing (see e.g. [10]).

In [9] Brijder et al. initiate an investigation of *causalities* in reaction systems [8,11]. Causalities deal with the ways entities of a reaction system influence each other. In [9], both static/structural causalities and dynamic causalities are discussed, introducing the idea of *predictor*. A predictor can be used to determine whether a molecule of interest s will be produced after k steps of execution of the reaction system, without executing the system itself.

The environment is the only source of non-determinism in a reaction system. Knowledge about the molecules which will be provided at each step by the environment is necessary to determine whether a molecule s will be produced after k steps. Moreover, not all molecules are relevant for the production of a molecule of interest s. On the basis of these two observations, a predictor is defined as the subset of molecules Q whose supply by the environment should be observed in order to determine whether s will be produced or not after k steps.

© Springer International Publishing AG 2018
M. Gheorghe et al. (Eds.): CMC 2017, LNCS 10725, pp. 54–73, 2018.
https://doi.org/10.1007/978-3-319-73359-3_4

In [1–4] we pushed forward the idea of predictors by defining the notion of *formula based predictor*. A formula based predictor consists in a propositional logic formula to be satisfied by the sequence of sets of molecules provided by the environment to the reaction system. Such a logic formula precisely discriminates the cases in which a particular molecule s will be produced after a given number of steps from the cases in which it will not.

P systems [13] are much more powerful and complex than reaction systems. They are based on multisets rather than sets and evolution rules are applied with *maximal parallelism* and with a non-deterministic competition for reactants.

The behaviour of a P system is determined only by the initial multiset and by the non-deterministic choices made at each maximally parallel step. In this context, a notion of predictor may correspond to a logical formula to be satisfied by the initial multiset (representing either a *sufficient condition* or a *necessary condition*) for a molecule of interest s to be present after a given number of evolution steps. Sufficient and necessary conditions have to be dealt with separately due to the intrinsically non-deterministic nature of P systems.

In this paper we propose a notion of *multiset pattern* as a way to express a logical formula on multisets: if the initial multiset of the P systems satisfies (*matches*) a given pattern, the molecule of interest will be *for sure* present after k steps; nothing can be said otherwise (sufficient condition). Moreover, we will define an operator that recursively computes the pattern for the production of a molecule of interest (actually, a multiset of molecules of interest) in k steps. The pattern obtained from the operator will be a sound predictor, but, in general, not a complete predictor. There can be multisets that do not match the pattern, but that always lead to the presence of the molecules of interest in k steps.

Section 2 introduces preliminary notions on multisets and membrane systems. The new notion of multiset patterns can be found in Sect. 3. In Sect. 4 we introduce the notion of predictor, an operator to compute it and we prove some properties. Section 5 presents an application of our approach.

2   Preliminaries

Let U be an arbitrary set. A *multiset* (over U) is a mapping $M : U \to \mathbb{N}$; with $|M|_a$, for $a \in U$, we denote the *multiplicity* of a in the multiset M. The *support* of a multiset M is the set $supp(M) = \{a \mid |M|_a > 0\}$. A multiset is empty when its support is empty and it is denoted by $\emptyset$.

In order to distinguish multiset operations from standard set operations we use the following notations: $\subseteq^*$ for multiset inclusion, $\cup^*$ for multiset union, $\cap^*$ for multiset intersection. For multisets defined over a set of molecules (an alphabet) V, we will use also the standard string representation, with ϵ representing the empty multiset and V^* representing the set of all multisets over V. With $\wp(V^*)$ we indicate the power set of the set V^*.

We consider *flat* P systems, namely in which the membrane structure consists only of the skin membrane. Flat P systems are defined as follows.

Definition 1. *A flat P system is a construct* $\Pi = (V, w, R)$ *where:*

- V is an alphabet *whose elements are called* molecules;
- $w \in V^*$ *is the* initial multiset;
- R *is a finite set of* evolution rules.

From [5] it follows that a P system with a standard membrane structure can be translated into an equivalent P system having a (flat) membrane structure that consists only of the skin.

In this paper we assume P systems to be closed computational devices, namely we assume that molecules cannot be sent out of the skin membrane (i.e. rules sending molecules out are not allowed in the skin membrane) and molecules cannot be received by the skin membrane from outside.

As a consequence, evolution rules will have the simple form $u \rightarrow v$ with $u, v \in V^*$. We denote with $\mathcal{R}$ the set of all evolution rules.

Given an evolution rule $r = u \rightarrow v$, we denote with $react(r)$ and $prod(r)$ its multisets of reactants u and products v, respectively. The same notations extend naturally to multisets of rules: given a multiset of rules $M \in \mathcal{R}^*$, we have $react(M) = \bigcup_{r \in supp(M)}^* react(r)^{|M|_r}$ and $prod(M) = \bigcup_{r \in supp(M)}^* prod(r)^{|M|_r}$.

We assume evolution rules to be applied with standard maximal parallelism. Since we consider P systems which do not send/receive molecules to/from the external environment, we obtain that the behaviour of a P system is determined only its initial multiset and by the non-deterministic choices made at each maximally parallel step.

3 Multiset Patterns

3.1 Definition

Given an alphabet V, a multiset pattern expresses a condition on multisets in V^*. A *basic* multiset pattern is denoted by a pair $(u, \{u_1, \ldots, u_n\})$ where $u, u_1, \ldots, u_n$ are multisets in V^*. More complex patterns can be obtained by composing basic patterns by using propositional logic connectives $\wedge$ and $\vee$. The syntax of multiset patterns is defined as follows.

Definition 2 (Multiset Patterns). *Given an alphabet V, $\mathcal{P}_V$ is the set of multiset patterns on V^* inductively defined as follows:*

- *true, false $\in \mathcal{P}_V$,*
- *if $p \in (V^* \times \wp(V^*))$ then $p \in \mathcal{P}_V$,*
- *if $p_1, p_2 \in \mathcal{P}_V$ then $p_1 \vee p_2, p_1 \wedge p_2 \in \mathcal{P}_V$.*

When the reference alphabet V is clear from the context, we will denote the set $\mathcal{P}_V$ simply as $\mathcal{P}$.

Now, we formally define the notion of satisfaction of a pattern by a multiset, that is the semantics of multiset patterns. The idea is that a multiset w satisfies a basic pattern $(u, \{u_1, \ldots, u_n\})$ if by removing from w the multisets $u_1, \ldots, u_n$ in any maximal way (i.e. so that what remains does not include any of $u_1, \ldots, u_n$) we always obtain a multiset that includes u. For example, multiset $A^4 B^2$ satisfies the pattern $(A, \{AB\})$ since after removing AB a maximal number of times (two times) we obtain A^2 that includes A.

The semantics of multiset patterns is formally defined as follows.

Definition 3. *Given an alphabet V, the* satisfaction relation $\models \subseteq V^* \times P_V$ *is the smallest relation inductively defined as follows:*

$$w \models true$$
$$w \models (u, \{u_1, \ldots, u_n\}) \text{ iff } \forall o_1, \ldots o_n \in \mathbb{N} \text{ such that } w \supseteq^* u_1^{o_1} u_2^{o_2} \ldots u_n^{o_n},$$
$$\text{it holds } w \supseteq^* uu_1^{o_1} u_2^{o_2} \ldots u_n^{o_n}$$
$$w \models p_1 \wedge p_2 \quad \text{iff } w \models p_1 \text{ and } w \models p_2$$
$$w \models p_1 \vee p_2 \quad \text{iff either } w \models p_1 \text{ or } w \models p_2$$

For the case of a basic pattern $(u, \{u_1, \ldots, u_n\})$, Definition 3 includes a requirement on all possible values $o_1, \ldots, o_n \in \mathbb{N}$ used as multiplicities of the occurrences of $u_1, \ldots, u_n$ in w. It is easy to see that the requirement can be checked by considering only the maximal combinations of values $o_1, \ldots, o_n$ such that $w \supseteq^* u_1^{o_1} u_2^{o_2} \ldots u_n^{o_n}$.

3.2   Multiset Patterns and Multiset Languages

Maximal patterns can be used to express complex conditions on multisets. For example, the pattern $p_1 = (AB, \{BC, BE\})$ is satisfied by multisets that contain at least one A and one B, and where the sum of the numbers of C and of E is smaller than the number of B. Indeed, the set of multisets satisfying the pattern corresponds to the multiset language

$$L_{p_1} = \{w \in V^* \mid |w|_A > 0, |w|_B > 0, |w|_B > |w|_C + |w|_E\}.$$

Patterns can express also conditions that are not in the "greater than" form. For example, pattern $(A, \{AA\})$ is satisfied by multisets with an odd number of A. Namely, it characterizes the language

$$L_{p_2} = \{w \in V^* \mid |w|_A \equiv_{mod\ 2} 1\}.$$

More generally, given any $n \in \mathbb{N}$, the multiset pattern $(A, \{A^n\})$ is such that $w \models (A, \{A^n\})$ iff w satisfies $|w|_A \not\equiv_{mod\ n} 0$.

The examples we have given show that multiset patterns could be used to characterize multiset languages. It could be interesting to investigate the classes of languages characterized by multiset patterns. Although such an investigation is out of the scope of this paper, we give a few more examples of patterns characterizing interesting languages.

Let us look for a pattern characterizing the language consisting only of the A^3 multiset. The pattern $p_3 = (A^3, \{\})$ is not correct, since it is satisfied by any multiset with *at least* three instances of A. We could combine p_3 with a pattern satisfied by multiset containing *at most* three instances of A. The latter pattern can be obtained by considering an additional molecule O, assumed to be present only once in the multiset, as follows: $p_4 = (O, \{OA^4\})$. By combining the two patterns (and by generalizing them to any fixed value $k \in \mathbb{N}$) we obtain $p_5 = (A^k, \{\}) \wedge (O, \{OA^{k+1}\})$ that is actually equivalent to $p_5' = (OA^k, \{OA^{k+1}\})$. The characterized language is

$$L_{p_5} = \{w \in V^* \mid |w|_O > 0, |w|_A = k + (|w|_O - 1)(k + 1)\}$$

that, by the assumption $|w|_O = 1$, becomes

$$L'_{p_5} = \{w \in V^* \mid |w|_O = 1, |w|_A = k\}.$$

A few more examples: $(A, \{AB\})$ characterizes the language $A^m B^n$ with $m > n$. Consequently, $(A, \{AB\}) \vee (B, \{AB\})$ characterizes the language $A^m B^n$ with $m \neq n$. It seems not possible to define a pattern that characterizes the complement of the previous language, namely $A^n B^n$, even if we consider additional molecules (like O in a previous example). This would be possible by including logical negation in the syntax of patterns.

3.3   Simplification of Multiset Patterns

Multiset patterns express logical conditions on multisets, hence they can be simplified using standard logic rules. For instance, a conjunction of basic patterns can be simplified to *false* every time the basic patterns implicitly express opposite constraints. Moreover, the following properties of the satisfaction relation $\models$ allow us to consider further simplification rules for multiset patterns. The proof of the two properties follows immediately from Definition 3.

Lemma 1. *Let* $(w, \{u_1, \dots, u_n\})$ *be a basic multiset pattern and* $v \in V^*$. *Then* $v \models (w, \{u_1, \dots, u_n\})$ *iff* $v \models (w, \{u_i \mid u_i \cap^* w \neq \emptyset\})$.

Using the previous result a basic pattern $(w, \{u_1, \dots, u_n\})$ can be always simplified into $(w, \{u_i \mid u_i \cap^* w \neq \emptyset\})$.

Lemma 2. *Let* $(w, \{u_1, \dots, u_n\})$ *be a basic pattern. If there exists* $i \in \{1, \dots, n\}$ *such that* $u_i \subseteq^* w$, *then for all* $v \in V^*$ *it holds* $v \not\models w\{u_1, \dots, u_n\}$.

Using the previous result a basic pattern $(w, \{u_1, \dots, u_n\})$ such that $u_i \subseteq^* w$ for some $i \in \{1, \dots, n\}$ can be simplified into *false*.

4   Multiset Patterns as Predictors

In this section we propose a methodology based on multiset patterns to compute a sufficient condition for the presence of a molecule s after k evolution steps of a given P system. The sufficient condition will be expressed as a pattern (called *predictor*) to be satisfied by the initial multiset w of the P system.

The idea is to define an operator that computes the predictor by starting from the pattern $(u, \{\})$ and by rewriting it by taking the set of rules of the P system into account. The pattern will be rewritten k times, each time simulating (in an abstract way) a backward step in the evolution of the P system. At each step, for each rule that is assumed to be applied the result will include information of the rules competing with it for application.

The definition of the operator that computes a predictor for a molecule s in k steps is quite complex. We start with the definition of a few auxiliary functions and sets. Then, we choose to introduce the concepts by giving several examples of incremental complexity. Examples will be alternated with definitions of functions that formalize the introduced concepts. The complete definition of the operator, together with the related theoretical results, will conclude this section.

4.1 Auxiliary Functions and Sets

Function *AppRules* gives the set of all the minimal multisets of rules necessary to produce v.

Definition 4. *Given a multiset $v \in V^*$ and a set of rules $R \in \wp(\mathcal{R})$, we define the function $AppRules : V^* \times \wp(\mathcal{R}) \to \wp(\mathcal{R}^*)$ as*

$$AppRules(v, R) = \{ M \in R^* \mid v \subseteq^* \bigcup_{r \in supp(M)}^* prod(r)^{|M|_r} \text{ and}$$
$$\nexists M' \subseteq^* M \text{ s.t. } v \subseteq^* \bigcup_{r \in supp(M')}^* prod(r)^{|M'|_r} \}$$

Example 1. Consider the P system $\Pi = (\{A, B, C, D, E\}, w, R)$ where evolution rules of the set R are:

$$r_0 : AB \to C \qquad r_1 : BD \to C \qquad r_2 : C \to AC \qquad r_3 : E \to A$$

We have: $AppRules(CCA, R) = \{r_0 r_0 r_3, r_0 r_1 r_3, r_1 r_1 r_3, r_0 r_2, r_1 r_2, r_2 r_2\}$.

In order to simulate a backward step in the evolution of a P system we have to take into account that a molecule might be obtained as the product of an applied evolution rule, but also might be obtained since it was present in the previous step and no rules used it. This is not possible if there is a rule in the P system having such a molecule as the only reactant. As a consequence, in order to simulate the backward step of a P system, we consider an extended set of evolution rules that includes also *self rules* rewriting each molecule into itself, for each molecule that is not the only reactant of a rule of the P system.

Definition 5. *Given a set of rules $R \subseteq \mathcal{R}$, the set of self rules $Self_R$ is*

$$Self_R = \{ v \to v \mid |v| = 1 \text{ and } \forall r \in R, \ react(r) \neq v \}$$

Example 2. For the P system of Example 1 we have

$$Self_R = \{ r_4 : A \to A, r_5 : B \to B, r_6 : D \to D \}$$

4.2 Competition for Reactants

Example 3. Consider the P system $\Pi_1 = (\{A, B, C, D\}, w, R_1)$ where the evolution rules R_1 are:

$$r_0 : AB \to D \qquad r_1 : BD \to C$$

A visual representation of evolution rules in $R_1 \cup Self_{R_1}$ is given by the graph in Fig. 1. The nodes in the top of the graph represent molecules used as reactants (associated with index 1), while the nodes in the bottom of the graph represent products (associated with index 2). Reactions are represented as nodes in the middle of the graph and by the arcs connecting such nodes to reactants and products. Solid arcs represent the evolution rules in R_1, while dashed arcs the evolution rules in $Self_{R_1} = \{r_2, r_3, r_4, r_5\}$.

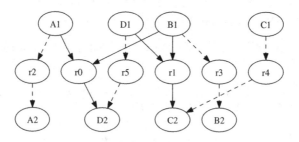

Fig. 1. Rules $R_1 \cup Self_{R_1}$

The graph representation helps us to reason on backward steps of the P system. For instance, in order to obtain D in one step, we need to have either A and B, or D itself in the previous step. Moreover, the graph makes explicit the competition of evolution rules on common reactants. For example, the production of D by rule r_0 competes with the application of rule r_1 since both rules have B as a reactant. Similarly, the self rule $r_5 : D \to D$ competes with rule r_1. Note however that the contrary does not hold, indeed rule r_1 does not compete with the self rule $r_5 : D \to D$ because self rules represent molecules which are not consumed by the evolutions steps of rule in R_1.

The information on evolution rules competition is essential. In order to be sure that D is present after one step we need to be sure that either r_0 has been applied or D was already present and it has not been consumed by any other evolution rule not producing D.

We now define the function $competitor_1$, which results in the set of evolution rules competing for reactants with a given evolution rule r which produces a molecule of interest s.

Definition 6. *Given a rule $r \in \mathcal{R}$, a set of rules $R \subseteq \mathcal{R}$ and a molecule $s \in V$ such that $s \in supp(prod(r))$, we define*

$$competitor_1(r, R, s) = \{r' \in R \mid react(r) \cap^* react(r') \neq \emptyset \text{ and } s \notin prod(r')\}.$$

A pattern that characterizes a sufficient condition for the presence of D after one step can be easily obtained by combining the reactants of evolution rules producing D (including self rules) with the information on the reactants of the other evolution rules that compete with them and do not produce D.

For the case of Example 3, we can express a pattern that characterizes a sufficient condition for the production of D in one step as follows

$$\bigvee_{r \in AppRules(D, R_1 \cup Self_{R_1})} (react(r), react(competitor_1(r, R_1, D)))$$

that corresponds to $(AB, \{BD\}) \vee (D, \{BD\})$. This pattern shows that D can be produced in two ways: through AB, that are the reactants of r_0, or through D itself. In both cases the only competitor is r_1, whose reactants are BD. So in both cases the pattern requires that AB or D remains after removing instances of BD in a maximal way. In other words, the pattern expresses the condition that either the multiset includes AB and the instances of B are more than the instances of D, or there is at least one D and the instances of D are more than the instances of B. Examples of multisets that satisfy the pattern (leading to the production of D) are ABB, AD, $ABBD$, etc.

Note that rule r_2 is not considered as a competitor since it is a self rule. Such a kind of rules cannot compete with other rules since they simply represent molecules that are not consumed by actual evolution rules of the P system.

In order to perform more than one backward step we will have to generalize the computation of the pattern representing the sufficient condition to the case in which we are interested in the production of *a multiset of molecules*, rather a single molecule. For instance, in the case of Example 3, performing one more backward step would require to compute the sufficient condition for the production of AB or of D, that will then be used to obtain D.

In order to show how to compute a pattern for the presence of a *multiset of molecules* after one step, consider, in the case of Example 3, the multiset DC. The pattern representing a sufficient condition for the presence of DC in one step could be obtained by combining the already seen pattern for the presence of D with analogous pattern for the presence of C, that is $(BD, \{AB\}) \vee (C, \{\})$. Since D and C are two different molecules (the case of repeated molecules is more complex and will be treated separately in Sect. 4.3) we can combine the two patterns by simply using a conjunction, thus obtaining:

$$((AB, \{BD\}) \vee (D, \{BD\})) \wedge ((BD, \{AB\}) \vee (C, \{\})).$$

Multisets satisfying the pattern are DC, ABC, ADC, $ABBD$, etc. Indeed, such multisets allow us to obtain DC after one step according to the rules in R_1. On the other hand, multisets not satisfying the pattern are for instance ABD, DCB and $ABDC$. The latter, in particular, could lead to the production of DC (actually DDC), but also to the production of ACC that does not include DC.

Example 4. Consider now a P system $\Pi_2 = (\{A, B, C, D\}, w, R_2)$ where R_2 (depicted in Fig. 2) is the same as R_1 of Example 3, but with r_0 extended with one more product, namely

$$r_0 : AB \rightarrow DC \qquad r_1 : BD \rightarrow C$$

While the sufficient conditions for molecule D to be present after one step are the same as in the previous example, the condition for the presence of C after one step has to take into account that now r_0 produces C, therefore it does not compete with r_1 for the production of C. This is correctly taken into account by the function $competitor_1$, indeed $competitor_1(r_0, R_2, C) = \emptyset$. Therefore, the pattern for the presence of C in one step, defined as

$$\bigvee_{r \in AppRules(C, R_2 \cup Self_{R_2})} (react(r), react(competitor_1(r, R_2, C))),$$

turns out to be $(AB, \{\}) \vee (BD, \{\}) \vee (C, \{\})$.

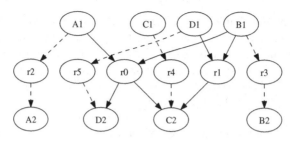

Fig. 2. Rules $R_2 \cup Self_{R_2}$

4.3   Competitors Dealing with Multiple Occurrences of Molecules

When multiple occurrences of the same molecule come into the picture, things get quickly more complicated.

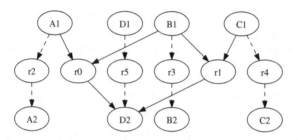

Fig. 3. Rules $R_3 \cup Self_{R_3}$

Example 5. Consider the P system $\Pi_3 = (\{A, B, C, D\}, w, R_3)$ where the evolution rules $R_3 = \{r_0, r_1\}$, depicted in Fig. 3, are

$$r_0 : AB \to D \qquad r_1 : BC \to D$$

Assume we are interested in the multiset DD. To produce DD in the P system Π_3 we may either apply one rule twice, or the two rules together. The pattern for the presence of DD in one step cannot be obtained just as a conjunction of a pattern p expressing the sufficient condition for D with itself, since $p \wedge p$ is equivalent to p.

In order to deal with multiple occurrences of molecules we have to consider, in the computation of the backward step, the possible *multisets of evolution rules* that could have been applied in order to produce such molecules. These multisets of rules are given by the auxiliary function *AppRules* defined in Sect. 4.1.

At a first glance one may think of defining the pattern for the presence of DD in one step as follows:

$$\bigvee_{n \in AppRules(DD, R_3 \cup Self_{R_3})} \bigwedge_{r \in supp(n)} (react(r)^{|n|_r}, react(competitor_1(r, R_3, D)))$$

that would give the following result:

$$(ABAB, \{\}) \vee ((AB, \{\}) \wedge (BC, \{\})) \vee ((AB, \{\}) \wedge (D, \{\}))$$
$$\vee ((BC, \{\}) \wedge (D, \{\})) \vee (BCBC, \{\}) \vee (DD, \{\}))$$

This pattern is however not correct, since it is satisfied by multiset ABC (because $ABC \models (AB, \{\}) \wedge (BC, \{\})$) that does not lead to DD in one step.

The point in this case is that there are two different rules that produce the same product D competing for the same reactant B. Since more than one instance of D has to be produced, we have to take also this form of competition into account. To this purpose, we define the function $competitor_2$.

Definition 7. *Given a rule $r \in \mathcal{R}$, a set of rules $R \subseteq \mathcal{R}$ and an multiset of rules $n \in R^*$, we define*

$$competitor_2(r, R, n) = \{r' \in R \mid r' \in supp(n), r' \neq r, react(r) \cap^* react(r') \neq \emptyset\}$$

Now, the pattern for DD can be expressed as

$$\bigvee_{n \in AppRules(DD, R_3 \cup Self_{R_3})} \bigwedge_{r \in supp(n)} (react(r)^{|n|_r}, react(C_{12}))$$

where $C_{12} = competitor_1(r, R_3, D) \cup competitor_2(r, R_3, n)$. The formula gives the following result:

$$(ABAB\{\}) \vee ((AB, \{BC\}) \wedge (BC, \{AB\})) \vee ((AB, \{\}) \wedge (D, \{\}))$$
$$\vee ((BC, \{\}) \wedge (D, \{\})) \vee (BCBC, \{\}) \vee (DD, \{\})$$

which now correctly models the required property.

4.4   Competition for Products

Example 6. Consider the P system $\Pi_4 = (\{A, B, C, D, E\}, w, R_4)$ where the evolution rules $R_4 = \{r_0, r_1, r_2, r_3\}$, depicted in Fig. 4, are

$$r_0 : AB \to D \qquad r_1 : BC \to D \qquad r_2 : BB \to DD \qquad r_3 : ACE \to D$$

Assume that, as in Example 5, we are interested in the presence of multiset DD after one step. The multiset DD can be produced by several combinations of rules in R_4. Rule r_2 has DD as product, but suffers from the competition of r_0 and of r_1 that, although producing the same kind of molecule, produce only one instance of such a molecule. Indeed, by starting from multisets ABB or BBC, we may obtain DD through r_2, but we may also obtain only one D, through r_0 or r_1, respectively.

Similarly, there are cases in which DD can be obtained by applying r_0 and r_1 together. Rule r_3, however, may compete with such a combination of rules, since in presence of E it may consume reactants necessary for the application of r_0 and r_1 giving only one D as a result.

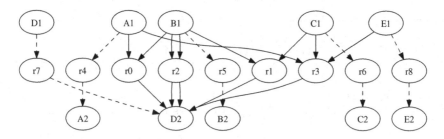

Fig. 4. Rules $R_4 \cup \mathit{Self}_{R_4}$

This example suggests that the concept of competitor has to be enriched with a definition that takes into account when a rule competes with a multiset of rules $n \in R^*$ that produce more than one occurrence of a molecule. Intuitively, this occurs when the use of such a rule prevents the application of a subset of the rules in n without producing an equivalent number of occurrences of the required molecule. This form of competition is formalized by the function $competitor_3$ defined as follows.

Definition 8. *Given a rule* $r \in \mathcal{R}$*, a set of rules* $R \subseteq \mathcal{R}$*, a multiset of rules* $n \in R^*$ *and a molecule* $s \in V$*, we define:*

$competitor_3(r, R, n, s) =$
$\{r' \in R \mid s \in prod(r'), r' \notin supp(n), react(r) \cap react(r') \neq \emptyset,$
$\qquad \exists m \subseteq^* n, \{r\} \subseteq^* m, react(m) \cap_* react(r') = react(n) \cap_* react(r'),$
$\qquad \forall m' \subset^* m, react(m') \cap_* react(r') \neq react(n) \cap_* react(r'),$
$\qquad |prod(m)|_s \supset^* |prod(r')|_s\}$

Assume as before that we are interested in the production of DD in one step. The pattern expressing a sufficient conditions is then

$$\bigvee_{n \in AppRules(DD, R_3 \cup Self_{R_3})} \bigwedge_{r \in supp(n)} (react(r)^{|n|_r}, react(C_{123}))$$

where

$C_{123} = competitor_1(r, R_3, D) \cup competitor_2(r, R_3, n) \cup competitor_3(r, R_3, n, D).$
The formula gives the following result:

$$((AB, \{BC, ACE\}) \wedge (BC, \{AB, ACE\})) \vee (BB, \{AB, BC\}) \vee$$
$$((AB, \{ACE, BC\}) \wedge (ACE, \{AB, BC\})) \vee$$
$$((BC, \{ACE, AB\}) \wedge (ACE, \{BC, AB\})) \vee (DD, \{\})$$

In the obtained pattern, conjunction $(AB, \{ACE, BC\}) \wedge (ACE, \{AB, BC\})$ is not satisfiable, since on the one hand it requires $ABACE$ to be included in the multiset, but at the same time it requires BC not to be included. The same holds for $(BC, \{ACE, AB\}) \wedge (ACE, \{BC, AB\})$ with $BCACE$ and AB. As a consequence, the pattern can be simplified into

$$((AB, \{BC, ACE\}) \wedge (BC, \{AB, ACE\})) \vee (BB, \{AB, BC\}) \vee (DD, \{\})$$

According to this pattern, for example, all multisets that contain BB lead to the presence of DD after one step as long as they contain enough instances of B (two more than the instances of A and C). As required, neither multiset ABB nor BBC satisfy the pattern.

This example shows also a situation in which the pattern does not describe multisets that actually lead to the presence of DD in one step, such as the multiset $ABBCE$. What happens in this case is that rule r_3 is identified as a competitor of both r_0 and r_1. However, in a multiset like $ABBCE$ the application of r_3 (that actually prevents r_0 and r_1 to be applied) causes also r_2 to be applied, obtaining DDD as result. This shows that the proposed notions of competitor are not able to characterize *all* multisets that lead to the presence of a required multiset in a given number of steps. In this case it is not able to recognize that the application of a competitor rule has as a side effect the application of some other rules that actually lead to the wanted result.

4.5   Multiple Backward Steps

We now describe how to obtain a pattern that expresses sufficient conditions for the presence of a molecule after two or more steps starting from patterns expressing sufficient conditions after one step.

Example 7. Let us consider the P system $\Pi_5 = (\{A, B, C, D, E, F\}, w, R_5)$ where the evolution rules in R_5, depicted in Fig. 5, are

$$r_0 : AB \rightarrow D \qquad r_1 : BD \rightarrow C \qquad r_2 : ED \rightarrow B$$

Note that rule r_0 and r_1 are the ones of Example 3 and the pattern for the presence of molecule D in one step is as in the previous example, namely $p = (AB, \{BD\}) \vee (D, \{BD, ED\})$. In order to obtain the pattern expressing the sufficient condition for the presence of D after two steps, intuitively we have to consider all the ways a multiset satisfying p can be obtained in one step.

The pattern p is satisfied by multiset containing A and B, or D. Hence, we could compute the patterns that predict the presence of A, B and D in one step, and use them to construct a pattern for the satisfaction of p after one step. In addition to this, we have to pay attention to the competitors of A, B and D mentioned in p, namely the set $\{BD, ED\}$. In order to construct the pattern for the satisfiability of p in one step we have to consider also all the ways the competitors BD and ED can be obtained in one step.

We formally define an operator that considers all the possible ways a set of multisets representing competitors can be obtained in one step.

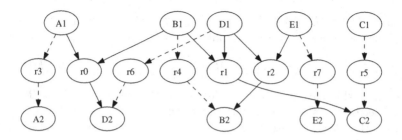

Fig. 5. Rules $R_5 \cup Self_{R_5}$

Definition 9. *Given a set of rules $R \subseteq \mathcal{R}$, a set of multiset $\{u_1, \ldots, u_n\}$ with each $u_i \in V^*$, we define*

$$Cr(R, \{u_1, \ldots, u_n\}) = \{react(n) \mid n \in AppRules(u_i, R \cup Self_R)) \\ and \; u_i \in \{u_1, \ldots, u_n\}\}$$

From the predictor of A in one step $(A, \{AB\})$, the predictor of B in one step $(ED, \{BD\}) \vee (B, \{AB, BD\})$, the predictor of D in one step $(AB, \{BD\}) \vee (D, \{BD\})$, $Cr(R_5, \{BD\}) = \{BD, EDD, ABB\} = C_5$ and $Cr(R_5, \{ED\}) = \{ED, EAB\} = C_6$ we can construct a pattern that predicts the presence of D in two steps as follows:

$$((A, \{AB, BD, EDD\}) \wedge (ED, \{BD\} \cup C_5)) \\ \vee (A, \{AB, BD, EDD\}) \wedge (B, \{AB, BD, EDD\})) \\ \vee (AB, \{BD\} \cup C_5 \cup \{ED\}) \vee (D, \{BD\} \cup C_5 \cup C_6)$$

The initial multiset AED satisfies the pattern, indeed, in one step we obtain AB using the only enabled rule r_2 and in two steps we obtain D applying the only enabled rule r_0. Consider $AEDD$ that does not satisfy the pattern, after one step we obtain ABD using the only enabled rule r_2 but also rule r_1 is enabled and by applying it we obtain AC that does not contain D.

4.6   Definition of the Main Operator and Theoretical Results

In the previous sections we have described the ingredients for the computation of a pattern expressing sufficient conditions for the presence of an molecule s after k steps. Now, we formally define an operator Sc_Π that performs such a computation.

Definition 10. *Let $\Pi = (V, w, R)$ be P system and $u \in V^*$. We define a function $Sc_\Pi : V^* \times \mathbb{N} \to \mathcal{P}$ as follows:*

$$Sc_\Pi(u, k) = Sca_\Pi((u, \{\}), k)$$

where the auxiliary function $\mathrm{Sca}_\Pi : \mathcal{P} \times \mathbb{N} \to \mathcal{P}$ *is recursively defined as follows:*

$$\mathrm{Sca}_\Pi(p, 0) = p$$
$$\mathrm{Sca}_\Pi(p_1 \vee p_2, k) = \mathrm{Sca}_\Pi(p_1, k) \vee \mathrm{Sca}_\Pi(p_2, k)$$
$$\mathrm{Sca}_\Pi(p_1 \wedge p_2, k) = \mathrm{Sca}_\Pi(p_1, k) \wedge \mathrm{Sca}_\Pi(p_2, k)$$
$$\mathrm{Sca}_\Pi((u, \{u_1, \ldots, u_m\}), k) = \mathrm{Sca}_\Pi\left(\bigwedge_{s \in supp(u)} p(s^{|u|_s}, \{u_1, \ldots, u_m\}), k-1 \right)$$

where

$$p(s^i, U) = \bigvee_{n \in AppRules(s^i, R \cup Self_R)} \left(\bigwedge_{r \in supp(n)} (react(r)^{|n|_r}, \bigcup_{r' \in C_{123}} \{react(r')\} \cup Cr(R, U)) \right)$$

and

$$C_{123} = competitor_1(r, R, s) \cup competitor_2(r, R, n) \cup competitor_3(r, R, n, s)$$

Now we present some lemmata that, step by step, lead to the main theorem stating that the $\mathrm{Sc}_\Pi(u, k)$ operator actually computes a pattern representing a sufficient condition for the presence of u after k steps. In the lemmata and in the main theorem, given two multisets w and w' and a set of evolution rules R, we will denote with $w \to_R w'$ the fact that w' can be obtained from w by applying rules in R in a maximally parallel way.

The first lemma states that the portion of the pattern computed by the operator and defined as $p(s^i, U)$ in Definition 10 is a predictor for the presence of i instances of molecule s after one step of evolution of the P system.

Lemma 3. *Given a P system* $\Pi = (V, w_0, R)$, $w \in V^*$ *and* $s^i \in V^*$ *with* $s \in V$ *and* $i > 0$, *if* $w \models p(s^i, \emptyset)$ *then* $\forall w' \in V^*$ *such that* $w \to_R w'$, *it holds* $s^i \subseteq^* w'$.

Proof. By definition, $Cr(R, \emptyset) = \emptyset$, therefore, in this case, we have $p(s^i, \emptyset) = \bigvee_{n \in AppRules(s^i, R \cup Self_R)} (\bigwedge_{r \in supp(n)} (react(r)^{|n|_r}, \{react(r')|r' \in C_{123}\}))$. Assume now, by contradiction, that $w \models p(s^i, \emptyset)$ but there exists w' such that $w \to_R w'$ and $s^i \not\subseteq^* w'$. This implies that $w \models \bigwedge_{r \in supp(n)}(react(r)^{|n|_r}, \{react(r')|r' \in C_{123}\})$ for at least one multiset n of rules in $R \cup Self_R$ such that $s^i \in prod(n)$.

Let us denote the conjunction $\bigwedge_{r \in supp(n)}(react(r)^{|n|_r}, \{react(r')|r' \in C_{123}\})$ simply as CP. Note that $w \models CP$ implies that, for each $r \in supp(n)$, $w \supseteq_* react(r)^{|n|_r}$. Intuitively, this means that w could be rewritten applying each rule $r \in supp(n)$ for the number of times required by the multiset n but we still are left to prove that all rules $r \in supp(n)$ could be applied *simultaneously* each one for the number of times required by the multiset n. Assume, by contradiction that this is not the case, then there exists at least two rules r and r'' belonging to n such that $react(r) \cap react(r'') \neq \emptyset$ and such that $w \not\supseteq_* react(r)^{|n|_r} react(r'')^{|n|_{r''}}$. Note that at most one can be a self rule $s \to s$. Assume that if one is a self rule than it is the one called r. As a consequence, we are sure that r'' does not belong to $Self_R$. Since $r'' \in R$ and, by hypothesis, it belongs to n and it is such that $react(r) \cap react(r'') \neq \emptyset$ then, by definition, we have that $r'' \in competitor_2(r, R, n)$. Therefore, when verifying that $w \models CP$, $react(r'')$ has to be maximally matched in w before matching with $react(r)^{|n|_r}$. Since $w \supseteq_* react(r'')^{|n|_{r''}}$ but $w \not\supseteq_* react(r)^{|n|_r} react(r'')^{|r''|_n}$, this gives a contradiction. Hence, we can conclude that $w \supseteq_* react(r_1)^{|n|_{r_1}} \ldots react(r_t)^{|n|_{r_t}}$ for $r_1, \ldots, r_t \in supp(n)$.

Now assume that w could be maximally rewritten with rules $\tilde{r}_1^{o_1} \ldots \tilde{r}_h^{o_h}$ (of R) that, by hypothesis, give a w' satisfying $v^j \in w' \Rightarrow j < i$.

Therefore, there exist some rules in $\{r_1, \ldots, r_t\}$ such that they are not applied with the multiplicity required by n, when applying $\tilde{r}_1^{o_1} \ldots \tilde{r}_h^{o_h}$. In more detail, the self rule $s \to s$ belongs to such set if the instances of s in w that are left unchanged when applying $\tilde{r}_1^{o_1} \ldots \tilde{r}_t^{o_h}$ are less than the multiplicity of the self rule $s \to s$ in n.

Among all the rules of $\{r_1, \ldots, r_t\}$ satisfying the above property, let us consider the case in which there exists r that also satisfies the following property:

$$\{\tilde{r} \mid \tilde{r} \in \{\tilde{r}_1, \ldots, \tilde{r}_h\}, s \in prod(\tilde{r}), \tilde{r} \notin supp(n), react(\tilde{r}) \cap react(r) \neq \emptyset\} \subseteq$$
$$competitor_3(r, R, n, s) \tag{1}$$

In this case, since $\tilde{r}_1^{o_1} \ldots \tilde{r}_h^{o_h}$ is a maximal rewriting of w such that r is not applied with the multiplicity required by n, it means that $w \not\models (react(r)^{|n|_r}, \{react(\tilde{r}) \mid \tilde{r} \in \{\tilde{r}_1, \ldots, \tilde{r}_t\}, \tilde{r} \neq r, react(r) \cap react(\tilde{r}) \neq \emptyset\})$. Since we have assumed that (1) holds, we have three cases for each $\tilde{r} \in \{\tilde{r}_1, \ldots, \tilde{r}_h\} \subseteq R$ such that $r \neq \tilde{r}$ and $react(r) \cap react(\tilde{r}) \neq \emptyset$:

1. $s \notin prod(\tilde{r})$ then, by definition, $\tilde{r} \in competitor_1(r, R, s)$.
2. $s \in prod(\tilde{r})$, $\tilde{r} \in n$, then, by definition, $\tilde{r} \in competitor_2(r, R, n)$.
3. $s \in prod(\tilde{r})$, $\tilde{r} \notin n$, in this case, since we have assumed that (1) holds, we can be sure that $\tilde{r} \in competitor_3(r, R, n, s)$.

As a consequence, we have that $\{react(\tilde{r}) \mid \tilde{r} \in \{\tilde{r}_1, \ldots, \tilde{r}_h\}, \tilde{r} \neq r, react(r) \cap react(\tilde{r}) \neq \emptyset\} \subseteq \{react(r') \mid r' \in C_{123}\}$. Then, we have a contradiction since, from the last reasoning, we can conclude that $w \not\models (react(r)^{|n|_r}, \{react(\tilde{r}) \mid \tilde{r} \in \{\tilde{r}_1, \ldots, \tilde{r}_t\}, \tilde{r} \neq r, react(r) \cap react(\tilde{r}) \neq \emptyset\})$ but, by hypothesis, $w \models CP$ and, as a consequence, since $r \in n$, $w \models (react(r)^{|n|_r}, \{react(r') \mid r' \in C_{123}\})$.

Assume now that does not exist an r satisfying (1). This implies that for each r_i (with $i = 1, \ldots, t$) there exist (at least one) $\hat{r}_1^i \ldots \hat{r}_{z_i}^i \in \{\tilde{r}_1, \ldots, \tilde{r}_h\}$ such that for $j = 1, \ldots z_i$, $\hat{r}_j^i \neq r_i$, $react(\hat{r}_j^i) \cap react(r_i) \neq \emptyset$, and $\hat{r}_j^i \notin C_{123}$. Therefore, for $i = 1, \ldots, t$ and $j = 1, \ldots z_i$, by definition, we have that it must be the case that $s \in prod(\hat{r}_j^i)$ (otherwise $\hat{r}_j^i$ would belong to C_1) and $\hat{r}_j^i \notin supp(n)$ (otherwise $\hat{r}_j^i$ would belong to C_2) and, for each combination m of rules of n that could not be maximally applied because we apply $\hat{r}_j^i$, we have that $prod(m) \subseteq^* prod(\hat{r}_j^i)$ (otherwise $\hat{r}_j^i$ would belong to C_3). For simplicity, let us say that a rule $\hat{r}$ covers a multiset $m \subseteq^* n$ iff $react(m) \cap_* react(\hat{r}) = react(n) \cap_* react(\hat{r})$ and, $\forall m' \subset^* m$, $react(m') \cap_* react(\hat{r}) \neq react(n) \cap_* react(\hat{r})$. It is worth noting that using a rule $\hat{r} \in \{\hat{r}_1^1 \ldots \hat{r}_{z_1}^1, \ldots, \hat{r}_1^t \ldots \hat{r}_{z_t}^t\}$ instead of rules $r_1, \ldots, r_t$ to rewrite w cannot give any w' that does not contain s^i. This is because for each multiset m of rules $r_1, \ldots, r_t$ such that $m \subseteq^* n$, if $\hat{r}$ covers m, then $|prod(\hat{r})|_s \subset^* |prod(m)|_s$. Therefore we have a contradiction.   □

The second lemma states that if a multiset w satisfies $p(s^i, U)$, then the multiset obtained after one evolution step will satisfy the basic pattern (s^i, U).

Lemma 4. *Given a P system* $\Pi = (V, w_0, R)$, $w \in V^*$ *and a basic pattern* (s^i, U) *with* $s \in V$ *and* $i > 0$, *if* $w \models p(s^i, U)$ *then* $\forall w' \in V^*$ *such that* $w \rightarrow_R w'$, *it holds* $w' \models (s^i, U)$.

Proof. By definition, from $w \models p(s^i, U)$, it follows $w \models p(s^i, \emptyset)$. By applying Lemma 3 we can conclude that $\forall w'$ such that $w \rightarrow_R w'$, $w' \supseteq^* s^i$. For simplicity assume that $w' \supseteq^* s^i$ but $w' \not\supseteq^* s^{i+1}$. The more general case can be obtained by applying the following reasoning more than once.

Assume now, by contradiction, that $w' \not\models (s^i, U)$. Then, there must be the case that $w' \supseteq^* u_1^{o_1}, \ldots, u_t^{o_t}$ for $\{u_1, \ldots, u_t\} = U$ but $w' \not\supseteq^* u_1^{o_1}, \ldots, u_t^{o_t} s^i$. This implies that there exists at least one u_j with $j \in \{1, \ldots, t\}$ such that $s \in u_j$ and $o_j > 0$, that is $u_j \subseteq^* w'$. Consider the multiset of rules $n = \tilde{r}_1^{\tilde{o}_1} \ldots \tilde{r}_p^{\tilde{o}_p}$, let us assume there is just one, used to obtain w' from w where the proper rule $\tilde{r} \in Self_R$ is used to indicate that an occurrence of a molecule is left unchanged. Then $w = pred(\tilde{r}_1)^{\tilde{o}_1}, \ldots, pred(\tilde{r}_p)^{\tilde{o}_p}$. Since $w' \supseteq^* u_j \supseteq^* s$ we can conclude that there exists a minimal multiset of rules $m \subseteq n$ such that $prod(m) \supseteq^* u^j$. Note that $m \in AppliedRules(u_j, R \cup Self_R)$, therefore $react(m) \in Cr(R, U)$ and $react(m) \subseteq^* w$. Since $s \in u_j$, there exists a rule in m, let us call it $\tilde{r}_h$, such that $s \in prod(\tilde{r}_h)$. By $react(m) \subseteq^* w$, we derive that also $react(\tilde{r}_h) \subseteq_* w$. Therefore, there exists at least one rule $\tilde{r}_h$ with $h \in \{1, \ldots, p\}$ such that $\tilde{r}_h \in supp(n)$ such that $w \not\models (react(\tilde{r})^{|n|_{\tilde{r}}}, \bigcup_{r' \in C_{123}} \{react(r')\} \cup Cr(R, U))$. Therefore $w \not\models \bigwedge_{r \in supp(n)} (react(r)^{|n|_r}, \bigcup_{r' \in C_{123}} \{react(r')\} \cup Cr(R, U))$.   □

The following result comes directly from the definition of multiset patterns.

Lemma 5. *If* $w \models (u, \{u_1, \ldots, u_s\})$ *and* $w \models (\bar{u}, \{u_1, \ldots, u_s\})$ *with* $u \cap \bar{u} = \emptyset$, *then* $w \models (u\bar{u}, \{u_1, \ldots, u_s\})$.

Finally, the following lemma states that if a multiset w satisfies the pattern $\bigwedge_{s \in supp(u)} p(s^{|u|_s}, U)$ with u a generic multiset, then the multiset obtained after one evolution step will satisfy the basic pattern (u, U).

Lemma 6. *Given a P system* $\Pi = (V, w_0, R)$, $u \in V^*$, $w \in V^*$ *and a basic pattern* (u, U) *with* $u \in V^*$, *if* $w \models \bigwedge_{s \in supp(u)} p(s^{|u|_s}, U)$ *then* $\forall w' \in V^*$ *such that* $w \rightarrow_R w'$, *it holds* $w' \models (u, U)$.

Proof. Assume that $w \models \bigwedge_{s \in supp(u)} p(s^{|u|_s}, U)$. This implies that $w \models p(s^{|u|_s}, U)$ for each $s \in supp(u)$. By Lemma 4 we have that $\forall w'$ such that $w \rightarrow_R w'$, $w' \models (s^{|u|_s}, U)$ with $s \in supp(u)$. Therefore, we can conclude that $\forall w'$ such that $w \rightarrow_R w'$, $w' \models \bigwedge_{s \in supp(u)} (s^{|u|_s}, U)$. Since $vs_1^{|u|_{s_1}} \cap s_2^{|u|_{s_2}} = \emptyset$ for $s_1, s_2 \in supp(u)$, $s_1 \neq s_2$, by Lemma 5, we can conclude that $w' \models (u, U)$.

Theorem 1. *Let* $\Pi = (V, w_0, R)$ *be* P *system and let* $p \in \mathcal{P}$ *be a multiset pattern. If* $w_0 \models \text{Sca}_\Pi(p, k)$ *then for any* $w_1, \ldots, w_k$ *such that* $w_{i \in \{1, \ldots, k\}} \in V^*$ *and* $w_0 \to_R w_1 \to_R \cdots \to_R w_k$, *it holds* $w_k \models p$.

Proof. Assume that $w_0 \models \text{Sca}_\Pi(p, k)$, the proof is by induction on the pair (p, k) considering the order $\sqsubseteq$ on $\mathcal{P} \times \mathbb{N}$ defined as $\mathcal{P} \times \mathbb{N}$, $(p_1, n_1) \sqsubseteq (p_2, n_2)$ iff $n_1 < n_2$ or $n_1 = n_2$ and p_2 is a multiset pattern that contains p_1.

The base case is when p is a basic multiset pattern $p = (u, U)$ and $k = 0$. In this case $\text{Sca}_\Pi((u, U), 0) = (u, \{\})$, therefore, since by hypothesis $w_0 \models \text{Sca}_\Pi(p, 0)$ we have that $w_0 \models p$.

For the inductive case, we have that either p is not a basic multiset pattern or $p = (u, U)$ and $k > 0$. We consider these cases separately.

- $p = p_1 \wedge p_2$. In this case since $\text{Sca}_\Pi(p, k) = \text{Sca}_\Pi(p_1, k) \wedge \text{Sca}_\Pi(p_2, k)$, if $w_0 \models \text{Sca}_\Pi(p, k)$ then $w_0 \models \text{Sca}_\Pi(p_1, k)$ and $w_0 \models \text{Sca}_\Pi(p_2, k)$. By induction hypothesis, for any $w_1, \ldots, w_k$ such that $w_{i \in \{1, \ldots, k\}} \in V^*$ and $w_0 \to_R w_1 \to_R \cdots \to_R w_k$, it holds $w_k \models p_1$ and for any $w_1, \ldots, w_k$ such that $w_{i \in \{1, \ldots, k\}} \in V^*$ and $w_0 \to_R w_1 \to_R \cdots \to_R w_k$, it holds $w_k \models p_1$ and $w_k \models p_2$. Hence, we can conclude that for any $w_1, \ldots, w_k$ such that $w_{i \in \{1, \ldots, k\}} \in V^*$ and $w_0 \to_R w_1 \to_R \cdots \to_R w_k$, it holds $w_k \models (p_1 \wedge p_2) = p$.
- $p = p_1 \vee p_2$. In this case the proof is analogous to the previous case.
- $p = (u, U)$ and $k > 0$. In this case since $\text{Sca}_\Pi(p, k) = \text{Sca}_\Pi(\bigwedge_{s \in supp(u)} p(s^{|u|_s}, \{u_1, \ldots, u_t\}), k - 1)$, if $w_0 \models \text{Sca}_\Pi(p, k)$ then $w_0 \models \text{Sca}_\Pi(\bigwedge_{s \in supp(u)} p(s^{|u|_s}, \{u_1, \ldots, u_t\}), k - 1)$. By induction hypothesis, we have that for any $w_1, \ldots, w_{k-1}$ such that $w_{i \in \{1, \ldots, k-1\}} \in V^*$ and $w_0 \to_R w_1 \to_R \cdots \to_R w_{k-1}$, it holds $w_{k-1} \models \bigwedge_{s \in supp(u)} p(s^{|u|_s}, \{u_1, \ldots, u_t\})$. By Lemma 6 we have that $\forall w_k \in V^*$ such that $w_{k-1} \to_R w_k$, it holds $w_k \models (u, U) = p$. □

We are now ready to state the main result of this paper based on Theorem 1.

Corollary 1 (Sufficient Condition). *Let* $\Pi = (V, w_0, R)$ *be* P *system and* $u \in V^*$. *If* $w_0 \models \text{Sc}_\Pi(u, k)$ *then for any* $w_1, \ldots, w_k$ *such that* $w_{i \in [1, k]} \in V^*$ *and* $w_0 \to_R w_1 \to_R \cdots \to_R w_k$, *it holds* $u \subseteq^* w_k$.

Proof. Since $\text{Sc}_\Pi(u, k) = \text{Sca}_\Pi((u, \{\}), k)$, if $w_0 \models \text{Sc}_\Pi(u, k)$ then we have that $w_0 \models \text{Sca}_\Pi((u, \{\}), k)$. By Theorem 1 we have that for any $w_1, \ldots, w_k$ such that $w_{i \in \{1, \ldots, k\}} \in V^*$ and $w_0 \to_R w_1 \to_R \cdots \to_R w_k$, it holds $w_k \models (u, \{\})$. By definition of multiset pattern note that $w_k \models (u, \{\})$ iff $w_k \supseteq^* u$. □

The corollary essentially states that the pattern computed by the Sc_Π operator is actually a *sound* sufficient predictor.

5 Applications

Let us consider again the example of the multiset language consisting only of the multiset A^3 we described in Sect. 3.2. An acceptor for such a language can be represented by the P system $\Pi_6 = (\{O, A, T, F\}, w_0, R_6)$, where R_6 consists of the following rules:

$$r_0 : OA^3 \to T \qquad r_1 : TA \to F$$

The acceptor works by assuming that $|w_0|_O = 1$ and $|w_0|_T = |w_0|_F = 0$. If $|w_0|_A = 3$, then in one step T is produced and it is left unchanged in the second step (actually, the P system terminates after one step). If $|w_0|_A \neq 3$, then either T is not produced, or it is replaced by F in the second step. As a consequence, T will be present after two steps iff $|w_0|_A = 3$.

Let us compute the predictor of T in two steps for the P system Π_6 by applying the Sc_{Π_6} operator:

$$
\begin{aligned}
\mathsf{Sc}_{\Pi_6}(T, 2) &= \mathsf{Sca}_{\Pi_6}((T, \{\}), 2) = \mathsf{Sca}_{\Pi_6}((OA^3, \{TA\}) \vee (T, \{TA\}), 1) \\
&= \mathsf{Sca}_{\Pi_6}((OA^3, \{TA\}), 1) \vee \mathsf{Sca}_{\Pi_6}((T, \{TA\}), 1) \\
&= \mathsf{Sca}_{\Pi_6}((OA^3, \{TA, OA^4\}), 0) \vee \mathsf{Sca}_{\Pi_6}((OA^3, \{TA, OA^4\}) \vee (T, \{TA\}), 0) \\
&= \mathsf{Sca}_{\Pi_6}((OA^3, \{TA, OA^4\}), 0) \vee \mathsf{Sca}_{\Pi_6}((OA^3, \{TA, OA^4\}), 0) \\
&\quad \vee \mathsf{Sca}_{\Pi_6}((T, \{TA\}), 0) \\
&= (OA^3, \{TA, OA^4\}) \vee (OA^3, \{TA, OA^4\}) \vee (T, \{TA\}) \\
&= (OA^3, \{TA, OA^4\}) \vee (T, \{TA\}).
\end{aligned}
$$

Assumptions $|w_0|_O = 1$ and $|w_0|_T = 0$ allow us to simplify the obtained pattern into $(OA^3, \{OA^4\})$ that is exactly the pattern p_5' we considered in Sect. 3.2.

We now consider an acceptor for the language $A^n B^n$. As in Sect. 3.2, we start by focusing on the complement of $A^n B^n$, namely $A^n B^m$ with $n \neq m$. Let $\Pi_7 = (\{O, D, A, B, C, T, F\}, w_0, R_7)$ be a P system where rules in R_7 are:

$$r_0 : AB \to C \quad r_1 : AD \to T \quad r_2 : BD \to T \quad r_3 : O \to D \quad r_4 : FT \to T$$

If we assume that the initial multiset w_0 contains exactly one F, one O and no instances of T and of D, namely $|w_0|_F = |w_0|_O = 1$ and $|w_0|_T = |w_0|_D = 0$. Under such an assumption, the evolution of the P system is as follows: in the first step a maximal number of AB pairs are consumed by rule r_0 and, at the same time, molecule O is transformed into D by rule r_3. In the second step, if either some A or some B is still present, that is if the number of A was not the same as the number of B in the initial multiset, then one instance of T is produced by either r_1 or r_2. If T is produced, it causes F to be removed in the third step due to the application of rule r_4. As a consequence, after three steps molecule T is present iff the initial multiset contained different numbers of A and of B. Otherwise, molecule F is present instead of T.

Let us compute the predictor of T after three steps for the P system Π_7 by applying the Sc_{Π_7} operator:

$$\begin{aligned}
\mathrm{Sc}_{\Pi_7}(T,3) &= \mathrm{Sca}_{\Pi_7}((T,\{\}),3) \\
&= \mathrm{Sca}_{\Pi_7}((T,\{\}) \vee (FT,\{\}) \vee (BD,\{AB\}) \vee (AD,\{AB\}),2) \\
&= \mathrm{Sca}_{\Pi_7}((T,\{\}),2) \vee \mathrm{Sca}_{\Pi_7}((FT,\{\}),2) \\
&\quad \vee \mathrm{Sca}_{\Pi_7}((BD,\{AB\}),2) \vee \mathrm{Sca}_{\Pi_7}((AD,\{AB\}),2) \\
&= \mathrm{Sca}_{\Pi_7}((T,\{\}),1) \vee \mathrm{Sca}_{\Pi_7}((FT,\{\}),1) \\
&\quad \vee \mathrm{Sca}_{\Pi_7}((BD,\{AB\}),1) \vee \mathrm{Sca}_{\Pi_7}((AD,\{AB\}),1) \\
&\quad \vee \mathrm{Sca}_{\Pi_7}((BO,\{AB\}),1) \vee \mathrm{Sca}_{\Pi_7}((AO,\{AB\}),1) \\
&= \mathrm{Sca}_{\Pi_7}((T,\{\}),0) \vee \mathrm{Sca}_{\Pi_7}((FT,\{\}),0) \\
&\quad \vee \mathrm{Sca}_{\Pi_7}((BD,\{AB\}),0) \vee \mathrm{Sca}_{\Pi_7}((AD,\{AB\}),0) \\
&\quad \vee \mathrm{Sca}_{\Pi_7}((BO,\{AB\}),0) \vee \mathrm{Sca}_{\Pi_7}((AO,\{AB\}),0) \\
&= (T,\{\}) \vee (FT,\{\}) \vee (BD,\{AB\}) \vee (AD,\{AB\}) \\
&\quad \vee (BO,\{AB\}) \vee (AO,\{AB\}) \\
&= (T,\{\}) \vee (BD,\{AB\}) \vee (AD,\{AB\}) \vee (BO,\{AB\}) \vee (AO,\{AB\}).
\end{aligned}$$

The assumptions on the absence of T and D and on the presence of B in the initial multiset make the obtained pattern equivalent to $(B,\{AB\}) \vee (A,\{AB\})$, that is exactly the pattern we identified in Sect. 3.2 for $A^n B^m$ with $n \neq m$.

For the same P systems Π_7, let us now compute the predictor for the presence of F after three steps. This actually should be a pattern characterizing $A^n B^n$ (that we have seen in Sect. 3.2 cannot be expressed by the version of multiset patterns as they are introduced in this paper).

$$\begin{aligned}
\mathrm{Sc}_{\Pi_7}(F,3) &= \mathrm{Sca}_{\Pi_7}((F,\{\}),3) = \mathrm{Sca}_{\Pi_7}((F,\{FT\}),2) \\
&= \mathrm{Sca}_{\Pi_7}((F,\{FT,FAD,FBD,FFT\}),1) \\
&= (F,\{FT,FAD,FBD,FFT,FAO,FBO\}).
\end{aligned}$$

From the assumption on the absence of T and D in the initial multiset we have that the obtained pattern corresponds to $(F,\{FAO,FBO\})$. Moreover, from the assumption on the presence of F and O we can conclude that the pattern is actually satisfied only when $|w_0|_A = |w_0|_B = 0$. Hence, the pattern is a correct predictor (since $A^0 B^0$ belongs to the $A^n B^n$ language), but it does not capture all the initial multisets that would lead to the presence of F in three steps.

The pattern obtained by the proposed operator represents a sufficient condition for the presence of some molecules after a given number of steps. The last example shows that there are cases in which a complete condition (without false negatives) cannot be expressed with the current definition of multiset patterns. However, the limited expressiveness of multiset patterns is not the only reason for the incompleteness of the Sc_{Π} operator. Indeed, there are also cases in which the operator fails in computing a complete pattern, even if the such a pattern could be expressed. We have shown this kind of situations in Example 6.

6   Conclusions and Further Developments

In this paper we have defined multiset patterns. Such patterns were exploited to express sufficient conditions on initial multisets that ensure the presence a multiset of molecules after a given number of evolution steps. Necessary conditions could also be expressed with multiset patterns and computed by a very simple operator that simulates the backward application of rules without considering any competition between different rules. For example, in the case of the P systems Π_4 of Example 6 the necessary condition for the presence of DD after 1 step is expressed by the following pattern $(AABCE, \{\}) \vee (ABCCE, \{\}) \vee (AACCEE, \{\}) \vee (BB, \{\})$.

Further developments of our work include the investigation of multiset patterns under the viewpoint of the multiset languages they characterize. Moreover, extensions of multiset patterns could be studied in order to enrich their expressiveness, this would be useful also to allow a new notion of predictor to be proposed which satisfies the completeness property (absence of false negatives).

References

1. Barbuti, R., Gori, R., Levi, F., Milazzo, P.: Specialized predictor for reaction systems with context properties. In: Proceedings of the 24th International Workshop on Concurrency, Specification and Programming, CS&P 2015, pp. 31–43 (2015)
2. Barbuti, R., Gori, R., Levi, F., Milazzo, P.: Investigating dynamic causalities in reaction systems. Theor. Comput. Sci. **623**, 114–145 (2016)
3. Barbuti, R., Gori, R., Levi, F., Milazzo, P.: Specialized predictor for reaction systems with context properties. Fundamenta Informaticae **147**(2–3), 173–191 (2016)
4. Barbuti, R., Gori, R., Levi, F., Milazzo, P.: Generalized contexts for reaction systems: definition and study of dynamic causalities. Acta Informatica (2017). https://doi.org/10.1007/s00236-017-0296-3
5. Barbuti, R., Maggiolo-Schettini, A., Milazzo, P., Tini, S.: Flat form preserving step-by-step behaviour. Fundamenta Informaticae **87**, 1–34 (2008)
6. Bodei, C., Gori, R., Levi, F.: An analysis for causal properties of membrane interactions. Electron. Notes Theor. Comput. Sci. **299**, 15–31 (2013)
7. Bodei, C., Gori, R., Levi, F.: Causal static analysis for brane calculi. Theor. Comput. Sci. **587**, 73–103 (2015)
8. Brijder, R., Ehrenfeucht, A., Main, M.G., Rozenberg, G.: A tour of reaction systems. Int. J. Found. Comput. Sci. **22**(7), 1499–1517 (2011)
9. Brijder, R., Ehrenfeucht, A., Rozenberg, G.: A Note on causalities in reaction systems. ECEASST **30** (2010)
10. Busi, N.: Causality in membrane systems. In: Eleftherakis, G., Kefalas, P., Păun, G., Rozenberg, G., Salomaa, A. (eds.) WMC 2007. LNCS, vol. 4860, pp. 160–171. Springer, Heidelberg (2007). https://doi.org/10.1007/978-3-540-77312-2_10
11. Ehrenfeucht, A., Rozenberg, G.: Reaction systems. Fundamenta Informaticae **75**(1–4), 263–280 (2007)
12. Gori, R., Levi, F.: Abstract interpretation based verification of temporal properties for bioambients. Inf. Comput. **208**(8), 869–921 (2010)
13. Păun, G.: Computing with membranes. J. Comput. Syst. Sci. **61**, 108–143 (2000)

Counting Membrane Systems

Luis Valencia-Cabrera, David Orellana-Martín$^{(\boxtimes)}$, Agustín Riscos-Núñez, and Mario J. Pérez-Jiménez

Research Group on Natural Computing,
Department of Computer Science and Artificial Intelligence, Universidad de Sevilla,
Avda. Reina Mercedes s/n, 41012 Sevilla, Spain
{lvalencia,dorellana,ariscosn,marper}@us.es

Abstract. A decision problem is one that has a yes/no answer, while a counting problem asks how many possible solutions exist associated with each instance. Every decision problem X has associated a counting problem, denoted by $\#X$, in a natural way by replacing the question *"is there a solution?"* with *"how many solutions are there?"*. Counting problems are very attractive from a computational complexity point of view: if X is an **NP**-complete problem then the counting version $\#X$ is **NP**-hard, but the counting version of some problems in class **P** can also be **NP**-hard. In this paper, a new class of membrane systems is presented in order to provide a natural framework to solve counting problems. The class is inspired in a special kind of non-deterministic Turing machines, called counting Turing machines, introduced by L. Valiant. A polynomial-time and uniform solution to the counting version of the SAT problem (a well-known $\#$**P**-complete problem) is also provided, by using a family of counting polarizationless P systems with active membranes, without dissolution rules and division rules for non-elementary membranes but where only very restrictive cooperation (minimal cooperation and minimal production) in object evolution rules is allowed.

Keywords: Membrane computing
Polarizationless P systems with active membranes · Cooperative rules
The **P** versus **NP** problem · $\#$SAT problem

1 Introduction

Membrane Computing is a computational paradigm inspired by the structure and functioning of the living cells as well as from the cooperation of cells in tissues, organs, and organisms. This paradigm provides distributed parallel and non-deterministic computing models. All of them share the main syntactical ingredients: a finite alphabet (the *working* alphabet whose elements are called *objects*), a finite set of processor units delimiting *compartments* (called *membranes, cells* or *neurons*) interconnected by a *graph-structure* in such manner that initially each processor contains a multiset of objects, a finite set of *evolution rules* which provides the dynamic of the system, and an *environment*.

© Springer International Publishing AG 2018
M. Gheorghe et al. (Eds.): CMC 2017, LNCS 10725, pp. 74–87, 2018.
https://doi.org/10.1007/978-3-319-73359-3_5

According with the type of structure underlying the systems, there are basically three approaches: *cell-like* P systems where the compartments are arranged in a hierarchical structure (formally, a rooted tree), like in a living cell [7]; *tissue-like* P systems with a directed graph structure associated inspired from the living tissues where cells bump into each other and communicate through pores or other membrane mechanisms [20]; and *neural-like* P systems with a directed graph structure associated which mimic the way that neurons communicate with each other by means of short electrical impulses, identical in shape (voltage), but emitted at precise moments of time [10]. In this paper, the term *membrane system* is used to refer to *cell-like* P systems, *tissue-like* P systems or *neural-like* P systems indistinctly.

Usually, in cell-like and neural-like P systems the environment plays a "passive" role in the sense that it only receives objects, but cannot contribute objects to the system. However, in tissue-like P systems the role played by the environment is "active" in the sense that it can receive objects from the system and also send objects inside the system, and the objects initially placed in the environment have an arbitrarily large number of copies.

Decision problems (those having a **yes**/**no** answer) have associated a language in a natural way (the set of instances having **yes** as an answer), in such manner that solving a decision problem is expressed in terms of the recognition of the language associated with it. In this context, recognizer membrane systems were introduced in order to define what solving a decision problem means in the framework of Membrane Computing [12]. P systems with active membranes were introduced in [8]. These cell-like models make use of electrical charges associated with membranes and rules of the following types: object evolution, send-in communication, send-out communication, dissolution and division rules. By means of these rules, membranes can change their electrical charges but not their label. P systems with active membranes can provide efficient solutions to computationally hard problems, by making use of an exponential workspace (expressed in terms of number of objects and number of membranes) created in a polynomial time. The class of decision problems which can be solved by families of P systems with active membranes with dissolution rules and which use division for elementary and non-elementary membranes is equal to **PSPACE** [14]. However, if electrical charges are removed from the usual framework of P systems with active membranes, then dissolution rules come to play a relevant role (without them, only problems in class **P** can be solved in an efficient way, even in the case that division for non-elementary membranes are permitted [5]). P systems with active membranes and without polarizations were initially studied in [1,2] by replacing electrical charges by the ability to change the label of the membranes.

Counting problems (those asking how many possible solutions exist associated with each instance) have a natural number instead of a **yes**/**no** as an answer. Each decision problem has associated a counting problem in a natural way by replacing "*there exists a solution*" with "*how many solutions*". For instance, the counting problem associated with the **SAT** problem, denoted by #**SAT**, is the following: *given a Boolean formula φ in conjunctive normal form, how many truth assignments make true φ?* It is worth pointing out that the counting problem $\#X$ associated with a decision problem X may be harder than the decision problem, from a complexity point of view.

The main goal of this paper is twofold. On the one hand, to provide a formal framework in Membrane Computing to solve counting problems by introducing *counting membrane systems*. This approach was first initiated by Alhazov et al. [3] and now, the computing model is formally defined inspired by *counting Turing machines* introduced by L. Valiant in 1979: *"a standard nondeterministic TM with an auxiliary output device that (magically) prints in binary notation on a special tape the number of accepting computations induced by the input"*. L. Valiant also introduced the complexity class $\#\mathbf{P}$ of functions that can be computed by *counting Turing machines* running in polynomial time [19]. The concept of $\#\mathbf{P}$-complete problems is defined in a natural way by considering *parsimonious reduction*, that is reduction which preserves the number of solutions.

On the other hand, following the works initiated in [15–17], a uniform and polynomial-time solution to the $\#\mathtt{SAT}$ problem, a well-known $\#\mathbf{P}$-complete problem, is provided by means of a family of counting membrane systems from $\mathcal{DAM}_{\mathbf{c}}^0(mcmp, +c, -d, -n)$ whose elements are (counting) polarizationless P systems with active membranes where labels of membranes keep unchanged by the application of rules, but where dissolution rules and division rules for non-elementary membranes are forbidden and some kind of very restrictive cooperation in object evolution rules is allowed.

The paper is structured as follows. Next, we shortly recall some preliminary basic definitions related to abstract problems. Section 3 introduces counting membrane systems, and the concept of uniform polynomial-time solvability of counting problems by means of families of counting membrane systems is presented (specifically, the class $\mathcal{DAM}_{\mathbf{c}}^0(mcmp, +c, -d, -n)$ is defined). Section 4 is devoted to showing a uniform and polynomial-time solution of the $\#\mathtt{SAT}$ by using a family of counting polarizationless P systems with active membranes, without dissolution rules and with division only for elementary membranes where minimal cooperation and minimal production is allowed in object evolution rules. The paper ends with some conclusions and final remarks.

2   Abstract Problems

Roughly speaking, an *abstract problem* is a "general question to be answered, usually possessing several parameters whose values are left unspecified" [4]. Solving an abstract problem consists of answering the question associated with it. Thus, an abstract problem consists of a (finite or infinite) set of *concrete problems*, called *instances*, obtained by specifying particular values for all parameters. Each instance has an associated set (eventually empty) of possible *solutions* and the answer to the general question of the problem is related to that set.

A *search problem* (or *function problem*) is an abstract problem such that the question is to identify/find *one* solution to the set of possible solutions associated with each instance. For example, given a Boolean formula φ in conjunctive normal form to find any truth assignment which makes it true, or if there is no such truth assignment, answer "no". That is, in this problem a "function" must be computed in such manner that for every input formula φ, this "function" may have many possible outcomes (any satisfying truth assignment) or none.

A *decision problem* is a particular case of search problem. Specifically, a decision problem can be viewed as an abstract problem that has a **yes** or **no** answer. This kind of problems can be formulated by specifying a generic instance of the problem and by stating a **yes**/**no** question concerning to the generic instance [4]. For example, the SAT problem is the following decision problem: *given a Boolean formula in conjunctive normal form, is there a truth assignment that makes the formula true?*

Informally, a *counting problem* is an abstract problem such that one asks how many possible solutions exist associated with each generic instance, that is, in this kind of problems the output is a natural number rather than just **yes** or **no** as in a decision problem. For example, the #SAT problem previously defined is a particular case of a counting problem.

In *optimization problems* we seek to find a *best solution* associated with each instance among a collection of feasible solutions, according to a concept of optimality given by an objective function associated with the problem. For example, the MIN-VERTEX-COVER problem is the following optimization problem: given an undirected graph, to find a smallest set of vertexes covering the graph.

Next, we formally define the previous concepts. A *search problem* (or *function problem*) X is a tuple (Σ_X, I_X, S_X) such that: (a) Σ_X is a finite alphabet; (b) I_X is a language over Σ_X whose elements are called *instances* of X; and (c) S_X is a function whose domain is I_X and for each $u \in I_X$, $S_X(u)$ is a set whose elements are called *solutions* for u. To *solve a search problem* X means the following: for each instance $u \in I_X$ return one element of $S_X(u)$ in the case that $S_X(u) \neq \emptyset$; otherwise, return "no". Each search problem $X = (\Sigma_X, I_X, S_X)$ has an associated binary relation Q_X defined as follows: $Q_X = \{(u, z) \mid u \in I_X \land z \in S_X(u)\}$. Then, solving the search problem X can be interpreted as follows: given an instance $u \in X$, find one element z such that $(u, z) \in Q_X$. We say that a deterministic Turing machine M solves a search problem X if, given as input any instance $u \in I_X$, the machine M with input u returns some element belonging to $S_X(u)$ (M accepts u) in the case that $S_X(u) \neq \emptyset$; otherwise, it returns "no" (M rejects u). That is, the Turing machine M computes a multivalued function F on I_X: this function may have many possible outcomes or none.

An *optimization problem* X is a tuple $(\Sigma_X, I_X, S_X, O_X)$ such that:

- (Σ_X, I_X, S_X) is a search problem.
- O_X is a function whose domain is I_X and for each instance $u \in I_X$ and for each possible solution $a \in S_X(u)$ associated with u, $O_X(u, a)$ is a positive rational number.

- For each instance $u \in I_X$ there exists a solution $a \in S_X(u)$ such that either $\forall b\,(b \in S_X(u) \Rightarrow O_X(u,b) \leq O_X(u,a))$ (we say that a is a *maximal solution* to instance u), or $\forall b\,(b \in S_X(u) \Rightarrow O_X(u,b) \geq O_X(u,a))$ (we say that a is a *minimal solution* to instance u).

To *solve an optimization problem* X means the following: for each instance $u \in I_X$ return a *maximal solution* or for each instance $u \in I_X$ return a *minimal solution*. We say that a deterministic Turing machine M solves an optimization problem X if, given an instance $u \in I_X$, the machine M with input u returns one *optimal* (maximal or minimal) solution associated with that instance.

A *decision problem* X is a search problem (Σ_X, I_X, S_X) such that for each instance $u \in I_X$, $S_X(u) = \{0\}$ or $S_X(u) = \{1\}$. In the case $S_X(u) = \{0\}$ we say that the answer of the decision problem is *negative* (**no**) for instance u. In the case $S_X(u) = \{1\}$ we say that the answer of the decision problem is *affirmative* (**yes**) for instance u. To *solve a decision problem* X means the following: for each instance $u \in I_X$, return **yes** in the case $S_X(u) = \{1\}$, otherwise, return **no**. Let us notice that a decision problem $X = (\Sigma_X, I_X, S_X)$ can be viewed as an optimization problem $(\Sigma_X, I_X, S_X, O_X)$ where $O_X(u,a)$ is constant, always equal to 1 (recall that for each instance $u \in I_X$ the set of possible solutions $S_X(u)$ is a singleton, either $\{0\}$ or $\{1\}$). Each decision problem $X = (\Sigma_X, I_X, S_X)$ has an associated language L_X defined as follows: $L_X = \{u \in \Sigma_X^* \mid S_X(u) = \{1\}\}$. Conversely, each language L over an alphabet Γ has an associated decision problem $X_L = (\Sigma_{X_L}, I_{X_L}, S_{X_L})$ defined as follows: $\Sigma_{X_L} = \Gamma$, $I_{X_L} = \Gamma^*$ and $S_{X_L}(u) = \{1\}$, for each $u \in L$, and $S_{X_L}(u) = \{0\}$, for each $u \notin L$. According with these definitions, for each decision problem X we have $X_{L_X} = X$ and for each language L we have $L_{X_L} = L$. A deterministic Turing machine M is said to solve a decision problem X if machine M *recognizes* or *decides* the language L_X associated with the problem X, that is, for any string u over Σ_X, if $u \in L_X$, then the answer of M on input u is **yes** (that is, M accepts u), and the answer is **no** otherwise (that is, M rejects u). A *non-deterministic* Turing machine M is said to solve a decision problem X if machine M *recognizes* L_X, that is, for any string u over Σ_X, $u \in L_X$ if and only if there exists <u>at least one</u> computation of M with input u such that the answer is **yes**.

A *counting problem* X is a tuple $(\Sigma_X, I_X, S_X, F_X)$ such that (Σ_X, I_X, S_X) is a search problem and F_X is the function whose domain is I_X, defined as follows: $F_X(u) = |S_X(u)|$, where $|S_X(u)|$ denotes the number of elements of the set $S_X(u)$, for each instance $u \in I_X$. A counting problem X can be considered as a particular case of a search problem expressed as follows: given an instance $u \in I_X$, how many z are there such that $(u, z) \in Q_X$? (where Q_X is the binary relation associated with the search problem). A counting Turing machine M solves a counting problem X if, given an instance $u \in I_X$, the number of the accepting computations of M with input u is equal to the number of elements of the set $S_X(u)$, i.e., the number of possible solutions associated with u.

3   Counting Membrane Systems

The main purpose of computational complexity theory is to provide bounds on the amount of computational resources necessary for any mechanical procedure that solves an abstract problem. Usually, this theory deals with languages encoding/representing decision problems. The solvability of decision problems is expressed in terms of recognize/decide the languages associated with them. In order to formally define what it means to solve decision problems in Membrane Computing, a new variant called *recognizer membrane systems* was introduced in [12] (so-called *accepting* P systems) for cell-like P systems, in [11] for tissue-like P systems, and in [6] for neural-like P systems (so-called *accepting* spiking neural P systems). Next, a new class of membrane systems, called *counting membrane systems*, is introduced as a framework where counting problems can be solved in a natural way. These systems are inspired from *counting Turing machines* introduced by Valiant [19] and from recognizer membrane systems where the Boolean answer of these systems is replaced by an answer encoded by a natural number expressed in a binary notation (placed in the environment associated with the halting configuration).

Definition 1. *A counting membrane system Π is a membrane system such that:*

- *There exist two distinguished disjoint alphabets Σ (input alphabet) and Φ (final alphabet) both of them strictly contained in the working alphabet Γ of Π. A total order in the final alphabet $\Phi = \{a_0, a_1, \ldots, a_n\}$ is also considered.*
- *The membrane system has an input compartment labelled by i_{in}.*
- *All computations of the system halt.*
- *For each computation of the system, the environment associated with the corresponding halting configuration, may contain objects from Φ, but each of them with multiplicity at most one.*

According to Definition 1, the *result of any computation $\mathcal{C}$* of a counting P system is a natural number whose binary expression is encoded by the objects from the final alphabet placed the environment associated with its halting configuration, according with the following criterion: (a) if the set of objects in Φ placed in the environment of the corresponding halting configuration is the nonempty set $\{a_{i_1}, \ldots, a_{i_r}\}$, then the answer of $\mathcal{C}$ is the natural number $2^{i_1} + \cdots + 2^{i_r}$; and (b) otherwise, the answer of $\mathcal{C}$ is 0.

For each finite multiset m over the input alphabet Σ, a *computation* of a counting membrane system Π with input multiset m starts from the initial configuration, where the input multiset m is added to the content of the input compartment i_{in}. That is, we have an initial configuration associated with each input multiset m over Σ in counting membrane systems. We denote by $\Pi + m$ the counting membrane system Π with input multiset m.

Many different classes of counting membrane systems depending on the kind of rules can be considered. For example, counting transition P systems, counting polarizationless P systems with active membranes, counting tissue P systems with symport/antiport rules can be defined in a natural way. Then, we will use a subscript **c** to emphasize that we are dealing with some kind of counting membrane system. For instance, $\mathcal{DAM}_{\mathbf{c}}^0(+e, +c, -d, -n)$ denotes the class of all counting polarizationless P systems with active membranes which use object evolution rules, communication rules and division rules only for elementary membranes, but dissolution rules are forbidden.

It is worth pointing out that any recognizer membrane system Π can be considered as a "particular case" of counting membrane system, where the final alphabet Φ is a singleton alphabet $\{a_0\}$ and the rules of the counting system are obtained from the rules of the recognizer system replacing **yes** with a_0 and replacing object **no** with a garbage object $\natural$ different of a_0.

3.1 Polynomial Complexity Classes for Counting Membrane Systems

The concept of polynomial encoding in recognizer membrane systems was introduced in [13] and polynomial encodings are stable under polynomial-time reductions. This concept can be translated to counting membrane systems in a natural way.

Definition 2. *Let X be a counting problem whose set of instances is I_X. Let $\mathbf{\Pi} = \{\Pi(t) : t \in \mathbb{N}\}$ be a family of counting membrane systems. A* polynomial encoding *of X in $\mathbf{\Pi}$ is a pair (cod, s) of polynomial-time computable functions over I_X such that $s(u)$ is a natural number (obtained by means of a reasonable encoding scheme) and $cod(u)$ is a multiset over the input alphabet of $\Pi(s(u))$, for each instance $u \in I_X$, and $s^{-1}(k)$ is a finite set, for each $k \in \mathbb{N}$.*

Definition 3. *A counting problem $X = (\Sigma_X, I_X, S_X, F_X)$ is solvable in polynomial time and in a uniform way by a family of counting membrane systems $\mathbf{\Pi} = \{\Pi(t) : t \in \mathbb{N}\}$ from a class $\mathcal{R}_c$, denoted by $X \in \mathbf{PCMS}_{\mathcal{R}_c}$, if the following holds:*

- *The family $\mathbf{\Pi}$ is polynomially uniform by Turing machines, that is, there exists a deterministic Turing machine working in polynomial time which constructs the system $\Pi(t)$ from $t \in \mathbb{N}$ (t is expressed in unary notation).*
- *There exists a polynomial encoding (cod, s) of X in $\mathbf{\Pi}$ such that:*
  - *The family $\mathbf{\Pi}$ is polynomially bounded with respect to (X, cod, s), that is, there exists a natural number $k \in \mathbb{N}$ such that for each instance $u \in I_X$, every computation of the system $\Pi(s(u))$ with input $cod(u)$ performs at most $|u|^k$ steps.*
  - *For each instance $u \in I_X$ and for each computation $\mathcal{C}$ of $\Pi(s(u))$ with input $cod(u)$ we have the result of $\mathcal{C}$ is $F_X(u)$.*

It is easy to prove that the class $\mathbf{PCMS}_{\mathcal{R}_c}$ is closed under polynomial-time reduction and under complement, by adapting the corresponding demostrations for $\mathbf{PMC}_{\mathcal{R}}$, being $\mathcal{R}$ any class of recognizer membrane systems [12].

Having in mind that any recognizer membrane system Π can be considered as a "particular case" of counting membrane system, we have $\mathbf{PMC}_{\mathcal{R}} \subseteq \mathbf{PCMS}_{\mathcal{R}}$, for any class of recognizer systems $\mathcal{R}$.

3.2   Counting Membrane Systems from $\mathcal{DAM}_c^0(mcmp, +c, -d, -n)$

Let us recall that $\mathcal{DAM}^0(+e, +c, -d, -n)$ denotes the class of all recognizer polarizationless P systems with active membranes (μ denotes the membrane structure, Γ denotes the working alphabet and H denotes the set of labels) such that the set of rules is of the following forms:

★ $[a \rightarrow u]_h$ for $h \in H$, $a \in \Gamma$, u is a finite multiset over Γ (*object evolution rules*).
★ $a [\ ]_h \rightarrow [b]_h$ for $h \in H$, $a, b \in \Gamma$ and h is not the label of the root of μ (*send-in communication rules*).
★ $[a]_h \rightarrow b [\ ]_h$ for $h \in H$, $a, b \in \Gamma$ (*send-out communication rules*).
★ $[a]_h \rightarrow [b]_h [c]_h$ for $h \in H$, $a, b, c \in \Gamma$ and h is the label of an elementary membrane different of the root of μ (*division rules for elementary membranes*).

It is well known [5] that only problems in class **P** can be solved in polynomial time (and in a uniform way) by means of families from $\mathcal{DAM}^0(+e, +c, -d, -n)$. Moreover, this holds even in the case that division rules for elementary and non-elementary membranes are permitted.

By incorporating a restricted cooperation in object evolution rules, a uniform polynomial-time solution to the SAT problem, a well-known **NP**-complete problem [4], has been provided [17]. Specifically, *minimal cooperation and minimal production* (**mcmp**) in object evolution rules has been considered, that is, rules of the forms $[a \rightarrow b]_h$ or $[a\, b \rightarrow c]_h$, where $a, b, c \in \Gamma$, but at least one object evolution rule is of the second type. The corresponding class of recognizer P systems was denoted by $\mathcal{DAM}^0(mcmp, +c, -d, -n)$. Then we denote by $\mathcal{DAM}_c^0(mcmp, +c, -d, -n)$ the class of all counting polarizationless P systems with active membranes, with minimal cooperation and minimal production in object evolution rules, with communication rules and division rules only for elementary membranes, but without dissolution rules.

4   A Solution to #SAT in $\mathcal{DAM}_c^0(mcmp, +c, -d, -n)$

In this section a polynomial-time uniform solution to the counting problem #SAT, a well-known #**P**-complete problem, is provided by means of a family of counting membrane systems from $\mathcal{DAM}_c^0(mcmp, +c, -d, -n)$. For that, the solution to SAT problem given in [17] by using a family of membrane systems from $\mathcal{DAM}^0(mcmp, +c, -d, -n)$ is adapted, basically, in the output stage.

Let us recall that the polynomial-time computable function (the *Cantor pair function*) defined as $\langle n, p \rangle = ((n + p)(n + p + 1)/2) + n$, is a primitive recursive and bijective function from $\mathbb{N} \times \mathbb{N}$ to $\mathbb{N}$. The family $\mathbf{\Pi} = \{\Pi(t) \mid t \in \mathbb{N}\}$ is defined in such a manner that system $\Pi(t)$ will process any Boolean formula φ in conjunctive normal form (CNF) with n variables and p clauses, where $t = \langle n, p \rangle$, provided that the appropriate input multiset $cod(\varphi)$ is supplied to the system (through the corresponding input membrane), and will answer how many truth assignments make true the input formula φ.

For each $n, p \in \mathbb{N}$, we consider the recognizer counting P system

$$\Pi(\langle n, p \rangle) = (\Gamma, \Sigma, \Phi, H, \mu, \mathcal{M}_1, \mathcal{M}_2, \mathcal{R}, i_{in})$$

from $\mathcal{DAM}^0(mcmp, +c, -d, -n)$, defined as follows:

(1) Working alphabet $\Gamma = \{\beta, \natural\} \cup \{a_i \mid 0 \leq i \leq 2n + 2p + 1\} \cup$
$\{a_{i,j}, \mid 0 \leq i \leq n - 1, 0 \leq j \leq i\} \cup \{a_i, \gamma_i \mid 0 \leq i \leq n - 1\} \cup$
$\{b_{i,k} \mid 1 \leq i \leq n, 1 \leq k \leq i\} \cup \{c_j \mid 1 \leq j \leq p\} \cup$
$\{d_j \mid 2 \leq j \leq p\} \cup \{t_{i,k}, f_{i,k} \mid 1 \leq i \leq n, i \leq k \leq n + p - 1\} \cup$
$\{T_{i,k}, F_{i,k} \mid 1 \leq i \leq n, 0 \leq k \leq n - 1\} \cup \{T_i, F_i \mid 1 \leq i \leq n\} \cup$
$\{x_{i,j,k}, \overline{x}_{i,j,k}, x_{i,j,k}^* \mid 0 \leq i \leq n, 1 \leq j \leq p, 0 \leq k \leq n + p\}$.

(2) Input alphabet $\Sigma = \{x_{i,j,0}, \overline{x}_{i,j,0}, x_{i,j,0}^* \mid 1 \leq i \leq n, 1 \leq j \leq p\}$.

(3) Final alphabet $\Phi = \{a_i \mid 0 \leq i \leq n - 1\}$.

(4) $H = \{1, 2\}$.

(5) Membrane structure: $\mu = [\,[\ \ ]_2\,]_1$, that is, $\mu = (V, E)$ where $V = \{1, 2\}$ and $E = \{(1, 2)\}$.

(6) Initial multisets: $\mathcal{M}_1 = \{a_0^n\}$, $\mathcal{M}_2 = \{\beta, b_{i,1}, T_{i,0}^p, F_{i,0}^p \mid 1 \leq i \leq n\}$.

(7) The set of rules $\mathcal{R}$ consists of the following rules:

7.1 Rules for a general counter.
$[\alpha_k \longrightarrow \alpha_{k+1}]_1$, for $0 \leq k \leq 2n + 2p$

7.2 Rules to generate all truth assignments.
$[b_{i,i}]_2 \longrightarrow [t_{i,i}]_2 \, [f_{i,i}]_2$, for $1 \leq i \leq n$
$[b_{i,k} \longrightarrow b_{i,k+1}]_2$, for $2 \leq i \leq n \wedge 1 \leq k \leq i - 1$

7.3 Rules to generate suitable objects in order to start the next stage.
$\left.\begin{array}{l} [t_{i,k} \longrightarrow t_{i,k+1}]_2 \\ [f_{i,k} \longrightarrow f_{i,k+1}]_2 \end{array}\right\} 1 \leq i \leq n - 1 \wedge i \leq k \leq n - 1$

$\left.\begin{array}{l} [T_{i,k} \longrightarrow T_{i,k+1}]_2 \\ [F_{i,k} \longrightarrow F_{i,k+1}]_2 \end{array}\right\} 1 \leq i \leq n, 0 \leq k \leq n - 2$

$\left.\begin{array}{l} [T_{i,n-1} \longrightarrow T_i]_2 \\ [F_{i,n-1} \longrightarrow F_i]_2 \end{array}\right\} 1 \leq i \leq n$

7.4 Rules to produce exactly p copies of each truth assignment.
$\left.\begin{array}{l} [t_{i,k} \, F_i \longrightarrow t_{i,k+1}]_2 \\ [f_{i,k} \, T_i \longrightarrow f_{i,k+1}]_2 \end{array}\right\} 1 \leq i \leq n \wedge n \leq k \leq n + p - 2$

$\left.\begin{array}{l} [t_{i,n+p-1} \, F_i \longrightarrow \natural]_2 \\ [f_{i,n+p-1} \, T_i \longrightarrow \natural]_2 \end{array}\right\} 1 \leq i \leq n$

7.5 Rules to prepare the input formula for check clauses:
$\left.\begin{array}{l} [x_{i,j,k} \longrightarrow x_{i,j,k+1}]_2 \\ [\overline{x}_{i,j,k} \longrightarrow \overline{x}_{i,j,k+1}]_2 \\ [x_{i,j,k}^* \longrightarrow x_{i,j,k+1}^*]_2 \end{array}\right\} 1 \leq i \leq n, \ 1 \leq j \leq p, \ 0 \leq k \leq n + p - 1$

7.6 Rules for the first checking stage.
$\left.\begin{array}{l} [T_i \, x_{i,j,n+p} \longrightarrow c_j]_2 \\ [T_i \, \overline{x}_{i,j,n+p} \longrightarrow \natural]_2 \\ [T_i \, x_{i,j,n+p}^* \longrightarrow \natural]_2 \\ [F_i \, x_{i,j,n+p} \longrightarrow \natural]_2 \\ [F_i \, \overline{x}_{i,j,n+p} \longrightarrow c_j]_2 \\ [F_i \, x_{i,j,n+p}^* \longrightarrow \natural]_2 \end{array}\right\} 1 \leq i \leq n \wedge 1 \leq j \leq p$

7.7 Rules for the second checking stage.

$[c_1 \, c_2 \longrightarrow d_2]_2$

$[d_j \, c_{j+1} \longrightarrow d_{j+1}]_2$, for $2 \leq j \leq p-1$

7.8 Rules to prepare objects in the skin membrane.

$[\beta \, d_p \longrightarrow \gamma_0]_2$

$[\gamma_0]_2 \longrightarrow \gamma_0 \, [\,]_2$, for $0 \leq i \leq n-1$

7.9 Rules to prepare objects encoding the binary output.

$[\gamma_i^2 \longrightarrow \gamma_{i+1}]_1$, for $0 \leq i \leq n-2$

$[\alpha_{2n+2p+1} \gamma_i \longrightarrow a_{i,0}]_1$, for $0 \leq i \leq n-1$

$[a_{i,j} \longrightarrow a_{i,j+1}]_1$, for $1 \leq i \leq n-1, 0 \leq j \leq i-1$

7.10 Rules to produce the output.

$[a_{i,i}]_1 \longrightarrow a_i \, [\,]_1$, for $0 \leq i \leq n-1$

(8) The input membrane is the membrane labelled by 2 ($i_{in} = 2$) and the output region is the environment.

4.1   An Overview of the Computation

It is easy to check that $\Pi(\langle n, p \rangle)$, previously defined, is a deterministic counting membrane system, for each $(n, p) \in \mathbb{N} \times \mathbb{N}$.

We consider the polynomial encoding (cod, s) from #SAT in Π defined as follows: let φ be a Boolean formula in conjunctive normal form. Let $Var(\varphi) = \{x_1, \cdots, x_n\}$ be the set of propositional variables and $\{C_1, \cdots, C_p\}$ the set of clauses of φ. Let us assume that both the number of variables and clauses of the input formula φ, are greater than or equal to 2. We define $s(\varphi) = \langle n, p \rangle$ and

$$cod(\varphi) = \{x_{i,j,0} \mid x_i \in C_j\} \cup \{\overline{x}_{i,j,0} \mid \neg x_i \in C_j\} \cup \{x_{i,j,0}^* \mid x_i \notin C_j, \neg x_i \notin C_j\}$$

Notice that $cod(\varphi)$ can be represented as a matrix, in such a way that the j-th row ($1 \leq j \leq p$) encodes the j-th clause C_j of φ, and the columns ($1 \leq i \leq n$) are associated with variables. We denote by $cod_k(\varphi)$ the multiset $cod(\varphi)$ when the third index of all objects is equal to k.

The Boolean formula φ will be processed by the system $\Pi(s(\varphi))$ with input multiset $cod(\varphi)$. Next, we informally describe how that system works.

The solution proposed is inspired in the solution provided to the SAT problem in [17], consisting of the following stages:

- *Generation stage*: by applying division rules from **7.2**, all truth assignments for the variables $\{x_1, \ldots, x_n\}$ associated with φ are produced. This stage takes exactly n computation steps and at the i-th step, $1 \leq i \leq n$, of this stage, division rule is triggered by object $b_{i,i}$, producing two new membranes with all its remaining contents replicated in the new membranes labelled by 2. Simultaneously to these divisions, objects $t_{i,k}, f_{i,k}, T_{i,k}, F_{i,k}$ (by applying rules from **7.3**) and objects $x_{i,j,k}, \overline{x}_{i,j,k}, x_{i,j,k}^*$ (by applying rules from **7.5**) evolve during this stage in such manner that at configuration $\mathcal{C}_n$:

(a) There is a membrane labelled by 1 which contains n copies of object α_n.

(b) There are 2^n membranes labelled by 2 such that each of them contains: a copy of object β, the set $cod_n(\varphi)$, the multiset $\{T_i^p, F_i^p \mid 1 \leq i \leq n\}$; and a different subset $\{r_{1,n}, \ldots, r_{n,n}\}$, being $r \in \{t, f\}$.

- *Production of enough copies for each truth assignment*: in this stage p copies (p is the number of clauses of φ) of each truth assignment are produced, to allow the checking of the literal associated with each variable in each clause. By using minimal cooperation and minimal production (applying rules from **7.4**), objects $t_{i,k}$ (respectively, object $f_{i,k}$) are used to remove all copies of F_i (respectively, T_i). This stage takes p steps and at configuration C_{n+p}:

(a) The root membrane (labelled by 1) contains n copies of object α_{n+p}.

(b) There are 2^n membranes labelled by 2 such that each of them contains: a copy of object β, n copies of the garbage object $\natural$, the set $cod_{n+p}(\varphi)$, and a different multiset $\{R_{1,n}^p, \ldots, R_{n,n}^p\}$, being $R \in \{T, F\}$.

- *First Checking stage*: by applying rules from **7.6**, we check whether or not each clause of the input formula φ is satisfied by the truth assignments generated in the previous stage, encoded by each membrane labelled by 2. This stage takes exactly one computation step and at configuration C_{n+p+1}:

(a) The root membrane (labelled by 1) contains n copies of object α_{n+p+1}.

(b) There are 2^n membranes labelled by 2 such that each of them contains: a copy of object β, many copies of the garbage object $\natural$ (which they will not evolve in the rest of the computation), and copies of objects c_j whose presence means that clause C_j is true for the truth assignment encoded by that membrane.

- *Second Checking stage*: by applying rules from **7.7**, we check whether or not all clauses of the input formula φ are satisfied by some truth assignment encoded by a membrane labelled by 2. This stage takes exactly $p - 1$ steps and at configuration C_{n+2p}:

(a) The root membrane (labelled by 1) contains n copies of object α_{n+2p}.

(b) There are 2^n membranes labelled by 2 such that each of them contains: a copy of object β, many copies of the garbage object $\natural$ (which they will not evolve in the rest of the computation), and copies of objects d_j and c_j, in such manner that the truth assignment encoded by such membrane makes true φ if and only if contains some object d_p.

- *Output stage. Negative answer*: if the input formula is not satisfiable, then any rule from **7.8** is not applicable and from C_{n+2p} on, no rules are applied in the system except those from **7.1** until reaching a halting configuration at $C_{2n+2p+1}$. Therefore, in this case, the system answers 0.

- *Output stage. Affirmative answer*: if the input formula is satisfiable, by applying rules from **7.8** some objects γ_0 are produced at membrane labelled by 1. Due to the semantics of these membrane systems, this stage takes exactly two steps. Thus, at configuration C_{n+2p+2} the multiplicity of γ_0 in the skin membrane equals to the number of truth assignment of variables $\{x_1, \ldots, x_n\}$ that makes true φ. Next, by applying rules from **7.9**, some objects γ_i, $0 \leq i \leq n-1$, with multiplicity 1 will be generated after, at most, $n - 1$ computation steps. Then, at configuration $C_{(n+2p+2)+n-1} = C_{2n+2p+1}$ at the skin membrane we have n copies of object $\alpha_{2n+2p+1}$ and some objects γ_i, $0 \leq i \leq n-1$, with multiplicity 1. By applying the second rule from **7.9**, some objects $a_{i,0}$ with multiplicity 1 are produced at that membrane. In order to make deterministic the system, objects $a_{i,0}$ evolves until $a_{i,i}$ by applying the third rules from **7.9**. Finally, the system sends to the environment the right answer according to the results of the previous stage, by applying rules from **7.10**, for instance, object $a_{i,i}$ is released to the environment as object a_i. This stage takes, at most, n computation steps. Specifically, if object $a_{i,0}$ appears in membrane 1 at configuration $\mathcal{C}_{2n+2p+2}$ then object a_i is sent out to the environment at $(i+1)$-th step of this stage.

5 Main Results

Theorem 1. #SAT $\in$ **PCMS**$_{\mathcal{DAM}_c^0(mcmp,+c,-d,-n)}$.

Proof. The family of P systems previously constructed verifies the following:

(a) Every system of the family $\mathbf{\Pi}$ belongs to $\mathcal{DAM}_c^0(mcmp, +c, -d, -n)$.
(b) The family $\mathbf{\Pi}$ is polynomially uniform by Turing machines because for each $n, p \in \mathbb{N}$, the amount of resources needed to build $\Pi(\langle n, p \rangle)$ is of a polynomial order in $\max\{n, p\}$:
  - Size of the alphabet: is of the order $O(n^2 \cdot p^2)$.
  - Initial number of membranes: $2 \in \Theta(1)$.
  - Initial number of objects in membranes: $2np + n + 1 \in \Theta(n \cdot p)$.
  - Number of rules: is of the order $O(n^2 \cdot p^2)$.
  - Maximal number of objects involved in any rule: $3 \in \Theta(1)$.
(c) The pair (cod, s) of polynomial-time computable functions defined fulfill the following: for each input formula φ of the #SAT problem, $s(\varphi)$ is a natural number, $cod(\varphi)$ is an input multiset of the system $\Pi(s(\varphi))$, and for each $k \in \mathbb{N}$, $s^{-1}(k)$ is a finite set.
(d) The family $\mathbf{\Pi}$ is polynomially bounded: indeed, for each input formula φ of the #SAT problem, the P system $\Pi(s(\varphi)) + cod(\varphi)$ takes at most $2n + 2p + 1$ computation steps in the case of the input formula is not satisfiable and, on the contrary, takes at most $2n + 2p + 2$ steps, n being the number of variables of φ and p the number of clauses.
(e) The family $\mathbf{\Pi}$ is sound and complete with regard to (X, cod, s): indeed, this can be deduced from the computations previously described.

Therefore, the family $\mathbf{\Pi}$ of P systems previously constructed solves the #SAT problem in polynomial time in a uniform way.

Corollary 1. #**P** $\subseteq$ **PCMS**$_{\mathcal{DAM}_c^0(mcmp,+c,-d,-n)}$.

Proof. It suffices to note that the #SAT problem is a #**P**-complete problem, #SAT $\in$ **PCMS**$_{\mathcal{DAM}_c^0(mcmp,+c,-d,-n)}$, and class **PCMS**$_{\mathcal{DAM}_c^0(mcmp,+c,-d,-n)}$ is closed under polynomial-time reduction and under complement.

6   Conclusions

In order to provided a natural framework to solve counting problems in the context of Membrane Computing, a new class of membrane systems, called *counting membrane systems*, is presented in this paper. The new kind of models is inspired from counting Turing machines [19] and from recognizer membrane systems [12].

The computational efficiency of the new variant has been explored. Specifically, a polynomial-time and uniform solution to the #SAT problem, a well-known #**P**-complete problem, is provided by using a family of counting polarizationless P systems with active membranes, without dissolution rules and division rules for non-elementary membranes but where very restrictive cooperation (minimal cooperation and minimal production) in object evolution rules is allowed.

As future works we suggest to analyze the computational efficiency of counting membrane systems from the previous class but where minimal cooperation and minimal production only is considered for communication rules (maybe only send-in rules or only send-out rules) instead of object evolution rules, following the work initiated in [18]. Besides, it would be interesting to explore the ability to use separation rules (*distribution of objects*) instead of division rules (*replication of objects*) in counting membrane systems, from a computational complexity point of view.

References

1. Alhazov, A., Pan, L.: Polarizationless P systems with active membranes. Grammars **7**, 141–159 (2004)
2. Alhazov, A., Pan, L., Păun, G.: Trading polarizations for labels in P systems with active membranes. Acta Informaticae **41**(2–3), 111–144 (2004)
3. Alhazov, A., Burtseva, L., Cojocaru, S., Rogozhin, Y.: Solving **PP**-complete and #**P**-complete problems by P systems with active membranes. In: Corne, D.W., Frisco, P., Păun, G., Rozenberg, G., Salomaa, A. (eds.) WMC 2008. LNCS, vol. 5391, pp. 108–117. Springer, Heidelberg (2009). https://doi.org/10.1007/978-3-540-95885-7_8
4. Garey, M.R., Johnson, D.S.: Computers and Intractability: A Guide to the Theory of NP-Completeness. W.H Freeman and Company, San Francisco (1979)
5. Gutiérrez–Naranjo, M.A., Pérez–Jiménez, M.J., Riscos–Núñez, A., Romero–Campero, F.J.: On the power of dissolution in P systems with active membranes. In: Freund, R., Păun, G., Rozenberg, G., Salomaa, A. (eds.) WMC 2005. LNCS, vol. 3850, pp. 224–240. Springer, Heidelberg (2006). https://doi.org/10.1007/11603047_16
6. Leporati, A., Mauri, G., Zandron, C., Păun, G., Pérez-Jiménez, M.J.: Uniform solutions to SAT and Subset Sum by spiking neural P systems. Nat. Comput. **8**(4), 681–702 (2009)
7. Păun, G.: Computing with membranes. J. Comput. Syst. Sci. **61**(1), 108–143 (2000)
8. Păun, G.: Computing with membranes: attacking NP-complete problems. In: Antoniou, I., Calude, C.S., Dinneen, M.J. (eds.) UMC'2K. DISCMATH. Springer, London (2000). https://doi.org/10.1007/978-1-4471-0313-4_7
9. Păun, G.: P systems with active membranes: attacking NP-complete problems. J. Automata Lang. Comb. **6**, 75–90 (2001)

10. Păun, G., Pérez-Jiménez, M.J., Rozenberg, G.: Spike trains in spiking neural P systems. Int. J. Found. Comput. Sci. **17**(4), 975–1002 (2006)
11. Păun, G., Pérez-Jiménez, M.J., Riscos-Núñez, A.: Tissue P systems with cell division. Int. J. Comput. Commun. Control **III**(3), 295–303 (2008)
12. Pérez-Jiménez, M.J., Romero-Jiménez, A., Sancho-Caparrini, F.: Complexity classes in models of cellular computing with membranes. Nat. Comput. **2**(3), 265–285 (2003)
13. Pérez-Jiménez, M.J., Romero-Jiménez, A., Sancho-Caparrini, F.: A polynomial complexity class in P systems using membrane division. J. Automata Lang. Comb. **11**(4), 423–434 (2006)
14. Sosík, P., Rodríguez-Patón, A.: Membrane computing and complexity theory: a characterization of PSPACE. J. Comput. Syst. Sci. **73**, 137–152 (2007)
15. Valencia-Cabrera, L., Orellana-Martín, D., Martínez-del-Amor, M.A., Riscos-Núñez, A., Pérez-Jiménez, M.J.: Polarizationless P systems with active membranes: Computational complexity aspects. J. Automata Lang. Comb. **21**(1–2), 107–123 (2016)
16. Valencia-Cabrera, L., Orellana-Martín, D., Riscos-Núñez, A., Pérez-Jiménez, M.J.: Minimal cooperation in polarizationless P systems with active membranes. In: Graciani, C., Păun, G., Orellana-Martín, D., Riscos-Núñez, A., Valencia-Cabrera, L. (eds.) Proceedings of the Fourteenth Brainstorming Week on Membrane Computing, 1–5 February 2016, Sevilla, Spain, pp. 327–356. Fénix Editora (2016)
17. Valencia-Cabrera, L., Orellana-Martín, D., Martínez-del-Amor, M.A., Riscos-Núñez, A., Pérez-Jiménez, M.J.: Reaching efficiency through collaboration in membrane systems: dissolution, polarization and cooperation. Theoret. Comput. Sci. (2017, in press). https://doi.org/10.1016/j.tcs.2017.04.015
18. Valencia-Cabrera, L., Orellana-Martín, D., Martínez-del-Amor, M.A., Riscos-Núñez, A., Pérez-Jiménez, M.J.: Cooperation in transport of chemical substances: a complexity approach. Fundamenta Informaticae **154**(1–4), 373–385 (2017)
19. Valiant, L.G.: The complexity of computing the permanent. Theoret. Comput. Sci. **8**(2), 189–201 (1979)
20. Zhang, G., Pérez-Jiménez, M.J., Gheorghe, M.: Real-life Applications with Membrane Computing. ECC, vol. 25. Springer, Cham (2017). https://doi.org/10.1007/978-3-319-55989-6. X + 367 p.

APCol Systems with Teams

Lucie Ciencialová[1], Luděk Ciencialá[1], and Erzsébet Csuhaj-Varjú[2]([✉])

[1] Institute of Computer Science and Research Institute of the IT4Innovations Centre of Excellence, Silesian University in Opava, Opava, Czech Republic
{lucie.ciencialova,ludek.cienciala}@fpf.slu.cz
[2] Department of Algorithms and Their Applications, Faculty of Informatics, ELTE Eötvös Loránd University, Pázmány Péter sétány 1/c, Budapest 1117, Hungary
csuhaj@inf.elte.hu

Abstract. We investigate the possibility of "going beyond" Turing in the terms of Automaton-like P Colonies (APCol systems, for short), variants of P colonies processing strings as their environments. We use the notion of teams of agents as a restriction for the maximal parallelism of the computation. In addition, we assign a colour to each team. In the course of the computation, the colour is changing according to the team that is currently active. We show that we can simulate red-green counter machines with APCol systems with two-coloured teams of minimal size. Red-green counter machines are computing devices with infinite run on finite input that exceed the power of Turing machines.

Keywords: Automaton-like P colonies · APCol systems · Red-green counter machine · Unbounded computation · Teams

1 Introduction

Recently, both unconventional Turing equivalent computing devices and computational models which "go beyond" Turing, i.e., which are able to compute more than recursively enumerable sets of strings or numbers are in the focus of interest. In membrane computing, we can find examples for both types of such constructs.

APCol systems (Automaton-like P colonies) were introduced in [4] as an extension of P colonies (introduced in [8]) - a very simple variant of membrane systems inspired by colonies of formal grammars. (The reader is referred to [12] for more information in membrane systems and to [9] and [6] for details on grammar systems theory.) An APCol system consists of a finite number of agents - finite collections of objects embedded in a membrane - and a shared environment. The agents are equipped with programs which are composed from rules that allow them to interact with their environment that is represented by a string. For this reason, the agents use their own objects and the objects of the environment. The number of objects inside each agent is set by definition and it

© Springer International Publishing AG 2018
M. Gheorghe et al. (Eds.): CMC 2017, LNCS 10725, pp. 88–104, 2018.
https://doi.org/10.1007/978-3-319-73359-3_6

is usually a very small number: 1, 2 or 3. The environmental string is processed by the agents and it is used as a communication channel for the agents as well. Through the string, the agents are able to affect the behaviour of another agent.

The activity of the agents is based on rules that can be rewriting, communication or checking rules [8]. A rewriting rule $a \rightarrow b$ allows the agent to rewrite (evolve) one object a to object b. Both objects are placed inside the agent. Communication rule $c \leftrightarrow d$ makes possible to exchange object c placed inside the agent with object d in the string. A checking rule is formed from two rules r_1, r_2 of type rewriting or communication. It sets a kind of priority between the two rules r_1 and r_2. The agent tries to apply the first rule and if it cannot be performed, then the agent executes the second rule. The rules are combined into programs in such a way that all objects inside the agent are affected by execution of the rules. Consequently, the number of rules in the program is the same as the number of objects inside the agent.

The interested reader can find more details on P colonies in [3, 7, 12].

In this paper, we focus on APCol systems with agents forming teams; the concept was first proposed in [5]. The team is a finite number of agents of the APCol system. These collections can be so-called prescribed teams (given together with the components of the APCol system) or so-called free teams where only the size of the teams, i.e., the number of the agents in the team is given in advance. The notion is inspired by the concept of team grammar systems (see [13]). APCol systems with prescribed or with free teams function in the following manner: in every computation step only one team is allowed to work (only one team is active) and all of its components should perform a program in parallel.

Another interesting extension is to assign colours to programs, instructions or rules and observing how the currently used colour changes under the computation. This method is well-known for observing unbounded computations. Motivated by the notion of red-green Turing machines [11] (red-green register machines) and related notions in P systems theory [2], we introduce the concept of APCol systems with coloured teams. These constructs are APCol systems with teams where each team is associated with a colour. A string is accepted by an APCol system with coloured teams, if starting with the string as initial string the computation is unbounded and its teams with the final colour are active in an infinite number of steps and the teams of the other colours are active only in a finite number of steps.

Red-green Turing machines, introduced in [11] exceed the power of Turing machines since they recognize exactly the Σ_2-sets of the Arithmetical Hierarchy. These machines are deterministic and their state sets are divided into two disjoint sets, called the set of red states and the set of green states. Red-green Turing machines work on finite input words with the following recognition criterion on infinite runs: no red state is visited infinitely often and one or more green states are visited infinitely often. A change from a green state to a red state or reversely is called a mind change; we may speak of a change of the "colour". In [11], it is shown that every recursively enumerable language can be recognized by a red-green Turing machine with one mind change. It is also proved that if more than one mind changes may take place, then red-green Turing machines are able to recognize the complement of any recursively enumerable language.

Our paper is structured as follows: the second section is devoted to definitions and notations used in the paper. The third section contains results obtained on APCol systems with coloured teams, namely, we show that any red-green counter machine can be simulated with an APCol system with coloured teams, where there are two colours. The teams either consist of only one agent and then the system works sequentially, or the APCol system has teams of at most two agents acting in parallel. Finally, some conclusions are derived.

2   Definitions

Throughout the paper we assume that the reader is familiar with the basics of formal language and automata theory; for further details consult [13]. We list the notations used in the paper.

We use $\mathbb{N} \cdot \mathsf{RE}$ to denote the family of recursively enumerable sets of natural numbers and $\mathbb{N}$ to denote the set of natural numbers.

For an alphabet Σ, Σ^* denotes the set of all words over Σ (including empty word ε). For the length of the word $w \in \Sigma^*$, we use notation $|w|$ and for the number of occurrences of symbol $a \in \Sigma$ in w notation $|w|_a$ is used.

A multiset of objects M is a pair $M = (V, f)$, where V is an arbitrary (not necessarily finite) set of objects and f is a mapping $f : V \to N$; f assigns to each object in V its multiplicity in M. The set of all multisets over the set of objects V is denoted by V^*. The set V' is called the support of M and denoted by $supp(M)$ if for all $x \in V'$ $f(x) \neq 0$. The cardinality of M, denoted by $card(M)$, is defined by $card(M) = \sum_{a \in V} f(a)$. Any multiset of objects M with the set of objects $V = \{a_i, \ldots, a_n\}$ can be represented as a string w over alphabet V with $|w|_{a_i} = f(a_i)$; $1 \leq i \leq n$. Obviously, all words obtained from w by permuting the letters can also represent M, and ε represents the empty multiset.

2.1   Register and Counter Machines

We briefly recall the basic notions, following the notations used in [2].

A register machine [10] is a construct $M = (m, B, l_0, l_h, P)$, where m is the number of registers, B is a set of labels, $l_0 \in B$ is the initial label, $l_h \in B$ is the final label, and P is the set of instructions bijectively labelled by elements of B. The instructions of M can be of the following forms:

- $l_1 : (ADD(r), l_2, l_3)$, with $l_1 \in (B - \{l_h\})$, $l_2, l_3 \in B, 1 \leq j \leq m$. It increases the value of register r by one and the next instruction to be performed is non-deterministically chosen, it is labelled by l_2 or l_3. This instruction is called increment.
- $l_1 : (SUB(r), l_2, l_3)$, with $l_1 \in (B - \{l_h\})$, $l_2, l_3 \in B, 1 \leq j \leq m$. If the value of register r is zero, then the label of the next instruction to be performed is l_3; otherwise, the value of register r is decreased by one and the label of the next instruction to be executed is l_2. The first case is called zero-test, the second case is called decrement.
- $l_h : HALT$. The register machine stops executing instructions.

A configuration of a register machine is described by the numbers stored in the registers and by the label of the next instruction to be performed. Computations start by executing the instruction l_0 of P, and terminate by execution of the $HALT$-instruction l_h.

This model of register machines can be extended by instructions for reading from an input tape and writing to an output tape containing strings over an input alphabet T_{in} and an output alphabet T_{out}, respectively, see [2]:

- $l_1 : (read(a), l_2)$, with $l_1 \in (B - \{l_h\}), l_2 \in B, a \in T_{in}$. This instruction reads symbol a from the input tape and the next instruction is l_2.
- $l_1 : (write(a), l_2)$, with $l_1 \in (B - \{l_h\}), l_2 \in B, a \in T_{out}$. This instruction writes symbol a to the output tape and the next instruction is l_2.

This extended register machine, working with strings is also called a counter automaton and is denoted by $M = (m, B, l_0, l_h, P, T_{in}, T_{out})$. If no output is written, T_{out} is not indicated. The language $L(M)$ accepted by a counter automaton $M = (m, B, l_0, l_h, P, T_{in})$ consists of all input words over T_{in} for which there is a halting computation by M.

It is known (see e.g. [10]) that register machines with (at most) three registers can compute all recursively enumerable sets of natural numbers. Counter automata with two registers can simulate the computations of Turing machines and thus characterize RE. All these results are obtained with deterministic register machines, where the ADD-instructions are of the form $l_1 : (ADD(r), l_2)$, with $l_1 \in (B - \{l_h\}), l_2 \in B, 1 \leq j \leq m$. More details can be found in [2].

2.2   Red-Green Turing Machines

We briefly recall the most important notions and statements concerning red-green Turing machines and their variants, following [1,2,11].

Red-green Turing machines, introduced in [11], exceed the power of the standard Turing machines, since they recognize exactly the Σ_2-sets of the Arithmetical Hierarchy. As we told before, they are deterministic and their state sets are divided into two disjoint sets, namely, the set of red states and the set of green states. Red-green Turing machines work on finite inputs with the recognition criterion on infinite runs that no red state is visited infinitely often and one or more green states are visited infinitely often. A change from a green state to a red state or reversely is called a mind change; we may speak of a change of the "colour". In [11], it was shown that every recursively enumerable language can be recognized by a red-green Turing machine with one mind change. It was also proved that if more than one mind change may take place, then they are able to recognize the complement of any recursively enumerable language.

In the analogy of the concept of red-green Turing machines, red-green counter machines (red-green register machines) were defined and examined [1]. The authors proved that the computations of a red-green Turing machine TM can be simulated by a red-green register machine RM with two registers and with string input in such a way that during the simulation of a transition of TM leading from a state p with colour c to a state p' with colour c' the simulating register machine uses instructions with labels (states) of colour c and only in the last step of the simulation changes the label (state) to colour c'. They showed that the reverse simulation works as well: the computations of a red-green register machine RM with an arbitrary number of registers and with string input can be simulated by a red-green Turing machine TM in such a way that during the simulation of a computation step of RM from an instruction with label (state) p with colour c to an instruction with label (state) p' with colour c', the simulating Turing machine TM are in states of colour c and only in the last step of the simulation changes to a state of colour c'. The language recognized by a red-green Turing machine is the set of input words on which the red-green TM has a computation which stabilizes in green, i.e., there is an infinite run that no red state is visited infinitely often and one or more green states are visited infinitely often.

In [2], the above notions were implemented for membrane systems: the notions of a red-green P automaton and its variants, as counterparts were introduced. It was shown that these devices are able to "go beyond" Turing, in the sense as red-green Turing machines are able to do.

2.3   APCol Systems

In the following we recall the concept of APCol systems, particular variants of P colonies, where the environment of the agents is given in the form of a string [4].

The agents of APCol systems contain objects, each object is an element of a finite alphabet. With every agent, a set of programs is associated. There are two types of rules in the programs. The first one is of the form $a \rightarrow b$ and it is called an evolution rule. It means that object a inside of the agent is rewritten (evolved) to object b. The second type of rules is called a communication rule and it is in the form $c \leftrightarrow d$. When this rule is performed, then the object c inside the agent and a symbol d in the string are exchanged. If $c = e$, then the agent erases d from the input string and if $d = e$, then the symbol c is inserted into the string.

During the work of the APCol system, the agents perform programs. The number of objects inside the agents remain unchanged during the functioning of the system, it is usually 2.

Since both rules in a program can be communication rules, an agent can work with two objects in the string in one step of the computation. In the case of program $\langle a \leftrightarrow b; c \leftrightarrow d \rangle$, a substring bd of the input string is replaced by string ac. If the program is of the form $\langle c \leftrightarrow d; a \leftrightarrow b \rangle$, then a substring db of the input string is replaced by string ca. That is, the agent can act only in one place in a computation step and the change of the string depends both on the order of the rules in the program and on the interacting objects. In particular, the following types of programs with two communication rules are considered:

- $\langle a \leftrightarrow b; c \leftrightarrow e \rangle$ - b in the string is replaced by ac,
- $\langle c \leftrightarrow e; a \leftrightarrow b \rangle$ - b in the string is replaced by ca,

- $\langle a \leftrightarrow e; c \leftrightarrow e \rangle$ - ac is inserted in a non-deterministically chosen place in the string,
- $\langle e \leftrightarrow b; e \leftrightarrow d \rangle$ - bd is erased from the string,
- $\langle e \leftrightarrow d; e \leftrightarrow b \rangle$ - db is erased from the string,
- $\langle e \leftrightarrow e; e \leftrightarrow d \rangle$; $\langle e \leftrightarrow e; c \leftrightarrow d \rangle$, ...- these programs can be replaced by programs of type $\langle e \rightarrow e; c \leftrightarrow d \rangle$.

The program is said to be *restricted* if it is formed from one rewriting and one communication rule. The APCol system is restricted if all of the programs of the agents are restricted.

To help the reader in the easier understanding the technical details of the paper, we recall the formal definition of an APCol system.

Definition 1 [4]. *An APCol system is a construct*

$$\Pi = (O, e, A_1, \dots, A_n), \ where$$

- *O is an alphabet; its elements are called the objects,*
- *$e \in O$, called the basic object,*
- *A_i, $1 \leq i \leq n$, are agents. Each agent is a triplet $A_i = (\omega_i, P_i, F_i)$, where*
  - *ω_i is a multiset over O, describing the initial state (content) of the agent, $|\omega_i| = 2$,*
  - *$P_i = \{p_{i,1}, \dots, p_{i,k_i}\}$ is a finite set of programs associated with the agent, where each program is a pair of rules. Each rule is in one of the following forms:*
    - *$a \rightarrow b$, where $a, b \in O$, called an evolution rule,*
    - *$c \leftrightarrow d$, where $c, d \in O$, called a communication rule,*
  - *$F_i \subseteq O^*$ is a finite set of final states (contents) of agent A_i.*

At the beginning of the computation of the APCol system is in initial configuration which is an $(n+1)$-tuple $c = (\omega; \omega_1, \dots, \omega_n)$ where ω is the initial state of the environment and the other n components are multisets of strings of objects, given in the form of strings, the initial states of the agents. The initial state of the environment does not contain object e.

A configuration of an APCol system Π is given by $(w; w_1, \dots, w_n)$, where $|w_i| = 2$, $1 \leq i \leq n$, w_i represents all the objects placed inside the i-th agent and $w \in (O - \{e\})^*$ is the string to be processed.

In each computation step every agent attempts to find one of its programs to use. If it has applicable programs, then it non-deterministically chooses one of them and applies it. As usual in membrane computing, APCol systems work in the maximally parallel manner, i.e., as many agents perform one of its programs in parallel as possible. We note that other working modes can also be defined.

By applying programs, the APCol system passes from one configuration to another configuration. A sequence of configurations starting from the initial configuration is called a computation. A configuration is halting if the APCol system has no applicable program.

A string ω is accepted by APCol system Π if there exists a computation by Π such that it starts in the initial configuration $(\omega; \omega_1, \dots, \omega_n)$ and ends by halting in a configuration $(\varepsilon; w_1, \ldots, w_n)$, where at least one of $w_i \in F_i$ for $1 \leq i \leq n$. The set of strings accepted by Π is its accepted language, denoted by $L(\Pi)$.

An APCol system Π can accept a set of numbers as well, i.e., $|L(\Pi)|$.

2.4   APCol Systems with Coloured Teams of Agents

As a restriction of the computation process, we can introduce teams into the concept of APCol system, as proposed in [5]. The team is a finite set of agents. These teams can be prescribed teams (given together with the components of the APCol system) or free teams where only the size of the teams, i.e., the number of agents in the team is given in advance. The notion is inspired by the concept of team grammar systems (see [13]).

APCol systems with prescribed or with free teams work in the following manner: at any computation step only one team is allowed to work (only one team is active) and all of its components should perform a program in parallel. We note that such a variant where a maximal number of components of the team should act in parallel can also be considered.

One other extension of the concept of APCol system is associating "colour" to the agents or, if the APCol system is with teams, to the teams. The concept is inspired by red-green Turing machines; the idea was first presented in [5], given in an informal manner, using only two colours, red and green.

Definition 2. *An APCol system with coloured teams is a construct*

$$\Pi = (O, e, A_1, \ldots, A_n, C, f, B, B_{colours}, B_{teams}), \text{ where}$$

- *O is an alphabet; its elements are called the objects,*
- *$e \in O$, called the basic object,*
- *A_i, $1 \leq i \leq n$, are agents. Each agent is a triplet $A_i = (\omega_i, P_i, F_i)$, where*
  - *ω_i is a multiset over O, describing the initial state (content) of the agent, $|\omega_i| = 2$,*
  - *$P_i = \{p_{i,1}, \ldots, p_{i,k_i}\}$ is a finite set of programs associated with the agent, where each program is a pair of rules. Each rule is in one of the following forms:*
    - *$a \rightarrow b$, where $a, b \in O$, called an evolution rule,*
    - *$c \leftrightarrow d$, where $c, d \in O$, called a communication rule,*
  - *$F_i \subseteq O^*$ is a finite set of final states (contents) of agent A_i,*
- *C is a set of labels of colours,*
- *$f \in C$ is the final colour,*
- *B is a set of labels of teams,*
- *B_{colour} is a set of pairs (B_s, c_t) assigning to every team its colour, where $B_s \in B$, $c_t \in C$,*
- *B_{teams} is a set of pairs (A_i, B_s) assigning the label of team $B_s \in B$ to each agent A_i.*

Infinite computations. Due to the results of the computational power of APCol systems, it can easily be seen that for finite computations colours and teams do not add more, they can only be used for defining restricted classes of APCol systems. However, this is not the case if we consider infinite computations.

We say that a string is recognized by an APCol system with coloured teams, if starting with the string as initial string the computation is infinite and its teams with the final colour are active in an infinite number of steps and the teams of the other colours are active only in a finite number of steps.

Now we provide an illustrative example of APCol system with coloured teams.

Example 1. We construct an APCol system with three teams assigned to three different colours - red, green and orange, simulating work of streets lights connected with speed radar. The green light is on the traffic light at the beginning. If the vehicle is approaching faster than allowed, the traffic light changes to orange and red. In the case that the vehicle stops before the traffic lights (or it drives away while the red is on), the traffic light lights up orange and then green again. The input string for computation is a sequence of signals coming from speed radar. The signals are encoded into symbols in such a way that F means fast speed over limit, S means slow speed within the limits, Z means that car stopped and finally E which means that street is empty. The signals are encoded and inserted into the string with given frequency. Every input string starts with special symbol $.

The constructed APCol system

$$\Pi = (\{e, E, Z, S, F, o, r, g, \$, R, P\}, e,$$
$$A_1, A_2, A_3, \{green, orange, red\}, green,$$
$$\{B_1, B_2, B_3\}, \{(B_1, green), (B_2, orange), (B_3, red)\},$$
$$\{(A_1, B_1), (A_2, B_2), (A_3, B_3)\})$$

has three teams - one green, one orange and one red. Each team is formed from only one agent. Agent A_1 has initial configuration ge and the following programs:

$1: \langle g \leftrightarrow \$; e \leftrightarrow X \rangle \quad X \in \{E, Z, S\}$
$2: \langle \$ \leftrightarrow g; X \to e \rangle$

The green team is active only if the current symbol is in accordance with the speed limit or the street is empty. When the speed of the arriving vehicle is over the speed limit, only the orange team can work.

The initial configuration of the agent A_2 is oe and it executes following programs:

$3: \langle o \leftrightarrow \$; e \leftrightarrow F \rangle$
$4: \langle \$ \to \$; F \to R \rangle$
$5: \langle \$ \to \$; R \leftrightarrow o \rangle$

The agent from the orange team consumes symbol F and replaces symbol $\$$ by R. When this symbol appears in the string, only the red team can work.

The initial configuration of the agent A_3 is re and it performs the following programs:

$6 : \langle r \leftrightarrow R; e \leftrightarrow X \rangle , \quad X \in \{E, F, S, Z\}$
$7 : \langle R \rightarrow R; Y \rightarrow e \rangle , \quad Y \in \{F, S\}$
$8 : \langle R \leftrightarrow r; e \rightarrow e \rangle$
$9 : \langle R \rightarrow P; K \rightarrow e \rangle , \quad K \in \{Z, E\}$
$10 : \langle P \leftrightarrow r; e \rightarrow e \rangle$

The agent from the red team consumes symbol R and the neighbouring symbol from the string. The following behaviour of the agent depends on consumed symbol. If the symbol is F or it is S, then the agent puts to the string symbol R and in this way it calls itself to work. In the case of symbol Z or E, (the vehicle stopped or the street is empty) then the agent puts the symbol P to the string and the agent from the orange team has an applicable program.

$11 : \langle \$ \rightarrow \$; o \leftrightarrow P \rangle$
$12 : \langle \$ \rightarrow \$; P \rightarrow e \rangle$
$13 : \langle \$ \leftrightarrow o; e \rightarrow e \rangle$

After executing program 13, symbol $\$$ appears in the string and it can be consumed by agent from the green team or the orange team. Although the computation over a finite string is not unbounded, but one can assume that if there is no output from the speed radar, encoder puts symbols E into the string with a given frequency (it is similar to the endless tape of Turing machine) and the computation can continue with executing programs of the agent from the green team.

3   APCol Systems with Coloured Teams and Red-Green Counter Machines

In this section we study the interconnection between red-green counter machines and APCol systems with coloured teams. First we present a result where the number of agents within every team is minimal, namely, one.

Theorem 1. *For every red-green counter machine*

$$CM = (m, B, B_{red}, B_{green}, l_0, P, T_{in})$$

we can construct an APCol system

$$\Pi = (O, e, A_1, \ldots, A_n, C, B, B_{colours}, B_{teams})$$

with teams having only one agent and being associated with two colours such that $L(\Pi) = \{\#\}L(CM)$, *where* $\# \notin T_{in} \cup \{e\}$.

Proof. Consider a red-green counter machine $CM = (2, B, B_{red}, B_{green}, l_0, P, T_{in})$ recognizing language $L(CM)$. To every such counter machine there exists a red-green counter machine $CM' = (2, B \cup \{l_0'\}, B_{red}', B_{green}', l_0', P, T_{in} \cup \{\#\})$ that recognizes language $L(CM') = \# \cdot L(CM)$, where $\{\#\} \cap T_{in} = \emptyset$ and the first instruction of CM' to be executed is instruction $l_0' : (read(\#), l_0)$. Then it continues the computation in the same way as machine CM. We construct an APCol system Π with coloured teams as follows: all labels from the set $B \cup T_{in}$ are objects of the APCol system. The content of register i is represented by the number of copies of objects i occurring in the string. All teams have one agent only. At the beginning of the computation only one team of agents can work - red team of one agent that generates symbols and puts them to the beginning of the string.

Team: B_1
Colour: Red
Agent: $A_1 = (ee, P_1, \emptyset)$
Programs: 1 : $\langle e \rightarrow \#_1; e \rightarrow O_1 \rangle$;   6 : $\langle \textcircled{R} \rightarrow \boxed{R}; R \leftrightarrow e \rangle$;

2 : $\langle \#_1 \leftrightarrow \#; O_1 \leftrightarrow e \rangle$;   7 : $\langle \boxed{R} \rightarrow \textcircled{G}; e \rightarrow G \rangle$;

3 : $\langle \# \rightarrow \#_2; e \rightarrow \$ \rangle$;   8 : $\langle \textcircled{G} \rightarrow \boxed{G}; G \leftrightarrow e \rangle$;

4 : $\langle \#_2 \leftrightarrow e; \$ \leftrightarrow O_1 \rangle$;   9 : $\langle \boxed{G} \rightarrow \textcircled{L}; e \rightarrow X_0 \rangle$;

5 : $\langle O_1 \rightarrow R; e \rightarrow \textcircled{R} \rangle$;   10 : $\langle \textcircled{L} \rightarrow \boxed{L}; X_0 \leftrightarrow e \rangle$;

Symbol X is an element from the set $\{l, r, g\}$ and it is selected as follows: let l_1 be the currently simulated instruction and let l_2 be the label of the next instruction. If l_2 is a read-instruction and the colour of instruction is red (or green) then $X = r$ (or $X = g$). Otherwise $X = l$.

The APCol system starts its computation on string $\#\omega$. Agent A_1 uses programs $1, 2, 3$ and 4 to replace symbol $\#$ by substring $\#_1\#_2\$$. Then it places three symbols (R, G, X_0) into random positions in the string.

Symbols R and G are consumed by two agents from two teams.

Team: B_2 Team: B_3
Colour: Red Colour: $Green$
Agent: $A_2 = (ee, P_2, \emptyset)$ Agent: $A_3 = (ee, P_3, \emptyset)$
Programs: 11 : $\langle e \leftrightarrow R; e \rightarrow e \rangle$;   Programs: 12 : $\langle e \leftrightarrow G; e \rightarrow e \rangle$;

Let l_1 be a read-instruction $l_1 : (read(a), l_2)$. We construct two similar teams of different colours to execute the first phase of the simulation of the read-instruction. The agent from such a team checks whether the symbol currently read from the input string is a or not. The team of the working agent has the same colour as the previously simulated instruction.

Team: B_{X_1} for $X \in \{r, g\}$ Team: B_2 or B_3
Colour: B_{r_1} is Red, B_{g_1} is $Green$ Colour: B_2 is Red, B_3 is $Green$
Agent: $A_{x_1} = (ee, P_{x_1}, \emptyset)$ Agent: A_2 or A_3; $d \in \{R, G\}$
Programs: 13 : $\langle e \leftrightarrow X_1; e \rightarrow e \rangle$;   Programs: 16 : $\langle d \leftrightarrow L_1'; e \rightarrow M_1 \rangle$;

14 : $\langle X_1 \rightarrow L_1'; e \rightarrow e \rangle$;   17 : $\langle L_1' \rightarrow N_1; M_1 \rightarrow M_1 \rangle$;

15 : $\langle L_1' \leftrightarrow \$; e \leftrightarrow y \rangle$;   18 : $\langle M_1 \leftrightarrow d; N_1 \leftrightarrow e \rangle$;
for all $y \in T_{in}$

When agent A_{X_1} successfully finishes its work, then agent from a team with the same colour as l_1 inserts symbol l_2 into the string in the same position. In the other case, when the read-instruction cannot be performed, agent from red team starts to be active for an unbounded number of steps.

Team: B_{X_1} for $X \in \{r, g\}$
Colour: B_{r_1} is *Red*, B_{g_1} is *Green*
Agent: A_{X_1}
Programs: $19 : \langle \$ \leftrightarrow M_1; a \rightarrow e \rangle$; $22 : \langle \$ \leftrightarrow M_1; y \leftrightarrow N_1 \rangle$; $y \in T_{in} - \{a\}$;
$\qquad\quad\ 20 : \langle M_1 \rightarrow Q_1; e \leftrightarrow N_1 \rangle$; $23 : \langle M_1 \rightarrow W; N_1 \rightarrow e \rangle$;
$\qquad\quad\ 21 : \langle Q_1 \leftrightarrow e; N_1 \rightarrow E \rangle$; $24 : \langle W \leftrightarrow e; e \rightarrow e \rangle$;

Team: B_{l_1}
Colour: *Red* or *Green* (depends on l_1)
Agent: $A_{l_1} = (ee, P_{l_1}, \emptyset)$
Programs: $25 : \langle e \leftrightarrow Q_1; e \rightarrow X_2 \rangle$;
$\qquad\quad\ 26 : \langle X_1 \leftrightarrow e; Q_1 \rightarrow e \rangle$;
$\qquad\qquad\ X \in \{l, r, g\}$

Team: B_4
Colour: *Red*
Agent: A_4
Programs: $27 : \langle e \leftrightarrow W; e \rightarrow e \rangle$;
$\qquad\quad\ 28 : \langle W \rightarrow W; e \rightarrow e \rangle$;

For each ADD-instruction $l_1 : (ADD(r), l_2)$, there are two teams of agents of the same colour as the ADD-instruction has.

Team: B_{l_1}
Colour: *Red* or *Green* (depends on the instruction colour)
Agent: A_{l_1}
Programs: $29 : \langle e \leftrightarrow l_1; a \rightarrow e \rangle$; $32 : \langle \#_r \leftrightarrow M_1; r \leftrightarrow e \rangle$;
$\qquad\quad\ 30 : \langle l_1 \rightarrow L_1; e \rightarrow e \rangle$; $33 : \langle M_1 \rightarrow X_2; e \rightarrow e \rangle$; $X \in \{l, r, g\}$
$\qquad\quad\ 31 : \langle L_1 \leftrightarrow \#_r; e \rightarrow r \rangle$; $34 : \langle X_2 \leftrightarrow e; e \rightarrow e \rangle$;

Team: B_2 or B_3
Colour: B_2 is *Red*, B_3 is *Green*
Agent: A_2 or A_3; $d \in \{R, G\}$
Programs: $35 : \langle d \leftrightarrow L_1; e \rightarrow M_1 \rangle$;
$\qquad\quad\ 36 : \langle M_1 \leftrightarrow d; L_1 \rightarrow e \rangle$;

The first agent consumes the corresponding symbol of the actually simulated instruction. At the following steps, the agent rewrites the symbol l_1 to L_1 and exchanges this symbol by $\#_r$. In the same time, the agent generates symbol r. Now it is time for the second team to work. The agent from the second team replaces symbol L_1 by R or G - it depends on the colour of the instruction, rewrites it to symbol M_1 and puts the symbol M_1 to the string instead of symbol R or G. When symbol M_1 appears in the string, then the agent B_1 exchanges it by two symbols - $\#_r$ and r.

For SUB-instruction $l_1 : (SUB(r), l_2, l_3)$, there are two teams of the same colour, too. The first team with one agent is for execution of the instruction and the second team is preparing the symbols for further use (symbol L_1 is replaced with M_1).

Team: B_{l_1} Team: B_2 or B_3
Colour: Red or Green   Colour: B_2 is Red, B_3 is Green
           (depends on the colour of l_1)   Agent: A_2 or A_3; $d \in \{R, G\}$
Agent: A_{l_1} Programs: $41 : \langle d \leftrightarrow L_1; e \to M_1 \rangle$;
Programs: $37 : \langle e \leftrightarrow l_1; e \to e \rangle$; $42 : \langle L_1 \leftrightarrow N_1; M_1 \to M_1 \rangle$;
          $38 : \langle l_1 \to L_1; e \to e \rangle$; $43 : \langle M_1 \leftrightarrow d; N_1 \leftrightarrow e \rangle$;
          $39 : \langle L_1 \leftrightarrow \#_r; e \leftrightarrow r \rangle$;
          $40 : \langle L_1 \leftrightarrow \#_r; e \leftrightarrow Z \rangle$;
          $Z \in \{\#_{r+1}, \$\}$

The idea of simulation of SUB-instruction is that the agent consumes symbol $\#_r$ together with symbol r - if the counter r is not empty -, or with symbol $\#_{r+1}$ (or $\$$) - if the counter r is empty and it is not the last counter (or it is the last counter). According to its content, the agent generates the label of the next instruction.

Team: B_{l_1}
Colour: Red or Green (depends on the colour of l_1)
Agent: A_{l_1}
Programs: $44 : \langle \#_r \to \#_r; r \to l_2' \rangle$; $49 : \langle \#_r \leftrightarrow M_1; Z \leftrightarrow N_1 \rangle$;
          $45 : \langle \#_r \leftrightarrow M_1; l_2' \to l_2'' \rangle$; $50 : \langle M_1 \to Y_3; N_1 \to e \rangle$;
          $46 : \langle M_1 \to e; l_2'' \to l_2''' \rangle$; $51 : \langle Y_3 \leftrightarrow e; e \to e \rangle$;
          $47 : \langle e \leftrightarrow N_1; l_2''' \to X_2 \rangle$; $X, Y \in \{l, r, g\}$;
          $48 : \langle N_1 \to e; X_2 \leftrightarrow e \rangle$; $Z \in \{\#_{r+1}, \$\}$

We construct the APCol system

$$\Pi = (O, e, A_1, \ldots, A_n, C, B, B_{colours}, B_{teams}) \text{ with:}$$

$- O = T_{in} \cup \{l_i, l_i', l_i'', l_i''', L_i, L_i', M_i, N_i, g_i, r_i, Q_i | l_i \in H\} \cup \{i | 1 \leq i \leq m\}$
  $\cup \{e, G, R, \textcircled{R}, \textcircled{G}, \boxed{R}, \boxed{G}, \textcircled{L}, \boxed{L}, W, \$, \#_1, \#2, O_i\}$,

$- n = |H| + 2 \times$ number of read-instructions $+ 4$
$- B = \{B_j\}, 1 \leq j \leq n$
$- C = \{Red, Green\}$
$-$ The sets $B_{colours}, B_{teams}$ and the agents $A_1, \ldots, A_n$
         are defined in the previous part of the text.

The computation of the APCol system starts with string $\#w$. The first steps are done by the red team B_1. Teams B_2 and B_3 must go through initialization before they are used the first time during simulation of the first red or green instruction. It can imply only a finite number of mind changes. After initialization of these two agents, the APCol system goes through the same mind changes as the red-green counter machine CM goes through during the corresponding computation. Therefore, if red-green counter machine CM recognizes string w, then APCol system Π recognizes it too and vice versa. $\square$

Although the APCol system from proof of Theorem 1. uses the maximally parallel working mode, its work is limited to the use of one team at each step, therefore, to one agent. As a matter of fact, it works sequentially.

Next we provide another simulation of the red-green counter machines with APCol systems with teams and colours where the parallelism is used.

Theorem 2. *For every red-green counter machine*

$$CM = (m, B, B_{red}, B_{green}, l_0, P, T_{in})$$

we can construct an APCol system

$$\Pi = (O, e, A_1, \ldots, A_n, C, B, B_{colours}, B_{teams})$$

with two colours and with at least one team formed from two agents such that $L(\Pi) = \{\#\}L(CM)$, *where* $\# \notin T_{in} \cup \{e\}$.

Proof. As in proof of Theorem 1, let us consider red-green counter machine

$$CM = (2, B, B_{red}, B_{green}, l_0, P, T_{in})$$

recognizing language $L(CM)$. To every such a red-green counter machine there exists a red-green counter machine

$$CM' = (2, B \cup \{l'_0\}, B'_{red}, B'_{green}, l'_0, P, T_{in} \cup \{\#\})$$

that recognizes language $L(CM') = \# \cdot L(CM)$, where $\{\#\} \cap T_{in} = \emptyset$ and the first instruction of the machine CM' to be executed is instruction $l'_0 : (read(\#), l_0)$. Then, it continues the computation in the same way as machine CM. We construct an APCol system Π with coloured teams as follows: All labels from the set $B \cup T_{in}$ are objects of the APCol system. The content of register i is represented by the number of copies of objects i in the string. At the beginning of the computation only one team of agents can work - red team of one agent that generates symbols to the beginning of the string.

Team: B_1
Colour: Red
Agent: $A_1 = (ee, P_1, \emptyset)$
Programs: 1 : $\langle e \rightarrow \#_1; e \rightarrow O_1 \rangle$;   4 : $\langle \#_2 \leftrightarrow e; \$ \leftrightarrow O_1 \rangle$;
           2 : $\langle \#_1 \leftrightarrow \#; O_1 \leftrightarrow e \rangle$;   5 : $\langle O_1 \rightarrow l_0; e \rightarrow T \rangle$;
           3 : $\langle \# \rightarrow \#_2; e \rightarrow \$ \rangle$;   6 : $\langle T \rightarrow T; l_0 \leftrightarrow e \rangle$;

The APCol system starts its computation on string $\#\omega$. Agent A_1 uses programs $1, 2, 3$ and 4 to replace symbol $\#$ by substring $\#_1\#_2\$$. Then it places symbol l_0 into some random position in the string.

Let l_1 be a read-instruction $l_1 : (read(a), l_2)$. We construct a team of the same colour as the read-instruction has. The team is formed from two agents. Because they work as a team, either they both execute their programs or none of them works.

Team: B_{l_1}
Colour: *Red* or *Green* (it depends on the colour of l_1)
Agent: $A_{a_1} = (ee, P_{a_1}, \emptyset)$ Agent: $A_{b_1} = (ee, P_{b_1}, \emptyset)$
Programs: $7 : \langle e \leftrightarrow l_1; e \to e \rangle$;   Programs: $11 : \langle e \to R_1; e \to e \rangle$;
           $8 : \langle l_1 \to \$; e \to e \rangle$; $12 : \langle R_1 \leftrightarrow \$; e \to x \rangle$;
           $9 : \langle \$ \leftrightarrow R_1; e \to e \rangle$;   for all $x \in T_{in}$
           $10 : \langle R_1 \to e; e \to e \rangle$; $13 : \langle \$ \to l_2; a \to e \rangle$;
                                                $14 : \langle \$ \to W; y \to e \rangle$;
                                                    for all $y \in T_{in} - \{a\}$
                                                $15 : \langle l_2 \leftrightarrow e; e \to e \rangle$;
                                                $16 : \langle W \leftrightarrow e; e \to e \rangle$;

Although agent A_{b_1} has an applicable program it must stay inactive until the first agent has an applicable program, too, i.e., until symbol l_1 appears in the string.

Team: B_1
Colour: *Red*
Agent: A_1
Programs: $17 : \langle e \leftrightarrow W; T \to T \rangle$;
           $18 : \langle W \to W; T \to T \rangle$;

When the read-instruction cannot be performed, agent A_1 from red team starts working for an unbounded number of steps.

For each ADD-instruction $l_1 : (ADD(r), l_2)$, there is one team of agents of the same colour as the ADD-instruction has.

Team: B_{l_1}
Colour: *Red* or *Green* (it depends on the colour of l_1)
Agent: $A_{a_1} = (ee, P_{a_1}, \emptyset)$ Agent: $A_{b_1} = (ee, P_{b_1}, \emptyset)$
Programs: $19 : \langle e \leftrightarrow l_1; e \to L_1 \rangle$;   Programs: $24 : \langle e \to r'; e \to e \rangle$;
           $20 : \langle L_1 \leftrightarrow \#_r; l_1 \to K_1 \rangle$; $25 : \langle r' \to r; e \to M_1 \rangle$;
           $21 : \langle \#_r \to \#_r; K_1 \to K_2 \rangle$; $26 : \langle M_1 \leftrightarrow L_1; r \leftrightarrow e \rangle$;
           $22 : \langle \#_r \leftrightarrow M_1; K_2 \to K_3 \rangle$; $27 : \langle L_1 \to l_2; e \to e \rangle$;
           $23 : \langle M_1 \to e; K_3 \to e \rangle$; $28 : \langle l_2 \leftrightarrow e; e \to e \rangle$;

The first agent consumes the symbol corresponding to the actually simulated instruction. In the same time, the second agent starts to generate symbol r. At the following steps, the first agent rewrites symbol l_1 to L_1 and exchanges this symbol by $\#_r$. The first agent can put symbol $\#_r$ back to the string only by replacing it by symbol M_1 generated by the second agent. The second agent inserts the label of the next instruction at some random place in the string.

For SUB-instruction $l_1 : (SUB(r), l_2, l_3)$, there is one team of the same colour as the instruction has.

Team: B_{l_1}
Colour: *Red* or *Green* (it depends on the colour of l_1)
Agent: $A_{a_1} = (ee, P_{a_1}, \emptyset)$ Agent: $A_{b_1} = (ee, P_{b_1}, \emptyset)$
Programs: $29 : \langle e \leftrightarrow l_1; e \rightarrow L_1 \rangle$;   Programs: $37 : \langle e \rightarrow M_1; e \rightarrow K_1 \rangle$;

$30 : \langle L_1 \leftrightarrow \#_r; l_1 \rightarrow K_1 \rangle$;

$31 : \langle \#_r \rightarrow \#_r; K_1 \rightarrow K_2 \rangle$;

$32 : \langle \#_r \leftrightarrow M_1; K_2 \rightarrow K_2 \rangle$;

$33 : \langle M_1 \rightarrow M'_1; K_2 \rightarrow K_2 \rangle$;

$34 : \langle M'_1 \leftrightarrow N_1; K_2 \rightarrow K_2 \rangle$;

$35 : \langle N_1 \rightarrow e; K_2 \rightarrow K_2 \rangle$;

$36 : \langle e \rightarrow e; K_2 \rightarrow e \rangle$;

$38 : \langle M_1 \rightarrow M_1; K_1 \rightarrow e \rangle$;

$39 : \langle M_1 \leftrightarrow L_1; e \leftrightarrow d \rangle$;

    for all $d \in \{r, \#_{r+1}, \$\}$

$40 : \langle L_1 \rightarrow N_1; r \rightarrow K_1 \rangle$;

$41 : \langle L_1 \rightarrow N_1; d' \rightarrow d' \rangle$;

    for all $d' \in \{\#_{r+1}, \$\}$

$42 : \langle N_1 \leftrightarrow \#_r; K_1 \rightarrow K_2 \rangle$;

$43 : \langle N_1 \leftrightarrow \#_r; d' \rightarrow d' \rangle$;

$44 : \langle \#_r \rightarrow \#_r; K_1 \rightarrow K_2 \rangle$;

$45 : \langle \#_r \rightarrow \#_r; K_2 \rightarrow K_3 \rangle$;

$46 : \langle \#_r \leftrightarrow M'_1; K_3 \rightarrow l_2 \rangle$;

$47 : \langle \#_r \rightarrow l_2; e \rightarrow e \rangle$;

$48 : \langle N_1 \leftrightarrow \#_r; d' \leftrightarrow e \rangle$;

$49 : \langle \#_r \rightarrow \#_r; e \rightarrow K \rangle$;

$50 : \langle \#_r \leftrightarrow M'_1; K \rightarrow l_3 \rangle$;

$51 : \langle l_2 \leftrightarrow e; M'_1 \rightarrow e \rangle$;

$52 : \langle l_3 \leftrightarrow e; M'_1 \rightarrow e \rangle$;

The idea of simulation of SUB-instruction is that agent consumes symbol $\#_r$ together with the right neighbouring symbol. According to content of the agent, it generates the label of the next instruction.

We construct the APCol system

$$\Pi = (O, e, A_1, \ldots, A_n, C, Green, B, B_{colours}, B_{teams}) \text{ with:}$$

- $O = T_{in} \cup \{l_i, L_i, M_i, M'_1, N_i, R_i | l_i \in H\} \cup \{i, i' | 1 \leq i \leq m\}$

  $\cup \{e, K_1, K_2, K_3, W, \$, \#_1, \#_2\}$,

- $n = 2 \times |H| + 1$
- $B = \{B_j\}, 1 \leq j \leq p; \ p = |H| + 1$
- $C = \{Red, Green\}$
-     The sets $B_{colours}, B_{teams}$ and the agents $A_1, \ldots, A_n$ are defined in the previous part of the text.

The computation of the APCol system starts with string $\$w$. The first steps are done by the red team B_1. After initialization, the APCol system goes through the same mind changes as the counter machine goes through during the corresponding computation. Therefore, if red-green counter machine CM recognizes string w, then APCol system Π recognizes string $\#w$ too, and vice versa. □

4   Conclusions

In this paper, we investigated the possibility of "going beyond" Turing in the terms of APCol systems. We introduced the notion of teams of agents as a restriction for the maximal parallelism of computation. In addition, we assigned a colour to each team. The unbounded computation was described by the sequence of the colours associated to the acting teams. We have shown that we can simulate red-green counter machines with APCol systems with two-coloured teams. Red-green counter machines are computing devices with infinite run on finite input that exceed the power of Turing machines.

As we mentioned in the Introduction, there are concepts in P systems theory which are motivated and mimic the behaviour of red-green Turing machines, for example [2]. The proofs of the theorems in Sect. 3 demonstrate that finite communities of very simple and very small computing devices (i.e. agents and programs) in a suitable environment and using a simple cooperation protocol (based on colours) can produce a behaviour which may not be computable in the sense of Turing machines. These results add further information on the behaviour of communities of agents and ideas to constructs networks of computing agents.

Acknowledgments. This work was supported by The Ministry of Education, Youth and Sports from the National Programme of Sustainability (NPU II) project IT4Innovations excellence in science - LQ1602, by SGS/13/2016 and by the National Research, Development, and Innovation Office - NKFIH, Hungary, Grant No. K 120558.

References

1. Alhazov, A., Aman, B., Freund, R., Păun, G.: Matter and anti-matter in membrane systems. In: Jürgensen, H., Karhumäki, J., Okhotin, A. (eds.) DCFS 2014. LNCS, vol. 8614, pp. 65–76. Springer, Cham (2014). https://doi.org/10.1007/978-3-319-09704-6_7

2. Aman, B., Csuhaj-Varjú, E., Freund, R.: Red–green P automata. In: Gheorghe, M., Rozenberg, G., Salomaa, A., Sosík, P., Zandron, C. (eds.) CMC 2014. LNCS, vol. 8961, pp. 139–157. Springer, Cham (2014). https://doi.org/10.1007/978-3-319-14370-5_9

3. Cienciala, L., Ciencialová, L.: P colonies and their extensions. In: Kelemen, J., Kelemenová, A. (eds.) Computation, Cooperation, and Life. LNCS, vol. 6610, pp. 158–169. Springer, Heidelberg (2011). https://doi.org/10.1007/978-3-642-20000-7_13

4. Cienciala, L., Ciencialová, L., Csuhaj-Varjú, E.: Towards on P colonies processing strings. In: Proceedings of the BWMC 2014, Sevilla, pp. 102–118. Fénix Editora, Sevilla (2014)

5. Csuhaj-Varjú, E.: Extensions of P colonies (extended abstract). In: Leporati, A., Zandron, C. (eds.) Proceedings of the CMC17, Milan, pp. 281–286. University Milano-Bicocca & IMCS, Italy (2014)

6. Csuhaj-Varjú, E., Kelemen, J., Păun, G., Dassow, J. (eds.): Grammar Systems: A Grammatical Approach to Distribution and Cooperation. Gordon and Breach Science Publishers Inc., Newark (1994)

7. Kelemenová, A.: P colonies. In: Păun, G., Rozenberg, G., Salomaa, A. (eds.) The Oxford Handbook of Membrane Computing, pp. 584–593. Oxford University Press, Oxford (2010). Chapter 23.1
8. Kelemen, J., Kelemenová, A., Păun, G.: Preview of P colonies: a biochemically inspired computing model. In: Workshop and Tutorial Proceedings of the Ninth International Conference on the Simulation and Synthesis of Living Systems (Alife IX), Boston, Mass, pp. 82–86 (2004)
9. Kelemen, J., Kelemenová, A.: A grammar-theoretic treatment of multiagent systems. Cybern. Syst. **23**(6), 621–633 (1992)
10. Minsky, M.L.: Computation: Finite and Infinite Machines. Prentice Hall, Englewood Cliffs (1967)
11. van Leeuwen, J., Wiedermann, J.: Computation as an unbounded process. Theor. Comput. Sci. **429**, 202–212 (2012)
12. Păun, G., Rozenberg, G., Salomaa, A. (eds.): The Oxford Handbook of Membrane Computing. Oxford University Press Inc., New York (2010)
13. Rozenberg, G., Salomaa, A. (eds.): Handbook of Formal Languages, vols. I–III. Springer, Berin/Heidelberg/New York (1997)

Bi-simulation Between P Colonies and P Systems with Multi-stable Catalysts

Erzsébet Csuhaj-Varjú[1(✉)] and Sergey Verlan[2]

[1] Department of Algorithms and Their Applications, Faculty of Informatics,
ELTE Eötvös Loránd University, Pázmány Péter sétány 1/c, Budapest 1117, Hungary
csuhaj@inf.elte.hu
[2] Université Paris Est, LACL (EA 4219), UPEC, 94010 Créteil, France
verlan@u-pec.fr

Abstract. The general concept, called the formal framework of P systems provides a representation to study and analyze different variants of P systems. In this paper, two well-known models, P colonies and P systems with multi-stable catalysts are considered. We show that the obtained representations are identical, thus both models can be related using a bi-simulation. This fact opens new approaches for studying both P colonies and catalytic P systems.

1 Introduction

Due to different motivations, there have been several variants of P systems introduced. However, all models have some common basic features as summarized in [5,9]. Among these characteristics we find

- a description of the initial structure or architecture (indicating the graph relation between the compartments and any additional information as labels, charges, etc.),
- a list of the initial multisets of objects present in each compartment at the beginning of the computation,
- a set of rules, acting over objects and/or over the structure.

Usually, the configuration of a P system is represented by the current contents of the compartments and the current structure of the system.

P systems work with transitions between configurations; a finite sequence of such transitions of a P system Π starting with the initial configuration and ending in some final configuration is called a computation. The final configuration is usually given by halting.

To give a more precise description of the semantics, the following notions (functions) were defined:

- $Applicable(\Pi, C, \delta)$ – the set of multisets of rules of Π applicable to the configuration C, according to some derivation mode δ.

© Springer International Publishing AG 2018
M. Gheorghe et al. (Eds.): CMC 2017, LNCS 10725, pp. 105–117, 2018.
https://doi.org/10.1007/978-3-319-73359-3_7

- $Apply(\Pi, \mathcal{C}, R)$ – the configuration obtained by the (usually parallel) application of the multiset of rules R to the configuration $\mathcal{C}$.
- $Halt(\Pi, \mathcal{C}, \delta)$ – a predicate that yields true if $\mathcal{C}$ is a halting configuration of the system Π using the derivation mode δ.
- $Result(\Pi, \mathcal{C})$ – a function giving the result of the computation of the P system Π when the halting configuration $\mathcal{C}$ has been reached. Usually, this is an integer function. However, generalizations as for example, Boolean or vector functions can also be considered.

We note that δ, above, differs from the dissolution symbol used in some P system models.

The transition of a P system Π according to the derivation mode δ (usually, the maximally parallel derivation mode) is defined as follows: the system changes from a configuration $\mathcal{C}$ to $\mathcal{C}'$ (written as $\mathcal{C} \Rightarrow \mathcal{C}'$) iff

$$\mathcal{C}' = Apply(\Pi, \mathcal{C}, R), \text{ for some } R \in Applicable(\Pi, \mathcal{C}, \delta)$$

The result of the computation of a P system is usually interpreted as the union of the results of all possible computations.

The precise interpretation of the four notions (functions) above depends on the chosen model of P systems. The goal of works [4,5,9] was to provide a concrete family of P systems based on the structure of *network of cells* together with a series of definitions of the functions above. The obtained model as well as the accompanying tools and methods together are called the *formal framework of P systems*. It has the property that most of the existing models of P systems could be obtained by a strong bi-simulation of a restricted version (eventually, using a simple encoding) of this formal framework with respect to different parameters, see [10] for some examples. We recall that a simulation of one transitional system by another one corresponds to an order relation on corresponding equivalent states [6]. Basically, this means that a step in the simulated system corresponds to one or several steps in the simulating one. In the case of a strong simulation, one step of the simulated system is performed using one step in the simulating system. If two systems can simulate each other, then we speak about bi-simulation.

In this paper, based on formal framework we provide a strong bi-simulation between two well-known models, namely P colonies and multi-stable (purely) catalytic P systems. P colonies are a finite collection of agents which interact with a shared environment via their own sets of programs. Each program is a limited number of very simple rules. Under functioning, the agents act in a maximally parallel manner and they change their own state and exchange symbols with the environment. Purely catalytic P systems are given with multiset rewriting rules where each rule has occurrences of distinguished symbols called catalysts. In the original model, catalysts cannot change, in case of multi-stable catalytic P systems catalysts are allowed to change only to some other, distinguished catalysts.

The bi-simulation we provide demonstrates that although the two models are formally different, one can be used to solve problems concerning the other one.

For example, both models are computationally complete, thus a proof for one of the models can be "translated" to a proof for the other one.

After providing the bi-simulation and some examples, we discuss the results and propose topics for future research.

2 Definitions and Notations

We assume that the reader is familiar with basic notions of formal language theory and membrane computing; for further details consult [7,8].

For a finite multiset of symbols M over an alphabet V, $supp(M)$ denotes the set of symbols in M (the support of M) and $|M|$ denotes its size, i.e., the total number of its symbols. By $|M|_x$, the number of occurrences of symbol x in M is denoted. By V° we denote the set of all finite multisets over V.

Throughout the paper, every finite multiset M is given as a string w, where M and w have the same number of occurrences of symbol a, for each $a \in V$.

2.1 Network of Cells

In this section we provide a summarized version of the definition of a *network of cells*, the class containing all networks of cells forming the structure of the formal framework. The definitions are based on those given in [5]. This version considers only static P systems where the membrane structure does not change under the computation (this also includes systems with the dissolution of membranes). We note that in [4], an extension of the formal framework to P systems with dynamically evolving structure is proposed. However, in order to have a more simple presentation, in this paper we will only consider the first variant. We remark that in the case of static structures both variants coincide, although the notation is slightly different.

Definition 1 [5]. *A network of cells of degree $n \geq 1$ is a construct*

$$\Pi = (n, V, w, Inf, R)$$

where

1. *n is the number of cells;*
2. *V is an alphabet;*
3. *$w = (w_1, \ldots, w_n)$ where $w_i \in V^\circ$, for all $1 \leq i \leq n$, is the finite multiset initially associated to cell i;*
4. *$Inf = (Inf_1, \ldots, Inf_n)$ where $Inf_i \subseteq V$, for all $1 \leq i \leq n$, is the set of symbols occurring infinitely often in cell i (in most of the cases, only one cell, called the* environment, *will contain symbols occurring with infinite multiplicity);*

5. R is a finite set of rules of the form

$$(X \to Y; P, Q)$$

where $X = (x_1, \ldots, x_n)$, $Y = (y_1, \ldots, y_n)$, $x_i, y_i \in V^\circ$, $1 \leq i \leq n$, are vectors of multisets over V and $P = (p_1, \ldots, p_n)$, $Q = (q_1, \ldots, q_n)$, p_i, q_i, $1 \leq i \leq n$ are finite sets of multisets over V. We will also use the notation

$$(1, x_1) \ldots (n, x_n) \to (1, y_1) \ldots (n, y_n); [(1, p_1) \ldots (1, p_n)]; [(1, q_1) \ldots (n, q_n)]$$

for a rule $(X \to Y; P, Q)$; moreover, if some p_i or q_i is an empty set or some x_i or y_i is equal to the empty multiset, $1 \leq i \leq n$, then we may omit it from the specification of the rule.

The semantics of the above rule is as follows: objects x_i from cells i are rewritten into objects y_j in cells j, $1 \leq i, j \leq n$, if every cell k, $1 \leq k \leq n$, contains all multisets from p_k and does not contain any multiset from q_k. In other words, the first part of the rule specifies the rewriting of symbols, the second part of the rule specifies permitting conditions and the third part of the rule specifies the forbidding conditions.

For a rule r of the form above, the set

$$\{i \mid x_i \neq \lambda \text{ or } y_i \neq \lambda \text{ or } p_i \neq \emptyset \text{ or } q_i \neq \emptyset\}$$

induces a (hypergraph) relation between the interacting cells. However, this relation does not need to give rise to a *structure* relation like a tree as in P systems or a graph as in tissue P systems.

A *configuration* C of Π is an n-tuple of multisets over V $(u_1, \ldots, u_n)$ satisfying $u_i \cap Inf_i = \emptyset$, $1 \leq i \leq n$.

In the sequel, networks of cells as intermediate models will assist to establish a bi-simulation between two variants of P systems, namely P colonies and P systems with multi-stable catalysts.

2.2   P Colonies

Next we provide the concept of a P colony, based on the formalism given in [7].

A P colony $\Pi = (O, e, f, C_1, \ldots, C_n)$, consists of n cells (agents) C_i, $1 \leq i \leq n$, each of them consisting of a multiset of exactly k symbols and an environment which consists initially of an unbounded number of copies of a distinguished symbol e. Every cell C_i has a set of programs $\{p_{i,1}, \ldots, p_{i,k_i}\}$, where each program $p_{i,j}$ consists of exactly k rules of the forms $a \to b$ (*evolution rule* or *internal point mutation*), $c \leftrightarrow d$ (*one object exchange* with the environment), or r_1/r_2 (*priority rule*, where r_1 and r_2 are arbitrary combinations of point mutation and/or exchange rules).

The computation starts in the initial configuration, i.e., the n-tuple of the initial contents of the cells. It can be performed in the maximally parallel (*par*) or in the sequential (*seq*) mode, the computation mode is assigned to the system at the beginning. If no more program is applicable, then the P colony halts and the result of the computation is collected as the number of distinguished symbols f in the environment. The result of the computation of Π is denoted by $N(\Pi)$.

We note that the result can also be defined in such a way that we consider the number of all symbols in the environment which are different from e.

The number of cells, the maximal number of programs in a cell, and the maximal number of rules in each program in a given P colony Π are called the degree, the height, and the capacity of Π, respectively.

The family of sets of numbers computed in the derivation mode x for $x \in \{par, seq\}$ by P colonies of capacity k, degree at most $n \geq 1$ and height at most $h \geq 1$, without (resp. with) using priority rules in their programs, is denoted by $NPCol_x(k, n, h)$ (resp. $NPCol_x K(k, n, h)$).

Notice that a strong bi-simulation of the P colony model and the formal framework can be given as follows.

- each rule $a \rightarrow b$ in p_{ij} becomes $r_{ij} : (i, a) \rightarrow (i, b)$;
- each rule $a \leftrightarrow b$ in p_{ij} becomes $r_{ij} : (i, a)(0, b) \rightarrow (i, b)(0, a)$;
- each rule r_1/r_2 in p_{ij} becomes:
  - $p^1_{ij} : r_1,\ p^2_{ij} : r_2; [\emptyset]; [\{(i, a)\}]$ if r_1 is an evolution rule $(a \rightarrow b)$
  - $p^1_{ij} : r_1,\ p^2_{ij} : r_2; [\emptyset]; [\{(i, a)(0, b)\}]$ if r_1 is an exchange rule $(a \leftrightarrow b)$.

For the derivation mode, each program becomes a rule partition and then the derivation mode requires to be maximal, but using exactly k rules from each partition (or using all rules from a partition). In the sequential case, the derivation mode prescribes to use only one partition (but all rules from that partition).

Example 1 [10]. Consider the following P colony Π having 3 cells. For simplicity, we provide only the initial multisets and the programs of the cells.

- C_1 contains the initial multiset aa and the following programs: $p_{11} : a \rightarrow b, a \leftrightarrow e$, $p_{12} : a \rightarrow c, a \leftrightarrow e$, $p_{13} : b \rightarrow a, e \rightarrow a$.
- C_2 contains the initial multiset be and the following program: $p_{21} : b \leftrightarrow e$, $e \rightarrow b$.
- C_3 contains the initial multiset ee and the following programs: $p_{31} : e \leftrightarrow a, e \leftrightarrow b$, $p_{32} : b \rightarrow f, a \rightarrow b$, $p_{33} : f \leftrightarrow a, b \rightarrow b$.

Figure 1 shows a graphical representation of this system.

We transform this system to a network of cells Π' having 4 cells (numbered from 0 to 3). Cell 0 corresponds to the environment. Cells 1, 2, 3 correspond to the cells of Π and have the same initial contents as the corresponding agent. We define $Info_0 = \{e\}$. System Π' contains the following rules:

Rules simulating programs from the first cell:

$$r_{111} : (1, a) \rightarrow (1, b) \qquad\qquad r_{112} : (1, a)(0, e) \rightarrow (1, e)(0, a)$$
$$r_{121} : (1, a) \rightarrow (1, c) \qquad\qquad r_{122} : (1, a)(0, e) \rightarrow (1, e)(0, a)$$
$$r_{131} : (1, b) \rightarrow (1, a) \qquad\qquad r_{132} : (1, e) \rightarrow (1, a)$$

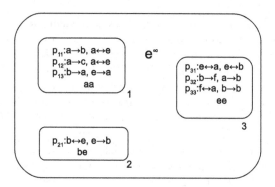

Fig. 1. The P colony from Example 1.

Rules simulating programs from the second cell:

$$r_{211} : (2, b)(0, e) \rightarrow (2, e)(0, b) \qquad r_{212} : (2, e) \rightarrow (2, b)$$

Rules simulating programs from the third cell:

$$r_{311} : (3, e)(0, a) \rightarrow (3, a)(0, e) \qquad r_{312} : (3, e)(0, b) \rightarrow (3, b)(0, e)$$
$$r_{321} : (3, b) \rightarrow (3, f) \qquad r_{322} : (3, a) \rightarrow (3, b)$$
$$r_{331} : (3, f)(0, a) \rightarrow (3, a)(0, f) \qquad r_{332} : (3, b) \rightarrow (3, b)$$

We remark that the derivation mode of P colonies groups rules corresponding to programs, uses maximal parallelism or sequential mode, and it requires that all rules from a group should be used. Since working with one symbol, the group r_{111} and r_{112} from the above example is equivalent to the application of a single rule $r_{11} : (1, aa)(0, e) \rightarrow (1, be)(0, a)$. Hence, we obtain that a program corresponds to a more complicated rule, and k is the size of the left-hand side (LSH) of this rule (and equal to the right-hand side, i.e., RHS). By considering such rules, the evolution of a P colony becomes just maximally parallel or sequential.

This consideration yields the following network of cells Π'' (working in sequential or maximally-parallel manner):

$$r_{11} : (1, aa)(0, e) \rightarrow (1, be)(0, a) \qquad r_{12} : (1, aa)(0, e) \rightarrow (1, ce)(0, a)$$
$$r_{13} : (1, be) \rightarrow (1, aa)$$
$$r_{21} : (2, be)(0, e) \rightarrow (2, be)(0, b)$$
$$r_{31} : (3, ee)(0, ab) \rightarrow (3, ab)(0, ee) \qquad r_{32} : (3, ab) \rightarrow (3, fb)$$
$$r_{33} : (3, bf)(0, a) \rightarrow (3, ab)(0, f)$$

Since the number of combinations of objects in an agent is finite, it can be represented by a single symbol, a state. Furthermore, symbol e from cell 0 can be ignored as it carries no information. This permits to deduce that a P colony corresponds to a cooperative rewriting mechanism with the size of LHS or RHS at most $k + 1$ and with forbidding conditions (if checking rules are present). In the next section we refine this observation by showing that the rewriting is performed in a catalytic-like manner.

2.3   P Systems with Multi-stable Catalysts

In this section we extend the notion of a P system with catalysts to that variant where the catalysts can have multiple states. For catalytic P systems, consult [7].

Let V and C be two disjoint alphabets, let $k > 0$, and let C have a partition $C = C_1 \cup \cdots \cup C_n$ such that $1 \leq |C_i| \leq k$. We say that each partition is a multi-stable catalyst and we define $Period(C_i) = |C_i|$ the *period* of the catalyst C_i, $1 \leq i \leq n$.

In the sequel, the elements of a multi-stable catalyst C_i having period k will be denoted by $c_i^{(j)}$, $1 \leq j \leq k$.

A k-states multi-stable (purely) catalytic P system with n catalysts is a construct $\Gamma = (V, C, R, w)$, where V is the set of non-catalytic objects of Γ, $C = C_1 \cup \cdots \cup C_n$ with catalysts C_i, having period at most k, $1 \leq i \leq n$.

R is a finite set of rules where each rule is of the following form

$$c_i^{(j)} u \rightarrow c_i^{(t)} v, \text{ where } 1 \leq j, t \leq Period(C_i), 1 \leq i \leq n \text{ and } u, v \in V^\circ.$$

The initial configuration of Γ, w is a multiset over $V \cup C$, with at most one element of each multi-stable catalyst C_i, i.e., $w \subseteq (V \cup C)^\circ$, with the condition that $\sum_{j=1}^{Period(C_i)} |w|_{c_i^{(j)}} \leq 1$, $1 \leq i \leq n$.

Notice that by [5,10] the rules of a multi-stable catalytic P system with multiple states can easily be represented in the formal framework as follows:

$$(0, c_i^{(j)} u) \rightarrow (0, c_i^{(t)} v), \text{ for all } c_i^{(j)} u \rightarrow c_i^{(t)} v \in R.$$

As standard P systems, the k-states multi-stable (purely) catalytic P systems Γ with n catalysts work by transitions of their configurations where the rules are applied in the maximally parallel manner. A successful computation performed by Γ is a finite sequence of transitions starting in its initial configuration and ending by halting; the result of the computation is the number of non-catalytic objects in the halting configuration. The result of the computation is denoted by $N(\Gamma)$.

3   Bi-simulation of the Two Models

In this section we demonstrate the equivalence of P colonies and multi-stable (purely) catalytic P systems by using their representation in the above formal framework.

We first show that any (recursively enumerable) set of numbers that can be computed by a P colony (in the sense defined above) can be computed by a multi-stable catalytic P system as well.

Theorem 1. *For any P colony* $\Pi = (O, e, w_0, P_1, \ldots, P_n)$ *of size* (k, n, h) *there exists a* h'-*states multi-stable purely catalytic P system* $\Gamma = (O, C, w, R)$ *with* n *catalysts with* $h' \leq h + 1$ *such that* $N(\Pi) = N(\Gamma)$.

Proof. To simplify the presentation, we consider P colonies that do not contain priority rules (checking rules), since P colonies both with and without checking rules are computationally complete (see [7]).

According to the discussion above (see also [10]), every P colony can be represented by the formal framework. To this goal, any program p located in cell i is replaced by a rule of the corresponding network of cells. Let $p = p_1 \cup p_2$, where p_c contains all the communication rules and p_r contains all the rewriting rules of p. Let $lhs_c(p)$ (resp. $rhs_c(p)$) denote the multiset of letters of all left-hand (resp. right-hand) sides of the communication rules; we consider the same notation for the rewriting rules, using the index r. For simplicity, we will speak of sum of the left-hand sides (resp. right-hand sides) of the rules in the sequel and we will use notation $+$.

Since the definition of the P colony requires that if a program is used, then all of its rules should be applied, therefore we obtain that the execution of a program p is equivalent to the following rule given in terms of the formal framework:

$$(i, x)(0, y) \rightarrow (i, x')(0, y'), \text{ where} \tag{1}$$
$$x = lhs_c(p) + lhs_r(p), y = rhs_c(p),$$
$$x' = rhs_c(p) + rhs_r(p), y' = lhs_c(p).$$

Since in every step of the computation every cell in a P colony contains a constant number of objects equal to its capacity k, each cell contents can be interpreted as a number z in base $k + 1$ having exactly $|O|$ bits. Alphabet O is equal to $\{o_1, \ldots, o_s\}$ and any o_i (and e) can appear in any contents in at most k copies. Thus $|O|$ bits represent the number of occurrences of object o_i in a cell contents c. Under this interpretation, the rules of a program specify some other number z' equal to the value of the contents of the cell after the application of the program. Since the number of rules in a program is exactly k, for each number z and program p there is exactly one number z' associated.

We remark that for a cell i having h programs there are at most $h+1$ different possible configurations of the cell contents. We number these configurations from 1 to i_h, where $i_h \leq h + 1$. Let f be a bijection between all possible values of cell configurations and $1, \ldots, i_h$. Thus, we can rewrite 1 as follows:

$$(i, c^{(f(z))})(0, y) \rightarrow (i, c^{(f(z'))})(0, y'), \text{ where} \tag{2}$$
$$y = rhs_c(p), y' = lhs_c(p), 1 \leq z, z' \leq i_h.$$

We can further transform this rule as follows:

$$(0, c_i^{(f(z))} y) \rightarrow (0, c_i^{(f(z'))} y') \tag{3}$$

It can clearly be seen that this rule corresponds to a rule of a multi-stable (purely) catalytic P system.

Hence, starting from the P colony Π, components of Γ can be constructed. We first remark that object e in P colonies acts as an empty symbol, so we replace all its occurrences by λ in the obtained catalytic rules. First, the initial multiset of Γ is determined from the initial configuration of Π. Since every rule $c_i^{(f(z))}y \rightarrow c_i^{(f(z'))}y'$ of Γ correspond to the application of a program p in Π described above, it can easily be seen that any transition from configuration c_1 to configuration c_2 of Π corresponds to the application of an m-tuple of rules in Γ, where $m \leq n$. Notice that depending on the applicability of their programs, some components may remain inactive. Since the initial multiset of Γ contains at most n catalysts, Γ has only catalytic rules, at any computation step as many catalytic rules are applied in parallel as possible, i.e. at most n. Since these rules correspond to programs of pairwise different components of Π, every computation in Γ corresponds to a computation in Π as well. Thus, it is easy to see that the number of non-catalytic objects at halting of Γ is equal to the number of objects in the environment of Π which are different from e at halting. □

Example 2. Let us consider P colony Π from Example 1. We recall the corresponding rules.

- C_1 contains the initial multiset aa and the following programs:
  $p_{11} : a \rightarrow b, a \leftrightarrow e, \; p_{12} : a \rightarrow c, a \leftrightarrow e, \; p_{13} : b \rightarrow a, e \rightarrow a.$
- C_2 contains the initial multiset be and the following program:
  $p_{21} : b \leftrightarrow e, e \rightarrow b.$
- C_3 contains the initial multiset ee and the following programs:
  $p_{31} : e \leftrightarrow a, e \leftrightarrow b, \; p_{32} : b \rightarrow f, a \rightarrow b, \; p_{33} : f \leftrightarrow a, b \rightarrow b.$

Let $O = \{a, b, c, e, f\}$, and let $o_1 = a, \ldots, o_5 = f$, in this order. The different cell contents are $A = (aa, be, ce, ee, ab, bf)$ which correspond to numbers 00002, 01010, 01100, 02000, 00011, 010010 in base $k + 1 = 6$. For simplicity, let us denote these numbers by s_1, s_2, s_3, s_4, s_5, and s_6, respectively.

Then by constructing the multi-stable catalytic P system we obtain the following rules:

- $C_1^{s_1} \rightarrow C_1^{s_2}a, \; C_1^{s_1} \rightarrow C_1^{s_3}a, \; C_1^{s_2} \rightarrow C_1^{s_1},$
- $C_2^{s_2} \rightarrow C_2^{s_2}b,$
- $C_3^{s_4}ab \rightarrow C_3^{s_5}, \; C_3^{s_5} \rightarrow C_3^{s_6}, \; C_3^{s_6}a \rightarrow C_3^{s_5}f.$

Next we show that the sets of numbers computed by multi-stable catalytic P systems can be computed by P colonies as well.

Theorem 2. *For any h-states multi-stable catalytic P system $\Gamma = (O, C, w, R)$ with n catalysts there exists a P colony $\Pi = (O, e, w_0, P_1, \ldots, P_n)$ of size (k, n, h) such that $N(\Pi) = N(\Gamma)$ holds.*

Proof. We construct Π as follows. P colony Π has n cells and each cell i has $Period(C_i)$ programs. Now we will show how these programs are constructed.

Consider a rule $c_i^j u \rightarrow c_i^t v \in R$. We suppose that $|u| = |v|$. If this is not the case, then we complement the smaller multiset by adding the needed amount of symbols e. That is, if $|u| < |v|$ then let $u' = u + e^{|v|-|u|}$. Suppose that $u = u_1 \ldots u_s$ and $v = v_1 \ldots v_s$. We will construct the program p_j corresponding to this rule. It will be composed from two parts. The first part will contain communication rules that simulate the rewriting of u to v in the above rule. The second part contains rewriting rules that allow to complement the encoding of the catalyst state by the contents of the cell.

In order to determine the corresponding rewriting rules we should first find an encoding for each state of the catalyst. This encoding can be obtained as a solution of the following integer optimization problem.

$$k \rightarrow min,$$

$$\sum_{a \in O} x_a^{i,j} = k, \quad 1 \leq j \leq Period(C_i),$$

$$x_a^{i,j} \geq |v|_a, \quad x_a^{i,t} \geq |u|_a, \quad \text{for any } c_i^j u \rightarrow c_i^t v \in R, \qquad (4)$$

$$x_a^{i,j} \in \mathbb{N}, \quad a \in O, 1 \leq i \leq n, 1 \leq j \leq Period(C_i).$$

The inequalities state that the symbols that are sent out (resp. received in) by the exchange rules of the P colony belong to the coding of state j (resp. t) of the catalyst C_i.

We remark that since inequalities 4 do not impose an upper bound value for $x_a^{i,j}$, there is always a solution for this system. In case of several possible solutions, we prefer solutions having the maximal number of symbols e.

The capacity of the P colony is the value k.

Let $x_a^{i,j}$, $a \in O$, $1 \leq j \leq Period(C_i)$ be a solution of the above problem. Let $Code(c_i^j) = \sum_{a \in O} a^{x_a^{i,j}}$. Let $c_i^j u \rightarrow c_i^t v \in R$ and let $|u| = |v| = s$, $d^j = Code(c_i^j) - v$ and $d^t = Code(c_i^t) - u$. Suppose that $d^l = d_1^l \ldots d_m^l, l \in \{j, t\}$. Then

$$p_j = (v_1 \leftrightarrow u_1; \ldots v_s \leftrightarrow u_s; d_1^j \rightarrow d_1^t; \ldots d_m^j \rightarrow d_m^t).$$

Now we are able to construct the colony: for every C_i, $1 \leq i \leq n$, P colony Π will have component P_i. The programs belonging to P_i are obtained from the rules $C_i^j u \rightarrow C_i^t v$, in the above described manner. Notice that any program of Π, determined above encodes the application of the corresponding catalytic rule, thus, the programs to be applied and the catalytic rules correspond to each other. Since at the beginning of the computation the initial state of Γ contains at most one element of each multi-stable catalyst and both systems apply the maximally parallel computation, we obtain that the two systems compute the same set of numbers.   □

Example 3. To demonstrate the previous construction, we add an example.
Consider the following multi-stable catalytic P system $\Pi = (O, C, w_1, R_1)$.

$$
\begin{array}{llll}
1.1: C_1^1 a \rightarrow C_1^2 bc & 2.1: C_2^1 \rightarrow C_2^2 & 3.1: C_3^1 \rightarrow C_3^2 a \\
1.2: C_1^1 a \rightarrow C_1^3 c & 2.2: C_2^2 b \rightarrow C_2^2 & 3.2: C_3^2 c \rightarrow C_3^1 b \\
1.3: C_1^2 ac \rightarrow C_1^1 aa & & 3.3: C_3^1 \rightarrow C_3^3
\end{array}
$$

We transform rules 1.1, 2.2 and 3.1 by adding symbol e in order to balance the number of symbols at both sides:

$$1.1 : C_1^1 ae \rightarrow C_1^2 bc \quad 2.2 : C_2^2 b \rightarrow C_2^2 e \quad 3.1 : C_3^1 \rightarrow C_3^2 a$$

Then the corresponding minimization problem is the following:

$$k \rightarrow min$$
$$x_a^{i,j} + x_b^{i,j} + x_c^{i,j} + x_e^{i,j} = k, \quad 1 \le i, j \le 3$$
$$x_b^{1,1} \ge 1, \ x_c^{1,1} \ge 1, \ x_a^{1,2} \ge 1, \ x_e^{1,2} \ge 1,$$
$$x_c^{1,1} \ge 1, \ x_a^{1,3} \ge 1,$$
$$x_a^{1,1} \ge 1, \ x_c^{1,1} \ge 1, \ x_a^{1,2} \ge 2$$
$$x_e^{2,2} \ge 1, \ x_b^{2,2} \ge 1$$
$$x_a^{3,1} \ge 1, \ x_e^{3,2} \ge 1, \ x_c^{3,1} \ge 1, \ x_b^{3,2} \ge 1$$
$$x_a^{i,j} \in \mathbb{N}, \quad a \in O, 1 \le i, j \le 3.$$

We can regroup inequalities by the corresponding state:

$$k \rightarrow min$$
$$x_a^{i,j} + x_b^{i,j} + x_c^{i,j} + x_e^{i,j} = k, \quad 1 \le i, j \le 3$$
$$x_a^{1,1} \ge 1, \ x_b^{1,1} \ge 1, \ x_c^{1,1} \ge 1$$
$$x_a^{1,2} \ge 2, \ x_e^{1,2} \ge 1$$
$$x_a^{1,3} \ge 1$$
$$x_b^{2,2} \ge 1, \ x_e^{2,2} \ge 1$$
$$x_a^{3,1} \ge 1, \ x_c^{3,1} \ge 1$$
$$x_b^{3,2} \ge 1, \ x_e^{3,2} \ge 1$$
$$x_a^{i,j} \in \mathbb{N}, \quad a \in O, 1 \le i, j \le 3.$$

The minimal value of k is equal to 3 and one of possible solutions yields to the following codes for c_i^j:

x	c_1^1	c_1^2	c_1^3	c_2^1	c_2^2	c_3^1	c_3^2	c_3^3
$Code(x)$	abc	aae	aaa	eee	bee	ace	bee	eee

We remark that catalysts C_2 and C_3 can be represented only using two symbols.

The obtained P colony is shown in Fig. 2.

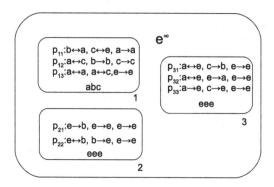

Fig. 2. The P colony constructed in Example 3.

4   Conclusions

In this paper we have shown a strong bi-simulation between the model of P colonies and pure multi-stable catalytic P systems. This result was obtained by using the formal framework for P systems as an intermediate step.

As an immediate consequence of the results of this paper, it is possible to rewrite existing results from the area of P colonies in terms of multi-stable catalytic P systems and conversely. These investigations are topics of future research. Another consequence is the possibility to conduct proofs in terms of purely catalytic P systems (that tend to be simpler) and automatically transform them to P colonies.

Furthermore, this article allows to establish the correspondence between different extensions of P colonies (see [3]) and particular variants of catalytic P systems. For example, the evolving environment extension [2] corresponds to the same multi-stable catalytic P systems, so it can be simulated by a P colony with a greater capacity. Homogeneous P colonies [1] correspond to catalytic P systems having same rules for all catalysts.

Other possible extensions can also be discussed. For example, non-pure catalytic systems would correspond to P colonies having special rules allowing to evolve objects by themselves in the environment. Another possibility that follows from our constructions is to consider P colonies where the capacity is different in each cell.

Acknowledgement. The work of E. CS-V. was supported by the National Research, Development, and Innovation Office - NKFIH, Hungary, Grant no. K 120558.

References

1. Cienciala, L., Ciencialová, L., Kelemenová, A.: Homogeneous P colonies. Comput. Inform. **27**(3), 481–496 (2008)
2. Ciencialová, L., Cienciala, L., Sosík, P.: P colonies with evolving environment. In: Leporati, A., Rozenberg, G., Salomaa, A., Zandron, C. (eds.) CMC 2016. LNCS, vol. 10105, pp. 151–164. Springer, Cham (2017). https://doi.org/10.1007/978-3-319-54072-6_10
3. Ciencialová, L., Csuhaj-Varjú, E., Cienciala, L., Sosík, P.: P colonies. Bull. Int. Membr. Comput. Soc. **1**(2), 119–156 (2016)
4. Freund, R., Pérez-Hurtado, I., Riscos-Núñez, A., Verlan, S.: A formalization of membrane systems with dynamically evolving structures. Int. J. Comput. Math. **90**(4), 801–815 (2013)
5. Freund, R., Verlan, S.: A formal framework for static (tissue) P systems. In: Eleftherakis, G., Kefalas, P., Păun, G., Rozenberg, G., Salomaa, A. (eds.) WMC 2007. LNCS, vol. 4860, pp. 271–284. Springer, Heidelberg (2007). https://doi.org/10.1007/978-3-540-77312-2_17
6. Milner, R.: An algebraic definition of simulation between programs. In: Proceedings of the 2nd International Joint Conference on Artificial Intelligence, IJCAI 1971, San Francisco, CA, USA, pp. 481–489. Morgan Kaufmann Publishers Inc. (1971)
7. Păun, G., Rozenberg, G., Salomaa, A. (eds.): The Oxford Handbook of Membrane Computing. Oxford University Press, Oxford (2009)
8. Rozenberg, G., Salomaa, A. (eds.): Handbook of Formal Languages, vols. 1–3. Springer, Heidelberg (1997)
9. Verlan, S.: Study of language-theoretic computational paradigms inspired by biology. Habilitation thesis, Université Paris Est (2010)
10. Verlan, S.: Using the formal framework for P systems. In: Alhazov, A., Cojocaru, S., Gheorghe, M., Rogozhin, Y., Rozenberg, G., Salomaa, A. (eds.) CMC 2013. LNCS, vol. 8340, pp. 56–79. Springer, Heidelberg (2014). https://doi.org/10.1007/978-3-642-54239-8_6

Computationally Complete Generalized Communicating P Systems with Three Cells

Erzsébet Csuhaj-Varjú[1]($\boxtimes$) and Sergey Verlan[2]

[1] Department of Algorithms and Their Applications, Faculty of Informatics,
ELTE Eötvös Loránd University, Pázmány Péter sétány 1/c, Budapest 1117, Hungary
`csuhaj@inf.elte.hu`
[2] Université Paris Est, LACL (EA 4219), UPEC, 94010 Créteil, France
`verlan@u-pec.fr`

Abstract. Generalized communicating P systems are particular variants of networks of cells where each rule moves only two objects. In this paper we show that GCPSs with three cells and with only join, or only split, or only chain rules are computationally complete computing devices. These bounds are improvements of the previous results.

1 Introduction

Purely communicating P systems are of particular interest in membrane computing [9]. These membrane systems work without any change of their objects but only with importing/exporting objects from and/or to the environment and communicating objects between their regions. A lot of these P system variants are computationally complete, demonstrating that rewriting can be replaced by communication with the environment where some objects are supposed to be found in an unbounded number of copies. This means that whenever to complete a transition the P system needs more (a finite number of new) objects than it has inside, then these objects are always available.

Generalized communicating P systems, introduced in [12] are such models, originally with the aim of providing a common generalization of various purely communicating models.

A generalized communicating P system, or a GCPS for short, is a tissue-like P system where each node represents a cell and each edge is represented by a rule. Every node contains a multiset of objects that can be communicated, i.e., it may move between the cells according to interaction (communication) rules.

The form of an interaction rule is $(a, i)(b, j) \rightarrow (a, k)(b, l)$ where a and b are objects and i, j, k, l are labels identifying the input and the output cells. Such a rule means that an object a from cell i and an object b from cell j move synchronously (in one step) to cell k and cell l, respectively. These rules are particularly simple, since they describe the move of only two objects.

The system is embedded in an environment, represented by cell 0, which may have certain objects in an infinite number of copies and certain objects only in a finite number of copies. The generalized communicating P system and

© Springer International Publishing AG 2018
M. Gheorghe et al. (Eds.): CMC 2017, LNCS 10725, pp. 118–128, 2018.
https://doi.org/10.1007/978-3-319-73359-3_8

the environment interact by using the communication (interaction) rules given above, with the restriction that at every computation step only a finite number of objects is allowed to enter in any cell from the environment.

The rules are applied in a maximally parallel manner, possibly changing the multisets representing the contents of the cells (the configuration of the GCPS). A computation in a GCPS is a sequence of configurations directly following each other, starting from the initial configuration and ending in a halting configuration. The result of the computation is the number of objects found in a distinguished cell, the output cell.

Due to their simplicity and relation to other fields like the theory of Petri nets, GCPSs have been studied in details. It has been shown that even restricted variants of these constructs (with respect to the form of rules) are able to generate any recursively enumerable set of numbers. Furthermore, several of them even with relatively small numbers of cells and with simple underlying hypergraph architectures are computationally complete [3,5–7]. It is also shown that the maximal expressive power can also be obtained with GCPSs where the alphabet of objects is a singleton [2]. Furthermore, computational completeness with small number of cells can also be obtained if the objects of the environment are provided step by step with a multiset generating system [1].

In the paper, we demonstrate that computational completeness of three restricted variants, namely, GCPSs with only three cells and with only join rules, or only split rules, or only chain rules are computationally complete. The proofs are based on simulating the register machines [8] and by using the formal framework of P systems [4].

2   Basic Notions

The reader is supposed to be familiar with formal language theory and membrane computing; for further details consult [9,10].

For a finite multiset of symbols M over an alphabet V, $supp(M)$ denotes the set of symbols in M (the support of M) and $|M|$ denotes the total number of its symbols (its size). The number of occurrences of symbol x in M is denoted by $|M|_x$. The set of all finite multisets over V is denoted by V°.

Throughout the paper, every finite multiset M is presented as a string w, where M and w have the same number of occurrences of symbol a, for each $a \in V$. The empty multiset is denoted by λ.

A register machine [8] is a 5-tuple $M = (Q, R, q_0, q_f, P)$, where Q is a finite non-empty set, called the set of states, $R = \{A_1, \ldots, A_k\}$, $k \geq 1$, is a set of registers, $q_0 \in Q$ is the initial state, and $q_f \in Q$ is the final state. P is a set of instructions of the following forms: $(p, A+, q, s)$, where $p, q, s \in Q, p \neq q_f, A \in R$, called an increment instruction, or $(p, A-, q, s)$, where $p, q, s \in Q, p \neq q_f, A \in R$, called a decrement instruction. For every $p \in Q$, $(p \neq q_f)$, there is exactly one instruction of the form either $(p, A+, q, s)$ or $(p, A-, q, s)$.

A configuration of a register machine M, defined above, is a $(k + 1)$-tuple $(q, m_1, \ldots, m_k)$, where $q \in Q$ and $m_1, \ldots, m_k$ are non-negative integers; q is the current state of M and $m_1, \ldots, m_k$ are the current numbers stored in the registers (the current contents of the registers or the value of the registers) $A_1, \ldots A_k$, respectively.

A transition of the register machine consists in executing an instruction. An increment instruction $(p, A+, q, s) \in P$ is performed if M is in state p, the number stored in register A is increased by 1, and after that M enters either state q or state s, chosen non-deterministically. A decrement instruction $(p, A-, q, s) \in P$ is performed if M is in state p, and if the number stored in register A is positive, then it is decreased by 1, and then M enters state q, and if the number stored in A is 0, then the contents of A remains unchanged and M enters state s.

A register machine $M = (Q, R, q_0, q_f, P)$, with k registers, given as above, generates a non-negative integer n if starting from the initial configuration $(q_0, 0, 0, \ldots, 0)$ it enters the final configuration $(q_f, n, 0, \ldots, 0)$. The set of non-negative integers generated by M is denoted by $N(M)$.

Next we recall the basic definitions concerning generalized communicating P systems [12].

A generalized communicating P system (a GCPS) of degree n, where $n \geq 1$, is an $(n + 4)$-tuple $\Pi = (O, E, w_1, \ldots, w_n, R, h)$ where

1. O is an alphabet, called the set of objects of Π;
2. $E \subseteq O$; called the set of environmental objects of Π;
3. $w_i \in O^*$, $1 \leq i \leq n$, is the multiset of objects initially associated to cell i;
4. R is a finite set of interaction rules or communication rules of the form $(a, i)(b, j) \rightarrow (a, k)(b, l)$, where $a, b \in O$, $0 \leq i, j, k, l \leq n$, and if $i = 0$ and $j = 0$, then $\{a, b\} \cap (O \setminus E) \neq \emptyset$; i.e., $a \notin E$ and/or $b \notin E$;
5. $h \in \{1, \ldots, n\}$ is the output cell.

The system consists of n cells, labeled by natural numbers from 1 to n, which contain multisets of objects over O. Initially, cell i contains multiset w_i (the initial contents of cell i is w_i). An additional special cell, labeled by 0 and called the environment is distinguished. The environment contains objects of E in an infinite number of copies.

The cells interact by means of the rules $(a, i)(b, j) \rightarrow (a, k)(b, l)$, with $a, b \in O$ and $0 \leq i, j, k, l \leq n$. As the result of the application of the rule, object a moves from cell i to cell k and b moves from cell j to cell l. If two objects from the environment move to some other cell or cells, then at least one of them must not appear in the environment in an infinite number of copies.

A configuration of a GCPS Π, as above, is an $(n + 1)$-tuple $(z_0, z_1, \ldots, z_n)$ with $z_0 \in (O \setminus E)^*$ and $z_i \in O^*$, for all $1 \leq i \leq n$; z_0 is the multiset of objects present in the environment in a finite number of copies, whereas, for all $1 \leq i \leq n$, z_i is the multiset of objects present inside cell i. The initial configuration of Π is the $(n + 1)$-tuple $(\lambda, w_1, \ldots, w_n)$.

Given a multiset of rules $\mathcal{R}$ over R and a configuration $u = (z_0, z_1, \ldots, z_n)$ of Π, we say that $\mathcal{R}$ is applicable to u if all its elements can be applied simultaneously to the objects of multisets $z_0, z_1, \ldots, z_n$ such that every object is used by at most one rule. Then, a configuration u' of Π is obtained from a configuration u by applying the rules of R in a non-deterministic maximally parallel manner if it is obtained by applying rules of an applicable multiset $\mathcal{R}$ over R to u and there is no other applicable multiset of rules $\mathcal{R}'$ over R which properly contains $\mathcal{R}$ and its application to u results in u'.

One such application of a multiset of rules satisfying the conditions listed above represents a transition in Π from configuration u to configuration u'. A transition sequence is said to be a successful generation by Π if it starts with the initial configuration of Π and ends with a halting configurations, i.e., with a configuration where no further transition step can be performed.

Π generates a non-negative integer n if there is a successful generation by Π such that n is the size of the multiset of objects present inside the output cell in the halting configuration. The set of non-negative integers generated by a GCPS Π in this way is denoted by $N(\Pi)$.

In the following we recall the notions of the possible restrictions on the interaction rules (modulo symmetry). We distinguish the following cases, called GCPSs with minimal interaction:

1. $i = j = k \neq l$: the conditional-uniport-out rule (the $uout$ rule) sends b to cell l provided that a and b are in cell i [11];
2. $i = k = l \neq j$: the conditional-uniport-in rule (the uin rule) brings b to cell i provided that a is in that cell;
3. $i = j,\ k = l,\ i \neq k$: the symport2 rule (the $sym2$ rule) corresponds to the minimal symport rule [9], i.e., a and b move together from cell i to k;
4. $i = l,\ j = k,\ i \neq j$: the antiport1 rule (the $anti1$ rule) corresponds to the minimal antiport rule [9], i.e., a and b are exchanged in cells i and k;
5. $i = k$ and $i \neq j,\ i \neq l,\ j \neq l$: the presence-move rule (the $presence$ rule) moves the object b from cell j to l, provided that there is an object a in cell i and i, j, l are pairwise different cells;
6. $i = j,\ i \neq k,\ i \neq l,\ k \neq l$: the $split$ rule sends a and b from cell i to cells k and l, respectively;
7. $k = l,\ i \neq j,\ k \neq i,\ k \neq j$: the $join$ rule brings a and b together to cell k;
8. $l = i,\ i \neq j,\ i \neq k$ and $j \neq k$: the $chain$ rule moves a from cell i to cell k while b is moved from cell j to cell i, i.e., to the cell where a located previously;
9. i, j, k, l are pairwise different numbers: the parallel-shift rule (the $shift$ rule) moves a and b from two different cells to another two different cells.

$NOtP_k(x)$ denotes the set of numbers generated by generalized communicating P systems with minimal interaction of degree k, $k \geq 1$, and with rules of type x, where $x \in \{uout, uin, sym2, anti1, presence, split, join, chain, shift\}$. $NOtP_*(x)$ is the notation for $\bigcup_{k=1}^{\infty} NOtP_k(x)$.

Generalized communicating P systems are particular variants of network of cells, constructs introduced in [4] as a formal framework of P systems.

A network of cells of degree $n \geq 1$ is a construct $\Pi = (n, O, w, Inf, R)$ where

- n is the number of cells;
- O is an alphabet;
- $w = (w_1, \ldots, w_n)$ where $w_i \in O^\circ$, for all $1 \leq i \leq n$, is the finite multiset initially associated to cell i;

– $Inf = (Inf_1, \ldots, Inf_n)$ where $Inf_i \subseteq O$, for all $1 \leq i \leq n$, is the set of symbols which may occur in infinitely many copies in cell i (in most of the cases, only one cell, called the environment, may contain symbols with infinite multiplicity);
– R is a finite set of rules of the form $(X \to Y; P, Q)$ where $X = (x_1, \ldots, x_n)$, $Y = (y_1, \ldots, y_n)$, $x_i, y_i \in V^\circ$, $1 \leq i \leq n$, are vectors of multisets over O and $P = (p_1, \ldots, p_n)$, $Q = (q_1, \ldots, q_n)$, p_i, q_i, $1 \leq i \leq n$ are finite sets of multisets over O. We will also use the notation

$$(1, x_1) \ldots (n, x_n) \to (1, y_1) \ldots (n, y_n); [(1, p_1) \ldots (1, p_n)]; [(1, q_1) \ldots (n, q_n)]$$

for a rule $(X \to Y; P, Q)$; moreover, if some p_i or q_i is an empty set or some x_i or y_i is equal to the empty multiset, $1 \leq i \leq n$, then we may omit it from the specification of the rule.

The above rule means the following: objects x_i from cells i are rewritten into objects y_j in cells j, $1 \leq i, j \leq n$, if every cell k, $1 \leq k \leq n$, contains all multisets from p_k and does not contain any multiset from q_k.

A configuration C of Π is an n-tuple of multisets $(u_1, \ldots, u_n)$ over O where $u_i \cap Inf_i = \emptyset$, $1 \leq i \leq n$.

Networks of cells compute sets of numbers; the result of the computation can be defined in several manners, among other by the number of objects in a distinguished cell in a halting configuration.

It is easy to see that GCPSs are particular variants of networks of cells: any rule $(a, i)(b, j) \to (a, k)(b, l)$ of a generalized communicating P system corresponds to a rule $(i, a)(j, b) \to (k, a)(l, b)$ in the corresponding network of cells. Obviously, if the GCPS is with minimal interaction, the form of the rules in the corresponding network of cells is modified accordingly.

Thus, without any proof, we may state that for any generalized communicating P system $\Pi = (O, E, w_1, \ldots, w_n, R, h)$, $1 \leq h \leq n$, there exists a network of cells $\Pi' = (n + 1, O, w, Inf, R)$ such that $N(\Pi) = N(\Pi')$ and Π and Π' strongly simulate each other. (In the case of a strong simulation, one step of the simulated system is performed using one step in the simulating system. If two systems can simulate each other, then we speak about bi-simulation.) Notice that the difference between the degree of Π and that of Π' is due to the fact that in the case of networks of cells the environment is counted as a cell.

3   Main Results

In the following we present the computational completeness results concerning generalized communicating P systems with minimal interaction. For simplicity, throughout the paper we follow the notations used for networks of cells.

In [3] it was shown that GCPSs with 7 cells and only join rules are computationally complete. The result was improved in [5,6] to bound 4. Here we present a further improvement.

Theorem 1. $NOtP_3(join) = NRE$.

Proof. Let us consider an arbitrary register machine $M = (Q, R, q_0, q_f, P)$ with $R = \{A_1, \ldots A_n\}$, $n \geq 1$, given as in Sect. 2. To prove the statement, we construct a generalized communicating P system $\Pi = (O, E, w_1, w_2, w_3, R_1, 2)$ with join rules such that $N(\Pi) = N(M)$. The proof is based on the simulation of M by Π and conversely, i.e., by showing that for any successful generation in M there exists a successful generation in Π and conversely such that the two generation processes yield the same number as result.

Since for every $p \in Q$, $(p \neq q_f)$, there is exactly one instruction of the form either $(p, A+, q, s)$ or $(p, A-, q, s)$, the set of instructions R of M can be labeled by the elements of Q in a one-to-one manner.

Let Q^+ and Q^- be the sets of labels of the increment instructions and the decrement instructions of M, respectively.

Let us define the alphabet of objects of Π as $O = Q \cup R \cup \{p' \mid p \in Q\} \cup \{\bar{p}, p_1 \mid p \in Q^-\} \cup \{C_i \mid A_i \in R\}$.

Let $E = Q \cup R \cup \{p' \mid p \in Q^+\} \cup \{p_1 \mid p \in Q^-\} \cup \{C_i \mid A_i \in R\}$. and $w_1 = \{q_0\}$, $w_2 = \emptyset$, $w_3 = \{\bar{p} \mid p \in Q^-\}$.

The set of rules R_1 of Π is defined as follows.

For any instruction (p, A_i+, q, s) of M we add the following rules to R_1:

$$p.1 : (1, p)(0, q') \rightarrow (3, pq') \qquad p.1' : (1, p)(0, s') \rightarrow (3, ps')$$
$$p.2 : (3, p)(0, A_i) \rightarrow (2, pA_i)$$

For any instruction (p, A_i-, q, s) of M we add the following rules to R_1:

$$p.1 : (1, p)(0, C_i) \rightarrow (3, pC_i) \qquad p.2 : (3, p)(0, p_1) \rightarrow (2, pp_1)$$
$$p.3 : (2, p_1)(3, \bar{p}) \rightarrow (0, p_1\bar{p}) \qquad p.4 : (0, \bar{p})(3, C_i) \rightarrow (1, \bar{p}C_i)$$
$$p.5 : (0, \bar{p})(1, C_i) \rightarrow (2, \bar{p}C_i) \qquad p.6 : (2, \bar{p})(0, q') \rightarrow (3, \bar{p}q')$$
$$p.7 : (1, \bar{p})(0, s'') \rightarrow (3, \bar{p}s'') \qquad p.8 : (3, s'')(1, C_i) \rightarrow (2, s''C_i)$$
$$p.9 : (2, s'')(0, s') \rightarrow (3, s''s') \qquad p.10 : (3, s'')(2, C_i) \rightarrow (0, s''C_i)$$

We also add the following rules to R_1:

$$p.p' : (3, p')(0, p) \rightarrow (1, p'p), \text{ for all } p \in Q$$
$$p.q : (2, p)(1, q') \rightarrow (0, pq'), \text{ for all } p, q \in Q$$
$$c_i.1 : (3, C_i)(2, A_i) \rightarrow (1, C_iA)$$
$$c_i.2 : (2, C_i)(1, A_i) \rightarrow (0, C_iA_i)$$

Now we prove that Π simulates M. For this, we show how the rules given above simulate the instructions of M. We first note that the simulation of any instruction of M starts with a symbol p in cell 1 which the corresponds to a state of M and no other symbol corresponding to a state of M can be found in this cell. However, cell 1 contains symbol $\bar{p}$ for any state p of M which appears in a decrement instruction. During the simulation of any instruction of M, Π cannot start the simulation of some other instruction, thus the simulating phases do not interfere. The contents of register A_i is represented by the number of symbols A_i appearing in the cells, symbol C_i assists the simulation of the decrement of register A_i, $1 \leq i \leq n$.

We start with the simulation of instructions of the form (p, A_i+, q, s). After applying rule $p.1$ or $p.1'$, respectively, symbols q' or s' move to cell 3. Then by applying rules $p.2$ and $p.p'$ in parallel, cell 2 will contain one more symbol A_i. In the next step, by applying rules $q.q'$ or $s.s'$ and $p.q$ or $p.s$, respectively, in parallel, symbol q or s enters cell 1 and q' or s' leave the system. Thus, the simulation of (p, A_i+, q, s) has completed.

The simulation of instruction (p, A_i-, q, s) is as follows: First rule $p.1$ is applied and thus p and C_i enter cell 3. Then, depending on whether or not cell 2 contains at least one copy of A_i (register A_i is empty or not) the following rules are applied. If cell 2 contains at least one A_i, then by rule $c_i.1$ symbols C_i and A_i move to cell 1. Meantime, by applying rule $p.2$, and then $p.3$ and $p.5$, $\bar{p}$ enters cell 2 and C_i moves from cell 1 to cell 2. Then, by rule $c_i.2$, symbols A_i and C_i leave the system and by rule $p.6$ symbol $\bar{p}$ introduces a copy of q' in cell 3. Then, by performing rule $q.q'$ and $p.q$, symbol q arrives in cell 1, and the simulation of the next instruction (if $q \neq q_f$) may start. If cell 2 does not contain any copy of A_i, then C_i in cell 3 introduces from the environment the copy of $\bar{p}$ that was sent out the system before. Then by rules $p.7$, $p.8$ and $p.9$ symbols s'' and s' move to cell 3 and C_i moves to cell 2. After that, by executing rule $p.10$, symbols C_i and s'' leave the system, meantime by rules $s.s'$ and $p.s$ symbol s moves to cell 1, and thus the simulation of the instruction ends.

The reader may notice that the rules can be performed only in the manner described above. This implies that any computation in M can correctly be simulated by Π and $N(M) = N(\Pi)$ holds. Since $N(M)$ is a recursively enumerable set of numbers, the statement of the theorem holds.

Next we show that three cells (and the environment) are sufficient to obtain computational completeness in case of GCPSs with only split rules. In [3] it was shown that GCPSs with 9 cells and only split rules are computationally complete, in [5,6] the bound was improved to 5.

Theorem 2. $NOtP_3(split) = NRE$.

Proof. Let us consider an arbitrary register machine $M = (Q, R, q_0, q_f, P)$ with $R = \{A_1, \ldots A_n\}$, $n \geq 1$, given as in Sect. 2. To prove the statement, we construct a generalized communicating P system $\Pi = (O, E, w_1, w_2, w_3, R_1, 2)$ with split rules such that $N(\Pi) = N(M)$. The proof is based on the simulation of M by Π and vice versa, i.e., by showing that for any successful generation in M there exists a successful generation in Π and conversely such that the two generation processes yield the same number as result.

Let Q^+ and Q^- be the sets of labels of the increment instructions and the decrement instructions of M, respectively.

Let us define the alphabet of objects of Π as $O = Q \cup R \cup \{p' \mid p \in Q\} \cup \{\bar{p}, p_1, p_2, p_3 \mid p \in Q^-\} \cup \{S_i \mid A_i \in R\} \cup \{Z, Z', Z''\}$.

Let $E = Q \cup R \cup \{Z''\}$ and $w_1 = \{q_0\} \cup \{S_i \mid A_i \in R\} \cup \{p_1 \mid p \in Q^-\}$, $w_2 = \{Z\}$, $w_3 = \{Z'\} \cup \{q' \mid q \in Q\} \cup \{p_2, p_3 \mid p \in Q^-\}$.

The set of rules R_1 of Π is defined as follows.

For any instruction (p, A_i+, q, s) of M we add the following rules to R_1:

$p.1 : (1, pS_i) \rightarrow (0, S_i)(3, p)$ $\qquad$ $p.2 : (0, S_iA_i) \rightarrow (1, S_i)(2, A_i)$

$p.3 : (3, pq') \rightarrow (2, p)(0, q')$ $\qquad$ $p.3' : (3, ps') \rightarrow (2, p)(0, s')$

$p.4 : (0, qq') \rightarrow (3, q')(1, q)$ $\qquad$ $p.4' : (0, ss') \rightarrow (3, s')(1, s)$

$p.5 : (2, pZ) \rightarrow (0, p)(3, Z)$ $\qquad$ $p.6 : (3, ZZ') \rightarrow (2, Z)(0, Z')$

$p.7 : (0, Z'Z'') \rightarrow (3, Z')(1, Z'')$

For any instruction (p, A_i-, q, s) of M we add the following rules to R_1:

$p.1 : (1, pp_1) \rightarrow (3, p)(2, p_1)$ $\qquad$ $p.2 : (2, p_1A_i) \rightarrow (3, p_1)(0, A_i)$

$p.3 : (3, pp_2) \rightarrow (0, p)(2, p_2)$ $\qquad$ $p.4 : (3, p_1p_3) \rightarrow (1, p_1)(2, p_3)$

$p.5 : (2, p_1p_2) \rightarrow (1, p_1)(0, p_2)$ $\qquad$ $p.6 : (0, p_2s) \rightarrow (3, p_2)(1, s)$

$p.7 : (2, p_2p_3) \rightarrow (0, p_3)(3, p_2)$ $\qquad$ $p.8 : (0, p_3q) \rightarrow (3, p_3)(1, q)$

Now we prove that any instruction of M can be simulated by a set of rules of Π. We first note that during the functioning of Π there is no more than one symbol $p \in Q$ in cell 1, and the simulation of any instruction of M can only start if an element of Q is in cell 1.

We start with instructions of the form (p, A_i+, q, s). The simulations starts with p in cell 1. Then rule $p.1$ is applied, after that $p.2$ and $p.3$ or p_2 and $p.3'$ are performed in parallel. At the end of this phase of the computation, p and one more copy of A_i will be in cell 2 and q' or s', respectively, moves to the environment. At the next moment, either rules $p.4$ and $p.5$ or $p.4'$ and $p.5$ are applied in parallel, resulting in symbols q or s in cell 1, p being sent out to the environment, and Z is in cell 3. Now, the simulation of a new instruction of M can start. However, two more rules are still applied in the next two steps, $p.6$ and $p.7$. These two rules provide Z in cell 2 and Z' in cell 3; these symbols will be needed later. Notice that the application of these rules does not interfere with the simulation of any instruction of M, thus they can be performed. We also note that during the computation symbols Z'' are accumulated in cell 1, but this fact does not influence the simulation. It is easy to see that the rules can be performed only in the order above and that this computation phase of Π corresponds to the execution of instruction (p, A_i+, q, s).

We continue with the simulation of instructions of the form (p, A_i-, q, s). At the first step, rule $p.1$ is applied which moves symbol p to cell 3 and symbol p_1 to cell 2. If cell 2 contains at least one copy of A_i, then in the next step rules $p.2$ and $p.3$ can be applied in parallel, otherwise only $p.3$ is applicable. Suppose that cell 2 contains at least one A_i. Then one copy of A_i and p leave the system, p_1 moves to cell 3 and p_2 to cell 2. After then rules $p.4$, $p.7$, and $p.8$ are applied, thus p_1 and symbol q enter cell 1, and symbols p_2 and p_3 return to their original location, namely to cell 3. If cell 2 does not contain any copy of A_i, then after applying rule $p.3$, rules $p.5$ and $p.6$ are applied one after each other. Thus, the zero check has been simulated since cell 1 contains symbols s and p_1 and cell 3 has p_2 and p_3. The reader may easily see that these rules of Π can be applied only in the order given above. This means that they simulate the instruction (p, A_i-, q, s) of Π and only that.

By the previous considerations, we obtain that any computation in M can correctly be simulated by Π and conversely and $N(M) = N(\Pi)$ holds. Since $N(M)$ is a recursively enumerable set of numbers, the statement of the theorem is valid.

As in the previous cases, generalized communicating P systems with three cells and with only chain rules are computationally complete computing devices. In [3] computational completeness was proved, however no size bound was presented.

Theorem 3. $NOtP_3(chain) = NRE$.

Proof. Let us consider an arbitrary register machine $M = (Q, R, q_0, q_f, P)$ with $R = \{A_1, \ldots A_n\}$, $n \geq 1$, given as in Sect. 2. To prove the statement, we construct a generalized communicating P system $\Pi = (O, E, w_1, w_2, w_3, R_1, 2)$ with chain rules such that $N(M) = N(\Pi)$. The proof is based on the bisimulation of M by Π, i.e., by showing that for any successful generation in M there exists a successful generation in Π and conversely such that the two generation processes yield the same number as result.

Let Q^+ and Q^- be the sets of labels of the increment instructions and the decrement instructions of M, respectively.

Let us define the alphabet of objects of Π as
$O = Q \cup R \cup \{p', \bar{p} \mid p \in Q\} \cup \{p_1, p_2 \mid p \in Q^-\} \cup \{Z\}$.

Let $E = Q \cup R \cup \{p' \mid p \in Q^+\} \cup \{p_1, p_2 \mid p \in Q^-\} \cup \{Z\}$ and $w_1 = \{q_0\} \cup \{\bar{p} \mid p \in Q\}$, $w_2 = \emptyset$, $w_3 = \emptyset$.

The set of rules R_1 of Π is defined as follows.

For any rule (p, A_i+, q, s) of M we add the following rules to R_1:

$p.1 : (1, p)(0, p') \rightarrow (2, p)(1, p')$ 　　 $p.2 : (1, p')(0, q) \rightarrow (2, p')(1, q)$

$p.2' : (1, p')(0, s) \rightarrow (2, p')(1, s)$ 　　 $p.3 : (2, p)(0, A_i) \rightarrow (3, p)(2, A_i)$

$p.4 : (3, p)(2, p') \rightarrow (0, p)(3, p')$ 　　 $p.5 : (0, Z)(3, p') \rightarrow (1, Z)(0, p')$

For any rule (p, A_i-, q, s) of M we add the following rules to R_1:

$p.1 : (1, p)(0, p_1) \rightarrow (3, p)(1, p_1)$ 　　 $p.2 : (1, p_1)(0, p_2) \rightarrow (2, p_1)(1, p_2)$

$p.3 : (3, p)(2, A_i) \rightarrow (0, p)(3, A_i)$ 　　 $p.4 : (3, A_i)(2, p_1) \rightarrow (0, A_i)(3, p_1)$

$p.5 : (3, p)(1, p_2) \rightarrow (0, p)(3, p_2)$ 　　 $p.6 : (0, q)(3, p_1) \rightarrow (2, q)(0, p_1)$

$p.7 : (3, p_2)(1, \bar{s}) \rightarrow (0, p)(3, \bar{s})$ 　　 $p.8 : (1, p_2)(2, q) \rightarrow (0, p_2)(1, q)$

$p.9 : (0, s)(3, \bar{s}) \rightarrow (1, s)(0, \bar{s})$ 　　 $p.10 : (0, \bar{s})(2, p_1) \rightarrow (1, \bar{s})(0, p_1)$

We show that any instruction of M can be simulated by applying rules of Π, and conversely, any successful computation in Π corresponds to a successful computation in M. We note that as in the proofs of the previous theorems, cell 1 contains at most one symbol that corresponds to a state of M.

Let us consider instructions of M of the form (p, A_i+, q, s). To simulate this instruction, first rule $p.1$ and after that either rule $p.2$ or rule $p.2'$ is applied (depending on whether the next state of M will be q or s) in parallel with rule $p.3$. Then, the number of symbols A_i in cell 2 is increased by one and the symbol representing the new state, i.e., q or s enters cell 1. (During the work of Π, cell 2 will store symbols A_i which represent the contents of the corresponding register.) Still we need to remove p and p' from the system. This is done by rules $p.4$ and $p.5$. Notice that the simulation of a new instruction may start before the application of rules $p.4$ and $p.5$, but these two rules do not interfere with any such computation phase, so these two rules may be applied. It can also be seen that the above rules, performed in the above order, simulate instruction (p, A_i+, q, s) and only that. We note that symbols Z are accumulated in cell 1, but the presence of these symbols in cell 1 has no effect on the simulation.

Now let us consider instructions of the form (p, A_i-, q, s). First rule $p.1$ is applied and then either rules $p.2$ and $p.3$ are applied in parallel (cell 2 contains at least one A_i) or only rule $p.2$ can be applied (cell 2 does not contain A_i). Suppose that cell 2 has at least one symbol A_i. Then, by applying rules $p.4$, $p.5$, $p.6$ and $p.8$ in this order, one copy of A_i leaves the system, symbol q enters the system and finally moves to cell 1, and assistant symbols p_1 and p_2 leave the systems as well. No other rule can be applied during this phase of the computation. Suppose now that cell 2 does not contain any occurrence of A_i. Then, only rule $p.2$ can be applied. Then, p is present in cell 3, p_1 in cell 2, and p_2 in cell 1. After then, rules $p.5$, $p.7$, $p.9$ and $p.10$ are applied in this order. As a result, s enters the system and enters cell 1, assistant symbols p_1 and p_2 leave the system, and the further assistant symbol $\bar{s}$ enters cell 1 and remains there. The presence of this symbol in cell 1 and the fact that rule $p.10$ is applied after s reaches its destination, cell 1, do not affect the computation.

We may easily notice that the rules can be performed only in the manner described above. Thus, any computation in M can correctly be simulated by Π and conversely, and $N(M) = N(\Pi)$ holds. Since $N(M)$ is a recursively enumerable set of numbers, the theorem holds.

4   Conclusion

In this paper we proved that GCPSs with three cells and with only join, or only split, or only chain rules are computationally complete computing devices. These bounds are improvements of the previous results. We guess that the number of cells can also be significantly reduced (to 3) in the case of other variants of generalized communicating P systems with minimal interaction, we plan investigations in this direction in the near future.

Acknowledgment. The work of E. CS-V. was supported by the National Research, Development, and Innovation Office - NKFIH, Hungary, Grant no. K 120558.

References

1. Balaskó, Á., Csuhaj-Varjú, E., Vaszil, G.: Dynamically changing environment for generalized communicating P systems. In: Rozenberg, G., Salomaa, A., Sempere, J.M., Zandron, C. (eds.) CMC 2015. LNCS, vol. 9504, pp. 92–105. Springer, Cham (2015). https://doi.org/10.1007/978-3-319-28475-0_7
2. Csuhaj-Varjú, E., Vaszil, G., Verlan, S.: On generalized communicating P systems with one symbol. In: Gheorghe, M., Hinze, T., Păun, G., Rozenberg, G., Salomaa, A. (eds.) CMC 2010. LNCS, vol. 6501, pp. 160–174. Springer, Heidelberg (2010). https://doi.org/10.1007/978-3-642-18123-8_14
3. Csuhaj-Varjú, E., Verlan, S.: On generalized communicating P systems with minimal interaction rules. Theor. Comput. Sci. **412**, 124–135 (2011)
4. Freund, R., Verlan, S.: A formal framework for static (tissue) P systems. In: Eleftherakis, G., Kefalas, P., Păun, G., Rozenberg, G., Salomaa, A. (eds.) WMC 2007. LNCS, vol. 4860, pp. 271–284. Springer, Heidelberg (2007). https://doi.org/10.1007/978-3-540-77312-2_17
5. Krishna, S.N., Gheorghe, M., Dragomir, C.: Some classes of generalised communicating P systems and simple kernel P systems. Technical report, CS-12-03, University of Sheffield (2013). http://staffwww.dcs.shef.ac.uk/people/M.Gheorghe/research/paperlist.html
6. Krishna, S.N., Gheorghe, M., Dragomir, C.: Some classes of generalised communicating P systems and simple kernel P systems. In: Bonizzoni, P., Brattka, V., Löwe, B. (eds.) CiE 2013. LNCS, vol. 7921, pp. 284–293. Springer, Heidelberg (2013). https://doi.org/10.1007/978-3-642-39053-1_33
7. Krishna, S.N., Gheorghe, M., Ipate, F., Csuhaj-Varjú, E., Ceterchi, R.: Further results on generalised communicating P systems. Theor. Comput. Sci. (2017, in press). https://doi.org/10.1016/j.tcs.2017.05.020
8. Minsky, M.: Finite and Infinite Machines. Prentice Hall, Englewood Cliffs (1967)
9. Păun, G., Rozenberg, G., Salomaa, A. (eds.): The Oxford Handbook of Membrane Computing. Oxford University Press, Oxford (2010)
10. Rozenberg, G., Salomaa, A. (eds.): Handbook of Formal Languages, vol. 1–3. Springer, Heidelberg (1997). https://doi.org/10.1007/978-3-642-59136-5
11. Verlan, S., Bernardini, F., Gheorghe, M., Margenstern, M.: Computational completeness of tissue P systems with conditional uniport. In: Hoogeboom, H.J., Păun, G., Rozenberg, G., Salomaa, A. (eds.) WMC 2006. LNCS, vol. 4361, pp. 521–535. Springer, Heidelberg (2006). https://doi.org/10.1007/11963516_33
12. Verlan, S., Bernardini, F., Gheorghe, M., Margenstern, M.: Generalized communicating P systems. Theor. Comput. Sci. **404**(1–2), 170–184 (2008)

Event-Based Life in a Nutshell: How Evaluation of Individual Life Cycles Can Reveal Statistical Inferences Using Action-Accumulating P Systems

Thomas Hinze[1][(✉)] and Benjamin Förster[2]

[1] Department of Bioinformatics, Friedrich Schiller University Jena,
Ernst-Abbe-Platz 2, 07743 Jena, Germany
thomas.hinze@uni-jena.de
[2] Institute of Computer Science, Brandenburg University of Technology,
Postfach 10 13 44, 03013 Cottbus, Germany
benjamin.foerster@b-tu.de

Abstract. A sequence of perceivable *events* or recorded observations over time commonly witnesses the *life cycle* of an individual at a macroscopic perspective. In case of a human being, birth could make the starting point followed by successive maturation along with increase of individual skills. Further events like foundation of a family, stages of career, coping with dramatic diseases, loss of abilities, and finally the death mark crucial events within a human life cycle. Even beyond biology, life cycles are present in various contexts, for instance when elucidating the quality of durable technical products such as cars. Social scenarios or games with several players incorporate consideration of life cycles as well. Provided by logfiles or monitoring reports, dedicated accumulation of events facilitates identification of life cycles whose statistical analysis promises valuable insights. To this end, we formalise an *individual* by a set of *attributes*. Based on its underlying initial assignment ("genetic potential"), events can *update* corresponding attribute values. Furthermore, events might *create* new individuals but also *kill* or *merge* existing ones. For modelling and evaluation of life cycles, we introduce *action-accumulating P systems* inspired by dealing with events which in turn result in actions at the system's level. Two case studies demonstrate practical benefits from our approach: We explore the survival of pieces in the board game *Mensch ärgere Dich nicht* (Man, don't get annoyed – a variation of Ludo). Secondly, we interpret pseudonymised data from 1,108 students who attended our *university course Introduction to Programming* stating main factors to improve the final grade with emphasis on the effect of passing a line of exercises and practical training offers.

1 Introduction and Background

In the end of 2016, the total amount of electronically stored data worldwide sums up to approximately $8 \cdot 10^{21}$ bytes (8 zettabytes) based on the overall capacity of

© Springer International Publishing AG 2018
M. Gheorghe et al. (Eds.): CMC 2017, LNCS 10725, pp. 129–150, 2018.
https://doi.org/10.1007/978-3-319-73359-3_9

sold storage media taking into account an average period of usage by five years [9]. Complementary studies conclude that this pool of data doubles every two up to three years which implies an exponential growth [14]. No doubt, generation and presence of processible data emerged as an essential part of modern life and for sciences in many facets during the last decades. Terms like *data mining* [13], *big data* [6,7], *knowledge retrieval* [1,5], or *machine learning* [16,25] reflect this development. Interestingly, a variety of different *sources* and contexts exists in which data have been produced. On the one hand, *human activities* in the internet, especially in social networks, newsgroups, or online services, originate a plethora of abundant data streams. On the other hand, more and more data come into existence by *measurement, technical cognition, smart devices*, and *monitoring*. It is said that one minute of autonomous driving induces more than 10 gigabytes [4].

It seems that the tremendous acceleration in throughput is closely connected with shortening the period of time in which new media, new tools, and new techniques for processing of corresponding data become established [23]. For the early mankind, it took more than 100,000 years to form spoken natural languages for individual communication. Handwriting dates back for nearly 7,000 years, while printing is available for more than 500 years now. Afterwards, the periods noticeably diminish: Around 120 years ago, the telephone was invented. Mobile phones needed less than 10 years to outperform the conventional telephone in use. The internet gave a further acceleration. First-generation social media platforms reduced its introductory phase to 5 years. Meanwhile, messenger applications have already found widespread practice after two years. What stands out is that each new innovation entails more and more *recorded data* accompanying everybody's life.

From a perspective exclusively focussing on data tracks, a typical human life consists of a sequence of *events* at different points in time in which every event contributes an additional record of data. In the long term, effects initiated by these events can accumulate in an appropriate manner. The underlying processes gradually imply the formation of a personality with an individual setting of skills, capabilities, properties, and qualities. Coinciding with a basic law of dialectics, quantitative change leads to qualitative change: A simple example is given by students attending a university course. During the course, they receive knowledge within the regular lectures. From time to time, taken as data-producing events, they submit solutions to mandatory or optional exercises whose degree of success becomes individually evaluated together with a feedback. After a certain period of training, most of the students possess new or extended abilities related to the topics of the course at various levels of quality, see Fig. 1.

In more general terms, the *life cycle* of an *individual* can be abstractly expressed by a temporal sequence of *events* in which each event might slightly modify one or more *attributes*. We assume that every individual is equipped with quantifiable attributes which stand for dedicated skills or qualities. For a majority of events, an update or reset of corresponding attribute values in a specific subset of individuals is sufficient in order to describe the underlying effect. But in some cases, an event affects the existence of individuals under study. To

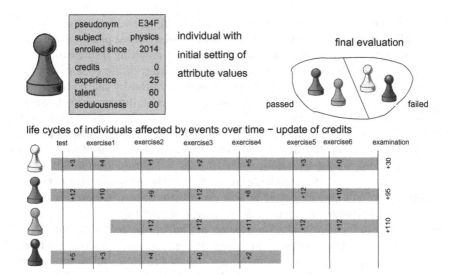

Fig. 1. Students attending a university course constitute individuals attached with attributes such as *subject* or *credits*. Initial attribute values symbolise the personal potential together with classifiable identity information. During the semester, several tests and exercises act as events at certain points in time. Events are able to update some attributes for a selection of students. Some students join the course late, others leave prematurely. Finally, the students can be classified according to an evaluation of their attribute values. The temporal evolution of attribute values opens employment of statistical analysis techniques.

this end, we distinguish several types of events whose effects enlarge or reduce the population of individuals in a dynamical manner. Event-based *creation* of a new individual enables scenarios in which controlled (re)production of individuals over time forms an essential feature. Attribute values of new individuals can be either *cloned* from present ones or alternatively set from scratch. In the opposite sense, an event might result in *killing* a specific subset of individuals from the population. Moreover, it appears to be helpful to have at hand a type of event able to *merge* two previously separate individuals into one individual whose attribute values arise from its precursors in a freely configurable way.

We start with a given multiset of individuals, each of them independently equipped with initial attribute values assuming that all individuals comprise the same composition of attributes. Additionally, we employ a set of events in which each event is characterised by its point in time, its type and necessary parameters and arithmetic functions in order to formalise its effect. A global clock controls progression of time. Processing of events follows the chronological order. Concurrent events are allowed iff they are independent from each other or they are confluent meaning that the final outcome of their effects remain the same. In the course of processing the events, the evolution of individuals and their specific attribute values gets permanently recorded at the granularity of a global clock tick. Based on this cumulative record, final evaluations as a part of the overall system might give new insights into behavioural patterns and their laws. Due to its principle of operation, we name the resulting framework *action-accumulating P systems* aimed at practical exploration of life cycles in various contexts but apart from pure theoretical aspects covered by temporal logics of actions [10, 19] or related formalisms. Instead, our contribution is dedicated to learn more about crucial indicators and indications responsible for clustering [17] or distribution of qualitative factors, their correlations and significance within a dynamical population of individuals. In consequence, this can lead to optimised and efficient behavioural strategies.

Within a large pool of comparable life cycles, statistical methods might allow identification of significant patterns able to substantiate prognoses and inferences. Social and medical sciences frequently practise this idea preferably by questionnaires or behavioural experiments acting in the role of events [8, 22]. Mainly inspired by this concept, our paper presents a way to utilise the framework of P systems in order to capture event-based life cycles for a dynamically managed multiset of attributed individuals together with purposive instruments for evaluation and hypothesis tests. Due to the algebraic nature of all relevant components and due to the fact that clusters of individuals with similar qualities constitute virtual membranes, we have an intuitive relation to the field of membrane computing. To our best knowledge, this is the first attempt to do so. Please note that an individual's membership in a membrane following the classical intention of membrane computing can be managed by a corresponding attribute as well without any loss of information or expressiveness.

Exploration of event-based life cycles is not restricted to studies in systems biology, medicine, and social sciences [12]. Modern technical products like cars or computers exhibit a high degree of inherent complexity. Commonly, they consist of numerous assembled components which in turn have been put together from subcomponents up to the level of elementary parts. Industry and customers are interested in getting detailed statistical information about durability of the entire product and about the resilience of components and parts on their own. As a result, the failure rate of a technical product over time can be obtained based on a representative sample [21]. Typically, the corresponding curve resembles the shape of a bathtub [26]: Shortly after putting into operation, some products fail at an early stage. For a long subsequent period, the failure rate remains low. Finally, failures agglomerate due to ascending wearout and worse connectivity between components. Having all relevant parameters at hand, questions like this can be answered: Which components form improvable bottlenecks? Is there any evidence for planned obsolescence [11]? From a practical point of view, underlying data represented by a pool of individuals together with temporally staggered events have been made available by logfiles or monitoring reports in tabular form ready for import and analysis. Using action-accumulating P systems, we open the potential of multisets in terms of membrane computing to a beneficial field of applications focusing on data mining.

When addressing related work, it makes sense to take into consideration different aspects from adjacent fields of research. Basically, our approach adopts some ideas from the *object-oriented paradigm of programming* [20]. Here, individuals called objects carry attributes able to get modified using dedicated methods. Objects can be created and destroyed. Indeed, this paradigm was invented to facilitate abstract modelling of real things for processing on a computer. Nevertheless, objects are typically managed as addressable entities instead of multisets. *Event-based simulation* by means of a queue of events is a well-known technique [2]. In contrast to our approach, events on their own produce further events in the future to keep the system running. Within the *world of P systems*, a loose relation to blotting P systems [15] and population P systems [3,18] becomes visible due to the consideration of individuals and groups of individuals forming populations. While migration between areas and membranes together with communication among individuals is mainly focussed in population P systems, we emphasise the notion of attributes and events. We are aware of the fact that a setting of attribute values can be interpreted as a location or position referred to a graph-based or nested membrane structure but we believe that attributes are more flexible and more intuitive for our purpose of application.

In Sect. 2, we familiarise the reader with the formal definition of action-accumulating P systems together with all required prerequisites. Hereafter, two case studies selected from different application scenarios demonstrate its practical use. First, as an introductory example, the popular board game "Mensch ärgere Dich nicht" (Man, don't get annoyed, a variation of Ludo) is taken under examination in Sect. 3. Survival, lifetime, and success of pieces running over the board follow specific distributions to be obtained. It is of interest whether a more protective/defensive or a more propulsive strategy offers higher chances to win. The second case study introduced in Sect. 4 is dedicated to our teaching experiences within the university course "Introduction to Programming" attended by 1,108 students from 2012 to 2016. We identify factors and training strategies suitable for improving the final grade. A final discussion concludes benefits and challenges raising open questions for future work.

2   Action-Accumulating P Systems

Formal Prerequisites

Let A and B be arbitrary sets, $\emptyset$ the empty set, $\mathbb{N}$ the set of natural numbers including zero and $\mathbb{R}$ the set of real numbers. A and B are disjoint (share no common elements) iff $A \cap B = \emptyset$. The Cartesian product $A \times B = \{(a, b) \mid a \in A \wedge b \in B\}$ collects all tuples from A and B. For $A \times A$, we write A^2 for short. A Cartesian product might result from more than two sets formalised by n-tuples:

$$\overset{n}{\underset{i=1}{\mathsf{X}}} A_i = \{(a_1, \ldots, a_n) \mid a_1 \in A_1 \wedge \ldots \wedge a_n \in A_n\}$$

The term card(A), also written as $|A|$, denotes the number of elements in A (cardinality). $\wp(A)$ symbolises the power set of A containing all $2^{|A|}$ subsets of A as elements. A multiset over A is a mapping $\mathcal{F} : A \longrightarrow \mathbb{N} \cup \{+\infty\}$. Multisets in general can be written as an elementwise enumeration of the form $\{(a_1, \mathcal{F}(a_1)), (a_2, \mathcal{F}(a_2)), \ldots\}$ since $\forall (a, b_1), (a, b_2) \in \mathcal{F} : b_1 = b_2$. A multiset can also be specified by unordered enumeration of multiple elements like for instance $\{a, a, b, a, b\}$ instead of $\{(a, 3), (b, 2)\}$. The support $\text{supp}(\mathcal{F}) \subseteq A$ of $\mathcal{F}$ is defined by $\text{supp}(\mathcal{F}) = \{a \in A \mid \mathcal{F}(a) > 0\}$. A multiset $\mathcal{F}$ over A is said to be empty iff $\forall a \in A : \mathcal{F}(a) = 0$. The cardinality $|\mathcal{F}|$ of $\mathcal{F}$ over A is $|\mathcal{F}| = \sum_{a \in A} \mathcal{F}(a)$.

Let $\mathcal{F}$ and $\mathcal{G}$ be multisets. It holds $\mathcal{F} \subseteq \mathcal{G}$ iff $\text{supp}(\mathcal{F}) \subseteq \text{supp}(\mathcal{G}) \wedge \forall f \in \text{supp}(\mathcal{F}) : (\mathcal{F}(f) \leq \mathcal{G}(f))$. Respectively, $\mathcal{F} \subset \mathcal{G}$ iff $\text{supp}(\mathcal{F}) \subseteq \text{supp}(\mathcal{G}) \wedge \exists f \in \text{supp}(\mathcal{F}) : (\mathcal{F}(f) < \mathcal{G}(f))$. $\mathcal{F}$ and $\mathcal{G}$ are equal, written as $\mathcal{F} = \mathcal{G}$, iff $\mathcal{F} \subseteq \mathcal{G} \wedge \mathcal{G} \subseteq \mathcal{F}$.

The multiset union $\mathcal{F} \cup \mathcal{G}$ is defined by
$\mathcal{F} \cup \mathcal{G} = \{(a, h) \mid a \in \text{supp}(\mathcal{F}) \cup \text{supp}(\mathcal{G}) \wedge h = \max(\mathcal{F}(a), \mathcal{G}(a))\}$,
the multiset intersection $\mathcal{F} \cap \mathcal{G}$ by
$\mathcal{F} \cap \mathcal{G} = \{(a, h) \mid a \in \text{supp}(\mathcal{F}) \cap \text{supp}(\mathcal{G}) \wedge h = \min(\mathcal{F}(a), \mathcal{G}(a))\}$,
the multiset sum $\mathcal{F} \uplus \mathcal{G}$ by
$\mathcal{F} \uplus \mathcal{G} = \{(a, h) \mid a \in \text{supp}(\mathcal{F}) \cup \text{supp}(\mathcal{G}) \wedge h = \mathcal{F}(a) + \mathcal{G}(a)\}$,
and the multiset difference $\mathcal{F} \ominus \mathcal{G}$ by
$\mathcal{F} \ominus \mathcal{G} = \{(a, h) \mid a \in \text{supp}(\mathcal{F}) \cup \text{supp}(\mathcal{G}) \wedge h = \max(\mathcal{F}(a) - \mathcal{G}(a), 0)\}$.

Definition of Systems Components

Let a domain be an arbitrary non-empty set. An action-accumulating P system $\Pi_\square$ is a construct

$$\Pi_\square = (C, n, D_1, \ldots, D_n, \mathcal{I}, R, E, m, S_1, \ldots, S_m, s_1, \ldots, s_m)$$

with its components
$C \subseteq \mathbb{N}$ .... domain of points in time (global clock)
$n \in \mathbb{N} \setminus \{0\}$ .... number of distinct attributes
D_i with $i = 1, \ldots, n$ .... domain of attribute i

$$\mathcal{I} : \underset{i=1}{\overset{n}{\times}} D_i \longrightarrow \mathbb{N} \cup \{+\infty\}$$

final multiset of initial individuals in which each individual is represented by the n-tuple of its initial attribute values in conjunction with the number of copies of the individual.

R .... set of actions available for events (see details in the next subsection)

$$E \subseteq C \times \wp\left(\left(\underset{i=1}{\overset{n}{\times}} D_i\right) \times (\mathbb{N} \cup \{+\infty\})\right) \times R$$

final set of events. Each event is described by its point in time $\in C$ followed by the multiset of affected individuals which is a subset of all individuals currently available within the system. Finally, a rule from R expresses the action initiated by the event.

$m \in \mathbb{N} \setminus \{0\}$ .... number of response functions

S_i with $i = 1, \ldots, m$ .... domain of response i

$$s_i : \left(\underset{i=1}{\overset{n}{\times}} D_i \longrightarrow \mathbb{N} \cup \{+\infty\} \right) \times C \longrightarrow S_i \text{ with } i = 1, \ldots, m$$

response function s_i. Each response function provides an output of the system taking into account the whole cumulative record tracing the evolution of individuals over time starting with the initial setting $\mathcal{I}$ up to the point in time in which all events from E have been processed and the corresponding actions are done. A typical response function might include statistical analysis.

Systems Behaviour and Available Types of Actions

The systems behaviour aims at *tracing* of the individuals together with their attribute values. In order to enable subsequent statistical analysis and interpretation of behavioural patterns, we emphasise the formulation of an algebraic framework able to have at hand the entire systems configuration record comprising the life cycles of all individuals together with the temporal progression of their attribute values. To do so, we define a *transition function*

$$\mathcal{Q} : \left(\underset{i=1}{\overset{n}{\times}} D_i \right) \times (\mathbb{N} \cup \{+\infty\}) \times \mathbb{N} \longrightarrow \left(\underset{i=1}{\overset{n}{\times}} D_i \right) \times (\mathbb{N} \cup \{+\infty\})$$

whose function value collects all individuals (including multiple copies) with their attribute values available in the system at time t. Along with the evolution of the system, $\mathcal{Q}(t+1)$ is obtained from $\mathcal{Q}(t)$ taking into account all events from E occurring at time t with $t \in C$. Initially, we set

$$\mathcal{Q}(0) = \mathcal{I}$$

In case there is *no event* in E at time t, a non-modifying transition is carried out which results in $\mathcal{Q}(t + 1) = \mathcal{Q}(t)$. For all other cases, the transition from $\mathcal{Q}(t)$ to $\mathcal{Q}(t + 1)$ needs to evaluate all events in E defined at time t. We distinguish different types of events which imply specific actions to perform the transition. Since each event from E comes with an action taken from the set R of available actions, we list the corresponding behaviour.

Let $(t, \mathcal{P}, r) \in E$ be an event at time $t \in C$ affecting a multiset of individuals captured by $\mathcal{P} \subseteq \left(\underset{i=1}{\overset{n}{\times}} D_i \right) \times (\mathbb{N} \cup \{+\infty\})$ and initiating an action $r \in R$, we specify the action types `modify`, `merge`, `create`, `kill`, and `clone` as follows:

$r = \mathtt{modify}\,(f_1, \ldots, f_n)$

> modifies the attribute values of all individuals from $\mathcal{P}$ using the update functions $f_i : D_1 \times \ldots \times D_n \longrightarrow D_i$ whereas $i = 1, \ldots, n$. Technically, the transition first removes those individuals from $\mathcal{Q}(t)$ whose attribute values have to be renewed followed by addition of corresponding individuals with the updated attribute values:

$$\mathcal{Q}(t+1) = \mathcal{Q}(t) \ominus \mathcal{V} \uplus \mathcal{W} \text{ with}$$
$$\mathcal{V} = \{v \in \mathcal{P} \mid (t, \mathcal{P}, \mathtt{modify}(f_1, \ldots, f_n)) \in E\}$$
$$\mathcal{W} = \{((f_1(a_1, \ldots, a_n), \ldots, f_n(a_1, \ldots, a_n)), \mu) \mid ((a_1, \ldots, a_n), \mu) \in \mathcal{V}\}$$

> Attention must be paid to the fact that several $\mathtt{modify}$ actions might take place simultaneously. In order to maintain a deterministic systems behaviour, we require a confluent course in which the sequence of processing the events does not matter. Formally, let $(t, \mathcal{P}_1, \mathtt{modify}(f_1, \ldots, f_n))$ and $(t, \mathcal{P}_2, \mathtt{modify}(g_1, \ldots, g_n))$ two concurrent events. It must hold either $\mathcal{P}_1 \cap \mathcal{P}_2 = \emptyset$ (disjoint individuals) or $f_1(g_1) = g_1(f_1), \ldots, f_n(g_n) = g_n(f_n)$ for all individuals in $\mathcal{P}_1 \cap \mathcal{P}_2$.

$r = \mathtt{merge}(f_1, \ldots, f_n)$

> removes all individuals in $\mathcal{P}$ and adds one new individual whose initial attribute values are composed from its ancestors in $\mathcal{P}$ using the recombination functions $f_i : (D_1 \times \ldots \times D_n)^{|\mathcal{P}|} \longrightarrow D_i$ whereas $i = 1, \ldots, n$.

$$\mathcal{Q}(t+1) = \mathcal{Q}(t) \ominus \mathcal{V} \uplus \mathcal{W} \text{ with}$$
$$\mathcal{V} = \{v \in \mathcal{P} \mid (t, \mathcal{P}, \mathtt{merge}(f_1, \ldots, f_n)) \in E\}$$
$$\mathcal{W} = \{((f_1(a_{1,1}, \ldots, a_{|\mathcal{P}|,n}), \ldots, f_n(a_{1,1}, \ldots, a_{|\mathcal{P}|,n})), 1)\}$$

> Analogously to $\mathtt{modify}$ actions, $\mathtt{merge}$ actions can influence each other and among others if they run simultaneously. To overcome this ambiguity, we technically process $\mathtt{merge}$ actions after concurrent $\mathtt{modify}$ actions. Furthermore, simultaneous $\mathtt{merge}$ actions are required to be independent from each other or confluent to each other. Formally, let $(t, \mathcal{P}_1, \mathtt{merge}(f_1, \ldots, f_n))$ and $(t, \mathcal{P}_2, \mathtt{merge}(g_1, \ldots, g_n))$ be two concurrent events. It must hold either $\mathcal{P}_1 \cap \mathcal{P}_2 = \emptyset$ (disjoint individuals) or $f_1(g_1) = g_1(f_1), \ldots, f_n(g_n) = g_n(f_n)$ for all individuals in $\mathcal{P}_1 \cap \mathcal{P}_2$.

$r = \mathtt{create}(a_1, \ldots, a_n)$

> creates a new individual with initial attribute values $a_1 \in D_1, \ldots, a_n \in D_n$ and adds this individual to the population.

$$\mathcal{Q}(t+1) = \mathcal{Q}(t) \uplus \{((a_1, \ldots, a_n), 1)\}$$

A $\mathtt{create}$ action cannot interact with other types of action.

$r = \texttt{kill}$

removes all individuals in $\mathcal{P}$ from the population.

$$\mathcal{Q}(t+1) = \mathcal{Q}(t) \ominus \mathcal{P}$$

A $\texttt{kill}$ action does not influence the resulting composition of the population if other actions occur at the same time.

$r = \texttt{clone}$

duplicates each individual from $\mathcal{P}$ with its attribute values.

$$\mathcal{Q}(t+1) = \mathcal{Q}(t) \uplus \mathcal{P}$$

It might happen that a $\texttt{clone}$ action interferes with one or more $\texttt{modify}$ or $\texttt{merge}$ actions at the same time. To avoid nondeterminism, we state that $\texttt{clone}$ actions get always executed after $\texttt{modify}$ and $\texttt{merge}$ actions.

In order to finalise the system's description, we still need to mention its response expressed by m freely definable response functions. In this context, we initiate response domains S_1 to S_m capturing all of the system's potential outputs. Based on that, each response function s_i $(i = 1, \ldots, m)$ is allowed to access the entire record $\mathcal{Q}(0), \mathcal{Q}(1), \mathcal{Q}(2), \ldots, \mathcal{Q}(\tau)$ of individuals present in the system over time whereas τ marks the temporally last event in E. Formulation of response functions might include statistical tests and/or some dedicated reasoning. Hence, their formal description within application scenarios might become rather extensive.

3 Board Game "Mensch ärgere Dich Nicht"

For more than 100 years, people worldwide enjoy the board game "Mensch ärgere Dich nicht" [24], a variation of the English Ludo developed in Germany following the notion of a *cross and circle* game. Its most popular version is made for four players. Here, the board consists of a directed ring forming a cross with 40 places, see Fig. 2. Every 10th place serves as a starting position for a player. Directly in front of each starting place is a junction to four consecutive goal places ("safe heaven") of the player according to the starting place. Each player controls four pieces of the same colour. His task is to maneuver all own pieces through the whole cross and place them afterwards inside the safe heaven. The winner is the player who succeeds in placing all of his pieces in the safe heaven before the competitors do. Remaining players continue in a way to successively complete the game on their own. The last one loses the game. The four players act in a cyclic order: black, yellow, green, red. Every player features four pieces initially not in the game but placed outside. The players throw a six-sided dice one after the other. At the beginning and in a situation when all own pieces are outside the game, the player is allowed to throw the dice up to three times. As soon as the dice shows 6 dots, the player sets one of his outside pieces into the game

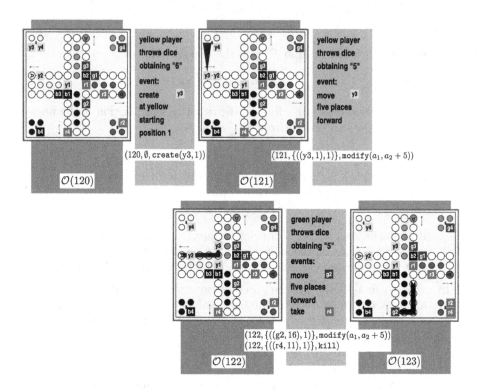

Fig. 2. Excerpt of the sample game course after 120 dice throws (upper left configuration of the board). The yellow player sets a new piece ($y3$) into the game and moves it 5 places forward. In the next step, piece $g2$ controlled by the green player reaches the place occupied by piece $r4$ which in turn is taken out of the game. Dice throws along with decisions of the player on which piece to move result in corresponding events depicted informally and in its formal notation. (Color figure online)

at the starting position and throws the dice again. After throwing the dice, the player is obliged to move one of his pieces in the game forward along the places by the exact number of dots on top of the dice. If the destination place of a move is occupied by a piece of his own, the move is not allowed. In case it is occupied by an opponent's piece, this one is taken out of the game and has to start the circle anew. Each player is free in choice to select among his pieces to move but two constraints have to be fulfilled: (1) The starting position has to be cleared up with highest priority if there are own pieces outside the game. (2) In case, a piece of another player can be taken out of the game, it is mandatory to do so. After finalising the whole ring, each piece enters its safe heaven. Pieces are not allowed to pass each other inside the safe heaven.

We utilise the toy example "Mensch ärgere Dich nicht" in order to illustrate descriptive and evaluative capabilities of action-accumulating P systems. Based on the common rules of the game together with a comprehensive set of monitoring data from a typical game course, we formulate the system

$$\Pi_\Box = (C, 2, D_1, D_2, \mathcal{I}, R, E, 4, S_1, s_1, S_2, s_2, S_3, s_3, S_4, s_4)$$

with its components:

$C = \{0, \dots, 360\}$

> Each time the dice is thrown, the global clock performs a tick increment-
> ing the point in time. The sample game ends after 360 time steps.

$D_1 = \{b1, b2, b3, b4, y1, y2, y3, y4, g1, g2, g3, g4, r1, r2, r3, r4\}$

> We distinguish a total amount of 16 individual pieces assigned to four
> players by colour. $b1$ to $b4$ stand for black pieces, $r1$ to $r4$ for red, $y1$ to
> $y4$ for yellow, and $g1$ to $g4$ for green.

$D_2 = \{0, \dots, 44\}$

> This attribute symbolises the place occupied by a piece. 0 marks the
> position outside the game. Inside the ring, the places have been consec-
> utively enumerated from the individual piece's starting position 1 up to
> 40. Values between 41 and 44 identify places within each player's safe
> heaven.

$\mathcal{I} = \emptyset$

> The game starts with an empty population. Pieces act as individuals.
> Once a piece is set into the game, the corresponding individual gets
> created. As soon as a piece is taken out of the game, its life cycle finishes.
> Pieces within the safe heaven remain in the population for the rest of
> the game course.

$R = \{\texttt{create}(\text{piece}, 1) \mid \text{piece} \in D_1\} \cup$
$\quad \{\texttt{modify}(a_1, a_2 + d) \mid d \in \{1, \dots, 6\}\} \cup \{\texttt{kill}\}$

> Piece's life cycles might be affected by three types of actions: Individuals
> enter the game by $\texttt{create}$ setting the name of the piece and its starting
> place 1 as attribute values. Moreover, a move of a piece is reflected by
> $\texttt{modify}$ in which the value of its second attribute a_2 gets increased by
> the number d shown on top of the dice.

$E = \{(0, \emptyset, \texttt{create}(b1, 1)),$
$\quad (1, \{((b1, 1), 1)\}, \texttt{modify}(a_1, a_2 + 3)),$
$\quad (6, \emptyset, \texttt{create}(g1, 1)),$
$\quad (7, \{((g1, 1), 1)\}, \texttt{modify}(a_1, a_2 + 2)),$
$\quad (11, \{((b1, 4), 1)\}, \texttt{modify}(a_1, a_2 + 1)),$
$\quad (15, \{((g1, 3), 1)\}, \texttt{modify}(a_1, a_2 + 2)),$
$$\vdots$$
$\quad (120, \emptyset, \texttt{create}(y3, 1)),$

$(121, \{((y3, 1), 1)\}, \texttt{modify}(a_1, a_2 + 5)),$
$(122, \{((g2, 16), 1)\}, \texttt{modify}(a_1, a_2 + 5)),$
$(122, \{((r4, 11), 1)\}, \texttt{kill}),$

$\vdots$

$(357, \{((b4, 36), 1)\}, \texttt{modify}(a_1, a_2 + 2)),$
$(358, \{((g3, 4), 1)\}, \texttt{modify}(a_1, a_2 + 5)),$
$(359, \{((b4, 38), 1)\}, \texttt{modify}(a_1, a_2 + 3)) \}$

Our sample game course comprises $|E| = 379$ events in total. In 32 cases, a piece is taken out of the game by $\texttt{kill}$.

Before finalisation of system's specification by four response domains S_1 to S_4 and dedicated response functions s_1 to s_4 for evaluation of the game, we illustrate the system's behaviour by means of the transition function over time. Inspired by the idea to attract more interest in the overall game course, the players follow different strategies. *Red* acts in a highly propulsive manner forcing one piece to run the ring as fast as possible while its further pieces reside outside the game or near the starting place. A more moderate but still propulsive strategy is exhibited by the *yellow* player who avoids setting its top piece onto places with a high risk of danger. The strategy of the *black* player is dominated by a defensive but present style of action. Keeping many pieces inside the game and close to each other, this strategy aims at mutual protection of pieces. In contrast to all others, the *green* "infant" player moves its pieces in a more or less naive way without any visible strategy.

By evolution of the transition function $\mathcal{Q}$ processing the events from E, we obtain the configuration of the game successively for all points in time:

$\mathcal{Q}(0) = \emptyset$
$\mathcal{Q}(6) = \mathcal{Q}(5) = \mathcal{Q}(4) = \mathcal{Q}(3) = \mathcal{Q}(2) = \mathcal{Q}(1) = \{((b1, 1), 1)\}$
$\mathcal{Q}(7) = \{((b1, 4), 1), ((g1, 1), 1)\}$
$\mathcal{Q}(8) = \{((b1, 4), 1), ((g1, 3), 1)\}$

$\vdots$

$\mathcal{Q}(120) = \{((b1, 5), 1), ((b2, 25), 1), ((b3, 6), 1), ((y1, 44), 1), ((y2, 2), 1), ((g1, 6), 1),$
$\quad ((g2, 16), 1), ((g3, 4), 1), ((r1, 44), 1), ((r3, 3), 1), ((r4, 11), 1)\}$

$\vdots$

$\mathcal{Q}(360) = \{((b1, 42), 1), ((b2, 43), 1), ((b3, 44), 1), ((b4, 41), 1), \ldots, ((r4, 41), 1)\}$

Evaluation 1: Identification of the ranking among all players

Having the transition function at hand, we can figure out the ranking of all players in the game. The ranking is determined by the point in time in which the last piece of a player enters its safe heaven. To this end, we formulate all necessary constraints to express the corresponding response function:

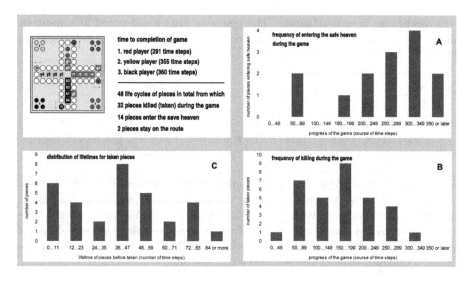

Fig. 3. Board game "Mensch ärgere Dich nicht", condensed representation of evaluation results. Upper left part: final configuration of the game captured by $\mathcal{Q}(360)$ and ranking of the players. Part A: frequency of entering safe heavens during the game corresponding to evaluation 2. Part B: frequency of taking out figures during the game (evaluation 3). Part C: distribution of lifetimes for taken pieces (evaluation 4). (Color figure online)

$$S_1 = C$$
$$s_1 \ : \ \{b, y, g, r\} \longrightarrow S_1$$
$$s_1 = \{(b, t_b), (y, t_y), (g, t_g), (r, t_r) \mid$$
$$\exists t_b \in C.\forall p \in \{b1, b2, b3, b4\}.[((p, z), 1) \in \mathcal{Q}(t_b) \wedge (z > 40) \wedge ((p, z), 1) \notin \mathcal{Q}(t_b - 1)] \vee$$
$$\exists t_y \in C.\forall p \in \{y1, y2, y3, y4\}.[((p, z), 1) \in \mathcal{Q}(t_y) \wedge (z > 40) \wedge ((p, z), 1) \notin \mathcal{Q}(t_y - 1)] \vee$$
$$\exists t_g \in C.\forall p \in \{g1, g2, g3, g4\}.[((p, z), 1) \in \mathcal{Q}(t_g) \wedge (z > 40) \wedge ((p, z), 1) \notin \mathcal{Q}(t_g - 1)] \vee$$
$$\exists t_r \in C.\forall p \in \{r1, r2, r3, r4\}.[((p, z), 1) \in \mathcal{Q}(t_r) \wedge (z > 40) \wedge ((p, z), 1) \notin \mathcal{Q}(t_r - 1)]\}$$

We obtain $s_1 = \{(b, 360), (y, 355), (r, 291)\}$. Thus, the red player was the winner followed by the yellow and then by the black player. The green player lost the game since he failed in placing all of his pieces in the save heaven. The ranking gives evidence to hypothesise that a highly propulsive strategy could be a promising way. Indeed, after performing an amount of 10 games, the most propulsive player succeeded in winning 8 times. A defensive strategy commonly prevents the player from losing the game but also from the winner state.

Evaluation 2: Frequency of entering safe heavens during the game

In this evaluation, we would like to answer the question about the distribution of arrivals of the pieces in the safe heavens during the game course. Obviously, from the beginning of the game it needs a certain amount of steps before the first piece reaches its final destination. The response function denoted as a multiset (allowed to be written as a set containing multiple copies of elements) reads as follows:

$$S_2 = \mathbb{N}$$

$$s_2 : \{p_0, \ldots, p_{360}\} \longrightarrow S_2$$

$$s_2 = \{p_{enter} \mid \exists enter \in C \ . \ \exists y, z \in D_2 \ . \ \exists x \in D_1 \ . [((x, y), 1) \in \mathcal{Q}(enter) \wedge (y > 40) \wedge$$
$$((x, z), 1) \in \mathcal{Q}(enter - 1) \wedge (z \leq 40) \wedge \forall t \in C \text{ with } (t > enter) \ . [((x, \alpha), 1) \in \mathcal{Q}(t)]]\}$$

Altogether, 14 out of 16 pieces in total finally reside inside one of the safe heavens. Response function $s_2 = \{p_{96}, p_{99}, p_{199}, p_{220}, p_{244}, p_{253}, p_{259}, p_{291}, p_{309}, p_{316}, p_{347}, p_{349}, p_{355}, p_{360}\}$ identifies all points in time in which a piece enters a safe heaven. It turns out that the majority of pieces arrives during the second half of the game course with the highest frequency in the last quarter. Figure 3A shows a more condensed view of the frequency distribution.

Evaluation 3: Frequency of killing during the game

In this study, we would like to know in which phase of the game most pieces get killed. To this end, we elaborate a distribution of the according frequencies over the game course resulting in the response function denoted as a multiset:

$$S_3 = \mathbb{N}$$

$$s_3 : \{p_0, \ldots, p_{360}\} \longrightarrow S_3$$

$$s_3 = \{p_{end} \mid \exists begin \in C \ . \ \exists end \in C \ . \ \exists y \in D_2 \ . \ \exists z \in D_2 \ . \ \exists x \in D_1 \ .$$
$$[((x, y), 1) \in \mathcal{Q}(begin) \wedge ((x, y), 1) \notin \mathcal{Q}(begin - 1) \wedge ((x, z), 1) \in \mathcal{Q}(end) \wedge$$
$$((x, z), 1) \notin \mathcal{Q}(end + 1) \wedge (y > 0) \wedge (y \leq 40) \wedge (z > 0) \wedge (z \leq 40) \wedge (z \geq y) \wedge$$
$$(\forall w \in \{begin, \ldots, end\} \ . \ [((x, \alpha), 1) \in \mathcal{Q}(w) \wedge (\alpha > 0) \wedge (\alpha \leq 40)])]\}$$

This evaluation categorises the life cycles of pieces whose lifetime terminates before the end of the game. For this purpose, the *trace* of prematurely killed individuals through the transition function has to be identified. Obviously, the life of a piece begins when set into the game. Prior to this point in time indicated by *begin*, the piece is not present. The death of this piece (taking out of the game) also occurs at a certain point in time called *end*. In between, the piece must persist without any interruption. Additionally, we require that the life cycle of a piece ends within the ring (places 1 to 40). After processing the evaluation, we obtain: $s_3 = \{p_{36}, p_{56}, p_{58}, p_{59}, p_{73}, p_{81}, p_{93}, p_{99}, p_{121}, p_{127}, p_{128}, p_{135}, p_{137}, p_{157}, p_{158}, p_{165}, p_{166}, p_{171}, p_{180}, p_{181}, p_{189}, p_{192}, p_{210}, p_{219}, p_{223}, p_{224}, p_{248}, p_{264}, p_{277}, p_{280}, p_{295}, p_{304}\}$. In total, 32 pieces get killed during the game. It stands out that pieces lose their life most frequently around half of the game. Within the first fifth and within the last fifth of the game, merely few pieces are taken. Figure 3B subsumes the underlying distribution in condensed form.

Evaluation 4: Lifetime distribution of killed pieces

In addition to evaluation 3, we focus on the distribution of age reached by those pieces killed during the game. This lifetime distribution resembles the shape of a bathtub in many real-world scenarios since a number of individuals dies shortly after birth while most individuals survive for a long time before they die as well. In our study, the lifetime distribution results from following response function denoted as a multiset by enumeration of its (multiple) elements:

$$S_4 = \mathbb{N}$$
$$s_4 : \{p_0, \ldots, p_{360}\} \longrightarrow S_4$$
$$s_4 = \{p_{end-begin} \mid \exists begin \in C . \exists end \in C . \exists y \in D_2 . \exists z \in D_2 . \exists x \in D_1 .$$
$$[((x,y),1) \in \mathcal{Q}(begin) \wedge ((x,y),1) \notin \mathcal{Q}(begin-1) \wedge ((x,z),1) \in \mathcal{Q}(end) \wedge$$
$$((x,z),1) \notin \mathcal{Q}(end+1) \wedge (y > 0) \wedge (y \leq 40) \wedge (z > 0) \wedge (z \leq 40) \wedge (z \geq y) \wedge$$
$$(\forall w \in \{begin, \ldots, end\} . [((x,\alpha),1) \in \mathcal{Q}(w) \wedge (\alpha > 0) \wedge (\alpha \leq 40)])]\}$$

Analogously to evaluation 3, for each piece x the time point of "birth" has been identified by $begin$ and the time point of "killing" by end, respectively. Moreover, we select those individuals taken inside the ring which means that their attribute value for the place must be between 1 and 40. Furthermore, we demand that every piece permanently exists from its birth to its death without any interruption. The outcome discloses the desired lifetime distribution taking into account all 32 prematurely killed pieces: $s_4 = \{p_4, p_5, p_6, p_8, p_9, p_{11}, p_{14}, p_{15}, p_{16}, p_{17}, p_{33}, p_{34}, p_{37}, p_{37}, p_{38}, p_{38}, p_{39}, p_{40}, p_{41}, p_{44}, p_{52}, p_{54}, p_{55}, p_{56}, p_{57}, p_{61}, p_{69}, p_{72}, p_{74}, p_{79}, p_{80}, p_{94}\}$. In contrast to the bathtub-shape, we observe three instead of two peaks due to the fact that pieces preferably get killed near the starting places of opponent players. For a more condensed illustrative representation of the lifetime distribution, see Fig. 3C.

4   University Course "Introduction to Programming"

A basic knowledge in computer programming and software development belongs to essential skills in many disciplines of engineering, natural, and life sciences. Thus, university courses addressing an introduction to programming using a popular programming language like Java have been regularly offered at more than 100 public universities in Germany. In this case study, we analyse the one-semester course held by us eight times within the period from autumn 2012 to summer 2016 having sole responsibility. In total, 1108 students attended this course from which 808 finally got graded. Each student participating in this course represents an individual whose life cycle indicates 10 consecutive *phases* of the course passed over 18 weeks. After the initial *enrolment* at the beginning of the semester, two lectures per week take place flanked by exercises and practical trainings in small groups. Approximately every two weeks, a written report with solutions and self-made source code to diverse tasks needs to be submitted whereas an annotated feedback about success (passed/failed) is given

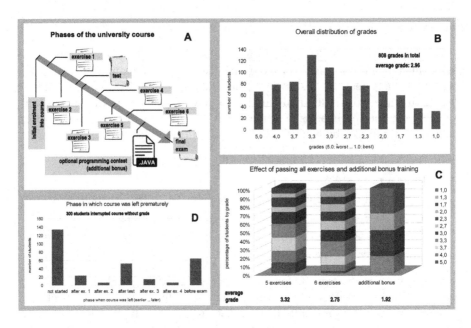

Fig. 4. Summary of evaluations for our one-semester university course "Introduction to Programming" held eight times from autumn 2012 to summer 2016. A: phases of the course, B: overall distribution of grades, C: effect of passing all exercises and additional bonus training, D: frequency of phases in which course was left prematurely

afterwards. Altogether, *six* separate submissions according to the topics of exercises are planned from which at least five have to be passed to finalise the course. In addition, around midterm a rated written *test* is carried out in which up to 30 scores can be reached. At the end of the lecture period, the students can take part in an optional programming contest for gaining an additional *bonus* of up to five scores if appropriate. At last, the final written *exam* is mandatory to graduate from the course. Here, up to 70 scores are available. Based on the individual number of scores in total $(0, \ldots, 105)$ in conjunction with the number of passed exercise submissions $(0, \ldots, 6)$, the final *grade* has been assigned. To this end, according to the common German classification system, the grades ordered from best to worst cover 1.0, 1.3 (excellent level), 1.7, 2.0, 2.3 (good), 2.7, 3.0, 3.3 (satisfactory), 3.7, 4.0 (fair), and 5.0 (fail). Beyond various informal and subjective quality indicators, a cumulative statistical evaluation taking into account pseudonymised quantifiable data from the participating students can support a comparison between different course offers among competing universities or departments. Having at hand the underlying recorded data organised into the structure of events associated with the predefined phases of the course, we create the corresponding action-accumulating P system as follows:

$$\Pi_\square = (C, 11, D_1, \ldots, D_{11}, \mathcal{I}, R, E, 3, S_1, s_1, S_2, s_2, S_3, s_3)$$

with its components:

$C = \{0, \ldots, 10\}$

> Points in time reflecting the consecutive phases of the course such as 0: enrolment; 1, 2: submission to exercise one and two; 3: midterm test, 4, 5, 6, 7: submission to exercise three, four, five, and six; 8: optional programming contest for additional bonus; 9: final examination and grade.

$D_1 = (\{A, \ldots, Z\} \cup \{0, \ldots, 9\})^*$

> Finite sequence of characters acting as pseudonym that identifies an individual. It uniquely results from the student's ID along with an indicator of the semester in which the course was attended (like summer term 2016) and a random number. A pseudonym is allowed to be empty.

$D_2 = D_3 = D_4 = D_5 = D_6 = D_7 = \{0, 1\}$

> For each exercise with report submission in ascending order, the corresponding attribute indicates either passed (1) or failed/skipped (0).

$D_8 = \{0, \ldots, 30\}$

> Number of scores reached in the midterm test.

$D_9 = \{0, \ldots, 5\}$

> Number of scores reached in the optional programming contest (additional bonus).

$D_{10} = \{0, \ldots, 70\}$

> Number of scores reached in the final examination.

$D_{11} = \{1.0, 1.3, 1.7, 2.0, 2.3, 2.7, 3.0, 3.3, 3.7, 4.0, 5.0\} \cup \{\infty\}$

> Range of grades. The auxiliary symbol ∞ stands for no grade.

$\mathcal{I} = \{((326C638, 0, 0, 0, 0, 0, 0, 0, 0, 0, \infty), 1), \ldots,$
$((2F56771, 0, 0, 0, 0, 0, 0, 0, 0, 0, \infty), 1)\}$

> Multiset of enrolled student's individuals, each at the begin of the course.

$R = \{\texttt{create}(d_1, \ldots, d_{11}) \mid d_1 \in D_1 \wedge \ldots \wedge d_{11} \in D_{11}\} \cup \{\texttt{kill}\} \cup \{\texttt{clone}\} \cup$
$\{\texttt{modify}(d_1, d_2 + e_1, \ldots, d_7 + e_6, z, d_9 + b, p, g) \mid e_1 \in D_2 \wedge \ldots \wedge e_6 \in D_7 \wedge$
$$z \in D_8 \wedge b \in D_9 \wedge s \in D_{10} \wedge g \in D_{11})\} \cup$$
$$\{\texttt{merge}(\bigotimes_{\substack{d_1 \text{ with} \\ (d_1, \ldots, d_{11}) \in \mathcal{P}}} d_1, \sum_{\substack{d_2 \text{ with} \\ (d_1, \ldots, d_{11}) \in \mathcal{P}}} d_2, \ldots, \sum_{\substack{d_7 \text{ with} \\ (d_1, \ldots, d_{11}) \in \mathcal{P}}} d_7, 0, 0, 0, \infty)\}$$

Events of type `create` enable addition of individuals joining the course late. By means of `modify`, the numerical attributes might get updated after each phase of the course. Individuals who leave the course prematurely imply `kill` events. The `merge` event allows for unification of individuals representing the same student attending the course more than once in a line of semesters. Here, $\otimes$ symbolises successive concatenation of underlying pseudonymous character strings. Events of type `clone` have been induced when a student continues the course after interruption one or more semesters later. In this case, the partial fulfilment of selected course phases can be approved by maintaining the corresponding attribute values.

$$E = \{(1, \{((342D5B8, 0, 0, 0, 0, 0, 0, 0, 0, 0, \infty), 1)\}, \mathtt{modify}(d_1, d_2 + 1, d_3, \ldots, d_{11})),$$

$$\vdots$$

$$(9, \{(((3356B8, d_2, \ldots, d_{10}, \infty), 1) \mid d_i \in D_i \wedge i = 2, \ldots, 10\}, \mathtt{modify}(d_1, \ldots,$$
$$d_{10}, 1.7))\}$$

The entire set of events consists of $7,219$ entries resulting from eight editions of the course.

Based on the aforementioned $\Pi_\square$ components, the transition function $\mathcal{Q}$ is determined revealing all system's configurations from $\mathcal{Q}(0)$ to $\mathcal{Q}(10)$. Now, we turn to three evaluation studies suitable to shed light on the course attractiveness for students and a potential for improvement of grades.

Evaluation 1: Overall distribution of grades

For gaining the overall distribution of grades, we define at first an auxiliary index function $g : \{1, \ldots, 11\} \longrightarrow D_{11} \setminus \{\infty\}$ with $g(1) = 1.0$, $g(2) = 1.3$, $g(3) = 1.7$, $g(4) = 2.0$, $g(5) = 2.3$, $g(6) = 2.7$, $g(7) = 3.0$, $g(8) = 3.3$, $g(9) = 3.7$, $g(10) = 4.0$, and $g(11) = 5.0$. Using this function, we can denote the response function s_1 representing a multiset whose elements may appear in multiple copies:

$$S_1 = \mathbb{N}$$
$$s_1 : D_{11} \setminus \{\infty\} \longrightarrow S_1$$
$$s_1 = \{g(i) \mid \exists x \in D_1 . \exists d_2 \in D_2 \ldots \exists d_{10} \in D_{10} . \exists grade \in D_{11} \setminus \{\infty\} . \exists i \in \{1, \ldots, 11\} .$$

$$[(((x, d_2, \ldots, d_{10}, grade), 1) \in \mathcal{Q}(10)) \wedge (grade = g(i)) \wedge \left(\sum_{k=2}^{7} d_k \geq 5\right)]\}$$

The evaluation result discloses the distribution of grades whose shape resembles a bell according to a Gaussian curve of distribution which is typical for the spread of talents, diligence, and motivation. The outcome of s_1 in detail reads: $s_1 = \{(5.0, 66), (4.0, 78), (3.7, 83), (3.3, 130), (3.0, 108), (2.7, 75), (2.3, 76), (2.0, 66), (1.7, 59), (1.3, 36), (1.0, 31)\}$. As a consequence, 742 out of 808 attendees – which is approximately 91.8% – taking part in the final examination successfully passed the course but merely 67 students (ca. 8.3%) graduated with an excellent mark. For a graphical illustration, see Fig. 4B. The overall average grade is:

$$avg = \frac{\sum\limits_{i=1}^{11} g(i) \cdot s_1(g(i))}{|s_1|} \approx 2.96$$

Evaluation 2: Impact of extensive training

It seems to be obvious that achievement of the best possible grade is closely related with the amount of practical training regardless of intrinsic factors like talent. Now, we disclose the impact of passing *all* six exercises and the optional programming contest for additional bonus. To this end, we divide the pool of individuals into *three* disjoint groups such that the first one (secondary index 1) contains all students passed the minimum number of five exercises without any significant additional bonus. The second group (2) comprises all students managed to finalise all six exercises, and the third group (3) in addition attained three or more bonus credits in the optional programming contest. We make use of the same auxiliary index function g introduced in the previous evaluation.

$S_{2,1} = \mathbb{N}$

$s_{2,1} : D_{11} \setminus \{\infty\} \longrightarrow S_{2,1}$

$s_{2,1} = \{g(i) \mid \exists x \in D_1 . \exists d_2 \in D_2 \dots \exists d_{10} \in D_{10} . \exists grade \in D_{11} \setminus \{\infty\} . \exists i \in \{1, \dots, 11\} .$

$\qquad [(((x, d_2, \dots, d_{10}, grade), 1) \in \mathcal{Q}(10)) \wedge (grade = g(i)) \wedge \left(\sum\limits_{k=2}^{7} d_k = 5 \right) \wedge (d_9 \leq 2)]\}$

$S_{2,2} = \mathbb{N}$

$s_{2,2} : D_{11} \setminus \{\infty\} \longrightarrow S_{2,2}$

$s_{2,2} = \{g(i) \mid \exists x \in D_1 . \exists d_2 \in D_2 \dots \exists d_{10} \in D_{10} . \exists grade \in D_{11} \setminus \{\infty\} . \exists i \in \{1, \dots, 11\} .$

$\qquad [(((x, d_2, \dots, d_{10}, grade), 1) \in \mathcal{Q}(10)) \wedge (grade = g(i)) \wedge \left(\sum\limits_{k=2}^{7} d_k = 6 \right) \wedge (d_9 \leq 2)]\}$

$S_{2,3} = \mathbb{N}$

$s_{2,3} : D_{11} \setminus \{\infty\} \longrightarrow S_{2,3}$

$s_{2,3} = \{g(i) \mid \exists x \in D_1 . \exists d_2 \in D_2 \dots \exists d_{10} \in D_{10} . \exists grade \in D_{11} \setminus \{\infty\} . \exists i \in \{1, \dots, 11\} .$

$\qquad [(((x, d_2, \dots, d_{10}, grade), 1) \in \mathcal{Q}(10)) \wedge (grade = g(i)) \wedge \left(\sum\limits_{k=2}^{7} d_k \geq 5 \right) \wedge (d_9 > 2)]\}$

It clearly turns out that the frequency of better grades increases with more practical training. Figure 4C subsumes the outcome. Corresponding average grades for the groups $k = 1, 2, 3$ by $avg_k = \frac{\sum\limits_{i=1}^{11} g(i) \cdot s_{2,k}(g(i))}{|s_{2,k}|}$ constitute $avg_1 \approx 3.32$, $avg_2 \approx 2.75$, $avg_3 \approx 1.92$ which results roughly spoken in a tremendous *improvement of two stages* from one group to the next one. Training matters.

Evaluation 3: Phase in which course was left prematurely

From 1,108 students in total, 808 got graded which implies a difference of exactly 300 individuals who left the course prematurely. In this study, we want to clarify in which phase this predominantly happens in order to propose adequate counteractions and stimuli. Formally, for each relevant phase of the course we accumulate the number of students dropping out directly afterwards by s_3.

$$S_3 = \mathbb{N}$$
$$s_3 \; : \; \{p_1, \ldots, p_8\} \longrightarrow S_3$$
$$s_3 = \{p_t \mid \exists t \in C \; . \; \forall i \in \{1, \ldots, 10\} \; . \; [\exists h_i \in D_{i+1}] \; . \; [(((x, h_1, \ldots, h_{10}), 1) \in \mathcal{Q}(t)) \wedge$$
$$(h_{10} = \infty) \wedge (h_t > 0) \wedge (\forall \tau \in \{t+1, \ldots, 9\} \; . \; [(((x, l_2, \ldots, l_{11}), 1) \in \mathcal{Q}(\tau)) \wedge (l_\tau = 0)])]\}$$

Figure 4D shows the resulting distribution. By detailed inspection of $s_3 = \{(p_1, 134), (p_2, 23), (p_3, 6), (p_4, 52), (p_5, 14), (p_6, 6), (p_7, 1), (p_8, 64)\}$ it becomes visible that 134 students enrolled but were absent from the beginning. 52 students left after the midterm test, and 64 students passed enough exercises but did not take part in the final examination. The number of students leaving the course in between is negligible.

5   Conclusions

Our concept of action-accumulating P systems is mainly motivated by interdisciplinary applications in data mining, data science, and information retrieval which benefits from the growing availability of logfiles and time-stamped data records. Gaining insights into hidden laws of life cycles and generalised behavioural patterns within complex systems exclusively from observed events promises a fascinating field opened for membrane computing. Particularly, the combination of multiset-based modelling with evaluation techniques incorporating predicate logic turns out to be an exploitably powerful tool to cope with descriptive and inferential statistics for bridging empirical knowledge with scientific expressiveness. We believe that our proposed framework of action-accumulating P systems provides a flexible toolbox able to be efficiently adopted in numerous scenarios. Future work will be directed at extension of our approach by *dynamical attributes* which might arise or disappear over time triggered by dedicated events.

References

1. Alhazov, A., Cojocaru, S., Colesnicov, A., Malahov, L., Petic, M.: A P system for annotation of Romanian affixes. In: Alhazov, A., Cojocaru, S., Gheorghe, M., Rogozhin, Y., Rozenberg, G., Salomaa, A. (eds.) CMC 2013. LNCS, vol. 8340, pp. 80–87. Springer, Heidelberg (2014). https://doi.org/10.1007/978-3-642-54239-8_7
2. Banks, J. (ed.): Handbook of Simulation. Wiley, Hoboken (1998)
3. Bernardini, F., Gheorghe, M.: Population P systems. J. Univ. Comput. Sci. **10**(5), 509–539 (2004)
4. Broggi, A., Buzzoni, M., Debattisti, S., Grisleri, P., Laghi, M.C., Medici, P., Versari, P.: Extensive tests of autonomous driving technologies. IEEE Trans. Intell. Transp. Syst. **14**(3), 1403–1415 (2013)

5. Bakir, M.E., Gheorghe, M., Konur, S., Stannett, M.: Comparative analysis of statistical model checking tools. In: Leporati, A., Rozenberg, G., Salomaa, A., Zandron, C. (eds.) CMC 2016. LNCS, vol. 10105, pp. 119–135. Springer, Cham (2017). https://doi.org/10.1007/978-3-319-54072-6_8

6. Chen, H., Chiang, R.H.L., Storey, V.C.: Business intelligence and analytics: from big data to big impact. MIS Q. **36**(4), 1165–1188 (2012)

7. Ciobanu, A., Ipate, F.: Implementation of P systems by using big data technologies. In: Alhazov, A., Cojocaru, S., Gheorghe, M., Rogozhin, Y., Rozenberg, G., Salomaa, A. (eds.) CMC 2013. LNCS, vol. 8340, pp. 117–137. Springer, Heidelberg (2014). https://doi.org/10.1007/978-3-642-54239-8_10

8. Cunha, F., Heckman, J.J., Lochner, L.J., Masterov, D.V.: Interpreting the evidence on life cycle skill formation. In: Handbook of the Economics of Education, Chap. 12, pp. 697–812. Elsevier (2006)

9. Erevelles, S., Fukawa, N., Swayne, L.: Big data consumer analytics and the transformation of marketing. Elsevier J. Bus. Res. **69**(2), 897–904 (2016)

10. Estrin, A., Kaminski, M.: The expressive power of temporal logic of actions. J. Logic Comput. **12**(5), 839–859 (2002)

11. Grout, P.A., Park, I.U.: Competitive planned obsolescence. RAND J. Econ. **36**(3), 596–612 (2005)

12. Guinee, J.B.: Handbook on life cycle assessment operational guide to the ISO standards. Int. J. Life Cycle Assess. **7**(3), 158–166 (2002)

13. Han, J., Kamber, M., Pei, J.: Data Mining Concepts and Techniques. Morgan Kaufmann and Elsevier, Burlington (2012)

14. Hilbert, M., Lopez, P.: The world's technological capacity to store, communicate, and compute information. Science **332**, 60–65 (2011)

15. Hinze, T., Grützmann, K., Höckner, B., Sauer, P., Hayat, S.: Categorised counting mediated by blotting membrane systems for particle-based data mining and numerical algorithms. In: Gheorghe, M., Rozenberg, G., Salomaa, A., Sosík, P., Zandron, C. (eds.) CMC 2014. LNCS, vol. 8961, pp. 241–257. Springer, Cham (2014). https://doi.org/10.1007/978-3-319-14370-5_15

16. Hinze, T., Weber, L.L., Hatnik, U.: Walking membranes: grid-exploring P systems with artificial evolution for multi-purpose topological optimisation of cascaded processes. In: Leporati, A., Rozenberg, G., Salomaa, A., Zandron, C. (eds.) CMC 2016. LNCS, vol. 10105, pp. 251–271. Springer, Cham (2017). https://doi.org/10.1007/978-3-319-54072-6_16

17. Jiang, Y., Peng, H., Huang, X., Zhang, J., Shi, P.: A novel clustering algorithm based on P systems. Int. J. Innov. Comput. Inf. Control **10**(2), 753–765 (2014)

18. Kefalas, P., Stamatopoulou, I., Eleftherakis, G., Gheorghe, M.: Transforming state-based models to P systems models in practice. In: Corne, D.W., Frisco, P., Păun, G., Rozenberg, G., Salomaa, A. (eds.) WMC 2008. LNCS, vol. 5391, pp. 260–273. Springer, Heidelberg (2009). https://doi.org/10.1007/978-3-540-95885-7_19

19. Lamport, L.: The temporal logics of actions. ACM Trans. Program. Lang. Syst. **16**(3), 872–923 (1994)

20. Meyer, B.: Object-Oriented Software Construction. Prentice Hall, New York (1997)

21. O'Leary, D.E.: Enterprise Resource Planning Systems: Systems, Life Cycle, Electronic Commerce, and Risk. Cambridge University Press, Cambridge (2000)

22. Neugarten, L.: Time, age, and the life cycle. Am. J. Psychiatry **136**(7), 887–894 (1979)

23. Stüber, G.L.: Principles of Mobile Communication. Springer, New York (2011). https://doi.org/10.1007/978-1-4614-0364-7

24. Wallhoff, F., Bannat, A., Gast, J., Rehrl, T., Dausinger, M., Rigoll, G.: Statistics-based cognitive human-robot interfaces for board games – let's play!. In: Salvendy, G., Smith, M.J. (eds.) Human Interface 2009. LNCS, vol. 5618, pp. 708–715. Springer, Heidelberg (2009). https://doi.org/10.1007/978-3-642-02559-4_77
25. Witten, I.H., Frank, E., Hall, M.A., Pal, C.J.: Data Mining: Practical Machine Learning Tools and Techniques. Morgan Kaufmann and Elsevier, Burlington (2017)
26. Yang, G.: Life Cycle Reliability Engineering. Wiley, Hoboken (2007)

On Evolution-Communication P Systems with Energy Having Bounded and Unbounded Communication

Richelle Ann B. Juayong$^{(\boxtimes)}$, Nestine Hope S. Hernandez,
Francis George C. Cabarle, Kelvin C. Buño, and Henry N. Adorna

Algorithms and Complexity Lab, Department of Computer Science,
University of the Philippines Diliman, Diliman, 1101 Quezon City, Philippines
{rbjuayong,fccabarle,hnadorna}@up.edu.ph,
{nshernandez,kcbuno}@dcs.upd.edu.ph

Abstract. We explore the computing power of Evolution-Communication P systems with energy (ECPe systems) considering dynamical communication measures, $ComN$, $ComR$ and $ComW$. These measures consider the number of communication steps, communication rules and total energy used per communication step, respectively. In this paper, we address a previous conjecture that states that only semilinear sets can be generated with bounded $ComX$, $X \in \{N, R, W\}$. Our result on bounded $ComW$ seems to support such conjecture while the conjecture is not true for bounded $ComN$ and $ComR$. We also show that the class of recursively enumerable sets can be computed using ECPe systems with two membranes. This improves a previous result that makes use of four membranes to show computational completeness.

Keywords: Membrane computing
Evolution-Communication P systems with energy
Dynamical communication measures

1 Introduction

Evolution-Communication P systems with energy (ECPe systems) is proposed in [1] as a model for studying communication complexity in a membrane system. ECPe system is similar to a variant called Evolution-Communication P systems (ECP systems) introduced in an earlier work [3]. These models are interesting variants for analyzing communication since distinct forms of rules are utilized for evolution and communication. However, in ECPe systems, a special object e, for energy, is presented as a form of communication cost. These e's can be earned or produced during evolution and consumed as requirement for every communication.

An approach adapted from classical communication complexity [11] was proposed to introduce a different way of analyzing communication in [1]. Specifically,

© Springer International Publishing AG 2018
M. Gheorghe et al. (Eds.): CMC 2017, LNCS 10725, pp. 151–166, 2018.
https://doi.org/10.1007/978-3-319-73359-3_10

dynamical communication measures were presented. For every successful computation, these measures consider the number of communication steps (or $ComN$), total number of communication rules (or $ComR$) and total energy used for all communication steps (or $ComW$). Several ways of using these measures for communication analysis were also proposed, e.g. determining the sets computed given these measures, using these measures as restrictions imposed on computations and determining problems decided given such measures, also explored in [4,5,7].

In this paper, we explore the set of numbers that can be computed with (un)bounded dynamical communication measures. First, we improve a previous result on computational completeness of ECPe systems. In [1], and in a follow-up work in [8], ECPe systems having four membranes were shown to be computationally complete. In this paper, we show computational completeness using only two membranes by simulating a matrix grammar with appearance checking. We also address a conjecture given in [1] stating that the set of numbers computed with bounded $ComX$, $X \in \{N, R, W\}$ are restricted to semilinear sets. We first show that only semilinear sets can be computed with bounded $ComW$ if the output region only acts as a receiver. We then show a class of non-semilinear sets that can be computed with only two membranes and bounded communication steps.

The paper is organized as follows: we first discuss some preliminaries, including the formal definition of ECPe systems in Sect. 2. We present our main results in Sect. 3 and provide our conclusions in Sect. 4.

2   Preliminaries

It is assumed that the readers are familiar with concepts in formal languages [6] and membrane computing [10]. We mention some concepts used throughout this paper.

Definition 1 (Matrix Grammar with appearance checking). *A matrix grammar with appearance checking is a tuple $G = (N, T, S, M, F)$ where N is a set of non-terminal symbols, T is a set of terminal symbols, $S \in N$ is the start symbol, and M is a set of matrices; each matrix has the form $(A_1 \to x_1, \ldots, A_n \to x_n)$ where $n \geq 1$, $A_i \in N$, $x_i \in (N \cup T)^*$ for $1 \leq i \leq n$. The set F is a set of occurrences of rules in the matrices of M, i.e. $A \to x \in F$, if and only if, there is a matrix $m \in M$ that contains the rule $A \to x$.*

Let $m\colon (A_1 \to x_1, \ldots, A_n \to x_n)$ be a matrix in a matrix grammar with appearance checking G. Matrix m derives z from w, denoted by $w \Rightarrow_m z$, if there is a set of strings $w_1, \ldots, w_n, w_{n+1}$ such that $w = w_1$, $z = w_{n+1}$, and for each $i = 1, 2, \ldots, n$, one of two cases hold: (a) $w_i = w_i' A_i w_i''$ and $w_{i+1} = w_i' x_i w_i''$ (b) $w_i = w_{i+1}$, A_i does not appear in w_i and $A_i \to x_i \in F$. When w results to z through some matrix, we write $w \Rightarrow z$. We write $w \Rightarrow^* z$ to denote the case when w results to z through zero or more applications of matrices in M. The language of G is then $L(G) = \{w \in T^* \mid S \Rightarrow^* w\}$.

Definition 2 (Matrix Grammar with appearance checking in binary normal form). *A matrix grammar with appearance checking in binary normal form is a matrix grammar* $G = (N, T, S, M, F)$ *where* $N = N_1 \cup N_2 \cup \{S, \#\}$, *these three sets are mutually disjoint and matrices are in the following forms:*

1. $(S \rightarrow XA)$ *where* $X \in N_1$, $A \in N_2$,
2. $(X \rightarrow Y, A \rightarrow x)$, *where* $X, Y \in N_1$, $A \in N_2$, $x \in (N_2 \cup T)^*$, $|x| \leq 2$,
3. $(X \rightarrow Y, A \rightarrow \#)$ *where* $X, Y \in N_1$, $A \in N_2$,
4. $(X \rightarrow \lambda, A \rightarrow x)$ *where* $X \in N_1, A \in N_2$, *and* $x \in T^*$, $|x| \leq 2$.

There is only one rule of type 1 and F consists of all rules $A \rightarrow \#$ *contained in matrices of type 3.*

The following are known results [10]: First, the length sets of family of languages computed using matrix grammars with appearance checking is equal to the class of recursively enumerable sets of numbers. Also, the language of any matrix grammar with appearance checking can be computed by a matrix grammar with appearance checking in binary normal form.

2.1   ECPe Systems

The following formal definition of ECPe systems is based on the definition given in [1]:

Definition 3 (ECPe systems). *An Evolution-Communication P system with energy (ECPe system) is a construct of the form* $\Pi = (O, e, \mu, w_1, \ldots, w_m, R_1,$ $R'_1, \ldots, R_m, R'_m, i_o)$ *where m is the total number of membranes; O is the alphabet of objects; $e \notin O$ is a special object, μ is a hierarchical membrane structure, w_h is the initial multiset over O^* in region h ($1 \leq h \leq m$).*

The set R_h consists of evolution rules for region h; each evolution rule has the form $a \rightarrow v$ where $a \in O$, $v \in (O \cup \{e\})^*$. The set R'_h is the set of communication rules for membrane h. There are three types of communication rules: symport-in, symport-out and antiport. A symport rule takes one of the following forms: (ae^i, in) or (ae^i, out), where $a \in O$, $i \geq 1$. An antiport rule takes the form $(ae^i, out; be^j, in)$ where $a, b \in O$ and $i, j \geq 1$. The value $i_o \in \{0, 1, \ldots, m\}$ is the output region. When $i_o = 0$, then the output region is the environment.

In an ECPe system, evolution rules are in the form of multiset-rewriting, however, only one object is located in the left-hand side of the rule (also called *non-cooperative*). Upon application of an evolution rule $a \rightarrow v \in R_h$, a copy of a in region h is removed and replaced with a multiset v. Note that while some copies of e can occur in the multiset v, the object a in the left-hand side cannot be e, i.e. this special object cannot evolve. The form of communication rules are adapted from a variant called P systems with symport and antiport [9]. Upon application of a symport-in rule $(ae^i, in) \in R'_h$, i copies of e outside of membrane h are consumed to transport inside region h a copy of a from the outside region. The reverse of such process is performed when applying a symport-out rule $(ae^i, out) \in R'_h$. We say that the *energy* of either symport rule (ae^i, in) or (ae^i, out) is equal to i. When applying an antiport rule $(ae^i, in; be^j, out) \in R'_h$, aside from a copy of a outside and a copy of b inside membrane h, there should be i copies of e outside and j copies of e inside membrane h. During application, a and b swap position, and the copies of e used are consumed. We say that the *energy* of antiport rule $(ae^i, in; be^j, out)$ is equal to $i + j$.

In this paper, we focus on ECPe systems that apply rules in the same manner as most P systems, i.e. rules are applied in a nondeterministic and maximally parallel manner. We say that a configuration is a state of an ECPe system, consisting of the multiset at each region. A transition from a configuration C to another configuration C' through a maximally parallel application of rules is denoted by $C \Rightarrow C'$; a sequence of zero or more transitions from a configuration C to another configuration C' is denoted by $C \Rightarrow^* C'$. The configuration of an ECPe system at a time unit i is denoted by C_i ($i \geq 0$). An ECPe system computes by starting from the initial configuration C_0 to a halting configuration C_h such that $C_0 \Rightarrow^* C_h$. We say that $C_0 \Rightarrow^* C_h$ is a *successful computation*. A halting configuration C_h is a configuration where no more rules can be applied to any copies of objects in each region.

A set of numbers can be computed by an ECPe system as follows: the natural number produced as output by a successful computation is the number of objects (including count of e's) in the output region of the halting configuration; the set of numbers generated in this way is exactly the set of numbers computed by an ECPe system. We shall denote this set by $N(\Pi)$.

2.2   Dynamical Communication Measures for ECPe Systems

The dynamical communication complexity parameters introduced in [1] are initially determined at the transition level:

$$ComN(C_i \Rightarrow C_{i+1}) = \begin{cases} 1 \text{ if at least one communication rule is used} \\ \quad \text{ in the transition } C_i \Rightarrow C_{i+1}, \\ 0 \text{ otherwise} \end{cases}$$

$$ComR(C_i \Rightarrow C_{i+1}) = \text{the number of communication rules}$$
$$\text{used in the transition } C_i \Rightarrow C_{i+1}$$

$$ComW(C_i \Rightarrow C_{i+1}) = \text{the total energy considering all applications}$$
$$\text{of communication rules used}$$
$$\text{in the transition } C_i \Rightarrow C_{i+1}$$

These parameters are related as follows: $ComN \leq ComR \leq ComW$. Let $X \in \{N, R, W\}$:

$$ComX(\delta) = \sum_{i=0}^{h-1} ComX(C_i \Rightarrow C_{i+1}) \text{ where } \delta : C_0 \Rightarrow C_1 \Rightarrow$$
$$\dots \Rightarrow C_h \text{ is a halting computation,}$$
$$ComX(n, \Pi) = \min\{ComX(\delta) \mid \delta : C_0 \Rightarrow C_1 \Rightarrow \dots \Rightarrow C_h \text{ in}$$
$$\Pi \text{ with the result } n\},$$
$$ComX(\Pi) = \max\{ComX(n, \Pi) \mid n \in N(\Pi)\}$$
$$ComX(Q) = \min\{ComX(\Pi) \mid Q = N(\Pi)\}$$

We let $NFComX_m(k, sym_p, anti_q)$ be the class of set of numbers computed by ECPe systems Π with at most $m \geq 1$ membranes, $ComX(\Pi) \leq k$, symport rules of maximal energy at most $p \geq 0$ and antiport rules of maximal energy at most $q \geq 0$. When one of the parameters m, k, p, q is not bounded, we replace the respective value by $*$. When $k = 0$, we simply omit sym_0 and $anti_0$. When $m = 1$, since it is obvious that no antiport rules can be applied, we simply omit $anti_0$.

In this study, we also explore ECPe systems with a particular restriction on output, i.e. when the output region is the environment ($out = env$), and when the output region only functions as a receiving region ($out = rec$). The class of set of numbers computed with such a restriction is represented by the following notation: $NFComX_m(k, sym_p, anti_q, out = \alpha)$ where $\alpha \in \{rec, env\}$. When $m = 2$ and $out = rec$, we simply omit $anti_0$.

The inclusions below directly follow from the definitions (as stated in [1]).

Lemma 1 [1]. $NFComX_m(k, sym_p, anti_q) \subseteq NFComX_{m'}(k', sym_{p'}, anti_{q'}) \subseteq NRE$ for $X \in \{N, R, W\}$ and for all $1 \leq m \leq m'$, $0 \leq p \leq p'$, $0 \leq q \leq q'$; each of m', p', q' can also be equal to $*$.

From [10] (and mentioned in [1]), the class of set of numbers computed by an ECPe system with no communication is the same as the class of semilinear sets.

Theorem 1 [10]. $NFComX_*(0) = NFComX_1(0) = SLIN$ for $X \in \{N, R, W\}$, $m \geq 1$.

The system considered in [10] is a one-membrane Transition P system where the output region is the skin membrane. The set of numbers computed in a single membrane system with no communication and counting objects in the skin, like the systems in Theorem 1, is exactly the class of semilinear sets. When assigning the environment as output region, the output numbers are determined from the set of communication rules. Thus, the following observation is true about bounded $ComW$.

Fact 1. $NFComW_1(k, sym_*, out = env) \subset NFIN$ for $k \geq 0$.

We now observe that when communication is unbounded, ECPe systems having environment as output holder can compute semilinear sets. We use the relation in Theorem 1.

Fact 2. $NFComW_1(*, sym_p, out = env) \supseteq SLIN$ for $p \geq 1$.

Proof. To prove this, we let Π be a one-membrane ECPe system without communication rules. We then show that there is a one-membrane ECPe system $\bar{\Pi}$ having environment as output region and $N(\Pi) = N(\bar{\Pi})$.

Given $\Pi = (O, e, [_1]_1, w_1, R_1, \emptyset, 1)$, we construct $\bar{\Pi} = (\bar{O}, e, [_1]_1, w_1, \bar{R}_1, \bar{R}'_1, 0)$ as follows: first, we replace all occurrences of e in Π with e'. We determine the set $O' = \{\alpha \mid \alpha \in O \cup \{e'\}$ and $\nexists r : \alpha \to v$, $v \in (O \cup \{e'\})^*\}$. The set O' is the set of all objects not used in the left hand side of any rule, thus, $N(\Pi)$ only considers the count of objects in O'. For every $\alpha \in O'$, the following rules are added: (a) $\alpha \to \bar{a}e \in \bar{R}_1$ (b) $(\bar{a}e, out) \in \bar{R}'_1$. This provides $\bar{O} = O \cup \{\bar{\alpha} \mid \alpha \in O'\}$. $\qquad\square$

Whether only semilinear sets can be generated by one-membrane ECPe systems with unbounded communication, i.e. $NFComW_1(*, sym_*, out = env) = SLIN$, is yet to be proven.

We now recall the results about the computing power of ECPe systems having unbounded communication.

Theorem 2 [1,8]. *For $X \in \{N, R, W\}$:*

- $NFComX_m(*, sym_p, anti_q) = NRE$ *for $m \geq 4$, $p \geq 2$, $q \geq 0$.*
- $NFComX_m(*, sym_p, anti_q) = NRE$ *for $m \geq 4$, $p \geq 1$, $q \geq 2$.*

As can be observed, the previous result shows that four membranes suffice to show computational completeness. When only symport rules are allowed, the maximum energy used in a rule is at most two, while when incorporating antiport rules the maximum energy for both symport and antiport rules are the lowest possible values.

3   Main Results

3.1   On ECPe Systems with Unbounded Communication

We now show that we can generate the class of recursively enumerable sets of numbers with two membranes and unbounded communication.

Theorem 3. *Let $G = (N, T, S, M, F)$ be a matrix grammar with appearance checking. There is a two-membrane ECPe system Π that computes the length-set of $L(G)$.*

Proof. We shall use a matrix grammar in binary normal form given in Definition 2 for our proof. We impose a total order on the matrices in M so that we can label each matrix from 1 to $|M|$ and uniquely label each matrix as m_i where $1 \leq i \leq |M|$. We construct an ECPe system Π as follows:

$$\Pi = (O, e, [_1[_2]_2]_1, w_1, w_2, R_1, \emptyset, R_2, R'_2, 1)$$

where $O = N \cup T \cup \{m_{ch}, \#\} \cup \{m_i, m_i^s, m_{ij}^v, m'_{ij}, m''_{ij}, m'''_{ij}, m_{i2}^{\bar{a}_1}, m_{i2}^{\bar{a}_2}, m_{i2}^{\bar{a}_3} \mid 1 \leq i \leq |M|, 1 \leq j \leq 2\}$, $w_1 = XA$ where $(S \to XA) \in M$ and $w_2 = m_{ch}$. The sets R_1, R'_2 and R_2 of rules include the rules given in Tables 1 and 2, as well as the following rules:

for region 1:	for membrane 2:	for region 2:	
$m_j^s \to \#$	$(Ae, in; m_{j2}^{\bar{a}_1}e, out)$	$m_{ch} \to m_i$	$m_{k2}^v \to \#$
$\# \to \#$		$m_{i1}^v \to \#$	$\# \to \#$

Table 1. Simulating a type 2 or 4 rule

Step	Region 1	Membrane 2	Region 2
1			$m_i \rightarrow m'_{i1} m''_{i1} e$
2		$(m'_{i1}e, out)$	$m''_{i1} \rightarrow m'''_{i1}$
3	$m'_{i1} \rightarrow e$		$m'''_{i1} \rightarrow m^v_{i1} m'_{i2} e$
4		$(Xe, in; m^v_{i1}e, out)$	$m'_{i2} \rightarrow m''_{i2}$
5	$m^v_{i1} \rightarrow e$		$X \rightarrow e \; m''_{i2} \rightarrow m^v_{i2}$
6		$(Ae, in; m^v_{i2}e, out)$	
7	$m^v_{i2} \rightarrow m^s_i \alpha e$ where $\alpha = Yx$ if type 2 or $\alpha = x$ if type 4		$A \rightarrow \lambda$
8		$(m^s_i e, in)$	
9			$m^s_i \rightarrow m_{ch}$

Table 2. Simulating a type 3 rule where a nonterminal symbol A does not occur in the current derivation

Step	Region 1	Membrane 2	Region 2
1			$m_i \rightarrow m'_{i1} m''_{i1} e$
2		$(m'_{i1}e, out)$	$m''_{i1} \rightarrow m'''_{i1}$
3	$m'_{i1} \rightarrow e$		$m'''_{i1} \rightarrow m^v_{i1} m'_{i2} e$
4		$(Xe, in; m^v_{i1}e, out)$	$m'_{i2} \rightarrow m''_{i2}$
5	$m^v_{i1} \rightarrow e$		$X \rightarrow e \; m''_{i2} \rightarrow m^{\bar{a}_1}_{i2} m^{\bar{a}_2}_{i2} e$
6		$(m^{\bar{a}_2}_{i2}e, out)$	
7	$m^{\bar{a}_2}_{i2} \rightarrow m^s_i Y$		
8		$(m^s_i e, in; m^{\bar{a}_1}_{i2}e, out)$	
9	$m^{\bar{a}_1}_{i2} \rightarrow \lambda$		$m^s_i \rightarrow m_{ch}$

where $1 \leq i \leq |M|$, m_j $(1 \leq j \leq |M|)$ is a type 3 matrix in M and m_k $(1 \leq k \leq |M|)$ is a type 2 or type 4 matrix in M. Computation of Π proceeds as follows:

Initially, region 1 contains two nonterminal symbols, X and A where the matrix $(S \rightarrow XA)$ occurs in M. This simulates the application of the first matrix in G. Region 2 contains an object m_{ch}. The system Π nondeterministically chooses a matrix in M that can be applied to the current derivation given in region 1. Shown in Table 1 is the step-by-step computation that simulates a type 2 or a type 4 rule, whereas Table 2 shows computations simulating a type 3 rule.

Suppose in a transition, a rule $m_{ch} \rightarrow m_i$ is in region 2 and m_i is a type 2 matrix where $m_i : (X \rightarrow Y, A \rightarrow x)$. In order for m_i to be correctly simulated, symbols X and A must be present in region 1. Steps 2 to 4 in Table 1 are used to validate and remove the occurrence of the symbol X in region 2 while steps 5 to 6 in the table validate and remove the occurrence A. The occurrence of the object m_i^s in region 2 at step 8 indicates a successful validation. The rule $m_i^s \to m_{ch}$ signals completion of simulating m_i. Shown below is the computation for a successful simulation of a type 2 matrix $m_i \colon (X \to Y, A \to x)$:

Step 0: $[_1 \; XA \; [_2 \; m_i]_2]_1$

Step 1: $[_1 \; XA \; [_2 \; m'_{i1} m''_{i1} e]_2]_1$

Step 2: $[_1 \; XAm'_{i1} \; [_2 \; m'''_{i1}]_2]_1$

Step 3: $[_1 \; XAe \; [_2 \; m^v_{i1} m'_{i2} e]_2]_1$

Step 4: $[_1 \; m^v_{i1} A \; [_2 \; X m''_{i2}]_2]_1$

Step 5: $[_1 \; eA \; [_2 \; em^v_{i2}]_2]_1$

Step 6: $[_1 \; m^v_{i2} \; [_2 \; A]_2]_1$

Step 7: $[_1 \; m_i^s Y x e \; [_2 \;]_2]_1$

Step 8: $[_1 \; Y x \; [_2 \; m_i^s]_2]_1$

Step 9: $[_1 \; Y x \; [_2 \; m_{ch}]_2]_1$

If m_i is a type 4 matrix $m_i \colon (X \to \lambda, A \to x)$, then Yx in steps 7 to 9 is replaced with x. Note that in cases where either X or A doesn't occur in region 1, the antiport rules $(Xe, in; m^v_{i1} e, out)$ or $(Ae, in; m^v_{i2} e, out)$, respectively, cannot be executed. Instead, rule $m^v_{i1} \to \#$ is executed in the former case while $m^v_{i2} \to \#$ is executed in the latter case. In both cases, the trap symbol $\#$ occurs in region 1. This signals a non-halting computation due to the evolution rule $\# \to \#$.

Suppose in a transition, a rule $m_{ch} \to m_i$ is in region 2 and m_i is a type 3 matrix where $m_i \colon (X \to Y, A \to \#)$. Since m_i is of type 3, the occurrence of both X and A in the current derivation leads to an unacceptable string when m_i is applied. In such case, A becomes $\#$ and any succeeding derivations will produce a non-acceptable string. When only X occurs and A does not exist in the current derivation, rule m_i is applied such that X becomes Y. Table 2 shows the sequence of rules that simulates matrix m_i when only X exists in the current derivation (i.e. when only X exists in region 1). Shown below is the computation for such successful simulation:

Step 0: $[_1 \; X \; [_2 \; m_i]_2]_1$

Step 1: $[_1 \; X \; [_2 \; m'_{i1} m''_{i1} e]_2]_1$

Step 2: $[_1 \; X m'_{i1} \; [_2 \; m'''_{i1}]_2]_1$

Step 3: $[_1 \; X e \; [_2 \; m^v_{i1} m'_{i2} e]_2]_1$

Step 4: $[_1 \; m^v_{i1} \; [_2 \; X m''_{i2}]_2]_1$

Step 5: $[_1 \; e \; [_2 \; em^{\bar{a}_1}_{i2} m^{\bar{a}_2}_{i2} e]_2]_1$

Step 6: $[_1 \; em^{\bar{a}_2}_{i2} \; [_2 \; em^{\bar{a}_1}_{i2}]_2]_1$

Step 7: $[_1 \; em_i^s Y \; [_2 \; em^{\bar{a}_1}_{i2}]_2]_1$

Step 8: $[_1 \; m^{\bar{a}_1}_{i2} Y \; [_2 \; m_i^s]_2]_1$

Step 9: $[_1 \; Y \; [_2 \; m_{ch}]_2]_1$

As can be observed, similar to simulating a type 2 or type 4 matrix, absence of X in region 2 leads to application of rule $m^v_{i1} \to \#$ in membrane 2 leading to a non-halting computation. In the case where both X and A occurs in region 2, the rule $(Ae, in; m^{\bar{a}_2}_{i2} e, out)$ is applied simultaneously with $(m^{\bar{a}_2}_{i2} e, out)$ in step 5 so that in step 6, both $m^{\bar{a}_1}_{i2}$ and $m^{\bar{a}_2}_{i2}$ are in region 1. This will prevent the application of the antiport rule $(m_i^s e, in; m^{\bar{a}_1}_{i2} e, out)$ in step 7. Instead, the evolution rule $m_i^s \to \#$ is applied, leading to a non-halting computation.

Corollary 1. $NFComX_m(*, sym_p, anti_q) = NRE$ for $X \in \{N, R, W\}$, $m \geq 2$, $p \geq 1$, $q \geq 2$.

Proof. Follows from Theorem 3.

3.2   On ECPe Systems with Bounded $ComW$

In this section, we consider systems where every communication always uses the output region as receiver.

Lemma 2. $NFComW_2(k, sym_*, out = rec) = SLIN$ for $k \geq 0$.

Proof. Let Π be a two-membrane ECPe system where $ComW(\Pi) = k$ and the output region is only a receiving region. We show that there is a one-membrane ECPe system $\bar{\Pi}$ having $ComW(\bar{\Pi}) = 0$ and $N(\Pi) = N(\bar{\Pi})$.

If the output region of Π is the environment, then this is true via Fact 1. Without loss of generality, let us assume the output region is the skin. Let $\Pi = (O, e, [_1[_2]_2]_1, w_1, w_2, R_1, R'_1, R_2, R'_2, 1)$. Suppose only one object is communicated so that $ComW(\Pi) = 1$. This also implies that only one communication rule is applied in a computation. Let this rule be $r : (ae, out) \in R'_2$, $a \in O$. Since evolution rules are non-cooperative, the communicated object a will be subjected to the same rules (and thus, production of the same multiset) regardless of the time it was communicated in the output region. If another computation exists such that rule r is used at a later or earlier time, the output region in the halting configurations of the two computation paths contain the same multiset. This same multiset is also obtained in the halting configuration when a is in the initial multiset of the output region. This means, $\bar{\Pi}$ can be generated having only the rules for the output region and including the object a in the initial multiset.

For cases where there is a halting computation path in Π without application of any communication rule, a rule $a \rightarrow \lambda$ can be included. For cases where there are several halting computation paths having distinct communication rules applied (e.g. (b_1e, out) in one computation path, (b_2e, out) in another, until (b_je, out) in the jth computation path), we can set an initial symbol, say α, in $\bar{\Pi}$. We then include the rules $\alpha \rightarrow b_1$, $\alpha \rightarrow b_2$ and $\alpha \rightarrow b_j$ in $\bar{\Pi}$.

To extend this to the case where $ComW(\Pi) = k$, we shall follow the same technique as discussed above. We construct a one-membrane ECPe system $\bar{\Pi}$ having the following characteristics: (a) Rules of its skin contain the rules in the output region of Π and (b) the initial multiset of its skin is composed of w_1 and an initial symbol α. Let V be the set of multisets communicated to the skin for all halting computations of Π. We add $|V|$ production rules $\alpha \rightarrow v$ where $v \in V$.

The set V can be obtained as follows: Suppose $R'_2 = \{r_1: (a_1e^{p_1}, out), r_2: (a_2e^{p_2}, out), \ldots, r_n: (a_ne^{p_n}, out)\}$. For each halting computation path δ, let $App(\delta) = (c_1, c_2, \ldots, c_n)$ where each value c_i refers to the total number of applications of rule r_i in the halting computation δ. Since $ComW(\Pi) = k$, the total energy used for communication in a halting computation is at most k. Thus, $App(\delta) = (c_1, c_2, \ldots, c_n)$ must follow the constraint:

$$0 \leq c_1 + c_2 + \ldots + c_n \leq k \tag{1}$$

Let $Q = \{(c_1, c_2, \ldots, c_n) \mid (c_1, c_2, \ldots, c_n)$ satisfies the Inequality (1)$\}$. Also, let $Q_v = \{v = a_1^{c_1} a_2^{c_2} \ldots a_n^{c_n} \mid (c_1, c_2, \ldots, c_n) \in Q\}$. Then, set V is a subset of Q_v $(V \subseteq Q_v)$.   □

This result can be extended to handle multiple membranes. In such a case, all neighboring regions will be considered in determining the set V of possible multisets communicated to the output region. Thus, the following theorem is given.

Theorem 4. $NFComW_*(k, sym_*, anti_*, out = rec) = SLIN$ for $k \geq 0$.

Let Π be an ECPe system having the following characteristics: (a) only symport rules are used, (b) $ComW(\Pi) = k$ and (c) communicated objects are not used in their respective receiving regions. The set V of all possible multisets communicated to the output region in Π can be obtained as a subset of multisets obtained via an inequality similar to Inequality (1). Since any multiset $v \in V$ is not influenced by the multiset communicated from the output region (and vice versa), we can use the same technique of Lemma 2 to construct a one-membrane ECPe system $\bar{\Pi}$ having the following characteristics: (a) Evolution rules of the skin of $\bar{\Pi}$ contain the evolution rules in the output region of Π and (b) the initial multiset of the skin of $\bar{\Pi}$ is composed of the initial multiset in the output region as well as a symbol α. We add $|V|$ production rules $\alpha \rightarrow v$ where $v \in V$ and R'_1 of $\bar{\Pi}$ is constructed in the following way: for all (ae^p, tar), $p \geq 1$ and $tar \in \{in, out\}$, having the output region as the sending region, $(ae^p, out) \in R'_1$. Thus, the following corollary is given.

Corollary 2. Let Π be an m-membrane ECPe system where $ComW(\Pi) = k$, only symport rules are used $(m \geq 2, k \geq 0)$ and all communicated objects are not used in their respective receiving regions. There is a one-membrane ECPe system $\bar{\Pi}$ having $N(\Pi) = N(\bar{\Pi})$ and $ComW(\bar{\Pi}) \leq k$.

Corollary 2 holds as long as the succeeding evolutions from the communicated objects do not produce e's or objects that can possibly be communicated in the succeeding transitions.

3.3   On ECPe Systems with Bounded $ComX$, $X \in \{N, R\}$

The example below shows a non-semilinear set that can be computed with bounded communication steps.

Example 1

$$\bar{\Pi} = (O, e, [_1[_2]_2]_1, w_1, w_2, R_1, \emptyset, R_2, R'_2, 1)$$

where $O = \{a', a, b, \alpha, \beta, \theta\} \cup \{c_i \mid 1 \leq i \leq 5\}$, $R_1 = \{a' \rightarrow ae, a \rightarrow c_1, c_5 \rightarrow aaee, b \rightarrow \beta, \theta \rightarrow \alpha\} \cup \{c_i \rightarrow c_{i+1} \mid 1 \leq i \leq 4\}$, $R_2 = \{a \rightarrow be, \beta \rightarrow \theta e, \alpha \rightarrow \alpha\}$, and $R'_2 = \{(ae, in), (be, out), (\beta e, in), (\theta e, out), (\alpha e, in)\}$.

Computation of Π proceeds as follows: Initially, the objects a' in region 1 evolve via rules $a' \rightarrow ae$.

These rules produce a copy of a and e in region 1. At time $t = 1$, the system nondeterministically chooses between application of rules $a \rightarrow c_1$ or applying the symport rule (ae, in). In the latter case, the e's produced from the previous rule will be consumed to transfer object a in region 2. In the next three time steps, the system reaches a halting configuration via consecutive use of rules $a \rightarrow be$, (be, out) and $b \rightarrow \beta$. Such computation produces the number 1 since only the object β is present in region 1.

When the symport rule is not used at time $t = 1$, the computation proceeds by continuously applying the sequence, $a \rightarrow c_1$, $c_i \rightarrow c_{i+1}$ $(1 \leq i \leq 4)$ and

$c_5 \rightarrow aaee$ in region 1. At step $1 + 6n$, $n \geq 0$, there are 2^n copies of a and $2^{n+1} - 1$ copies of e in region 1. A successful computation applies the symport rule (ae, in) to all copies of a so that in the next step, there are $2^n - 1$ copies of e in region 1 and 2^n copies of a in region 2. In the next two time steps, the copies of a in region 2 evolve via consecutive use of rules $a \rightarrow be$ and (be, in) so that there will be an additional 2^n copies of b in region 1.

The copies of b in region 1 will evolve via the rule $b \rightarrow \beta$. Since there are only $2^n - 1$ copies of e in region 1, there will only be $2^n - 1$ applications of rule $(\beta e, in)$ in the succeeding step. After such applications, there will only be one copy of β in region 1 and $2^n - 1$ copies of β in region 2. The next two steps proceeds as follows: the copies of β in region 2 evolve via rule $\beta \rightarrow \theta e$ and the θs are communicated to region 1 via rule $(\theta e, out)$. The copies of θ in region 1 evolve via rule $\theta \rightarrow \alpha$. At this point, no more rules are applicable, leading the system to a halting state. Region 1 has $2^n - 1$ copies of α and one copy of β, thus the system outputs 2^n.

We now look at the case where copies of a in region 1 are not communicated at the same time. Let step $1+6n$ be the step where the first symport rule (ae, in) is applied. Also, let us say there are only $k < 2^n$ applications of this symport rule. The next sequence of transitions proceeds as follows:

1. At step $1 + 6n + 3$, there are k copies of b $(k < 2^n)$ and the remaining copies of e are at least 2^n in region 1.
2. At step $1 + 6n + 4$, each b produces β.
3. At step $1 + 6n + 5$, since there are at least 2^n copies of e and less than 2^n copies of β, there are some e's left in region 1 after the application of rule $(\beta e, in)$.
4. At step $1 + 7n$, rule $\beta \rightarrow \theta e$ is applied in region 2 and at step $1 + 7n + 1$, the rule $(\theta e, out)$ is applied in membrane 2. At step $1 + 7n + 2$, the rule $\theta \rightarrow \alpha$ is applied in region 1.
5. At step $1+7n+3$, since there are some e's left in region 1, the communication rule $(\alpha e, in)$ is applied, leading the system to a non-halting computation due to the rule $\alpha \rightarrow \alpha$ in region 2.

Note that since not all copies of a are communicated at step $1 + 6n$, at step $1 + 7n$ there are some copies of a and additional copies of e in region 1. If some of these copies trigger the rule (ae, in) in the next step, application of rule $(\beta e, in)$ happens at step $1 + 7n + 5$, which occurs after item 5.

The description of the above computation shows that $N(\bar{\Pi}) = \{2^n \mid n \geq 0\}$. For each successful computation, exactly four communication steps were used, and in each communication step, only one communication rule is used. Thus, $ComN(\bar{\Pi}) = ComR(\bar{\Pi}) = 4$.

The example above leads to the following theorem.

Theorem 5. *$NFComX_m(k, sym_p, anti_q) - SLIN \neq \emptyset$ for $X \in \{N, R\}$, $m \geq 2$, $k \geq 4$, $p \geq 1$, $q \geq 0$.*

In the next theorem, we extend the construction in Example 1 to generate any set composed of powers of j.

Theorem 6. *For $N_j = \{j^n \mid n \geq 0\}$, $j > 1$:*

1. $ComN(N_j) = ComR(N_j) \leq 4$.
2. $N_j \in NFComX_m(k, sym_p, anti_0)$ for $X \in \{N, R\}$, $m \geq 2$, $k \geq 4$, $p \geq j - 1$.

Proof. For every $j > 1$, we construct an ECPe system $\bar{\Pi}_j$:

$$\bar{\Pi}_j = (O, e, [_1[_2]_2]_1, w_1, w_2, R_1, \emptyset, R_2, R'_2, 1)$$

where $O = \{a', a, b, \alpha, \beta, \theta\} \cup \{c_i \mid 1 \leq i \leq 5\}$, $R_1 = \{a' \to ae^{j-1}, a \to c_1, c_5 \to a^j e^{j(j-1)}, b \to \beta, \theta \to \alpha\} \cup \{c_i \to c_{i+1} \mid 1 \leq i \leq 4\}$, $R_2 = \{a \to be, \beta \to \theta e, \alpha \to \alpha\}$, and $R'_2 = \{(ae^{j-1}, in), (be, out), (\beta e, in), (\theta e, out), (\alpha e, in)\}$. It can be observed that $\bar{\Pi}_j = \{j^n \mid n \geq 0\}$ and $ComN(\Pi) = ComR(\Pi) = 4$.

The idea for how the system computes is similar to the ECPe system given in Example 1 for generating 2^n. At step $1 + 6n$, $n \geq 0$, there are j^n copies of a and $j^{n+1} - 1$ copies of e in region 1. The latter value is computed as

$$\sum_{i=0}^{n}(j^i)(j-1) = (j-1)\sum_{i=0}^{n}(j^i)$$
$$= (j-1)\left(\frac{1 - j^{n+1}}{1 - j}\right)$$
$$= j^{n+1} - 1$$

A successful computation applies the symport rule (ae^{j-1}, in) to all copies of a so that in the next step, there are j^n copies of a in region 2 and $j^n - 1$ copies of e in region 1. The value $j^n - 1$ is computed as $(j^n(j) - 1) - j^n(j - 1)$ where the subtrahend is obtained from the copies of e consumed due to applications of rule r'_{21}. The copies of a in region 2 becomes b and gets transported back to region 1 via the rule $a \to be$ and (be, out), respectively. The copies of b in region 1 becomes β via rule r_{18}. Since there are only $j^n - 1$ copies of e in region 1, there will only be $j^n - 1$ applications of rule $(\beta e, in)$ in the succeeding step. This leaves one copy of β in region 1. The copies of β in region 2 becomes θ and gets transported back to region 1 via the rule $\beta \to \theta e$ and $(\theta e, out)$, respectively. Afterwards, no more rules are applicable leaving region 1 with one copy of β and $j^n - 1$ copies of θ.

In the event that the symport rule (ae^{j-1}, in) is not applied to all copies of a in region 1 at the same time, then after the first application of this symport rule, say at time step $1 + 6n$, there will be less than j^n copies of β and at least j^n copies of e at step $1 + 6n + 5$. As a consequence, not all e's will be used for the rule $(\beta e, in)$. The extra e's will be used in executing at least one application of rule $(\alpha e, in)$ at step $1 + 7n + 3$ leading the system to a non-halting state. $\square$

Although a bounded number of communication steps is enough to compute any set $\{j^n \mid n \geq 0\}$, the ECPe system constructed for Theorem 6 needed a symport rule having energy $j - 1$ to compute j^n. It is interesting to determine whether computing the set $\{j^n \mid n \geq 0\}$ using four communication steps can be done using rules with maximum energy of less than $j - 1$.

The next theorem shows that classes of sets of numbers involving summation of exponential terms with several distinct bases can still be computed with four communication steps. However, the number of communication rules depends on the number of bases. Let $Q \in NFComNR_m(k, k', sym_p, anti_q)$ if and only if $Q \in NFComN_m(k, sym_p, anti_q)$ and $Q \in NFComR_m(k', sym_p, anti_q)$.

Theorem 7. *Let* $N \in SLIN$ *and* $Q = \left\{ \sum_{t=1}^{s} j_t^n + \alpha \mid n \geq 0,\ j_t > 1, \alpha \in N \right\}.$
Then $Q \in NFComNR_m(k, k', sym_p, anti_q)$ *for* $m \geq 2,\ k \geq 4,\ k' \geq s + 3$, $p \geq j - 1,\ q \geq 0,\ j = \max\{j_1, \ldots, j_s\}.$

Proof. We construct a 2-membrane ECPe system Π generating Q as follows: first, since $N \in SLIN$, there is a set of evolution rules that can be defined in the output region in order to produce α objects in a halting configuration. For each j_t^n, we shall use multisets and rules similar to those given in Example 1. Also, for each object a, a', c_1 to c_5, we append a subscript t e.g. a becomes a_t. In the first communication step of a successful computation, rules $(a_i e^{j-1}, in)$ for $1 \leq i \leq s$ are used. In the next three communication steps, rule (be, out), $(\beta e, in)$ and $(\theta e, out)$ are used, respectively.   □

3.4   The Power of Including Antiport Rules

Notice that we use symport rules only in the ECPe system constructions described in the previous section. In the next theorem, we reduce the values of $ComN$ and $ComR$ in Theorem 6 (from four to two) by including an antiport rule.

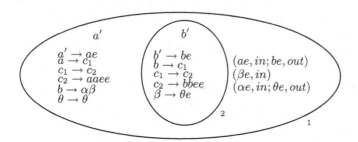

Fig. 1. An ECPe system generating $\{2^n + 1 \mid n \geq 0\}$. The output region is the skin.

Theorem 8. *For* $N_j = \{j^n + 1 \mid n \geq 0\}, j > 1:$

1. $ComN(N_j) = ComR(N_j) \leq 2.$
2. $N_j \in NFComX_m(k, sym_p, anti_q)$ *for* $X \in \{N, R\}, m \geq 2, k \geq 2, p \geq 1$, $q \geq j.$

Proof. For this theorem, we construct an ECPe system Π_j generating $N_j = \{j^n + 1 \mid n \geq 0\}$ for $j > 1$ as follows: $\Pi_j = (O, e, [_1[_2]_2]_1, a', b', R_1, \emptyset, R_2, R'_2, 1)$ where $O = \{a', b', a, b, c_1, c_2, \alpha, \beta, \theta\}$, $R_1 = \{a' \rightarrow ae^{j-1}, a \rightarrow c_1, c_1 \rightarrow c_2, c_2 \rightarrow a^j e^{j(j-1)}, b \rightarrow \alpha\beta, \theta \rightarrow \theta\}$, $R_2 = \{b' \rightarrow be, b \rightarrow c_1, c_1 \rightarrow c_2, c_2 \rightarrow b^j e^j, \beta \rightarrow \theta e\}$, and $R'_2 = \{(ae^{j-1}, in; be, out), (\beta e, in), (\alpha e, in; \theta e, out)\}$. Figure 1 shows the description of an ECPe system Π_j when $j = 2$.

Computation for Π_j with $j > 1$ proceeds as follows: At step $1 + 3n$, $n \geq 0$, there are j^n copies of a and $j^{n+1} - 1$ copies of e in region 1. In region 2, there are j^n copies of b and at least j^n copies of e. A successful computation applies the antiport rule $(ae^{j-1}, in; be, out)$ to all copies of a so that in the next step, there are j^n copies of b and $j^n - 1$ copies of e in region 1. (The a's transported in region 2 as well as the remaining e's in the region will no longer be used in the next steps). The copies of b in region 1 will evolve via the rule $b \rightarrow \alpha\beta$. Since there are only $j^n - 1$ copies of e in region 1, there will only be $j^n - 1$ applications of rule $(\beta e, in)$ in the succeeding step. The remaining copies of objects in region 1 will then be j^n copies of α and a copy of β. After the production of copies of θ via rule $\beta \rightarrow \theta e$, no more rules are applicable in the next step.

In the event that antiport rule $(ae^{j-1}, in; be, out)$ is not applied to all copies of a in region 1 at the same time, then after the first application of the antiport rule, say at time step $1 + 3n$, there will be less than j^n copies of β at step $1 + 4n$ and at least j^n copies of e. The extra e's will be used in executing at least one application of rule $(\alpha e, in; \theta e, out)$ leading the system to a non-halting state. □

The idea for how ECPe systems for Theorem 8 compute is similar to the ECPe systems given in Theorem 6. Combining separate symport rules (ae, in) and (be, out) into one antiport rule $(ae, in; be, out)$ results to a reduction of steps from four to two. However, the resulting output of the system is increased by one (generating $j^n + 1$ instead of j^n). Note also that the construction for Theorem 8 requires an antiport rule having energy j to compute $j^n + 1$ in just two communication steps.

The proof for the next theorem is similar to the proof given in Theorem 7.

Theorem 9. *Let* $N \in SLIN$ *and* $Q = \left\{ \sum_{t=1}^{s} (j_t^n + 1) + \alpha \mid n \geq 0, \ j_t > 1, \alpha \in N \right\}$. *Then* $Q \in NFComNR_m(k, k', sym_p, anti_q)$ *for* $m \geq 2$, $k \geq 2$, $k' \geq s+1$, $p \geq 1$, $q \geq j$, $j = \max\{j_1, \ldots, j_s\}$.

4   Summary

We analyze the computing power of ECPe systems with (un)bounded dynamical communication measures $ComX$, where $X \in \{N, R, W\}$. We provide insights on the class of numbers computed for one-membrane ECPe systems where the environment is set as output region. When using bounded $ComW$, only a finite set of numbers can be computed. When using unbounded $ComW$, semilinear sets of numbers can be computed. Whether only semilinear sets of numbers can be generated by such systems remains an open problem. Also, the class of sets of numbers computed using one-membrane ECPe systems that use skin as output region and (un)bounded non-zero communication has not been addressed.

Our result about computational completeness using only two membranes is an improvement from the results given in [1,8] that use four membranes. The resources used are almost similar to universality proofs in ECP systems, e.g. as presented in [2]. We now ask the following question: can we construct computationally complete two-membrane ECPe systems that only make use of symport rules? We know that a four-membrane ECPe system is computationally complete even using only symport rules (as presented in [1]). Note, however, that the energy required in the rules are not optimal.

We presented result on ECPe systems having bounded $ComW$ and where the output region only acts as a receiving end of communication. We have shown that:

$$SLIN = NFComW_*(0) = NFComW_*(k, sym_*, anti_*, out = rec)$$

We also extended such result to two-way communication with bounded $ComW$ where the communicated objects are not used in their receiving regions. Any set of numbers computed by such systems can also be computed by a one-membrane ECPe system.

Shown below is a hierarchy of relations considering our results and the results given in [1,8]. Let $X \in \{N, R\}$,

$$SLIN = NFComX_*(0) \subset NFComX_2(4, sym_1, anti_0) \subseteq$$
$$NFComX_4(*, sym_2, anti_0) = NRE$$
$$SLIN = NFComX_*(0) \subset NFComX_2(2, sym_1, anti_2) \subseteq$$
$$NFComX_2(*, sym_1, anti_2) = NRE$$

Contrary to a previous conjecture (in [1]), this shows that the class of numbers computed with bounded $ComX$ is strictly greater than the numbers computed with no communication. The relation between no communication and only one $ComX$ remains an open problem. It is also interesting to determine the exact class of sets of numbers computed with $ComX$ of two and $ComX$ greater than two.

In showing the power of bounded communication, we are able to explore a class of set of numbers computed with increasing maximum energy cost, as shown below. Let $j > 1$ and $X \in \{N, R\}$:

$$\{j^n \mid n \geq 0\} \in NFComX_2(4, sym_{j-1}, anti_0)$$
$$\{j^n + 1 \mid n \geq 0\} \in NFComX_2(2, sym_1, anti_j)$$

It is interesting to determine if we can reduce the cost of the energy used in the rules when computing these sets with two membranes and $ComX$ having the same bounded values. Specifically, is $\{j^n \mid n \geq 0\} \notin NFComX_2(4, sym_{j-2}, anti_0)$? Is $\{j^n + 1 \mid n \geq 0\} \notin NFComX_2(2, sym_1, anti_{j-1})$? Can computing powers of j, $j > 1$ be done using only one communication step?

Acknowledgements. R. Juayong would like to thank the DOST-ERDT Scholarship Program, OVPAA-OIL and the College of Engineering, UP Diliman. N. Hernandez is supported by the Vea Family Technology for All Centennial professorial chair. F.G.C. Cabarle is grateful for a Faculty Research Incentive Award (2016–2017) from the College of Engineering of UP Diliman, the PhDIA Project No. 161606 and RLC grant 2016–2017 both from the UP Diliman OVCRD, and the Soy and Tess Medina Professorial Chair Award for 2016–2017. H. Adorna is supported by the Semirara Mining Corp. professorial chair, UP Diliman.

References

1. Adorna, H.N., Păun, G., Pérez-Jiménez, M.J.: On communication complexity in evolution-communication P systems. Rom. J. Inf. Sci. Technol. **13**(2), 113–130 (2010)

2. Alhazov, A.: Communication in membrane systems with symbol objects. Ph.D. thesis, Universitat Rovira I Virgili (2006)

3. Cavaliere, M.: Evolution–communication P systems. In: Păun, G., Rozenberg, G., Salomaa, A., Zandron, C. (eds.) WMC 2002. LNCS, vol. 2597, pp. 134–145. Springer, Heidelberg (2003). https://doi.org/10.1007/3-540-36490-0_10

4. Donor, B., Juayong, R.A.B., Adorna, H.N.: On the communication complexity of sorting in evolution-communication P systems with energy. In: 12th Philippine Computing Science Congress (PCSC 2012), Canlubang, Laguna, pp. 15–25 (2002)

5. Francia, S.L., Francisco, D.A.A., Juayong, R.A.B., Adorna, H.N.: On communication complexity of some hard problems in ECPe systems with priority. Philipp. Comput. J. **9**(2), 14–25 (2014)

6. Garey, M.R., Johnson, D.S.: Computers and Intractability: A Guide to the Theory of NP-Completeness. W. H. Freeman & Co., New York (1990)

7. Hernandez, N.H.S., Juayong, R.A.B., Adorna, H.N.: On communication complexity of some hard problems in ECPe systems. In: Alhazov, A., Cojocaru, S., Gheorghe, M., Rogozhin, Y., Rozenberg, G., Salomaa, A. (eds.) CMC 2013. LNCS, vol. 8340, pp. 206–224. Springer, Heidelberg (2014). https://doi.org/10.1007/978-3-642-54239-8_15

8. Juayong, R.A.B., Adorna, H.N.: A note on the universality of EC P systems with energy. In: 2nd International Conference on Information Technology Convergence and Services (ITCS), pp. 1–6, August 2010

9. Păun, A., Păun, G.: The power of communication: P systems with symport/antiport. New Gener. Comput. **20**(3), 295–305 (2002)

10. Păun, G.: Membrane Computing. Springer, Heidelberg (2002). https://doi.org/10.1007/978-3-642-56196-2

11. Yao, A.C.: Some complexity questions related to distributed computing. In: ACM Symposium on Theory of Computing, pp. 209–213 (1979)

Generalized P Colony Automata and Their Relation to P Automata

Kristóf Kántor and György Vaszil$^{(\boxtimes)}$

Department of Computer Science, Faculty of Informatics, University of Debrecen,
Kassai út 26, Debrecen 4028, Hungary
{kantor.kristof,vaszil.gyorgy}@inf.unideb.hu

Abstract. We investigate genPCol automata with input mappings that can be realized through the application of finite transducers to the string representations of multisets. We show that using unrestricted programs, these automata characterize the class of recursively enumerable languages. The same holds for systems with all-tape programs, having capacity at least *two*. In the case of systems with com-tape programs, we show that they characterize language classes which are closely related to those characterized by variants of P automata.

1 Introduction

Cells and their life cycle interactions through a common and shared environment are modeled by P colonies. They are tissue-like membrane systems, where cells represent a community of very simple computing agents, see [20,21]. In the theory of grammar systems (see [7]), a field so called *colony of grammars* exists, where the name *colony* comes from. These colonies of grammars (see also [19]) consist of a collection of simple generative grammars (generating finite languages each), even so their behavior is cooperating, creating a system able to generate fairly complicated languages. The computing power of the whole system is a lot more complex compared to the power of the individual components.

This behavioral complexity is modeled by P colonies in the framework of membrane computing. This model is very much like tissue-like membrane systems, where multisets of objects are used to describe the contents of the cells and environment and then are processed by the cells in the corresponding colony using rules which enable the evolution of the objects present in the cells and the exchange of objects between the environment and the cells. These computing agents have a very confined functionality: they can store a restricted amount of objects at a given time (this is called the capacity of the system) and they can process a restricted amount of information. The way the information processing

Supported in part by project no. K 120558, implemented with the support provided from the National Research, Development and Innovation Fund of Hungary, financed under the K_16 funding scheme. Also supported by the construction EFOP-3.6.3-VEKOP-16-2017-00002, a project supported by the European Union, co-financed by the European Social Fund.

M. Gheorghe et al. (Eds.): CMC 2017, LNCS 10725, pp. 167–182, 2018.
https://doi.org/10.1007/978-3-319-73359-3_11

is done is really simple: The rules are either of the form $a \rightarrow b$ (for changing an object a into an object b inside the cell), or $a \leftrightarrow b$ (for exchanging an object a inside a cell with an object b in the environment). A rule set is often called a program, that consists exactly the same number of rules as the capacity of the system. When a program gets executed, the k (the capacity of the system) rules that it contains are applied to the k objects simultaneously. A sequence of program executions where in each step a program is applied for every cell is called a computation. During a computational step, every colony member cell execute one of their programs in parallel. A computation ends when the system reaches one of its the final configurations (usually given as the set of halting configurations, that is, those situations when no programs can be applied by any of the cells). The result of the computation is a multiset, thus multiplicities of different objects present in each cell and the environment. It is natural to observe these results as sets of vectors, or sets of numbers.

There are many theoretical results concerning P colonies. Despite the fact that they are extremely simple computing systems, they are computationally complete, even with very restricted size parameters and other syntactic or functioning restrictions. For these, and more topics, results, see [3–6,10,11,15,16].

P colony automata were introduced in [1] for a sole purpose, that is, the capability of describing sets of strings. P colony automata accept string languages by assuming an initial input tape and an input string in the environment and extending the available types of rules by tape rules. These types of rules in addition to their non-tape counterparts, also read the processed objects from the input tape. This computational model comes with a difficulty: The possibility of applying more than one tape rule simultaneously, that is, the possibility of reading several different objects in the same computational step. Even so, [1] and later [2] provides adequate proofs in regard of several variants of P colony automata being computationally complete.

To overcome this difficulty, generalized P colony automata were introduced in [18] and studied further in [17]. The main idea of this computational model was to get the process of input reading closer to other kinds of membrane systems, especially to antiport P systems and P automata. The latter, introduced in [12] (see also [8]) are P systems using symport and antiport rules (see [23]), characterizing string languages. They do this not by having an input tape, but rather associating strings to their computations by keeping track of the communication with the environment. In this model, membranes communicate freely with the environment and each object that could be requested for input by the communication rules is assumed to be available in an unlimited supply. During every computational step, a multiset of objects enter the system from the environment. The computation is a sequence of computational steps, therefore a sequence of multisets, which defines the accepted strings by mapping the sequence of multisets to a string.

This generality is used in the generalized P colony automata theory, that is, the idea of characterizing strings through the sequences of multisets processed during computations. A computation in this model defines accepted multiset sequences, which are transformed into accepted symbol sequences/strings. In this model there is no input string, but there are tape and non-tape rules equally for evolution and communication rules. In a single computational step, this system is able to read more than one symbol, thus reading a multiset. This way generalized P colony automata are able to avoid the conflicts present in P Colony automata, where simultaneous usage of tape rules in a single computational step can arise problems. After getting the result of a computation, that is, the accepted sequence of multisets, it is possible to map them to strings in a similar way as shown in P automata.

In [18], some basic variants of the model were introduced and studied from the point of view of their computational power. In [17] we continued the investigations structuring our results around the capacity of the systems, and different types of restrictions imposed on the use of tape rules in the programs of the systems. We considered three possible ways of dealing with tape rules in the programs: (1) the unrestricted case, (2) the case when all programs must contain at least one tape rule (all-tape programs), and (3) the case when all communication rules are tape rules (com-tape programs).

2   Generalized P Colony Automata

Let V be a finite alphabet, let the set of all words over V be denoted by V^*, and let ε be the empty word. We denote the number of occurrences of a symbol $a \in V$ in w by $|w|_a$.

A multiset over a set V is a mapping $M : V \to \mathbb{N}$ where $\mathbb{N}$ denotes the set of non-negative integers. This mapping assigns to each object $a \in V$ its multiplicity $M(a)$ in M. The set $supp(M) = \{a \mid M(a) \geq 1\}$ is the support of M. If V is a finite set, then M is called a finite multiset. A multiset M is empty if its support is empty, $supp(M) = \emptyset$. The set of finite multisets over the alphabet V is denoted by $\mathcal{M}(V)$. A finite multiset M over V will also be represented by a string w over the alphabet V with $|w|_a = M(a)$, $a \in V$, the empty multiset will be denoted by $\emptyset$.

We say that $a \in M$ if $M(a) \geq 1$, and the cardinality of M, $card(M)$ is defined as $card(M) = \Sigma_{a \in M} M(a)$. For two multisets $M_1, M_2 \in \mathcal{M}(V)$, $M_1 \subseteq M_2$ holds, if for all $a \in V$, $M_1(a) \leq M_2(a)$. The union of M_1 and M_2 is defined as $(M_1 \cup M_2) : V \to \mathbb{N}$ with $(M_1 \cup M_2)(a) = M_1(a) + M_2(a)$ for all $a \in V$, the difference is defined for $M_2 \subseteq M_1$ as $(M_1 - M_2) : V \to \mathbb{N}$ with $(M_1 - M_2)(a) = M_1(a) - M_2(a)$ for all $a \in V$.

A *genPCol automaton* of capacity k and with n cells, $k, n \geq 1$, is a construct

$$\Pi = (V, e, w_E, (w_1, P_1), \ldots, (w_n, P_n), F)$$

where

- V is an *alphabet*, the alphabet of the automaton, its elements are called *objects*;
- $e \in V$ is the *environmental object* of the automaton, the only object which is assumed to be available in an arbitrary, unbounded number of copies in the environment;

- $w_E \in (V - \{e\})^*$ is a string representing a multiset from $\mathcal{M}(V - \{e\})$, the multiset of objects different from e which is found in the environment initially;
- $(w_i, P_i), 1 \leq i \leq n$, specifies the i-th *cell* where w_i is (the representation of) a multiset over V, it determines the initial contents of the cell, and its cardinality $|w_i| = k$ is called the *capacity* of the system. P_i is a set of *programs*, each program is formed from k rules of the following types (where $a, b \in V$):

  - *tape rules* of the form $a \xrightarrow{T} b$, or $a \xleftrightarrow{T} b$, called rewriting tape rules and communication tape rules, respectively; or
  - *nontape rules* of the form $a \rightarrow b$, or $a \leftrightarrow b$, called rewriting (nontape) rules and communication (nontape) rules, respectively.

  A program is called a *tape program* if it contains at least one tape rule.
- F is a set of *accepting configurations* of the automaton which we will specify in more detail below.

A genPCol automaton reads an input word during a computation. A part of the input (possibly consisting of more than one symbols) is read during each configuration change: the processed part of the input corresponds to the multiset of symbols introduced by the tape rules of the system.

A *configuration* of a genPCol automaton is an $(n+1)$-tuple $(u_E, u_1, \ldots, u_n)$, where $u_E \in \mathcal{M}(V - \{e\})$ is the multiset of objects different from e in the environment, and $u_i \in \mathcal{M}(V)$, $1 \leq i \leq n$, are the contents of the i-th cell. The *initial configuration* is given by $(w_E, w_1, \ldots, w_n)$, the initial contents of the environment and the cells. The elements of the set F of *accepting configurations* are given as configurations of the form $(v_E, v_1, \ldots, v_n)$, where

- $v_E \in \mathcal{M}(V - \{e\})$ denotes a multiset of objects different from e being in the environment, and
- $v_i \in \mathcal{M}(V)$, $1 \leq i \leq n$, is the contents of the i-th cell.

In order to describe the functioning of genPCol automata, let us define the following multisets. Let r be a rewriting or a communication rule (tape or nontape), and let us denote by $left(r)$ and $right(r)$ the objects on the left and on the right side of r, respectively. Let also, for $\alpha \in \{left, right\}$ and for any program p, $\alpha(p) = \bigcup_{r \in p} \alpha(r)$ where the union denotes multiset union (as defined above), and for a rule r and program $p = \langle r_1, \ldots, r_k \rangle$, the notation $r \in p$ denotes the fact that r is one of the rules of the program, that is, $r = r_j$ for some j, $1 \leq j \leq k$.

Moreover, for any tape program p we also define $read(p)$ as the multiset of symbols (different from e) on the right side of rewriting tape rules and on the left side of communication tape rules, that is, $read(p) = \bigcup_{r \in p, r = a \xrightarrow{T} b, b \neq e} right(r) \cup \bigcup_{r \in p, r = a \xleftrightarrow{T} b, a \neq e} left(r)$.

Let us also denote by $export(p)$ and $import(p)$ the multiset of objects that are sent out to the environment and brought inside the cell when applying the program p, respectively, that is, $export(p) = \bigcup_{r \in p} left(r)$, $import(p) = \bigcup_{r \in p} right(r)$ for all communication rules r of the program p. Moreover, by $create(p)$ we denote the multiset of symbols produced by the rewriting rules of program p, thus, $create(p) = \bigcup_{r \in p} right(p)$ for the rewriting rules r of p.

Let $c = (u_E, u_1, \ldots, u_n)$ be a configuration of a genPCol automaton Π, and let $U_E = u_E \cup \{e, e, \ldots\}$, thus, the multiset of objects found in the environment (together with the infinite number of es which are always present). The *set of programs*, P_c is *applicable in configuration* c, if the following conditions hold.

- At most one program is selected for each cell, that is, if $p, p' \in P_c, p \neq p'$ and $p \in P_i, p' \in P_j$, then $i \neq j$;
- The selected programs are applicable in the cells (the left sides of the rules contain the same symbols that are present in the cell), that is, for each $p \in P_c$, if $p \in P_i$ then $left(p) = u_i$;
- The symbols to be brought inside the cells by the programs are present in the environment, that is, $\bigcup_{p \in P_c} import(p) \subseteq U_E$;
- P_c is maximal, that is, if any other program is added to it, then some of the above conditions are not satisfied.

Let $c = (u_E, u_1, \ldots, u_n)$ be a configuration of the genPCol automaton. By applying a set P_c of applicable programs, the configuration c is *changed* to a configuration $c' = (u'_E, u'_1, \ldots, u'_n)$, denoted by $c \overset{P_c}{\Longrightarrow} c'$, if the following properties hold:

- If there is a $p \in P_c$ such that $p \in P_i$, then $u'_i = create(p) \cup import(p)$, otherwise $u'_i = u_i$, $1 \leq i \leq n$; and
- $U'_E = U_E - \bigcup_{p \in P_c} import(p) \cup \bigcup_{p \in P_c} export(p)$ (where U'_E again denotes $u'_E \cup \{e, e, \ldots\}$ with an infinite number of es).

Thus, in genPCol automata, we apply the programs in the maximally parallel way, that is, in each computational step, every component cell nondeterministically applies one of its applicable programs. Then we collect all the symbols that the tape rules "read" (these multisets are denoted by $read(p)$ for a program p above): this is the multiset read by the system in the given computational step. For any P_c, a set of applicable programs in a configuration c, let us denote by $read(P_c)$ the multiset of objects read by the tape rules of the programs of P_c.

Then we can also define the set of multisets which can be read in any configuration of the genPCol automaton Π as

$$in(\Pi) = \{read(P_c) \mid P_c \text{ is a set of applicable programs in a configuration } c\}.$$

Remark 1. Although the set of configurations of a genPCol automaton Π is infinite (because the multiset corresponding to the contents of the environment is not necessarily finite), the set $in(\Pi)$ is finite. To see this, note that the applicability of a program by a component cell also depends on the contents of the particular component. Since at most one program can be applied in a component in one computational step, and the number of programs associated to each component is finite, the number of different sets of applicable programs in any configuration, that is, the set $\{P_c \mid c \text{ is a configuration of } \Pi\}$ is also finite.

A successful computation defines this way an accepted sequence of multisets: $u_1 u_2 \ldots u_s$, $u_i \in in(\Pi)$, for $1 \leq i \leq s$, that is, the sequence of multisets entering the system during the steps of the computation.

Let $\Pi = (V, e, w_E, (w_1, P_1), \ldots, (w_n, P_n), F)$ be a genPCol automaton. The *set of input sequences accepted by Π* is defined as

$$A(\Pi) = \{ u_1 u_2 \ldots u_s \mid u_i \in in(\Pi), \ 1 \leq i \leq s, \text{ and there is a configuration}$$
$$\text{sequence } c_0, \ldots, c_s, \text{ with } c_0 = (w_E, w_1, \ldots, w_n), \ c_s \in F, \text{ and}$$
$$c_i \xRightarrow{P_{c_i}} c_{i+1} \text{ with } u_{i+1} = read(P_{c_i}) \text{ for all } 0 \leq i \leq s-1 \}.$$

Remark 2. Note that this way of functioning is different from the computational modes used for P colony automata in [1] where only one symbol can be read by the system in one computational step, so all tape rules that are applied simultaneously must read one and the same symbol.

Let Π be a genPCol automaton, and let $f : in(\Pi) \to 2^{\Sigma^*}$ be a mapping, such that $f(u) = \{\varepsilon\}$ if and only if u is the empty multiset.

The *language accepted by Π* with respect to f is defined as

$$L(\Pi, f) = \{ f(u_1) f(u_2) \ldots f(u_s) \in \Sigma^* \mid u_1 u_2 \ldots u_s \in A(\Pi) \}.$$

We define the following language classes.

- $\mathcal{L}(\text{genPCol}, \mathcal{F}, \text{com-tape}(k))$ is the class of languages accepted by generalized PCol automata with capacity k and with mappings from the class $\mathcal{F}$ where all the communication rules are tape rules,
- $\mathcal{L}(\text{genPCol}, \mathcal{F}, \text{all-tape}(k))$ is the class of languages accepted by generalized PCol automata with capacity k and with mappings from the class $\mathcal{F}$ where all the programs must have at least one tape rule,
- $\mathcal{L}(\text{genPCol}, \mathcal{F}, *(k))$ is the class of languages accepted by generalized PCol automata with capacity k and with mappings from the class $\mathcal{F}$ where unrestricted programs are used, that is, where programs with any kinds of rules are allowed.

Let V and Σ be two alphabets, and let $\mathcal{M}_{FIN}(V) \subseteq \mathcal{M}(V)$ denote the set of finite subsets of the set of finite multisets over an alphabet V. Consider a mapping $f : D \to 2^{\Sigma^*}$ for some $D \in \mathcal{M}_{FIN}(V)$. We say that $f \in \mathcal{F}_{TRANS}$, if for any $v \in D$, we have $|f(v)| = 1$, and we can obtain $f(v) = \{w\}$, $w \in \Sigma^*$ by applying a deterministic finite transducer to any string representation of the multiset v, (as w is unique, the transducer must be constructed in such a way that all string representations of the multiset v as input result in the same $w \in \Sigma^*$ as output, and moreover, as f should be nonerasing, the transducer produces a result with $w \neq \varepsilon$ for any nonempty input).

Besides the above defined class of mappings, we also use the so called permutation mapping. Let $f_{perm} : \mathcal{M}(V) \to 2^{\Sigma^*}$ where $V = \Sigma$ be defined as follows. For all $v \in \mathcal{M}(V)$, we have

$$f(v) = \{ a_1 a_2 \ldots a_s \mid |v| = s, a_1 a_2 \ldots a_s \text{ is a permutation of the elements of } v \}.$$

We denote the language classes that can be characterized with these types of input mappings as $\mathcal{L}_X(\text{genPCol}, Y(k))$, where $X \in \{f_{perm}, \text{TRANS}\}$, $Y \in \{\text{com-tape, all-tape}, *\}$.

Now we present an example to demonstrate the above defined notions.

Example 1. Let $\Pi = (\{a, b, c\}, e, \emptyset, (ea, P), F)$ be a genPCol automaton where

$$P = \{\langle e \to a, a \overset{T}{\leftrightarrow} e \rangle, \langle e \to b, a \overset{T}{\leftrightarrow} e \rangle, \langle e \to b, b \overset{T}{\leftrightarrow} a \rangle, \langle e \to c, b \overset{T}{\leftrightarrow} a \rangle,$$
$$\langle a \to b, b \overset{T}{\leftrightarrow} a \rangle, \langle a \to c, b \overset{T}{\leftrightarrow} a \rangle\}$$

with all the communication rules being tape rules. Let also $F = \{(v, ca) \mid a \notin v\}$ be the set of final configurations.

A possible computation of this system is the following:

$$(\emptyset, ea) \Rightarrow (a, ea) \Rightarrow (aa, ea) \Rightarrow (aaa, eb) \Rightarrow (aab, ba) \Rightarrow (bba, ba) \Rightarrow (bbb, ac)$$

where the first three computational steps read the multiset containing an a, the last three steps read a multiset containing a b, thus the accepted multiset sequence of this computation is $(a)(a)(a)(b)(b)(b)$.

It is not difficult to see that similarly to the one above, the computations which end in a final configuration (a configuration which does not contain the object a in the environment) accept the set of multiset sequences

$$A(\Pi) = \{(a)^n(b)^n \mid n \geq 1\}.$$

The set of multisets which can be read by Π is $in(\Pi) = \{a, b\}$ (where a and b denote the multisets containing one copy of the object a and b, respectively). If we consider f_{perm} as the input mapping, we have

$$L(\Pi, f_{perm}) = \{a^n b^n \mid n \geq 1\}.$$

On the other hand, if we consider the mapping $f_1 \in \mathcal{F}_{\text{TRANS}}$ where $f_1 : in(\Pi) \to 2^{\Sigma^*}$ with $\Sigma = \{c, d, e, f\}$ and $f_1(a) = \{cd\}$, $f_1(b) = \{ef\}$, we get the language

$$L(\Pi, f_1) = \{(cd)^n(ef)^n \mid n \geq 1\}.$$

3   Results on Systems with Unrestricted or All-Tape Programs

In [17] we have examined the power of genPCol automata with the permutation mapping, but it is also not difficult to see that in the general case, that is, for any class of mappings $\mathcal{F}$, we have the following.

1. $\mathcal{L}(\text{genPCol}, \mathcal{F}, \text{com-tape}(k)) \subseteq \mathcal{L}(\text{genPCol}, \mathcal{F}, *(k))$ and
   $\mathcal{L}(\text{genPCol}, \mathcal{F}, \text{all-tape}(k)) \subseteq \mathcal{L}(\text{genPCol}, \mathcal{F}, *(k))$ for $k \geq 1$; and
2. $\mathcal{L}(\text{genPCol}, \mathcal{F}, X(k)) \subseteq \mathcal{L}(\text{genPCol}, \mathcal{F}, X(k + 1))$ for $k \geq 1$, where $X \in \{\text{com-tape, all-tape}, *\}$.

The computational capacity of genPCol automata with input mapping f_{perm} was also investigated in [18]. It was shown that with unrestricted programs systems of capacity *one* generate any recursively enumerable language, that is,

$$\mathcal{L}_{perm}(\text{genPCol}, *(k)) = \mathcal{L}(\text{RE}), \ k \geq 1. \tag{1}$$

The same holds also for the class of mappings $\mathcal{F}_{\text{TRANS}}$.

Theorem 1

$$\mathcal{L}_{TRANS}(genPCol, *(k)) = \mathcal{L}(RE), \ k \geq 1.$$

Proof. The statement (1) is proved in Theorem 1 of [17] by showing how genPCol automata of capacity one can simulate the computations of so called register machines with input tape. Such machines characterize the class of recursively enumerable languages. They are similar to register machines introduced in [22], but instead of processing a numerical input from an input counter, they process an input string which is present on an input tape. To be able to read the input string, besides the usual instructions of the types $l_i : (\text{ADD}(r), l_j)$ (add 1 to register r and then go to the instruction with label l_j), $l_i : (\text{SUB}(r), l_j, l_k)$ (if the value of register r is not zero, subtract one from it and go to instruction l_j, otherwise leave it unchanged and go to l_k), and $l_h : \text{HALT}$ (stop the machine), they also have instructions of a different type

- $l_i : (\text{READ}(a), l_j)$ for a symbol $a \in \Sigma$ of the input alphabet Σ.

The purpose of these instructions is to read symbol a from the input tape, and then go to the instruction with label l_j. Such an instruction can be applied if the reading head scans a symbol $a \in \Sigma$ on the input tape, and the head moves to the next tape cell after the application of the instruction.

It is not difficult to see that register machines with input tape characterize the class of recursively enumerable languages, as they can simulate two-counter machines. Two-counter machines (see [14]) are Turing machines with an input tape (which is read only from left to right in one direction), and worktapes which are only used as counters (by moving the reading heads left or right without writing anything to the tape cells).

Let $L \subseteq \Sigma^*$ be an arbitrary recursively enumerable language and let Π be the genPCol automaton constructed in [17] with $L(\Pi, f_{perm}) = L$. The idea of the simulation is to have an object in the environment corresponding to the label of the instruction which is to be simulated next. The cells of the system "process" the instruction label in such a way that the necessary modifications of the configuration are implemented, and the label of the next instruction is sent to the environment. By observing the components which are responsible for the simulation of the tape reading instructions, we may notice that there is one simulating component constructed for each such instruction $l_i : (\text{READ}(a), l_j)$ with label l_i

$$P_{l_i} = \{\langle e \leftrightarrow l_i \rangle, \ \langle l_i \xrightarrow{T} a \rangle, \ \langle a \rightarrow l_j \rangle, \ \langle l_j \leftrightarrow e \rangle\}.$$

These programs can be applied when l_i appears in the environment. They read an input symbol a while exchanging l_i for l_j in the environment. Notice that the actual "reading" of the input symbol is realized by the tape program $\langle l_i \xrightarrow{T} a \rangle$, and note also, that the system is constructed in such a way that at most one such program might be applied in any computational step. This means, that the set of input multisets of Π correspond to the singleton multisets consisting of the symbols of the input alphabet of Π, that is, $in(\Pi) = \{a \in \mathcal{M}(\Sigma) \mid a \in \Sigma\}$. Thus, if we define $f_1 \in \mathcal{F}_{\mathrm{TRANS}}$ as $f_1 : in(\Pi) \to 2^{\Sigma^*}$ with $f_1(a) = \{a\}$ for any $a \in \Sigma$, then we have $L = L(\Pi, f_{perm}) = L(\Pi, f_1)$. This implies that $L \in \mathcal{L}_{TRANS}(\mathrm{genPCol}, *(1))$, and since $\mathcal{L}(\mathrm{genPCol}, \mathcal{F}, *(k)) \subseteq \mathcal{L}(\mathrm{genPCol}, \mathcal{F}, *(k + 1))$ for $k \geq 1$, our statement holds.

A similar result holds for all-tape systems with capacity at least two. From [17] we have that $\mathcal{L}_{perm}(\mathrm{genPCol}, \text{all-tape}(k)) = \mathcal{L}(\mathrm{RE})$ for $k \geq 2$, and we can show the same for systems with input mappings from $\mathcal{F}_{\mathrm{TRANS}}$.

Theorem 2

$$\mathcal{L}_{TRANS}(genPCol, \text{all-tape}(k)) = \mathcal{L}(RE) \text{ for } k \geq 2.$$

Proof. The proof is based on the construction of the proof of Theorem 1 above. For any recursively enumerable language $L \subseteq \Sigma^*$, we can obtain a genPCol automaton of capacity *two* accepting L with all-tape type of programs by simply putting one more e object into each cell, and adding the dummy tape rules $e \xrightarrow{T} e$ or $e \xleftrightarrow{T} e$ to every program. This way we get that $\mathcal{L}_{TRANS}(\mathrm{genPCol}, \text{all-tape}(2)) = \mathcal{L}(\mathrm{RE})$. Since $\mathcal{L}(\mathrm{genPCol}, \mathcal{F}, \text{all-tape}(k)) \subseteq \mathcal{L}(\mathrm{genPCol}, \mathcal{F}, \text{all-tape}(k + 1))$ for any $k \geq 1$, the statement also holds for any $k > 2$.

As we have seen above, systems of capacity at least *two* with all-tape programs are as powerful as Turing machines. For the case of capacity *one*, we are able to show that all regular languages, and also some non-regular ones, can be characterized not only with all-tape, but also with com-tape programs.

Theorem 3

$$\mathcal{L}(\mathrm{REG}) \subset \mathcal{L}_{\mathrm{TRANS}}(genPCol, \mathrm{X}(1)), \text{ for } \mathrm{X} \in \{\text{all-tape, com-tape}\}.$$

Proof. To prove that any regular language can be described by genPCol automata of capacity one having all-tape or com-tape type of programs, consider an arbitrary regular language L, and the finite automaton $M = (Q, \Sigma, q_0, A, \delta)$ with $L(M) = L$, where Q is the set of internal states, Σ is the input alphabet, $q_0 \in Q$ is the initial state, A is the set of final states, and $\delta : Q \times \Sigma \to Q$ is the transition function.

Consider the genPCol automaton

$$\Pi_1 = (V, e, \emptyset, (w_0, P), F)$$

with $V = \{(q, a, s) \mid \delta(q, a) = s\} \cup \{(q_0)\}$, $w_0 = (q_0)$ where q_0 is the initial state and the set of accepting configurations is $F = \{(\emptyset, (s, a, q)), (\emptyset, (q)) \mid q \in A\}$.

The set of all-tape programs is as follows

$$P = \{\langle (q_0) \xrightarrow{T} (q_0, a, s) \rangle \mid \delta(q_0, a) = s\} \cup$$
$$\{\langle (q, a, s) \xrightarrow{T} (s, b, r) \rangle \mid \delta(q, a) = s, \delta(s, b) = r\}.$$

The sets of accepted multiset sequences of Π_1 are

$$A(\Pi_1) = \{(q_0, a_1, q_1) \ldots (q_n, a_{n+1}, q_{n+1}) \mid q_0, q_1, \ldots, q_{n+1} \text{ is a sequence}$$
of states ending in an accepting configuration while reading
the string $a_1 \ldots a_{n+1}\}.$

Now, if we define $f_1 : in(\Pi) \to 2^{\Sigma^*}$ by $f_1(q, a, s) = \{a\}$, then we have $f_1 \in \mathcal{F}_{\text{TRANS}}$ and $L(\Pi_1, f_1) = L(M) = L$.

For the case of com-tape programs, we construct the following system,

$$\Pi_2 = (V, e, (q_0), (e, P), F)$$

with $V = \{(q, a, s) \mid \delta(q, a) = s\} \cup \{(q_0)\}$, where q_0 is the initial state and the set of accepting configurations is $F = \{((s, a, q), u), ((q), u) \mid q \in A\}$.

The set of com-tape programs is as follows

$$P = \{\langle e \to (q, a, s) \rangle, \langle (s, b, r) \xleftrightarrow{T} (q, a, s), \langle (q_0, a, s) \xleftrightarrow{T} (q_0) \rangle,$$
$$\langle (q_0) \to (q, a, s) \rangle \mid \delta(q, a) = s, \delta(q_0, a) = s, \delta(s, b) = r\}.$$

The sets of accepted multiset sequences of Π_2 are again

$$A(\Pi_2) = \{(q_0, a_1, q_1) \ldots (q_n, a_{n+1}, q_{n+1}) \mid q_0, q_1, \ldots, q_{n+1} \text{ is a sequence}$$
of states ending in an accepting configuration while reading
the string $a_1 \ldots a_{n+1}\}.$

Taking the same f_1 input mapping as above, we have $L(\Pi_2, f_1) = L(M) = L$. As Π_1 and Π_2 are systems with all-tape and com-tape programs, respectively, we have shown that genPCol automata of capacity one with both of these types of programs and input mappings from $\mathcal{F}_{\text{TRANS}}$ are able to characterize any regular language.

To see that the inclusion is strict, we recall the genPCol automaton from Theorem 2 of [17]

$$(\Sigma \cup \{e\}, e, w_E, (e, P_1), (e, P_2), (e, P_3), F),$$

with the sets of programs as

$$P_1 = \{\langle e \xrightarrow{\alpha} \$ \rangle, \langle \$ \xleftrightarrow{\beta} e \rangle\},$$
$$P_2 = \{\langle e \xrightarrow{\alpha} a \rangle, \langle a \xleftrightarrow{\beta} e \rangle, \langle e \xrightarrow{\alpha} b \rangle, \langle b \xleftrightarrow{\beta} \$ \rangle\},$$
$$P_3 = \{\langle e \xleftrightarrow{\beta} b \rangle, \langle b \xleftrightarrow{\beta} a \rangle, \langle a \xrightarrow{\alpha} b \rangle\},$$

where α, β can be empty, or they also can be T, that is, the rules are either non-tape rules or tape rules, and set of accepting configurations

$$F = \{(u, \$, \$, a) \mid u \in \mathcal{M}(\Sigma - \{a\}), \ u \neq \emptyset\}.$$

If we have com-tape programs, that is, if α is empty and $\beta = T$, then let the resulting system be denoted by Π_1. It accepts the sequences of multisets

$$A(\Pi_1) = \{(\$a)^n (\$b)^{n+1} (\$)^m \mid n \geq 1, m \geq 0\}.$$

Thus, if we take $f_1 : in(\Pi_1) \rightarrow 2^{\{c,d,e\}^*}$ with $f_1(\$a) = c$, $f_1(\$b) = d$, and $f_1(\$) = g$, then we obtain the language

$$L(\Pi_1, f_1) = \{c^n d^{n+1} g^m \mid n \geq 1, m \geq 0\},$$

which is not a regular language.

If $\alpha = \beta = T$, that is, if we have all-tape programs, then let the resulting system be denoted by Π_2. The accepted sequences of multisets are

$$A(\Pi_2) = \{(\$a)^{2n} (\$b)^{2n+1} (\$)^m \mid n \geq 1, m \geq 0\}.$$

In this case, taking the same f_1 as above, the accepted language is

$$L(\Pi_2, f_1) = \{c^{2n} d^{2n+1} g^m \mid n \geq 1, m \geq 0\}.$$

The accepted language is non-regular, in any of the cases, so the strictness of the inclusion in the statement follows.

The examination of the case of systems with com-tape programs is an interesting research direction which is still mostly open. What we are able to show, is the following. Similarly to systems with input mapping f_{perm}, languages that can be characterized (with any capacity) are included in the class r-1LOGSPACE, the class of languages characterized by so-called *restricted one-way logarithmic space* bounded Turing machines. (For more on this complexity class, see [8].)

Recall that a nondeterministic Turing machine with a one-way input tape is *restricted logarithmic space bounded*, if for every accepted input of length n, there is an accepting computation where the number of nonempty cells on the work-tape(s) is bounded by $O(\log d)$ where $d \leq n$ is the number of input tape cells already read, that is, the *distance* of the reading head from the left end of the one-way input tape. The class of languages accepted by such machines is denoted by r-1LOGSPACE.

In [9] it is shown that this class is strictly included in 1LOGSPACE, the class of languages accepted by Turing machines with a one-way input tape using logarithmic space on the worktapes.

4   P Automata and genPCol Automata

Now we are going to compare the power of genPCol automata and P automata. A P automaton is an antiport P system where, similarly to P colony automata, the accepted string language is defined by mapping the accepted multiset sequence (that is, the sequence of multisets entering the skin membrane during the steps of an accepting computation) to symbols of a given alphabet.

More formally, a *P automaton*, see [8]

$$\Pi = (V, \mu, w_1, \ldots, w_k, P_1, \ldots, P_k, F)$$

is a membrane system with object alphabet V, membrane structure μ, initial contents (multisets) of the ith region $w_i \in V^*$, $1 \leq i \leq k$, sets of antiport rules P_i, $1 \leq i \leq k$, and a set of accepting configurations F.

An antiport rule is of the form $(u, in; v, out)$, where $u, v \in \mathcal{M}(V)$ are finite multisets over V. If such a rule is applied in a region, then the objects of u enter from the parent region and, in the same step, objects of v leave to the parent region.

The configurations of the P automaton can be changed by transitions where the rules are applied in the sequential mode (*seq*) or in the non-deterministic maximally parallel mode (*par*). In the first case one rule is applied in each region in every step, in the second case as many rules are applied simultaneously in the regions at the same step as possible. Thus, a transition in the P automaton Π is $(v_1, \ldots, v_k) \in \delta_\Pi(u_0, u_1, \ldots, u_k)$, where δ_Π denotes the transition relation, $u_1, \ldots, u_k$ are the contents of the k regions, u_0 is the multiset entering the system from the environment, and $v_1, \ldots, v_k$, respectively, are the contents of the k regions after performing the transition.

In this way, there is a sequence of multisets which enter the system from the environment during the steps of its computation. If the computation is accepting, that is, if it reaches a configuration from F, the set of accepting configurations, then this multiset sequence is called an accepted multiset sequence, and denoted by $A(\Pi)$ for a P automaton Π.

The language accepted by a P automaton Π is defined with the use of input mappings in the same way as in the case of genPCol automata. Let Π be a P automaton, let $in(\Pi)$ the set of possible input multisets, and let $f : in(\Pi) \rightarrow 2^{\Sigma^*}$ be a mapping, such that $f(u) = \{\varepsilon\}$ if and only if u is the empty multiset. The accepted language is defined as

$$L_X(\Pi, f) = \{f(u_1) \ldots f(u_s) \in \Sigma^* \mid u_1 \ldots u_s \in A(\Pi)\}, \ X \in \{par, seq\}$$

where *par* and *seq* denotes maximally parallel or sequential application of the antiport rules, respectively.

The class of languages belonging to r-1LOGSPACE is important from the point of view of P automata, as the following results are known. If we denote by $\mathcal{L}_X(PA, f_{perm})$, $X \in \{par, seq\}$ the class of languages characterized by P automata with input mapping f_{perm} (using maximal parallel or sequential rule application), then we have from [13]

$$\mathcal{L}_X(PA, f_{perm}) \subset \text{r-1LOGSPACE}, \ X \in \{par, seq\}.$$

We also know from [13] that

$$\mathcal{L}_{perm}(\text{genPCol}, \text{com-tape}(k)) \subseteq \text{r-1LOGSPACE for any } k \geq 1,$$

and moreover,

$$\mathcal{L}_{perm}(\text{genPCol, com-tape}(2))\backslash\mathcal{L}_X(PA, f_{perm}) \neq \emptyset \ X \in \{par, seq\}.$$

Thus, the relationship of languages accepted by P automata and genPCol automata with com-tape rules using the mapping f_{perm} is still not clear. We only know that they are both contained in r-1LOGSPACE, and that genPCol automata can accept languages that P automata cannot.

Now we examine the case of mappings from $\mathcal{F}_{TRANS}$. We show that the class of languages that characterized by genPCol automata with com-tape rules is also included in r-1LOGSPACE.

Theorem 4

$$\mathcal{L}_{TRANS}(genPCol, com\text{-}tape(k)) \subseteq r\text{-}1LOGSPACE, \text{ for } k \geq 1.$$

Proof. We have shown in [17] that a similar inclusion holds for systems with permutation mappings. The idea is based on the proof in [18] where the same result was shown for capacity *two*. Consider the number of different configurations that a genPCol automaton can reach during its computations. The number of different possible states of the component cells is $(m^k)^l$ where we have an alphabet of cardinality m, and l cells having the capacity k.

To take into account also the different states of the environment, we need to count how many objects have been exported from the component cells, since all symbols different from e that are present in the environment during any configuration must have been exported from the cells with the use of communication rules. Since all communication rules are tape rules, the number of objects inside the multisets of the multiset sequence read by the system cannot be less than the number of non-e objects present in the environment.

Let us examine now the relationship of the length of the multiset sequence read and the corresponding string obtained by applying the input mapping to the multiset sequence. Since the cardinality of the read multisets is at most $l \cdot k$, the input mapping is from $\mathcal{F}_{TRANS}$, and each nonempty multiset is mapped to a nonempty string, the number of objects in the environment is at most $c_1 \cdot n$ where n is the length of the string obtained by the input mapping from the multiset sequence that is read so far, and $c_1 \in \mathbb{N}$ is an appropriate constant. Thus, after reading a string of length n, there can be at most $c_1 \cdot n$ non-e symbols in the environment, that is, the number of different states of the environment is at most $(c_1 \cdot n)^m$ where m is the cardinality of the object alphabet.

Summing up the number of different configurations possible, we can conclude that after reading a string of length n, the genPCol automaton can be in at most $(m^k)^l \cdot (c_1 \cdot n)^m$ different configurations, where m is the size of the object alphabet, k is the capacity, l is the number of cells of the system, and $c_1 \in \mathbb{N}$ is an appropriate constant.

Such a system can be simulated by a Turing machine in restricted logarithmic space by creating a Turing machine program that is able to store the encodings of the genPCol automaton configurations on the worktapes, and based on the currently stored configuration, is able to simulate its computation by computing and storing the next configuration and reading the necessary input symbols from the input tape.

As the number of different configurations that are needed to be stored after reading n symbols of the input string is $(m^k)^l \cdot (c_1 \cdot n)^m = c_2 \cdot n^m$, we can encode a configuration on the worktapes in such a way that it uses $c_3 \cdot \log(c_2 \cdot n^m)$ tape cells for some constants $c_2, c_3 \in \mathbb{N}$, that is, the corresponding language has restricted logarithmic space complexity.

As P automata with sequential rule application and mappings from $\mathcal{F}_{TRANS}$ characterize exactly the class r-1LOGSPACE (see [9]), we also have the following.

Corollary 1

$$\mathcal{L}_{TRANS}(genPCol, com\text{-}tape(k)) \subseteq \mathcal{L}_{seq}(PA, \mathcal{F}_{TRANS}), \ k \geq 1.$$

The precise relationship of the power of sequential P automata and genPCol automata with $\mathcal{F}_{TRANS}$, however, remains an open problem.

5   Conclusions

We have investigated genPCol automata with input mappings from the class $\mathcal{F}_{TRANS}$, the class of mappings between multisets and strings that can be realized through the application of finite transducers to the string representations of multisets.

We have shown that using unrestricted programs, these automata characterize the class of recursively enumerable languages. The same holds for systems with all-tape programs, having capacity at least *two*. The situation is more complicated in the case of systems with com-tape programs, we have shown that they characterize language classes which are closely related to those characterized by variants of P automata.

Besides clarifying the power of com-tape programs, the effect of using *checking rules*, as defined in [20] for P colonies, is also an interesting topic for further investigations. The study of systems with other classes of input mappings would be an interesting research topic as well.

References

1. Cienciala, L., Ciencialová, L., Csuhaj-Varjú, E., Vaszil, G.: PCol automata: recognizing strings with P colonies. In: Martínez Del Amor, M.A., Păun, G., Pérez Hurtado, I., Riscos Nuñez, A. (eds.) Eighth Brainstorming Week on Membrane Computing, Sevilla, 1–5 February 2010, pp. 65–76. Fénix Editora (2010)
2. Cienciala, L., Ciencialová, L.: P colonies and their extensions. In: Kelemen, J., Kelemenová, A. (eds.) Computation, Cooperation, and Life. LNCS, vol. 6610, pp. 158–169. Springer, Heidelberg (2011). https://doi.org/10.1007/978-3-642-20000-7_13

3. Cienciala, L., Ciencialová, L., Kelemenová, A.: On the number of agents in P colonies. In: Eleftherakis, G., Kefalas, P., Păun, G., Rozenberg, G., Salomaa, A. (eds.) WMC 2007. LNCS, vol. 4860, pp. 193–208. Springer, Heidelberg (2007). https://doi.org/10.1007/978-3-540-77312-2_12

4. Cienciala, L., Ciencialová, L., Kelemenová, A.: Homogeneous P colonies. Comput. Inform. **27**(3+), 481–496 (2008)

5. Ciencialová, L., Cienciala, L.: Variations on the theme: P colonies. In: Kolăr, D., Meduna, A. (eds.) Proceedings of the 1st International Workshop on Formal Models, pp. 27–34, Ostrava (2006)

6. Ciencialová, L., Csuhaj-Varjú, E., Kelemenová, A., Vaszil, G.: Variants of P colonies with very simple cell structure. Int. J. Comput. Commun. Control **4**(3), 224–233 (2009)

7. Csuhaj-Varjú, E., Dassow, J., Kelemen, J., Păun, G.: Grammar Systems - A Grammatical Approach to Distribution and Cooperation. Gordon and Breach, London (1994)

8. Csuhaj-Varjú, E., Oswald, M., Vaszil, G.: P automata. In: Paun, G., Rozenberg, G., Salomaa, A. (eds.) The Oxford Handbook of Membrane Computing. Oxford University Press, Inc. (2010)

9. Csuhaj-Varjú, E., Ibarra, O.H., Vaszil, G.: On the computational complexity of P automata. In: Ferretti, C., Mauri, G., Zandron, C. (eds.) DNA 2004. LNCS, vol. 3384, pp. 76–89. Springer, Heidelberg (2005). https://doi.org/10.1007/11493785_7

10. Csuhaj-Varjú, E., Kelemen, J., Kelemenová, A.: Computing with cells in environment: P colonies. Mult.-Valued Log. Soft Comput. **12**(3–4), 201–215 (2006)

11. Csuhaj-Varjú, E., Margenstern, M., Vaszil, G.: P colonies with a bounded number of cells and programs. In: Hoogeboom, H.J., Păun, G., Rozenberg, G., Salomaa, A. (eds.) WMC 2006. LNCS, vol. 4361, pp. 352–366. Springer, Heidelberg (2006). https://doi.org/10.1007/11963516_22

12. Csuhaj-Varjú, E., Vaszil, G.: P automata or purely communicating accepting P systems. In: Păun, G., Rozenberg, G., Salomaa, A., Zandron, C. (eds.) WMC 2002. LNCS, vol. 2597, pp. 219–233. Springer, Heidelberg (2003). https://doi.org/10.1007/3-540-36490-0_14

13. Csuhaj-Varjú, E., Vaszil, G.: P automata with restricted power. Int. J. Found. Comput. Sci. **25**(4), 391–408 (2014)

14. Fischer, P.: Turing machines with restricted memory access. Inf. Control **9**, 231–236 (1966)

15. Freund, R., Oswald, M.: P colonies working in the maximally parallel and in the sequential mode. In: Zaharie, D., Petcu, D., Negru, V., Jebelean, T., Ciobanu, G., Cicortas, A., Abraham, A., Paprzycki, M. (eds.) Seventh International Symposium on Symbolic and Numeric Algorithms for Scientific Computing (SYNASC 2005), Timisoara, Romania, 25–29 September 2005, pp. 419–426. IEEE Computer Society (2005)

16. Freund, R., Oswald, M.: P colonies and prescribed teams. Int. J. Comput. Math. **83**(7), 569–592 (2006)

17. Kántor, K., Vaszil, G.: On the class of languages characterized by generalized P colony automata. Theoret. Comput. Sci. (to appear)

18. Kántor, K., Vaszil, G.: Generalized P colony automata. J. Autom. Lang. Comb. **19**(1–4), 145–156 (2014)

19. Kelemen, J., Kelemenová, A.: A grammar-theoretic treatment of multiagent systems. Cybern. Syst. **23**, 621–633 (1992)

20. Kelemen, J., Kelemenová, A., Păun, G.: Preview of P colonies: a biochemically inspired computing model. In: Workshop and Tutorial Proceedings, Ninth International Conference on the Simulation and Synthesis of Living Systems, ALIFE IX, Boston, Massachusetts, pp. 82–86 (2004)
21. Kelemenová, A.: P colonies. In: Paun, G., Rozenberg, G., Salomaa, A. (eds.) The Oxford Handbook of Membrane Computing, pp. 584–593. Oxford University Press, Inc. (2010)
22. Minsky, M.: Computation: Finite and Infinite Machines. Prentice Hall, Upper Saddle River (1967)
23. Păun, A., Păun, G.: The power of communication: P systems with symport/antiport. New Gener. Comput. **20**(3), 295–306 (2002)

Modelling and Validating an Engineering Application in Kernel P Systems

Raluca Lefticaru[1,2(✉)], Mehmet Emin Bakir[3], Savas Konur[1], Mike Stannett[3], and Florentin Ipate[2]

[1] School of Electrical Engineering and Computer Science, University of Bradford, Bradford, West Yorkshire BD7 1DP, UK
{r.lefticaru,s.konur}@bradford.ac.uk
[2] Department of Computer Science, University of Bucharest, Str. Academiei nr. 14, 010014 Bucharest, Romania
florentin.ipate@ifsoft.ro
[3] Department of Computer Science, The University of Sheffield, Regent Court, 211 Portobello, Sheffield S1 4DP, UK
{mebakir1,m.stannett}@sheffield.ac.uk

Abstract. This paper illustrates how kernel P systems (*kP systems*) can be used for modelling and validating an engineering application, in this case a cruise control system of an electric bike. The validity of the system is demonstrated via formal verification, carried out using the kPWORKBENCH tool. Furthermore, we show how the kernel P system model can be tested using automata and X-machine based techniques.

Keywords: Membrane computing · Kernel P systems
Cruise control · Electric bike · Bicycle · Verification · Testing

1 Introduction

Nature inspired computational approaches have been the focus of research for several decades. Membrane computing [21] is one of these paradigms that has recently been through significant developments and achievements. For the most up to date results, we refer the reader to [22]. The main computational models are called *P systems*, inspired by the functioning and structure of the living cells.

In recent years, various types or classes of P systems have been introduced and applied to different problems. While these variants provide more flexibility in modelling, this has inevitably resulted in a large pool of P system variants, which do not have a coherent integrating view.

Kernel P (kP) systems have been introduced to unify many variants of P system models, and combine a blend of various P system features and concepts, including (i) complex guards attached to rules, (ii) flexible ways to specify the system structure and dynamically change it and (iii) various execution strategies for rules and compartments.

© Springer International Publishing AG 2018
M. Gheorghe et al. (Eds.): CMC 2017, LNCS 10725, pp. 183–195, 2018.
https://doi.org/10.1007/978-3-319-73359-3_12

Kernel P systems are supported by a software suite, called kPWORKBENCH [5]. The platform integrates several tools to simulate and verify kP systems models written in a modelling language, called *kP-Lingua*, capable of mapping the kernel P system specification into a machine readable representation.

The usability and efficiency of kP systems have been illustrated by a number of representative case studies, ranging from systems and synthetic biology, e.g. quorum sensing [18], genetic Boolean gates [23] and synthetic pulse generators [1], to some classical computational problems, e.g. sorting [6], broadcasting [10] and subset sum [5].

Here, as an engineering application, we focus on an *e-bike cruise control system*. An *e-bike* (electric bicycle) is a bicycle that uses an integrated rechargeable battery and an electric motor, which provides propulsion. A *cruise control* is an advanced driver-assistance system technology that automatically regulates the speed of a transportation system (such as motor vehicle or electric bicycle) set by the user. From a system design perspective, the validation of the operational safety of any component/feature is very crucial [24].

In this paper, we will model an e-bike cruise control system using kernel P systems and verify its behaviour using the kPWORKBENCH verification environment. We also show how the kernel P system model can be tested using automata and X-machine based techniques.

This paper is structured as follows: Sect. 2 introduces the preliminaries and theoretical background. Section 3 presents our modelling approach using kernel P systems, while Sects. 4 and 5 present the verification and testing approaches. Finally, conclusions and further work are presented in Sect. 6.

2   Background

This section briefly presents the cruise control system, then gives the basic definitions regarding kernel P systems [9], a presentation of the kPWORKBENCH software suite, and previous testing approaches for membrane systems.

2.1   Cruise Control System for an Electric Bicycle

In this paper, we focus on an e-bike cruise control system. By controlling the speed of the e-bike (or other transportation system), this feature makes the driving experience easier as the user does not have to use the accelerator or brake. For an e-bike system a cruise control feature also assists the user by improving the control of the journey time and controlling the level of exercise undertaken.

From a system design point of view, however, adding a new feature brings in new challenges for the operational safety of the new functionality [24]. Thus validation of additional functionalities of any new technology and their impact on other components of an existing system is important. This will be our focus in this paper. The behaviour of the e-bike cruise control considered in this paper is shown in Fig. 1.

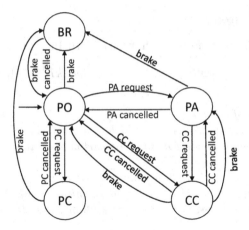

Fig. 1. The state machine representing the behaviour of the e-bike cruise control system considered in this paper. The system works as follows:

- At any time, the system can be at any of the following states:
  (i) pedal bike (Pedal Only – PO, for short)
  (ii) pedal bike with power assistance (Pedal Assist – PA)
  (iii) maintain constant speed (Cruise Control – CC)
  (iv) pedal to charge battery (Pedal Charge – PC)
  (v) brake (Brake – BR).
- CC can be activated from PO or PA.
- If CC is cancelled, the system returns to the state from where it was activated i.e., PO or PA, respectively.
- Pedal assist can be requested when the user is pedalling.
- Pedal charge can be requested when the user is pedalling.
- When the user brakes from CC mode, the system returns to PA/PO before going to BR (if brake is still held).
- BR can be reached from PO, PA or PC.
- If the user releases the brake, the system goes to PO, no matter which was the state before Brake. This happens because from the Brake state, after releasing the brake lever, one can only start to pedal and enter in PO mode. In order to enter in PA mode, the user must first start to pedal and then make a pedal assist request.

In a previous paper [20], a similar e-bike case study has been used to illustrate an integrated approach, combining software engineering methodologies (verification and model-based testing) with notations and methods from system engineering. Although the two state machines corresponding to the e-bike system (from current paper and from [20]) have many similarities, the current approach adopts kernel P systems as modelling formalism and further illustrates how these can be used for simulating and validating an engineering application.

2.2   Kernel P Systems

We first begin recalling the formal definition of kernel P systems (or kP systems).

Definition 1. *A kP system of degree n is a tuple $k\Pi = (A, \mu, C_1, \ldots, C_n, i_0)$, where*

- *A is a finite set of elements called objects;*
- *μ defines the membrane structure, which is a graph, (V, E), where V is a set of vertices representing components (compartments), and E is a set of edges, i.e., links between components;*
- *$C_i = (t_i, w_{i,0})$, $1 \le i \le n$, is a compartment of the system consisting of a compartment type, t_i, from a set T and an initial multiset, $w_{i,0}$ over A; the type $t_i = (R_i, \rho_i)$ consists of a set of evolution rules, R_i, and an execution strategy, ρ_i;*
- *i_0 is the output compartment where the result is obtained.*

Kernel P systems have features inspired by object-oriented programming: one *compartment type* can have one or more *instances*. These instances share the same set of rules and execution strategies (so will deliver the same functionality), but they may contain different multisets of objects and different neighbours according to the graph relation specified by (V, E). Within the kP systems framework, the following types of evolution rules have been considered so far:

- *rewriting and communication* rule: $x \longrightarrow y\{g\}$, where $x \in A^+$ and y represents a multiset of objects over A^* with potential different compartment type targets (each symbol from the right side of the rule can be sent to a different compartment, specified by its type; if multiple compartments of the same type are linked to the current compartment, then one is randomly chosen to be the target). Unlike cell-like P systems, the targets in kP systems indicate only the types of compartments to which the objects will be sent, not particular instances. Also, for kP systems, complex *guards* can be represented, using multisets over A with relational and Boolean operators [9].
- *structure changing* rules: membrane division, membrane dissolution, link creation and link destruction rules, which all may also incorporate complex guards and that are covered in detail in [9].

In addition to its evolution rules, each compartment type in a kP system has an associated *execution strategy*. The rules corresponding to a compartment can be grouped in blocks, each having one of the following strategies:

- *sequential*: if the current rule is applicable, then it is executed, advancing towards the next rule/block of rules; otherwise, the execution terminates;
- *choice*: a non-deterministic choice within a set of rules. One and only one applicable rule will be executed if such a rule exists, otherwise the whole block is simply skipped;
- *arbitrary*: the rules from the block can be executed zero or more times by non-deterministically choosing any of the applicable rules;
- *maximal parallel*: the classic execution mode used in membrane computing.

These execution strategies and the fact that in any compartment several blocks with different strategies can be composed and executed offer a lot of flexibility to the kP system designer, similarly to procedural programming.

2.3 kPWORKBENCH

Kernel P systems are supported by an integrated software suite, kPWORKBENCH [5], which employs a set of simulation and formal verification tools and methods that permit simulating and verifying kP system models, written in kP-Lingua.

The verification component of kPWORKBENCH checks the correctness of kP system models by exhaustively analysing all possible behaviours. In order to facilitate the specification of system requirements, kPWORKBENCH features a property language, called *kP-Queries*, which comprises a list of property patterns written as natural language statements. The properties expressed in *kP-Queries* are verified using the SPIN [13] and NuSMV [3] model checkers after being translated into corresponding *Linear Temporal Logic (LTL)* and *Computation Tree Logic (CTL)* syntax.

The simulation component features a native simulator [2,19], which allows the users to simulate kP system models efficiently. In addition, kPWORKBENCH integrates the FLAME simulator [4,23], a general purpose large scale agent based simulation environment, based on a method that allows users to express kP systems as a set of communicating X-machines [11].

2.4 Kernel P Systems Testing

When testing a kP system model, an automata model needs to be constructed first, based on the computation tree of the kP system. As, in general, the computation tree may be infinite and cannot be modelled by a finite automaton, an approximation of the tree is used. This approximation is obtained by limiting the length of any computation to an upper bound k and considering only computations up to k transitions in length. This approximation is then used to construct a deterministic finite cover automaton (DFCA) of the model [6–8].

However, in the case of the e-bike, this can be naturally modelled by a state-based formalism and, furthermore, the kP system was derived from such a model (Fig. 1). Therefore one can use this state-based model in testing. It can be observed, however, that the model is not exactly a finite automaton since an additional variable is used to decide to which state (PO or PA) the e-bike returns when the Cruise Control facility is cancelled[1]. Such a formalism, that

---

[1] One could build a Finite State Automaton with two extra states (CCPO and CCPA, that allow to come back to PO and PA, respectively, when CC facility is cancelled), plus other necessary transitions from/to these states, in order to simulate the same behaviour of the e-bike model. However, the corresponding X-machine model, having one memory variable instead of the 2 extra states, has the advantage of keeping the control structure simpler; having less states it's easier to be read and the states correspond exactly to the device modes.

combines a finite state machine like control with data structures is the *stream X-machine* [12].

A stream X-machine (SXM) is like a finite automaton in which the transitions are labelled by partial functions (or, more generally, relations) instead of mere symbols. Formally,

Definition 2. *A* stream X-Machine *(abbreviated* SXM*) is a tuple*

$$Z = (\Sigma, \Gamma, Q, M, \Phi, F, q_0, m_0),$$

where:

- Σ *is the finite* input alphabet.
- Γ *is the finite* output alphabet.
- Q *is the finite set of* states.
- M *is a (possibly infinite) set called* memory.
- Φ *is a finite set of distinct* processing functions; *a processing function is a non-empty (partial) function of type* $M \times \Sigma \longrightarrow \Gamma \times M$.
- F *is the (partial)* next-state function, $F : Q \times \Phi \longrightarrow Q$.
- $q_0 \in Q$ *is the initial state.*
- $m_0 \in M$ *is the initial memory value.*

Intuitively, an SXM Z can be thought as a finite automaton with the arcs labelled by functions from the set Φ. The automaton $A_Z = (\Phi, Q, F, q_0)$ over the alphabet Φ is called *the associated finite automaton* (abbreviated *associated FA*) of Z and is usually described by a state-transition diagram. As with any automaton, the function F may be extended to take sequences from Φ^*, to form the function $F^* : Q \times \Phi^* \longrightarrow Q$. We will write $L_{A_Z}(q) = \{p \in \Phi^* \mid (q, p) \in dom\ F^*\}$ to denote the set of paths that can be traced out of state q. When $q = q_0$, this will be called the *language accepted* by Z and denoted L_{A_Z}.

3   KP Model for e-bike Cruise Control

In [20], the e-bike cruise control system has been manually coded into different formal models for verification and model-based testing, which is a very challenging and time consuming process. Also, any change in the system model requires the modification of all formal models. This issue, the direct coding from the system description, has been highlighted in various engineering applications, e.g. real-time systems [15], safety critical systems [16], pervasive systems [17].

Using kernel P systems as modelling language provides some practical advantages. Namely, several verification and simulation methods integrated into kPWORKBENCH are readily available; hence several complementary analyses can be performed, which allows more in-depth analysis of the system. Since kPWORKBENCH automatically translates a kP system model written in kP-Lingua into the corresponding formal syntax, users do not need to carry out manual encoding to access the tools. In addition, kP-Lingua has a simple language, which makes it much easier to express system models.

In this section we present a kP system model for the cruise control system described as a state machine in Fig. 1. The corresponding kP system has two compartment types: (1) *tEvent*, in charge of generating all possible events (or inputs from the user) and sending them to *tEBike*; (2) *tEBike*, receiving these events and processing them according to state machine rules. The *tEBike* will always contain only one element of the set $\{PO, CC, PC, PA, BR\}$ representing the current state of the machine, and might have other elements such as $\{pa, pc, cc, br, pac, pcc, ccc, brc\}$ representing the event received from *tEvent* or $\{po2cc, pa2cc\}$ as objects recording which was the previous state before CC. The event names are lower case always, compared to their upper case states counterparts, e.g. *pa*, *cc* for pedal assist, cruise control request, while *brc*, *pcc* represent brake cancelled or pedal charge cancelled.

Figure 2 presents the kP-Lingua source code corresponding to our model of e-bike cruise control. The execution strategy is *choice* for both compartment

```
type tEvent{                          PC, br -> BR.
 choice{                              PC, cc -> PC.
   g -> g, br(tEBike).                PC, pa -> PC.
   g -> g, cc(tEBike).                PC, pc -> PC.
   g -> g, pa(tEBike).                PC, brc -> PC.
   g -> g, pc(tEBike).                PC, ccc -> PC.
   g -> g, brc(tEBike).               PC, pac -> PC.
   g -> g, ccc(tEBike).               PC, pcc -> PO.
   g -> g, pac(tEBike).
   g -> g, pcc(tEBike).               CC, br, pa2cc -> PA.
   }                                  CC, br, po2cc -> PO.
 }                                    CC, cc -> CC.
                                      CC, pa -> CC.
 type tEBike{                         CC, pc -> CC.
  choice{                             CC, brc -> CC.
  PO, br -> BR.                       CC, ccc, po2cc -> PO.
  PO, cc -> CC, po2cc.                CC, ccc, pa2cc -> PA.
  PO, pa -> PA.                       CC, pac -> CC.
  PO, pc -> PC.                       CC, pcc -> CC.
  PO, brc -> PO.
  PO, ccc -> PO.                      BR, br -> BR.
  PO, pac -> PO.                      BR, cc -> BR.
  PO, pcc -> PO.                      BR, pa -> BR.
                                      BR, pc -> BR.
  PA, br -> BR.                       BR, brc -> PO.
  PA, cc -> CC, pa2cc.                BR, ccc -> BR.
  PA, pa -> PA.                       BR, pac -> BR.
  PA, pc -> PA.                       BR, pcc -> BR.
  PA, brc -> PA.                       }
  PA, ccc -> PA.                      }
  PA, pac -> PO.                      cEvent {g} (tEvent).
  PA, pcc -> PA.                      cEBike {PO} (tEBike).
                                      cEvent - cEBike.
```

Fig. 2. kP-Lingua code for the e-bike cruise control system

types, but in this particular case the maximal parallelism strategy would have provided the same functionality. The computation is infinite and due to the non-determinism of the model we would like to check if some properties hold for any possible computation. The kP-Lingua model and verification files discussed here are available for download on the kPWORKBENCH website[2].

4   Verification

In this section, we check various properties of the e-bike model to verify that the model satisfies the system requirements using the verification component of kPWORKBENCH. The tool translates the kP-Lingua model of the e-bike system into the NuSMV modelling language. Similarly, the properties written in kP-Queries (using natural language statements) are translated into the NuSMV property specification language (the translation can be in LTL or CTL).

Table 1 shows the verification results of the e-bike model properties. The first column shows the property id; the second column describes the properties informally; the third column shows the formal properties expressed in kP-Queries (which are then translated into LTL and CTL in NuSMV syntax); and the last column illustrates the verification result.

The first property checks whether BR is reachable from any state after brake requested. The property holds because BR can be activated directly from PO, PA and PC, and there are paths from CC to BR, too, over PO and PA. The second property verifies that after BR is activated, the system will either stay in BR or move to PO. As expected, this property also holds, because BR cannot request any states other than itself or PO. The properties from 3 to 8 test different transitions from/to the CC state. For example, properties 4 and 5 verify that after CC is cancelled, the system will return to the state from which it was activated, i.e., PO or PA. Properties 3–8 all hold, except for property 8, which is false. This property checks the existence of states (other than PO and PA) from which we may have direct access to the CC state. However, only PO and PA can access CC, so the property does not hold. The remaining properties, 9–12, check the existence/absence of transitions from/to PC. Again, all properties hold except property 11. This property asserts that PC can be activated from a state other than PO, whereas in fact only PO can activate PC. Therefore, it does not hold. The verified properties validate that the e-bike system works as desired.

5   Testing

In this section we show how the kernel P system model from Sect. 3 can be tested using automata and X-machine based techniques.

For the kP system described in Sect. 3, the associated stream X-machine (SXM) will be defined as follows:

---

[2] http://kpworkbench.org/index.php/case-studies.

Table 1. Verified properties

#	Description	kP-queries	Res.
1	Whenever brake is requested, it will eventually be activated	CTL: cEBike.br > 0 **followed-by** cEBike.BR > 0	T
2	BR either stays same or it can activate only PO	LTL: **always** ((cEBike.BR > 0) **implies** (**next** (cEBike.PO > 0 **or** cEBike.BR > 0)))	T
3	The user should be able to request/activate CC only from PO or PA	LTL: **never** ((cEBike.BR > 0 **or** cEBike.PC > 0) **and** (**next** (cEBike.CC > 0)))	T
4	If CC activated from PO, then the system will return to PO after CC cancel or brake request	LTL: **always** ((cEBike.CC > 0 **and** cEBike.po2cc > 0) **and** (cEBike.ccc > 0 **or** cEBike.br > 0) **implies** (**next**(cEBike.PO > 0)))	T
5	If CC activated from PA, then the system will return to PA after CC cancel or brake request	LTL: **always** ((cEBike.CC > 0 **and** cEBike.pa2cc > 0) **and** (cEBike.ccc > 0 **or** cEBike.br > 0) **implies** (**next**(cEBike.PA > 0)))	T
6	When brake is requested in CC the system returns to PA or PO	LTL: **always** ((cEBike.CC > 0 **and** cEBike.br > 0) **implies** (cEBike.BR > 0 **preceded-by** (cEBike.PO > 0 **or** cEBike.PA > 0)))	T
7	The system should not transit directly from CC to brake directly	LTL: **never** ((cEBike.CC > 0 **and** cEBike.br > 0) **and** (**next** (cEBike.BR > 0)))	T
8	CC can be activated from a state other than PO or PA	CTL: (**not** (cEBike.PO > 0 **or** cEBike.PA > 0)) **until** cEBike.CC > 0	F
9	PA and PC cannot directly activate each other	LTL: **never** ((cEBike.PA > 0 **and** (**next** (cEBike.PC > 0))) **or** (cEBike.PC > 0 **and** (**next** (cEBike.PO > 0))))	T
10	CC and PC cannot directly activate each other	LTL: **never** ((cEBike.CC > 0 **and** (**next** (cEBike.PC > 0))) **or** (cEBike.PC > 0 **and** (**next** (cEBike.CC > 0))))	T
11	PC can be activated from a state other than PO	CTL: (**not** (cEBike.PO > 0)) **until** cEBike.PC > 0	F
12	PC can activate PC, PO or BR only	LTL: **always** (cEBike.PC > 0 **implies** (**next** (((((cEBike.PC > 0) **or** (cEBike.PO > 0)) **or** (cEBike.BR > 0)))))	T

- the set of states is $Q = \{PO, PA, PC, CC, BR\}$;
- the set of inputs is $\Sigma = \{pa, cc, pc, br, brc, pac, ccc, pcc\}$
- there are no explicit outputs; in order to make the transition observable we consider the output to be the next state for each transition, so the set of outputs is the same as the set of states, $\Gamma = Q$.
- the memory is $M = \{m\}$, $m \in \{\lambda, pa2cc, po2cc\}$ (one memory variable m, where λ represents an undefined value, and $pa2cc, po2cc$ are used to record the last state before enabling the CC feature);
- each processing function is determined by a rewriting rule in $tEBike$, e.g., the $PO, pa \rightarrow PA$ rule induces the processing function $\phi_{PO,pa,PA}$ defined by $\phi_{PO,pa,PA}(m, pa) = (PA, m)$, $m \in M$; the $PO, cc \rightarrow CC, po2cc$ rule induces processing function $\phi_{PO,cc,CC}(m, cc) = (CC, po2cc)$, $m \in M$; the $CC, ccc, po2cc \rightarrow PO$ rule induces processing function $\phi_{CC,ccc,PO}(po2cc, ccc)$ $= (PO, \lambda)$;
- the next-state function is defined by $F(q, \phi_{q,\sigma,q'}) = q'$ for every $q, q' \in Q$, $\sigma \in \Sigma$ such that $\phi_{q,\sigma,q'} \in \Phi$;
- the initial state is $q_0 = PO$;
- the initial memory is $m_0 = \lambda$.

Now, suppose we want to test an implementation of a system specified as an SXM. The testing techniques presented in [12, 14] generate test suites that guarantee that the implementation conforms to the model, provided that some *design for test* conditions are satisfied and the tester is able to estimate the maximum number of states the implementation may have. We denote by β the difference between this estimated upper bound on the number of states of the implementation under test and the number of states of the model.

In order to generate a test suite from a SXM, two set of paths from the associated automaton will have to be constructed: a state cover and a characterisation set.

A *transition cover* of a SXM Z is a set $S \subseteq \Phi^*$ such that for every state $q \in Q$ of Z there is $p \in S$ such that p reaches state q, i.e. $F^*(q_0, p) = q$. In our example, the empty sequence λ reaches the initial state PO, $\phi_{PO,pa,PA}$ reaches PA, $\phi_{PO,pc,PC}$ reaches PC, $\phi_{PO,cc,CC}$ reaches CC and $\phi_{PO,br,BR}$ reaches BR, thus $S = \{\lambda, \phi_{PO,pa,PA}, \phi_{PO,pc,PC}, \phi_{PO,cc,CC}, \phi_{PO,br,BR}\}$ is a state cover of Z.

A *characterization set* of a SXM Z is a set $W \subseteq \Phi^*$ such that for every two distinct states $q, q' \in Q$ there is $p \in W$ such that p distinguishes between q and q', i.e. $F^*(q, p)$ is defined and $F^*(q', p)$ is not defined or $F^*(q, p)$ is not defined and $F^*(q', p)$ is defined. In our example, $\phi_{PO,br,BR}$ distinguishes PO from any other state of Z, $\phi_{PA,br,BR}$ distinguishes PA from any other state of Z, $\phi_{PC,br,BR}$ distinguishes PC from any other state of Z and $\phi_{CC,br,PO}$ distinguishes CC from any other state of Z, so $W = \{\phi_{PO,br,BR}, \phi_{PA,br,BR}, \phi_{PC,br,BR}, \phi_{CC,br,PO}\}$ is a characterization set of Z. Once a transition cover and a characterization set have been constructed, the test suite is given by the formula

$$S(\Phi^0 \cup \Phi^1 \cup \cdots \cup \Phi^{\beta+1})W,$$

where S is a transition cover, W is a characterization set, and (as already noted) β denotes the difference between the estimated maximum number of states of the implementation under test and the number of states of the model.

In order for the successful application of the test suite to guarantee the conformance of the implementation to the model, the SXM model has to satisfy two design for test conditions: output-distinguishability and input-completeness. The set of processing functions Φ is called *output-distinguishable* if, for every two processing functions $\phi_1, \phi_2 \in \Phi$, if there exists $m, m_1, m_2 \in M$, $\sigma \in \Sigma$, $\gamma \in \Gamma$ such that $\phi_1(m, \sigma) = (\gamma, m_1)$ and $\phi_2(m, \sigma) = (\gamma, m_2)$ then $\phi_1 = \phi_2$. In our example, Φ is not output-distinguishable since, for example, both $\phi_{PO,br,BR}$ and $\phi_{PA,br,BR}$ produce the output BR while processing any memory value m and input br. The set Φ can be transformed into one that is output-distinguishable by suitably augmenting the output alphabet. In our running example we may enlarge Γ by considering as output for each transition a pair formed by both the current and the next state of the transition.

The set of processing functions Φ is called input-complete if, for every processing function $\phi \in \Phi$ and every memory $m \in M$, there exists an input symbol $\sigma \in \Sigma$ such that (m, σ) is in the domain of ϕ. In our running example, Φ is not input-complete since, for example, for $\phi_{CC,br,PA} \in \Phi$ and $po2cc \in M$, there is no input $\sigma \in \Sigma$ such that $(po2cc, \sigma)$ is in the domain of $\phi_{CC,br,PA}$. The set Φ can be transformed into one that is input-complete by suitably augmenting the input alphabet and the processing functions. In our running example, $\phi_{CC,br,PA}$ can be augmented by introducing an extra input symbol, say σ_e, and setting $\phi_{CC,br,PA}(po2cc, \sigma_e) = (\lambda, PA)$. Naturally, the extra inputs, outputs and transitions will be removed after testing has been completed.

6   Conclusions and Further Work

In this paper, we have presented our current work, focusing on an application of membrane computing to modelling and analysing engineering systems. As our initial attempt, we have considered the cruise control system of e-bike as our case study. We have modelled an e-bike cruise control system using kernel P systems and validated its behaviour using the kPWORKBENCH verification environment. We have also illustrated how the automata and X-machine testing methodologies can be applied on the kP model of the cruise control system.

As future work, we are planning to show how more complex engineering problems can be solved, tested and verified by using kP systems.

Acknowledgements. The work of SK is supported by Innovate UK (project no: KTP010551). MB is supported by a PhD studentship provided by the Turkey Ministry of Education. FI is supported by a grant of the Romanian National Authority for Scientific Research, CNCS-UEFISCDI, project number PN-III-P4-ID-PCE-2016-0210.

References

1. Bakir, M.E., Ipate, F., Konur, S., Mierla, L., Niculescu, I.: Extended simulation and verification platform for kernel P systems. In: Gheorghe, M., Rozenberg, G., Salomaa, A., Sosík, P., Zandron, C. (eds.) CMC 2014. LNCS, vol. 8961, pp. 158–178. Springer, Cham (2014). https://doi.org/10.1007/978-3-319-14370-5_10
2. Bakir, M.E., Konur, S., Gheorghe, M., Niculescu, I., Ipate, F.: High performance simulations of kernel P systems. In: 2014 IEEE International Conference on High Performance Computing and Communications, HPCC 2014, pp. 409–412 (2014)
3. Cimatti, A., Clarke, E., Giunchiglia, E., Giunchiglia, F., Pistore, M., Roveri, M., Sebastiani, R., Tacchella, A.: NuSMV 2: An OpenSource tool for symbolic model checking. In: Brinksma, E., Larsen, K.G. (eds.) CAV 2002. LNCS, vol. 2404, pp. 359–364. Springer, Heidelberg (2002). https://doi.org/10.1007/3-540-45657-0_29
4. Coakley, S., Gheorghe, M., Holcombe, M., Chin, S., Worth, D., Greenough, C.: Exploitation of high performance computing in the FLAME agent-based simulation framework. In: 14th IEEE International Conference on High Performance Computing and Communication, HPCC 2012, pp. 538–545 (2012)
5. Dragomir, C., Ipate, F., Konur, S., Lefticaru, R., Mierla, L.: Model checking kernel P systems. In: Alhazov, A., Cojocaru, S., Gheorghe, M., Rogozhin, Y., Rozenberg, G., Salomaa, A. (eds.) CMC 2013. LNCS, vol. 8340, pp. 151–172. Springer, Heidelberg (2014). https://doi.org/10.1007/978-3-642-54239-8_12
6. Gheorghe, M., Ceterchi, R., Ipate, F., Konur, S.: Kernel P systems modelling, testing and verification - sorting case study. In: Leporati, A., Rozenberg, G., Salomaa, A., Zandron, C. (eds.) CMC 2016. LNCS, vol. 10105, pp. 233–250. Springer, Cham (2017). https://doi.org/10.1007/978-3-319-54072-6_15
7. Gheorghe, M., Ceterchi, R., Ipate, F., Konur, S., Lefticaru, R.: Kernel P systems: from modelling to verification and testing. Theoretical Computer Science (accepted for publication). http://hdl.handle.net/10454/11720
8. Gheorghe, M., Ipate, F.: On testing P systems. In: Corne, D.W., Frisco, P., Păun, G., Rozenberg, G., Salomaa, A. (eds.) WMC 2008. LNCS, vol. 5391, pp. 204–216. Springer, Heidelberg (2009). https://doi.org/10.1007/978-3-540-95885-7_15
9. Gheorghe, M., Ipate, F., Dragomir, C., Mierla, L., Valencia-Cabrera, L., García-Quismondo, M., Pérez-Jiménez, M.J.: Kernel P systems - Version I. In: Eleventh Brainstorming Week on Membrane Computing (11BWMC), pp. 97–124 (2013)
10. Gheorghe, M., Konur, S., Ipate, F., Mierla, L., Bakir, M.E., Stannett, M.: An integrated model checking toolset for kernel P systems. In: Rozenberg, G., Salomaa, A., Sempere, J.M., Zandron, C. (eds.) CMC 2015. LNCS, vol. 9504, pp. 153–170. Springer, Cham (2015). https://doi.org/10.1007/978-3-319-28475-0_11
11. Holcombe, M.: X-machines as a basis for dynamic system specification. Softw. Eng. J. **3**(2), 69–76 (1988)
12. Holcombe, M., Ipate, F.: Correct Systems: Building a Business Process Solution. Applied computing. Springer, Heidelberg (1998)
13. Holzmann, G.J.: The model checker SPIN. IEEE Trans. Softw. Eng. **23**(5), 275–295 (1997)
14. Ipate, F., Holcombe, M.: An integration testing method that is proved to find all faults. Int. J. Comput. Math. **63**(3–4), 159–178 (1997)
15. Konur, S.: An event-based fragment of first-order logic over intervals. J. Logic Lang. Inf. **20**(1), 49–68 (2011)
16. Konur, S.: Specifying safety-critical systems with a decidable duration logic. Sci. Comput. Program. **80**(Part B), 264–287 (2014)

17. Konur, S., Fisher, M.: A roadmap to pervasive systems verification. Knowl. Eng. Rev. **30**(3), 324–341 (2015)
18. Konur, S., Gheorghe, M., Dragomir, C., Mierla, L., Ipate, F., Krasnogor, N.: Qualitative and quantitative analysis of systems and synthetic biology constructs using P systems. ACS Synth. Biol. **4**(1), 83–92 (2015)
19. Konur, S., Kiran, M., Gheorghe, M., Burkitt, M., Ipate, F.: Agent-based high-performance simulation of biological systems on the GPU. In: 17th IEEE International Conference on High Performance Computing and Communications, HPCC 2015, pp. 84–89 (2015)
20. Lefticaru, R., Konur, S., Yildirim, U., Uddin, A., Campean, F., Gheorghe, M.: Towards an integrated approach to verification and model-based testing in system engineering. In: The International Workshop on Engineering Data- & Model-driven Applications (EDMA-2017) within the IEEE International Conference on Cyber, Physical and Social Computing (CPSCom), pp. 131–138 (2017). http://hdl.handle.net/10454/12322
21. Păun, G.: Computing with membranes. J. Comput. Syst. Sci. **61**(1), 108–143 (2000)
22. The P systems website. http://ppage.psystems.eu. Accessed 30 Oct 2017
23. Sanassy, D., Fellermann, H., Krasnogor, N., Konur, S., Mierla, L., Gheorghe, M., Ladroue, C., Kalvala, S.: Modelling and stochastic simulation of synthetic biological boolean gates. In: 2014 IEEE International Conference on High Performance Computing and Communications, HPCC 2014, Paris, France, August 20–22, 2014, pp. 404–408 (2014)
24. Varadarajan, A.V., Romijn, M., Oosthoek, B., van de Mortel-Fronczak, J.M., Beijer, J.: Development and validation of functional model of a cruise control system. In: Proceedings of the 13th International Workshop on Formal Engineering Approaches to Software Components and Architectures, pp. 45–58. EPTCS (2016)

Solving a Special Case of the P Conjecture Using Dependency Graphs with Dissolution

Alberto Leporati, Luca Manzoni, Giancarlo Mauri,
Antonio E. Porreca, and Claudio Zandron$^{(\boxtimes)}$

Dipartimento di Informatica, Sistemistica e Comunicazione,
Università degli Studi di Milano-Bicocca, Viale Sarca 336/14, 20126 Milano, Italy
{leporati,luca.manzoni,mauri,porreca,zandron}@disco.unimib.it

Abstract. We solve affirmatively a new special case of the *P conjecture* by Gh. Păun, which states that P systems with active membranes without charges and without non-elementary membrane division cannot solve **NP**-complete problems in polynomial time. The variant we consider is *monodirectional*, i.e., without send-in communication rules, *shallow*, i.e., with membrane structures consisting of only one level besides the external membrane, and *deterministic*, rather than more generally confluent. We describe a polynomial-time Turing machine simulation of this variant of P systems, exploiting a generalised version of dependency graphs for P systems which, unlike the original version introduced by Cordón-Franco et al., also takes membrane dissolution into account.

1 Introduction

The original variant of P systems with active membranes, which includes membrane charges (or polarisations), solves in polynomial time exactly the problems in the complexity class **PSPACE** [13]. However, the variant without charges appears to be significantly weaker. This led Păun to formulate the P conjecture in 2005 [11, Problem F], one of the long-standing open problems in membrane computing:

> *Can the polarizations be completely avoided?* [...] *The feeling is that this is not possible — and such a result would be rather sound: passing from no polarization (which, in fact, means one polarization) to two polarizations amounts to passing from nonefficiency to efficiency.*

While this general formulation of P conjecture is actually false, as P systems without charges still characterise **PSPACE** when both non-elementary membrane division and dissolution rules are allowed [2], the statement is true when dissolution rules are forbidden [6].

This work was partially supported by Fondo d'Ateneo 2016 of Università degli Studi di Milano-Bicocca, project 2016-ATE-0492 "Sistemi a membrane: classi di complessità spaziale e temporale".

© Springer International Publishing AG 2018
M. Gheorghe et al. (Eds.): CMC 2017, LNCS 10725, pp. 196–213, 2018.
https://doi.org/10.1007/978-3-319-73359-3_13

The intermediate case, where dissolution is allowed but non-elementary division is not, is still open. The best known upper bound is $\mathbf{P}^{\#\mathbf{P}}$, the class of problems solved in polynomial time by Turing machines with an oracle for a counting problem [7]. However, some restricted special cases actually *do* have a **P** upper bound; this can be proved for P systems having only *symmetric* division rules [9], i.e., of the form $[a]_h \rightarrow [b]_h[b]_h$, or when the initial membrane structure is linear, and *only* dissolution and elementary division are allowed [14]. We refer the reader to Gazdag and Kolonits [4] for a more detailed survey of related results.

In this paper we consider another special case of the P conjecture, proving a **P** upper bound for P systems with active membranes without charges with the following three restrictions:

– *monodirectional*, that is, without send-in communication rules, as previously investigated for membranes with charges [8];
– *shallow*, that is, having only one level of elementary membranes in addition to the outermost one;
– *deterministic*, that is, having only one computation, instead of having multiple computations with the same result as in the usual *confluent* mode.

We believe that these constraints are quite natural and interesting, since monodirectional shallow deterministic P systems with active membranes have long been known to solve **NP**-complete problems in polynomial time with only two membrane charges [1]. Furthermore, they have been recently [8] proved to characterise $\mathbf{P}_{\parallel}^{\mathbf{NP}}$, which allows parallel queries to an **NP** oracle, with three charges[1]; clearly, the $\mathbf{P}_{\parallel}^{\mathbf{NP}}$ upper bound also applies to the variant without charges considered in this paper.

Among the three assumptions above, the most fundamental one is monodirectionality. As we will prove later, this restriction implies that the result of the computation only depends on at most one elementary membrane, although establishing *which one* is nontrivial. We hope, instead, to relax the latter two constraints in future works.

Besides the **P** upper bound itself, the main contribution of this paper is the tool we exploit in order to prove the upper bound. This is a generalisation of the *dependency graphs*, introduced by Cordón-Franco et al. [3] to establish the result of P systems without charges and without dissolution rules, to P systems which do include dissolving membranes. This generalisation has the potential to be extended to other variants of P systems for proving upper bounds to the complexity classes they characterise.

2   Basic Notions

The P systems analysed in this paper are *monodirectional* P systems with active membranes [8] without charges [6], using object evolution rules $[a \rightarrow w]_h$, send-out communication rules $[a]_h \rightarrow [\ ]_h\, b$, membrane dissolution rules $[a]_h \rightarrow b$

---

[1] The determinism of the P systems is not explicitly stated in the original paper [8], but can be easily checked by inspection of the rules.

and elementary membrane division rules $[a]_h \rightarrow [b]_h[c]_h$. These P systems do not use send-in communication rules $a[\ ]_h \rightarrow [b]_h$, or division rules for non-elementary membranes, either of the "weak" form $[a]_h \rightarrow [b]_h[c]_h$ or the "strong" form $[[\ ]_k[\ ]_\ell]_h \rightarrow [[\ ]_k]_h\ [[\ ]_\ell]_h$.

Furthermore, we focus on *shallow* P systems, which have membrane structures of depth at most 1, that is, at most one level of elementary membranes besides the outermost membrane.

Finally, we require our P systems to be *deterministic*, that is, each configuration reachable from the initial one has at most one successor configuration. Notice that this condition, although much stronger than the usual confluence requirement (where multiple computations can exist, as long as they all agree on the result), does not require a single multiset of rules to be applicable at each computation step, but only that all applicable multisets of rules produce the same result.

For brevity, in this paper we refer to monodirectional, shallow, deterministic P systems as MSD P systems.

In particular, we are dealing with *recogniser P systems* [12], whose alphabet includes the distinguished result objects yes and no; exactly one result object must be sent out from the outermost membrane to signal acceptance or rejection, and only at the last computation step.

A decision problem, or language $L \subseteq \Sigma^\star$, is solved by a *family* of P systems $\Pi = \{\Pi_x : x \in \Sigma^\star\}$, where Π_x accepts if and only if $x \in L$. In that case, we write $L(\Pi) = L$. As usual, we require a uniformity condition [10] on families of P systems:

Definition 1. *A family of P systems $\Pi = \{\Pi_x : x \in \Sigma^\star\}$ is (polynomial-time) uniform if the mapping $x \mapsto \Pi_x$ can be computed by two polynomial-time deterministic Turing machines E and F as follows:*

- *$F(1^n) = \Pi(n)$ is a common P system for all inputs of length n, with a distinguished input membrane.*
- *$E(x) = w_x$ is an input multiset for $\Pi(|x|)$, encoding the specific input x.*
- *Finally, Π_x is simply $\Pi(|x|)$ with w_x added to its input membrane.*

The family Π is said to be (polynomial-time) semi-uniform if there exists a single deterministic polynomial-time Turing machine H such that $H(x) = \Pi_x$ for each $x \in \Sigma^\star$.

We denote the class of problems solved by uniform (resp., semi-uniform) families of deterministic P systems of type $\mathcal{D}$ as $\mathbf{DMC}_\mathcal{D}$ (resp., $\mathbf{DMC}_\mathcal{D}^\star$). We denote the corresponding class of problems solved *in polynomial time* by $\mathbf{DPMC}_\mathcal{D}$ (resp., $\mathbf{DPMC}_\mathcal{D}^\star$).

3   Properties of MSD P Systems

We begin our analysis of MSD P systems by proving that their overall behaviour, acceptance or rejection, is actually governed by *just one or two objects*, which must moreover be located inside a single membrane. In order to be able to succinctly formalise this result, we first define a notion of restricted configuration similar, but more general than the one previously used by the authors [8, Definition 3].

Definition 2. *Given two configurations C, D of a P system, we say that C is a restriction of D, in symbols $C \sqsubseteq D$, if C is obtained from D by deleting zero or more membranes, including their whole content (both objects and children membranes), and zero or more of the remaining objects.*

Being based on the subtree partial ordering of membrane structures and on the submultiset partial order, the relation $\sqsubseteq$ is also a partial order.

For the purposes of this paper, we consider as valid restricted configurations even those obtained by only keeping part of the environment and ignoring the membrane structure altogether. For instance, given the configuration

$$D = \big[[a\,b]_k, [c\,c]_\ell d\,d\,d\big]_h \, e\, f$$

the following are all valid restrictions of D:

$$C_1 = [[a\,b]_k d\,d]_h \qquad C_2 = [[c\,c]_\ell]_h \qquad C_3 = [d\,d\,d]_h \, e \qquad C_4 = e\,f$$

A subclass of restricted configurations that we will focus on in this paper consists of the "small" configurations, which contain only one object, or up to two objects, if they are both located inside an internal membrane.

Definition 3. *We call a configuration C of an MSD P system Π a small configuration if it consists of the isolated object* yes *or* no *in the environment, or if it is of one of the forms $[a]_h$, $\big[[a]_k\big]_h$, or $\big[[a\,b]_k\big]_h$ where h is the outermost membrane of Π, k is the label of an internal membrane, and a, b are objects of the alphabet.*

A simple counting argument shows that the number of small configurations for an MSD P system is bounded by $(m^2 + m)\ell + 2 \in O(m^2\ell)$, where m is the size of the alphabet, and ℓ the number of labels, which corresponds to the initial number of membranes.

The following result shows that a halting computation of an MSD P system contains a sequence of small configurations which, alone, suffice to establish the result of the computation. This theorem is a stronger version of an analogous result for monodirectional P systems with charges [8, Lemma 1], where a *polynomial* number of objects and membranes were necessary and sufficient to decide the result of the computation.

Theorem 1. *Let Π be an accepting (resp., rejecting) MSD P system, and let C_1 be a configuration reachable in any number of steps from the initial configuration C_0 of Π. Let $\vec{C} = (C_1, C_2, \cdots, C_t)$ be the halting subcomputation starting at C_1. Then, there exists a sequence of small configurations $\vec{D} = (D_1, \ldots, D_t)$ with $D_i \sqsubseteq C_i$ for $1 \le i \le t$ and $D_t =$ yes (resp., $D_t =$ no) and a sequence of configurations $\vec{E} = (E_2, \ldots, E_t)$ such that $D_i \to E_{i+1}$ and $D_{i+1} \sqsubseteq E_{i+1} \sqsubseteq C_{i+1}$ for all $1 \le i < t$.*

Proof. We construct the sequences $\vec{\mathcal{D}} = (\mathcal{D}_1, \ldots, \mathcal{D}_t)$ and $\vec{\mathcal{E}} = (\mathcal{E}_2, \ldots, \mathcal{E}_t)$ by recursion on t. If $t = 1$ then $\mathcal{C}_1$ is already an accepting (resp., rejecting) configuration, and thus $\mathcal{D}_1 = \mathsf{yes} \sqsubseteq \mathcal{C}_1$ (resp, $\mathcal{D}_1 = \mathsf{no} \sqsubseteq \mathcal{C}_1$); in this case, the sequence $\vec{\mathcal{E}}$ is empty.

Now suppose $t > 1$. Then, the sub-computation $\vec{\mathcal{C}'} = (\mathcal{C}_2, \ldots, \mathcal{C}_t)$, i.e., the same computation as $\vec{\mathcal{C}}$ but starting from the second step, is a halting computation starting at a configuration reachable from the initial configuration $\mathcal{C}_0$ of Π. By induction hypothesis, there exists a sequence $\vec{\mathcal{D}'} = (\mathcal{D}_2, \ldots, \mathcal{D}_t)$ of small configurations and a sequence $\vec{\mathcal{E}'} = (\mathcal{E}_3, \ldots, \mathcal{E}_t)$ of configurations satisfying the statement of the theorem.

We construct $\mathcal{D}_1$ and $\mathcal{E}_2$ according to the form of $\mathcal{D}_2$ and the choice of rules that may have produced that configuration. The following list exhausts all possibilities.

(1) If $\mathcal{D}_2 = \mathsf{yes}$ (resp., $\mathcal{D}_2 = \mathsf{no}$), then there necessarily exists a send-out rule $[a]_h \to [\,]_h\,\mathsf{yes}$ (resp., $[a]_h \to [\,]_h\,\mathsf{no}$) which is applied in the step $\mathcal{C}_1 \to \mathcal{C}_2$. In this case, we let $\mathcal{D}_1 = [a]_h$ and $\mathcal{E}_2 = [\,]_h\,\mathsf{yes}$ (resp., $\mathcal{E}_2 = [\,]_h\,\mathsf{no}$).

(2) If $\mathcal{D}_2 = [a]_h$ and object a is produced by an object evolution rule $[b \to a\,w]_h$, then let $\mathcal{D}_1 = [b]_h$ and $\mathcal{E}_2 = [a\,w]_h$.

(3) If $\mathcal{D}_2 = [a]_h$ and object a is produced by a send-out rule $[b]_k \to [\,]_k\,a$, then let $\mathcal{D}_1 = \left[[b]_k\right]_h$ and $\mathcal{E}_2 = [[\,]_k\,a]_h$.

(4) If $\mathcal{D}_2 = [a]_h$ and object a is produced by a dissolution rule $[b]_k \to a$, then let $\mathcal{D}_1 = \left[[b]_k\right]_h$ and $\mathcal{E}_2 = [a]_h$.

(5) If $\mathcal{D}_2 = [a]_h$ and object a appeared inside an internal membrane k in $\mathcal{C}_1$, but fell out due to another object b applying a dissolution rule $[b]_k \to c$, then let $\mathcal{D}_1 = \left[[a\,b]_k\right]_h$ and $\mathcal{E}_2 = [a\,c]_h$.

(6) If $\mathcal{D}_2 = [a]_h$ and object a evolved from an object b appearing inside an internal membrane k in $\mathcal{C}_1$ using the rule $[b \to a\,w]_k$, and fell out due to another object c applying a dissolution rule $[c]_k \to d$, then let $\mathcal{D}_1 = \left[[b\,c]_k\right]_h$ and $\mathcal{E}_2 = [a\,w\,d]_h$.

(7) If $\mathcal{D}_2 = \left[[a]_k\right]_h$ and object a is produced by an evolution rule $[b \to a\,w]_k$, then let $\mathcal{D}_1 = \left[[b]_k\right]_h$ and $\mathcal{E}_2 = \left[[a\,w]_k\right]_h$.

(8) If $\mathcal{D}_2 = \left[[a]_k\right]_h$ and object a is produced by a division rule $[c]_k \to [a]_k\,[b]_k$, then let $\mathcal{D}_1 = \left[[c]_k\right]_h$ and $\mathcal{E}_2 = [[a]_k\,[b]_k]_h$.

(9) If $\mathcal{D}_2 = \left[[a\,b]_k\right]_h$ and objects a, b are produced by an object evolution rule $[c \to a, b, w]_k$, then let $\mathcal{D}_1 = \left[[c]_k\right]_h$ and $\mathcal{E}_2 = \left[[a\,b\,w]_k\right]_h$.

(10) If $\mathcal{D}_2 = \left[[a\,b]_k\right]_h$ and objects a, b are produced by two object evolution rules $[c \to a\,v]_k$ and $[d \to b\,w]_k$, then let $\mathcal{D}_1 = \left[[c\,d]_k\right]_h$ and $\mathcal{E}_2 = \left[[a\,v\,b\,w]_k\right]_h$.

(11) If $\mathcal{D}_2 = \left[[a\,b]_k\right]_h$, object a is produced by an object evolution rule $[c \to a\,w]_k$, and object b already appeared inside membrane k, then let $\mathcal{D}_1 = \left[[c\,b]_k\right]_h$ and $\mathcal{E}_2 = \left[[a\,w\,b]_k\right]_h$.

(12) If $\mathcal{D}_2 = \left[[a\,b]_k\right]_h$, object a is produced by a division rule $[c]_k \to [a]_k[d]_k$, and object b is produced by an object evolution rule $[e \to b, w]_k$, then let $\mathcal{D}_1 = \left[[c\,e]_k\right]_h$ and $\mathcal{E}_2 = [[a\,b\,w]_k, [d\,b\,w]_k]_h$.

(13) If $\mathcal{D}_2 = \big[[a\,b]_k\big]_h$, object a is produced by a division rule $[c]_k \rightarrow [a]_k[d]_k$, and object b already appeared inside membrane k, then let $\mathcal{D}_1 = \big[[c\,b]_k\big]_h$ and $\mathcal{E}_2 = [[a\,b]_k\,[d\,b]_k]_h$.

It is easy to check by inspection that in all cases (1)–(13) we have $\mathcal{D}_1 \sqsubseteq \mathcal{C}_1$, $\mathcal{D}_1 \rightarrow \mathcal{E}_2$, and $\mathcal{D}_2 \sqsubseteq \mathcal{E}_2 \sqsubseteq \mathcal{C}_2$ as required.   □

Figure 1 shows the relationship between the computation $\vec{\mathcal{C}}$ and the sequences of configurations $\vec{\mathcal{D}}$ and $\vec{\mathcal{E}}$ in the statement of Theorem 1.

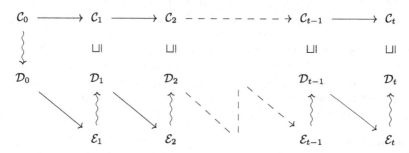

Fig. 1. A computation $\vec{\mathcal{C}} = (\mathcal{C}_0, \mathcal{C}_1, \mathcal{C}_2, \ldots, \mathcal{C}_{t-1}, \mathcal{C}_t)$ of Π and a sequence of configurations $\mathcal{C}_0 \rightsquigarrow \mathcal{D}_0 \rightarrow \mathcal{E}_1 \rightsquigarrow \mathcal{D}_1 \rightarrow \mathcal{E}_2 \rightsquigarrow \mathcal{D}_2 \rightarrow \cdots \rightarrow \mathcal{E}_{t-1} \rightsquigarrow \mathcal{D}_{t-1} \rightarrow \mathcal{E}_t \rightsquigarrow \mathcal{D}_t$ alternating restriction steps ($\rightsquigarrow$) and application of the rules from the corresponding steps of $\vec{\mathcal{C}}$ ($\rightarrow$) limited to the objects in $\mathcal{D}_i$. The diagram "commutes" in the sense that, starting from $\mathcal{C}_0$, the two paths either both lead to accepting configurations, or both to rejecting configurations. Notice that $\mathcal{E}_i \sqsubseteq \mathcal{C}_i$ for all i, since $\mathcal{E}_i$ is obtained from $\mathcal{D}_{i-1} \sqsubseteq \mathcal{C}_{i-1}$ and the P system is deterministic.

Notice that Theorem 1 does not directly provide an algorithm for computing *which* sequence $\vec{\mathcal{D}} = (\mathcal{D}_0, \ldots, \mathcal{D}_t)$ of small configurations gives the result of the computation. Furthermore, as will be shown in Sect. 4, it is not even sufficient to check that $\mathcal{D}_0 \sqsubseteq \mathcal{C}_0$ and $\mathcal{D}_t = \mathsf{yes}$ to guarantee the acceptance of Π, due to the possible interference from objects in $\vec{\mathcal{C}}$ not appearing in $\vec{\mathcal{D}}$.

Another fundamental limitation of MSD P systems is that they always halt in linear time with respect to the size of the alphabet, otherwise they would enter an infinite loop.

Theorem 2. *Every MSD P system halts within $2m$ steps, where m is the size of its alphabet.*

Proof. Assume that the P system is accepting, as the rejecting case is symmetrical. The object yes descends from an object a contained in the initial configuration of the P system via a sequence of rule applications. The object a is initially either inside the outermost membrane, or inside an elementary membrane immediately contained therein; in the latter case, either it reaches the outermost membrane via communication or by dissolving the membrane, or it reaches the outermost membrane due to *another* object dissolving the membrane.

If a is initially located inside the outermost membrane, then it can be rewritten a number of times by object evolution rules until an object b with an associated send-out rule $[b]_h \to [\ ]_h$ yes is produced; notice that object evolution is the only way to produce b, as the outermost membrane cannot divide. In the shortest possible computation, the object b appears after a sequence of at most $m - 1$ rewriting steps, where at least one new object is introduced at each step: indeed, since object evolution rules are context-free, each object either (i) becomes b within $m - 1$ steps, or (ii) it stops evolving before $m - 1$ steps without ever becoming b, or (iii) it enters an infinite rewriting loop. Case (iii) is impossible, since the P system is a recogniser; case (ii) is also impossible, since reaching b is necessary in order to send out the result yes. Hence case (i) must hold, and the computation accepts in at most m steps.

An analogous argument shows that a rule of the form $[a]_k \to [\ ]_k\, b$ or $[a]_k \to b$ is applied inside the elementary membrane containing a after at most $m-1$ steps, if a is not initially located inside the outermost membrane. After further $m - 1$ steps, the result is then sent out by a rule $[c]_h \to [\ ]_h$ yes as detailed above. In this case, the accepting computation has a length at most $2m$.   □

This result implies that the class of languages recognised by MSD P systems with no restriction on computation resources is the same as the class of languages they recognise in polynomial time.

Corollary 1. DPMC$_{\mathcal{D}}$ = DMC$_{\mathcal{D}}$ and DPMC$_{\mathcal{D}}^\star$ = DMC$_{\mathcal{D}}^\star$, *where $\mathcal{D}$ is the class of MSD P systems.*   □

4   Dependency Graphs with Dissolution

Dependency graphs for P systems were introduced by Cordón-Franco et al. [3] as a way to track the objects in a P system without charges with non-cooperative rules and fixed membrane structures, and were later extended to membrane division rules [5], leaving out only membrane dissolution.

A dependency graph for a P system Π of this kind has, as vertices, all possible configurations of the form $\left[[\cdots [a]_{h_d} \cdots]_{h_1}\right]_{h_0}$, consisting of a linear sub-membrane structure of the membrane structure of Π, and a single object contained in the innermost membrane; a single object a in the environment (i.e., without any surrounding membrane) is also allowed[2]. Two configurations $\mathcal{V}, \mathcal{W}$ of the dependency graph are connected by an oriented edge if, when applying the rules of Π from configuration $\mathcal{V}$ (recall that, for a confluent P system, multiple choices are generally possible), we can reach a configuration $\mathcal{V}'$ containing $\mathcal{W}$, or $\mathcal{W} \sqsubseteq \mathcal{V}'$ in our notation (Definition 2).

The usefulness of the dependency graph for a P system Π without dissolution lies in the fact that it can be constructed in polynomial time from the description

---

[2] In the original notation [3,5] the surrounding membranes are left implicit, and thus the vertex $\left[[\cdots [a]_{h_d} \cdots]_{h_1}\right]_{h_0}$ is simply denoted by (a, h_d); an object a in the environment is denoted by (a, env).

of Π, and that Π accepts if and only if there exists a vertex $\mathcal{V}$ contained in the initial configuration $\mathcal{C}_0$, in symbols $\mathcal{V} \sqsubseteq \mathcal{C}_0$, that is connected with a path to the node yes, representing the positive answer object in the environment[3]. This property can be easily checked in polynomial time, and this proves that the P conjecture is indeed true *limited to P systems without dissolution* [5].

The reason why checking reachability on dependency graphs suffices is due to the fact that such P systems lack *cooperation*, or, in other words, the only interaction between objects is due to the fact that the rules (excluding object evolution) can compete for the same membrane. Indeed, a theorem analogous to our Theorem 1, but stating that the result of the entire computation depends only on "very small configurations" containing *exactly one single object*, can be easily inferred from the above-mentioned result [5].

Allowing membrane dissolution breaks the entire reasoning, by introducing cooperation (or context-sensitiveness). Indeed, consider a configuration $\big[[a\,u]_k\big]_h$ with a dissolution rule $[a]_k \to b$ and zero or more object evolution rules rewriting the multiset u into v. This configuration leads to $[b\,v]_h$ in one step, and now the objects in v are subject to a potentially completely different set of rules, since the label of the membrane containing them was changed by the object a dissolving k. Thus, the objects in v have been affected by a, which is not possible in a P system without charges and without dissolution; furthermore, the influence of a on v cannot be represented by a standard dependency graph, as this tracks each object separately.

A way to generalise dependency graphs in order to take cooperation into account is to use larger configurations as vertices, containing multiple objects; as an extreme case, the whole set of configurations of Π could be kept as set of vertices. The side effect of this choice is the growth of the dependency graph. In general, a dependency graph keeping track of n objects per vertex has $\Theta(n^m)$ vertices, where m is the size of the alphabet; this value is exponential if $n \in \Theta(m)$. If there is no bound on the number of objects per vertex, the dependency graph might even become infinite.

In the case of MSD P systems, however, we can exploit Theorem 1 to keep the vertices of the dependency graph small, and thus reducing their number to polynomial, since at most two objects per vertex are needed even in the presence of dissolution.

Definition 4. *The* dependency graph *$G(\Pi) = \big(V(\Pi), E(\Pi)\big)$ for an MSD P system has as vertices $V(\Pi)$ all small configurations of Π and, as edges, the set $E(\Pi) = \big\{(\mathcal{U}, \mathcal{V}) : \mathcal{U} \to \mathcal{C}$ for some configuration $\mathcal{C}$ and $\mathcal{V} \sqsubseteq \mathcal{C}\big\}$. We denote by $Y(\Pi)$ the subset of $V(\Pi)$ consisting of all vertices connected with a path to the small configuration* yes.

Figure 2 shows the dependency graph for a simple MSD P system using all available types of rule.

Notice that yes $\sqsubseteq \mathcal{C}$ if and only if the object yes is located in the environment of configuration $\mathcal{C}$, that is, if and only if $\mathcal{C}$ is an accepting configuration. Hence,

---

[3] That is, node (yes, env) in the original notation.

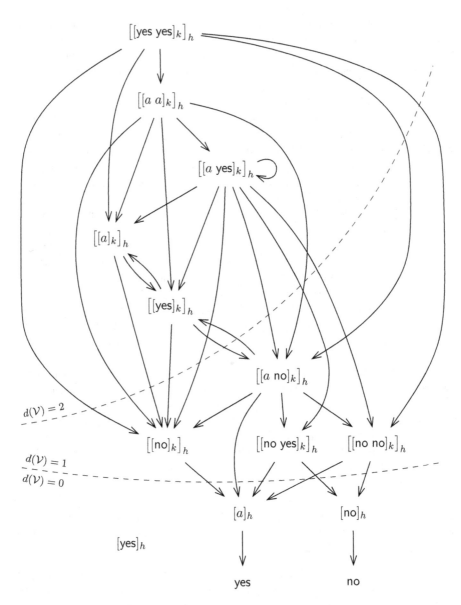

Fig. 2. Dependency graph for an MSD P system Π having alphabet $\Gamma = \{a, \text{yes}, \text{no}\}$ and rules $[a]_k \rightarrow [\text{yes}]_k[\text{no}]_k$, $[\text{no}]_k \rightarrow a$, $[\text{yes} \rightarrow a \ \text{no}]_k$, $[\text{no}]_h \rightarrow [\ ]_h \text{no}$, $[a]_h \rightarrow [\ ]_h \text{yes}$. Notice that this dependency graph is neither connected (the vertex $[\text{yes}]_h$ is isolated), nor acyclic (it even includes a self-loop). Also notice that some vertices, such as $[[a \ \text{no}]_k]_h$, show nondeterministic behaviour, since two rules can be applied; this does not necessarily contradict the determinism of Π, since these vertices $\mathcal{V}$ might not satisfy $\mathcal{V} \sqsubseteq \mathcal{C}$ for any configuration $\mathcal{C}$ reachable from the initial configuration. This P system accepts, for instance, from the initial configuration $\mathcal{C}_0 = [[\text{no}]_k]_h$, but rejects from $\mathcal{C}_0 = [\text{no}]_h$. The dashed lines are isolines grouping together the vertices by distance d (Definition 5).

the small configurations $\mathcal{V} \in Y(\Pi)$ are those that allow a configuration $\mathcal{C} \sqsupseteq \mathcal{V}$ to ultimately reach an accepting configuration, under certain conditions. Unfortunately, the mere inclusion $\mathcal{V} \sqsubseteq \mathcal{C}$, which allowed us to establish the result of P systems without dissolution, does not suffice in the case of MSD P systems, as shown by the following example.

Example 1. Consider an MSD P system Π with the rules

$$[a \to c]_k \qquad [b \to d]_k \qquad [c \to e]_k \qquad [d]_k \to f$$
$$[c]_h \to [\,]_h \text{ no} \qquad [e]_h \to [\,]_h \text{ yes} \qquad [g]_k \to f$$

The dependency graph for Π includes the following path:

$$\vec{\mathcal{D}} = \left(\left[[a\,b]_k\right]_h, \left[[c\,d]_k\right]_h, [e]_h, \text{yes} \right)$$

If the initial configuration of Π is $\mathcal{C}_0 = \left[[a\,b]_k\right]_h$, then Π has indeed the accepting computation

$$\left[[a\,b]_k\right]_h \quad \to \quad \left[[c\,d]_k\right]_h \quad \to \quad [e\,f]_h \quad \to \quad [f]_h \text{ yes}$$

If, on the other hand, the initial configuration is $\mathcal{C}_0 = \left[[a\,b\,g]_k\right]_h$, i.e., also including the object g, the resulting computation is rejecting:

$$\left[[a\,b\,g]_k\right]_h \quad \to \quad [c\,d\,f]_h \quad \to \quad [d\,f]_h \text{ no}$$

This shows that it is not sufficient to find a vertex $\mathcal{V}$, in this case $\mathcal{V} = \left[[a\,b]_k\right]_h$, such that $\mathcal{V} \sqsubseteq \mathcal{C}_0$ and there exists a path from $\mathcal{V}$ to yes if dissolution rules are allowed, since objects such as d may interfere with the path leading to yes.

As a consequence, the use of small configurations alone does not suffice to correctly determine the result of P systems where dissolution is allowed. A property more complex than "being connected via a path to the vertex yes" needs to be checked for the vertices contained in the initial configuration $\mathcal{C}_0$. The rest of this section is devoted to establishing this property.

We refer to objects such as g in Example 1, which do *not* appear in a small configuration $\mathcal{V}$ connected by a path to the vertex yes, and yet interfere with that path, as *troublemakers for* $\mathcal{V}$. In order to give a formal definition of troublemakers, we first define a few related notions.

First of all, notice that when the current configuration of the P system contains a vertex $\mathcal{V}$ of the form $[a]_h$, with an object located inside the outermost membrane, then no troublemaker can exist, since the outermost membrane cannot be dissolved. This applies, of course, also when $\mathcal{V} = \text{yes}$, that is, after having reached the halting configuration. For the remaining vertices, we define a notion of distance from such vertices without troublemakers.

Definition 5. *Let Π be an MSD P system; define the function $d\colon Y(\Pi) \to \mathbb{N}$ by letting $d(\mathcal{V}) = 0$ if $\mathcal{V} = \text{yes}$ or $\mathcal{V} = [a]_h$ for some $a \in \Gamma$, and letting $d(\mathcal{V})$ be the distance (in terms of oriented edges) of $\mathcal{V}$ to the nearest small configuration of the form $[a]_h$ in the subgraph of $G(\Pi)$ induced by $Y(\Pi)$, otherwise.*

Figure 2 also shows the distances of each node of the example dependency graph.

Among the troublemakers for a small configuration of the form $\mathcal{V} = \big[[a]_k\big]_h$ or $\mathcal{V} = \big[[a\,b]_k\big]_h$ there are the objects that dissolve membrane k, unless a or b themselves have dissolution rules. We refer to these objects with the symbol

$$\mathrm{dis}(k) = \{a \in \Gamma : \text{there exists a rule } [a]_k \rightarrow b \text{ for some } b \in \Gamma\}.$$

Other troublemakers do not dissolve membrane k immediately, but rather produce the set of objects X that are troublemakers for vertices reachable from $\mathcal{V}$ with an edge. These may be produced either by object evolution rules, and we denote them by

$$\mathrm{evo}_k(X) = \{a \in \Gamma : \text{there exists a rule } [a \rightarrow b\,w]_k \text{ for some } b \in X\}$$

or by division rules, and we denote them by

$$\mathrm{div}_k(X) = \{a \in \Gamma : \text{there exists a rule } [a]_k \rightarrow [b]_k[c]_k \text{ for some } b, c \in X\}$$

Notice that send-out rules cannot produce troublemakers for any connected vertex, since the outermost membrane, where the result of the send-out appears, cannot be dissolved.

Now let $\mathcal{V}$ be a small configuration of the form $\big[[a]_k\big]_h$ or $\big[[a\,b]_k\big]_h$. In order to recursively compute its set of troublemakers, let us consider all vertices $\mathcal{W}$ with an edge $(\mathcal{V}, \mathcal{W}) \in E(\Pi)$. Among these, we keep only the vertices $\mathcal{W}_1, \ldots, \mathcal{W}_n$ having distance $d(\mathcal{W}_i) = d(\mathcal{V}) - 1$. The reason to exclude adjacent vertices $\mathcal{W}$ with $d(\mathcal{W}) \geq d(\mathcal{V})$ is that these require more computation steps to reach a troublemaker-free small configuration and, intuitively, the set of troublemakers of a vertex can increase with its distance. Furthermore, the troublemakers of $\mathcal{V}$ only depend on the *intersection* of the troublemakers of $\mathcal{W}_1, \ldots, \mathcal{W}_n$; indeed, a troublemaker for $\mathcal{W}_i$ that is not simultaneously a troublemaker for some $\mathcal{W}_j$ can be bypassed by following the edge $(\mathcal{V}, \mathcal{W}_j)$.

Based on this intuition we can now define, for each small configuration $\mathcal{V}$ on a path to yes, the notion of *set of troublemakers* $\mathrm{tm}(\mathcal{V})$ by recursion on the distance $d(\mathcal{V})$.

Definition 6. *Let Π be an MSD P system and let 2^Γ be the power set of its alphabet. Define the function* $\mathrm{tm}\colon Y(\Pi) \rightarrow 2^\Gamma$ *as*

$$\mathrm{tm}(\mathcal{V}) = \varnothing \tag{1}$$

if $d(\mathcal{V}) = 0$ or $d(\mathcal{V}) = 1$, and

$$\mathrm{tm}(\mathcal{V}) = \mathrm{dis}(k) \cup \mathrm{evo}_k\left(\bigcap_{i=1}^{n} \mathrm{tm}(\mathcal{W}_i)\right) \cup \mathrm{div}_k\left(\bigcap_{i=1}^{n} \mathrm{tm}(\mathcal{W}_i)\right) \tag{2}$$

if $d(\mathcal{V}) \geq 2$, where $\mathcal{W}_1, \ldots, \mathcal{W}_n$ are all vertices in $Y(\Pi)$ such that $(\mathcal{V}, \mathcal{W}_i) \in E(\Pi)$ and $d(\mathcal{W}_i) = d(\mathcal{V}) - 1$.

In fact, we can actually prove that the set of troublemakers $\mathrm{tm}(\mathcal{V})$ depends only on the distance $d(\mathcal{V})$ and on the label of the internal membrane, but not on the actual objects it contains.

Lemma 1. *Let Π be an MSD P system, let $\mathcal{U}, \mathcal{V}$ be two small configurations of Π such that, if both $\mathcal{U}$ and $\mathcal{V}$ contain two nested membranes, then the internal ones have the same label, and assume that $d(\mathcal{U}) = d(\mathcal{V})$. Then $\mathrm{tm}(\mathcal{U}) = \mathrm{tm}(\mathcal{V})$.*

Proof. By induction on $d(\mathcal{U})$. If $d(\mathcal{U}) = d(\mathcal{V}) = 0$ or $d(\mathcal{U}) = d(\mathcal{V}) = 1$, then $\mathrm{tm}(\mathcal{U}) = \varnothing = \mathrm{tm}(\mathcal{V})$. If $d(\mathcal{U}) = d(\mathcal{V}) \geq 2$ then, according to Eq. (2), we have

$$\mathrm{tm}(\mathcal{U}) = \mathrm{dis}(k) \cup \mathrm{evo}_k \left(\bigcap_{i=1}^n \mathrm{tm}(\mathcal{W}_i) \right) \cup \mathrm{div}_k \left(\bigcap_{i=1}^n \mathrm{tm}(\mathcal{W}_i) \right)$$

$$\mathrm{tm}(\mathcal{V}) = \mathrm{dis}(k) \cup \mathrm{evo}_k \left(\bigcap_{i=1}^m \mathrm{tm}(\mathcal{Z}_i) \right) \cup \mathrm{div}_k \left(\bigcap_{i=1}^m \mathrm{tm}(\mathcal{Z}_i) \right)$$

with $d(\mathcal{W}_1) = \cdots = d(\mathcal{W}_n) = d(\mathcal{Z}_1) = \cdots = d(\mathcal{Z}_m) < d(\mathcal{U})$. Hence, by induction hypothesis we have $\mathrm{tm}(\mathcal{W}_1) = \cdots = \mathrm{tm}(\mathcal{W}_n) = \mathrm{tm}(\mathcal{Z}_1) = \cdots = \mathrm{tm}(\mathcal{Z}_m)$, which implies $\mathrm{tm}(\mathcal{U}) = \mathrm{tm}(\mathcal{V})$. □

The following monotonicity result formalises the intuitive notion that, with the increase of $d(\mathcal{V})$, the possibilities for external objects to interfere with a path on the dependency graph may also increase.

Lemma 2. *Let Π be an MSD P system, let $\mathcal{U}, \mathcal{V}$ be two small configurations of Π such that, if both $\mathcal{U}$ and $\mathcal{V}$ contain two nested membranes, the internal ones have the same label, and assume that $d(\mathcal{U}) \leq d(\mathcal{V})$. Then $\mathrm{tm}(\mathcal{U}) \subseteq \mathrm{tm}(\mathcal{V})$.*

Proof. It suffices to show that $\mathrm{tm}(\mathcal{U}) \subseteq \mathrm{tm}(\mathcal{V})$ when $d(\mathcal{U}) = d(\mathcal{V}) - 1$. We prove it by induction on $d(\mathcal{U})$. If $d(\mathcal{U}) = 0$ or $d(\mathcal{U}) = 1$, then $\mathrm{tm}(\mathcal{U}) = \varnothing$, which is always a subset of $\mathrm{tm}(\mathcal{V})$.

If $d(\mathcal{U}) \geq 2$ then $d(\mathcal{V}) > 2$, and both $\mathrm{tm}(\mathcal{U})$ and $\mathrm{tm}(\mathcal{V})$ are computed using Eq. (2):

$$\mathrm{tm}(\mathcal{U}) = \mathrm{dis}(k) \cup \mathrm{evo}_k \left(\bigcap_{i=1}^n \mathrm{tm}(\mathcal{W}_i) \right) \cup \mathrm{div}_k \left(\bigcap_{i=1}^n \mathrm{tm}(\mathcal{W}_i) \right)$$

$$\mathrm{tm}(\mathcal{V}) = \mathrm{dis}(k) \cup \mathrm{evo}_k \left(\bigcap_{i=1}^m \mathrm{tm}(\mathcal{Z}_i) \right) \cup \mathrm{div}_k \left(\bigcap_{i=1}^m \mathrm{tm}(\mathcal{Z}_i) \right)$$

Since $d(\mathcal{Z}_1) = \cdots = d(\mathcal{Z}_m) = d(\mathcal{V}) - 1 = d(\mathcal{U})$, then by Lemma 1 we have $\mathrm{tm}(\mathcal{Z}_1) = \cdots = \mathrm{tm}(\mathcal{Z}_m) = \mathrm{tm}(\mathcal{U})$, and thus

$$\mathrm{tm}(\mathcal{V}) = \mathrm{dis}(k) \cup \mathrm{evo}_k \left(\bigcap_{i=1}^m \mathrm{tm}(\mathcal{U}) \right) \cup \mathrm{div}_k \left(\bigcap_{i=1}^m \mathrm{tm}(\mathcal{U}) \right)$$

$$= \mathrm{dis}(k) \cup \mathrm{evo}_k \left(\mathrm{tm}(\mathcal{U}) \right) \cup \mathrm{div}_k \left(\mathrm{tm}(\mathcal{U}) \right)$$

Since $d(\mathcal{W}_1), \ldots, d(\mathcal{W}_n) = d(\mathcal{U}) - 1$, we have $\mathrm{tm}(\mathcal{W}_1), \ldots, \mathrm{tm}(\mathcal{W}_n) \subseteq \mathrm{tm}(\mathcal{U})$ by induction hypothesis, and thus $\bigcap_{i=1}^{n} \mathrm{tm}(\mathcal{W}_i) \subseteq \mathrm{tm}(\mathcal{U})$, which implies

$$\mathrm{tm}(\mathcal{V}) \supseteq \mathrm{dis}(k) \cup \mathrm{evo}_k \left(\bigcap_{i=1}^{n} \mathrm{tm}(\mathcal{W}_i) \right) \cup \mathrm{div}_k \left(\bigcap_{i=1}^{n} \mathrm{tm}(\mathcal{W}_i) \right) = \mathrm{tm}(\mathcal{U})$$

as needed.   □

We call a configuration $\mathcal{C}$ of an MSD P system Π *untroubled* if it contains a vertex $\mathcal{V} \in V(\Pi)$ that is connected via a path to the vertex yes, and none of the troublemakers of $\mathcal{V}$. Notice, however, that a vertex can be contained multiple times in a given configuration, and each occurrence may or may not be subject to interference by its troublemakers. For instance, let $\mathcal{V} = \big[[a\,b]_k\big]_h$ with $\mathrm{tm}(\mathcal{V}) = \{c\}$ and $\mathcal{C} = \big[[a\,a\,b]_k\,[a\,b\,c]_k\big]_h$; the small configuration $\mathcal{V}$ occurs three times in $\mathcal{C}$ (twice in the left membrane k, and once in the right one), but only one occurrence may have interference, since the troublemaker c does not occur in the left membrane k. In order to formalise the notion of untroubled membrane, given a configuration of an MSD P system

$$\mathcal{C} = \big[[w_1]_{k_1}, \cdots, [w_n]_{k_n}, w_0\big]_h \, w$$

we say that $\mathcal{L} \sqsubseteq \mathcal{C}$ is a *linear restriction* of $\mathcal{C}$ if either $\mathcal{L} = w$, or $\mathcal{L} = [w_0]_h$, or $\mathcal{L} = \big[[w_i]_{k_i}\big]_h$ for some $1 \leq i \leq n$. In a linear restriction $\mathcal{L}$, only one membrane contains objects, and thus the occurrences of a small configuration $\mathcal{V} \sqsubseteq \mathcal{L}$ are either all subject to interference from a troublemaker, or none of them is.

Definition 7. *We say that a configuration $\mathcal{C}$ of an MSD P system is* untroubled *if there exists a linear restriction $\mathcal{L} \sqsubseteq \mathcal{C}$ and a small configuration $\mathcal{V} \in Y(\Pi)$ such that $\mathcal{V} \sqsubseteq \mathcal{L}$ and no object $a \in \mathrm{tm}(\mathcal{V})$ appears in $\mathcal{L}$.*

The following results show that the property of being untroubled propagates forwards along a computation step and thus, recursively, all the way to the halting configuration.

Lemma 3. *Let Π be an MSD P system, let $\mathcal{C}$ be an untroubled configuration reachable from the initial configuration $\mathcal{C}_0$, and let $\mathcal{C} \to \mathcal{D}$. Then $\mathcal{D}$ is also untroubled.*

Proof. Since $\mathcal{C}$ is untroubled, there exists a linear restriction $\mathcal{L} \sqsubseteq \mathcal{C}$ and a small configuration $\mathcal{V} \sqsubseteq \mathcal{L}$ such that no object of $\mathrm{tm}(\mathcal{V})$ belongs to $\mathcal{L}$.

If $d(\mathcal{V}) \leq 2$, then there exists a small configuration $\mathcal{W}$ with $d(\mathcal{W}) \leq 1$ such that $\mathcal{V} \to \mathcal{V}' \sqsupseteq \mathcal{W}$ for some configuration $\mathcal{V}'$, otherwise $d(\mathcal{V})$ would be at least 3. But then $\mathrm{tm}(\mathcal{W}) = \varnothing$ and thus $\mathcal{D}$ is untroubled.

If $d(\mathcal{V}) \geq 3$, then $\mathcal{V} \to \mathcal{V}' \sqsupseteq \mathcal{W}$ for some $\mathcal{W}$ such that $d(\mathcal{W}) = d(\mathcal{V}) - 1 \geq 2$, and there exists a linear restriction $\mathcal{M} \sqsubseteq \mathcal{D}$ with $\mathcal{W} \sqsubseteq \mathcal{M}$. By contradiction suppose that, for all such $\mathcal{W}$, there exists $a \in \mathrm{tm}(\mathcal{W})$ with a belonging to $\mathcal{M}$.

This object a itself cannot appear in $\mathcal{L}$: since we have $\mathrm{tm}(\mathcal{W}) \subseteq \mathrm{tm}(\mathcal{V})$ by Lemma 2, we would have simultaneously $a \in \mathrm{tm}(\mathcal{V})$ and a in $\mathcal{L}$, contradicting our assumptions on $\mathcal{V}$. Hence, the object a must be generated by an object evolution or division rule triggered by an object b in $\mathcal{L}$.

If it is generated by an object evolution rule, then $b \in \text{evo}_k\left(\text{tm}(\mathcal{W})\right)$; since tm only depends on the distance d (Lemma 1), this means that we have $b \in \text{evo}_k\left(\text{tm}\left(\bigcap_{i=1}^n \mathcal{W}_i\right)\right)$, where the $\mathcal{W}_i$ are all small configurations, including $\mathcal{W}$, such that $(\mathcal{V}, \mathcal{W}_i) \in E(\Pi)$ with $d(\mathcal{W}_i) = d(\mathcal{V}) - 1$. But then $b \in \text{tm}(\mathcal{V})$ while simultaneously appearing in $\mathcal{L}$, once again contradicting the hypotheses on $\mathcal{V}$.

Suppose, instead, that the object a is generated by a division rule of the form $[b]_h \rightarrow [a]_h[c]_h$. We necessarily have $c \in \text{tm}(\mathcal{W})$, because otherwise there would exist a linear restriction $\mathcal{M}' \sqsubseteq \mathcal{D}$ distinct from $\mathcal{M}$ with $\mathcal{M}'$ containing the other copy of $\mathcal{W}$ resulting from the division, but without any object in $\text{tm}(\mathcal{W})$. But then we have both $a, c \in \text{tm}(\mathcal{W})$, which implies that

$$b \in \text{div}_k\left(\text{tm}(\mathcal{W})\right) = \text{div}_k\left(\bigcap_{i=1}^n \text{tm}(\mathcal{W}_i)\right) \subseteq \text{tm}(\mathcal{V})$$

once again contradicting the hypotheses on $\mathcal{V}$.

This shows that no object $a \in \text{tm}(\mathcal{W})$ can belong to $\mathcal{M}$, and thus $\mathcal{D}$ is untroubled. $\qquad\square$

Lemma 4. *Let Π be an MSD P system with untroubled initial configuration $\mathcal{C}_0$. Then Π accepts.*

Proof. Suppose that Π has the halting computation $\vec{\mathcal{C}} = (\mathcal{C}_0, \ldots, \mathcal{C}_t)$ with untroubled $\mathcal{C}_0$. By Lemma 3, all other configurations of $\vec{\mathcal{C}}$, and in particular $\mathcal{C}_t$, are also untroubled. This means that there exist a linear restriction $\mathcal{L} \sqsubseteq \mathcal{C}_t$ and a small configuration $\mathcal{V} \in Y(\Pi)$ such that $\mathcal{V} \sqsubseteq \mathcal{L}$ and no $a \in \text{tm}(\mathcal{V})$ appears in $\mathcal{L}$. The only small configuration in $Y(\Pi)$ where no rule is applicable is **yes**. This proves that the P system accepts. $\qquad\square$

The property of being untroubled does not only propagate forwards, but also *backwards*, all the way to the initial configuration.

Lemma 5. *Let Π be an MSD P system, let $\mathcal{C}$ be a configuration reachable from the initial configuration $\mathcal{C}_0$, and let $\mathcal{C} \rightarrow \mathcal{D}$ with $\mathcal{D}$ untroubled. Then $\mathcal{C}$ is also untroubled.*

Proof. Since $\mathcal{D}$ is untroubled, there exist a linear restriction $\mathcal{M} \sqsubseteq \mathcal{D}$ and a small configuration $\mathcal{W} \sqsubseteq \mathcal{M}$ such that no object $a \in \text{tm}(\mathcal{W})$ appears in $\mathcal{M}$.

Since $\mathcal{W}$ contains at most two objects, it is generated by at most two rules applied in $\mathcal{C}$; this means that there exist a linear restriction $\mathcal{L} \sqsubseteq \mathcal{C}$ and a small configuration $\mathcal{V} \sqsubseteq \mathcal{L}$ such that $\mathcal{V} \rightarrow \mathcal{V}' \sqsupseteq \mathcal{W}$ for some configuration $\mathcal{V}'$. Let us consider the set $\text{tm}(\mathcal{V})$. If $d(\mathcal{V}) \leq 1$, this set is computed according to Eq. (1), and then $\text{tm}(\mathcal{V}) = \varnothing$ and $\mathcal{C}$ is untroubled.

If $d(\mathcal{V}) \geq 2$, the set $\text{tm}(\mathcal{V})$ is computed according to Eq. (2):

$$\text{tm}(\mathcal{V}) = \text{dis}(k) \cup \text{evo}_k\left(\bigcap_{i=1}^n \text{tm}(\mathcal{W}_i)\right) \cup \text{div}_k\left(\bigcap_{i=1}^n \text{tm}(\mathcal{W}_i)\right)$$

In this case we have $\mathcal{W} = \big[[a]_k\big]_h$ or $\mathcal{W} = \big[[a\,b]_k\big]_h$. Let us consider an object $a \in \text{tm}(\mathcal{V})$. If $a \in \text{dis}(k)$, then a does not appear in $\mathcal{L}$, because membrane k survived the transition $\mathcal{V} \to \mathcal{V}' \sqsupseteq \mathcal{W}$. If $a \in \text{evo}_k\left(\bigcap_{i=1}^n \text{tm}(\mathcal{W}_i)\right)$ appeared in $\mathcal{L}$, then it would evolve into an object of $\mathcal{M}$ belonging to $\bigcap_{i=1}^n \text{tm}(\mathcal{W}_i) \subseteq \text{tm}(\mathcal{W})$, which contradicts the hypotheses on $\mathcal{W}$ and is thus impossible. Similarly, if $a \in \text{div}_k\left(\bigcap_{i=1}^n \text{tm}(\mathcal{W}_i)\right)$ appeared in $\mathcal{L}$, then $\mathcal{M}$ would contain one of the two objects on the right-hand side of the division rule involving a, and that object would belong to $\text{tm}(\mathcal{W})$; this contradicts the hypotheses on $\mathcal{W}$, and thus is also impossible. Hence, no object in $\text{tm}(\mathcal{V})$ appears in $\mathcal{L}$, and thus $\mathcal{C}$ is untroubled. $\square$

Lemma 6. *Let Π be an MSD P system with troubled initial configuration $\mathcal{C}_0$. Then Π rejects.*

Proof. Suppose that Π has the accepting computation $\vec{\mathcal{C}} = (\mathcal{C}_0, \ldots, \mathcal{C}_t)$. Then $\text{yes} \sqsubseteq \mathcal{C}_t$ and $\text{tm}(\text{yes}) = \varnothing$, which means that $\mathcal{C}_t$ is untroubled. But we have $\mathcal{C}_0 \to \mathcal{C}_1 \to \cdots \to \mathcal{C}_t$, and by Lemma 5 all previous configurations, including $\mathcal{C}_0$, are untroubled, which contradicts our hypotheses. $\square$

Hence, deciding whether an MSD P system accepts coincides with checking the troublemakers in its initial configuration.

Theorem 3. *An MSD P system accepts if and only if its initial configuration is untroubled.* $\square$

If membrane dissolution rules are disallowed, the term $\text{dis}(k)$ is always empty in Eq. (2), and thus $\text{tm}(\mathcal{V}) = \varnothing$ for all small configurations $\mathcal{V}$; this implies that all configurations are untroubled (Definition 7). Furthermore, the small configurations of the form $\big[[a\,b]_k\big]_h$ can be ignored in favour of the smaller configurations $\big[[a]_k\big]_h$ and $\big[[b]_k\big]_h$, since a configuration with two objects is only required when the dissolution caused by one allows the other object to eventually evolve into yes (cases 5 and 6 of Theorem 1). This shows that, in the absence of dissolution, the acceptance condition of Theorem 3 corresponds to the existence of a path from a small configuration of the form $[a]_h$ or $\big[[a]_k\big]_h$, included in the initial configuration of the P system, to the small configuration yes. This is exactly the original acceptance condition for standard dependency graphs [3,5].

An analysis of the computational resources required in order to check the condition of Theorem 3 finally allows us to show that MSD P systems characterise the complexity class **P**.

Theorem 4. $\textbf{DMC}_{\mathcal{D}}^{[\star]} = \textbf{DPMC}_{\mathcal{D}}^{[\star]} = \textbf{P}$, *where $\mathcal{D}$ is the class of MSD P systems and $[\star]$ denotes optional semi-uniformity.*

Proof. Since the following inclusions hold

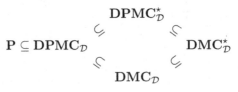

it suffices to prove $\mathbf{DMC}^\star_{\mathcal{D}} \subseteq \mathbf{P}$. Let Π be a semi-uniform family of recogniser MSD P systems constructed in polynomial time by Turing machine H.

Given an input string $x \in \Sigma^\star$, simulate H on x in polynomial time in order to obtain the description of the P system Π_x.

The alphabet of Π_x and its set of rules have polynomial size, and thus the dependency graph $G(\Pi)$ can be constructed in polynomial time (see Gutiérrez-Naranjo et al. [5] for more details).

The set of vertices $Y(\Pi)$ connected to the vertex yes, and thus the subgraph of $G(\Pi)$ induced by them, can be computed in polynomial time by exploring the transposed dependency graph (i.e., with all edges reversed) starting from the vertex yes.

The value $d(\mathcal{V})$ can then be computed in polynomial time for each $\mathcal{V} \in Y(\Pi)$ by using an all-pairs shortest path algorithm on the subgraph induced by $Y(\Pi)$, and then choosing the distance from the closest vertex of the form $[a]_h$ or yes.

The troublemakers $\mathrm{tm}(\mathcal{V})$ are computed recursively in polynomial time using Eqs. (1) and (2) on the subgraph induced by $Y(\Pi)$ and based on the distance function d.

Finally, for each of the (polynomially many) small configurations $\mathcal{V}$ and all (polynomially many) linear restrictions $\mathcal{L} \sqsubseteq \mathcal{C}_0$, where $\mathcal{C}_0$ is the initial configuration of Π, we can check whether $\mathcal{V} \sqsubseteq \mathcal{L}$ and simultaneously no object $a \in \mathrm{tm}(\mathcal{V})$ appears in $\mathcal{L}$. If this happens at least once, the input string x is accepted, and otherwise rejected. □

5   Conclusions and Open Problems

We have proved that families of monodirectional, deterministic, shallow P systems with active membranes without charges (MSD P systems) characterise the complexity class $\mathbf{P}$, both with a polynomial-time uniformity and a polynomial-time semi-uniformity condition. This solves an open special case of the P conjecture and shows that dissolution does not always allow us to break the $\mathbf{P}$ barrier, even if object evolution, send-out, and membrane division rules are allowed.

In order to prove this result, we developed a generalisation of an important membrane computing tool, already exploited for several $\mathbf{P}$ upper bound results for P systems without charges: namely, dependency graphs. By proving that a constant number of objects govern the result of the computation, we were able to construct polynomial-size dependency graphs that include dissolving membranes. By checking a property of dependency graphs more complex than the original one, but still verifiable in polynomial time, we can establish the result of the computation of an MSD P system without resorting to expensive full simulations.

Even if we only focused on P systems of depth at most one in this paper, our approach should be straightforward to generalise to MSD P systems of any constant depth, as long as membrane division is only applicable to the initial elementary membranes, by tracking a constant number of objects larger than two. If elementary division rules are associated to membranes that only become elementary during the computation, there is the additional problem of establishing when this is the case for the membranes we are tracking (since "being elementary" depends on untracked membranes having dissolved). Here, we believe it is worth investigating a combination of our approach with the one proposed by Woods et al. [14], which deals correctly with dissolution and elementary division in P systems of arbitrary depth in the absence of other types of rules.

We further conjecture that it is possible to replace the determinism constraint with the standard confluence condition. This seems, however, to make the forwards and backwards propagation of the property of being untroubled harder to prove, due to the possibility of multiple computations.

We also remarked that several other generalisations of dependency graphs, for use with other variants of P systems, are possible. Although it is unclear whether this approach is powerful enough to solve the remaining open cases of the P conjecture, an interesting open problem is establishing which classes of P systems admit polynomial-size dependency graphs with polynomial-time computable accepting conditions. A related question is whether it is possible to find classes of P systems with larger-than-polynomial dependency graphs that do not require a complete exploration, and thus still allow their result to be established in polynomial time.

References

1. Alhazov, A., Freund, R.: On the efficiency of P systems with active membranes and two polarizations. In: Mauri, G., Păun, G., Pérez-Jiménez, M.J., Rozenberg, G., Salomaa, A. (eds.) WMC 2004. LNCS, vol. 3365, pp. 146–160. Springer, Heidelberg (2005). https://doi.org/10.1007/978-3-540-31837-8_8
2. Alhazov, A., Pérez-Jiménez, M.J.: Uniform solution of QSAT using polarizationless active membranes. In: Durand-Lose, J., Margenstern, M. (eds.) MCU 2007. LNCS, vol. 4664, pp. 122–133. Springer, Heidelberg (2007). https://doi.org/10.1007/978-3-540-74593-8_11
3. Cordón-Franco, A., Gutiérrez-Naranjo, M.A., Pérez-Jiménez, M.J., Riscos-Núñez, A.: Exploring computation trees associated with P systems. In: Mauri, G., Păun, G., Pérez-Jiménez, M.J., Rozenberg, G., Salomaa, A. (eds.) WMC 2004. LNCS, vol. 3365, pp. 278–286. Springer, Heidelberg (2005). https://doi.org/10.1007/978-3-540-31837-8_16
4. Gazdag, Z., Kolonits, G.: Remarks on the computational power of some restricted variants of P systems with active membranes. In: Leporati, A., Rozenberg, G., Salomaa, A., Zandron, C. (eds.) CMC 2016. LNCS, vol. 10105, pp. 209–232. Springer, Cham (2017). https://doi.org/10.1007/978-3-319-54072-6_14
5. Gutiérrez-Naranjo, M.A., Pérez-Jiménez, M.J., Riscos-Núñez, A., Romero-Campero, F.J.: P systems with active membranes, without polarizations and without dissolution: a characterization of P. In: Calude, C.S., Dinneen, M.J., Păun, G., Pérez-Jímenez, M.J., Rozenberg, G. (eds.) UC 2005. LNCS, vol. 3699, pp. 105–116. Springer, Heidelberg (2005). https://doi.org/10.1007/11560319_11
6. Gutiérrez–Naranjo, M.A., Pérez–Jiménez, M.J., Riscos–Núñez, A., Romero–Campero, F.J.: On the power of dissolution in P systems with active membranes. In: Freund, R., Păun, G., Rozenberg, G., Salomaa, A. (eds.) WMC 2005. LNCS, vol. 3850, pp. 224–240. Springer, Heidelberg (2006). https://doi.org/10.1007/11603047_16

7. Leporati, A., Manzoni, L., Mauri, G., Porreca, A.E., Zandron, C.: Simulating elementary active membranes. In: Gheorghe, M., Rozenberg, G., Salomaa, A., Sosík, P., Zandron, C. (eds.) CMC 2014. LNCS, vol. 8961, pp. 284–299. Springer, Cham (2014). https://doi.org/10.1007/978-3-319-14370-5_18

8. Leporati, A., Manzoni, L., Mauri, G., Porreca, A.E., Zandron, C.: Monodirectional P systems. Nat. Comput. **15**(4), 551–564 (2016). https://doi.org/10.1007/s11047-016-9565-2

9. Murphy, N., Woods, D.: Active membrane systems without charges and using only symmetric elementary division characterise P. In: Eleftherakis, G., Kefalas, P., Păun, G., Rozenberg, G., Salomaa, A. (eds.) WMC 2007. LNCS, vol. 4860, pp. 367–384. Springer, Heidelberg (2007). https://doi.org/10.1007/978-3-540-77312-2_23

10. Murphy, N., Woods, D.: The computational power of membrane systems under tight uniformity conditions. Nat. Comput. **10**(1), 613–632 (2011)

11. Păun, G.: Further twenty six open problems in membrane computing. In: Gutíerrez-Naranjo, M.A., Riscos-Nuñez, A., Romero-Campero, F.J., Sburlan, D. (eds.) Proceedings of the Third Brainstorming Week on Membrane Computing, pp. 249–262. Fénix Editora (2005)

12. Pérez-Jiménez, M.J., Romero-Jiménez, A., Sancho-Caparrini, F.: Complexity classes in models of cellular computing with membranes. Nat. Comput. **2**(3), 265–284 (2003)

13. Sosík, P., Rodríguez-Patón, A.: Membrane computing and complexity theory: a characterization of PSPACE. J. Comput. Syst. Sci. **73**(1), 137–152 (2007)

14. Woods, D., Murphy, N., Pérez-Jiménez, M.J., Riscos-Núñez, A.: Membrane dissolution and division in P. In: Calude, C.S., Costa, J.F., Dershowitz, N., Freire, E., Rozenberg, G. (eds.) UC 2009. LNCS, vol. 5715, pp. 262–276. Springer, Heidelberg (2009). https://doi.org/10.1007/978-3-642-03745-0_28

Most Common Words – A cP Systems Solution

Radu Nicolescu[✉]

Department of Computer Science, University of Auckland,
Private Bag, 92019 Auckland, New Zealand
r.nicolescu@auckland.ac.nz

Abstract. Finding the most common words in a text file is a famous "programming pearl", originally posed by Jon Bentley (1984). Several interesting solutions have been proposed by Knuth (an exquisite model of literate programming, 1986), McIlroy (an engineering example of combining a timeless set of tools, 1986), Hanson (an alternate efficient solution, 1987). Here we propose a concise efficient solution based on the fast parallel and associative capabilities of cP systems. We also check their parallel sorting capabilities and propose a dynamic version of the classical pigeonhole algorithm.

Keywords: Literate programming · Most common words
Membrane computing · P systems · cP systems
Associative data structures · Inter- and intra-cell parallelism
Prolog terms and unification · Parallel sorting · Pigeonhole algorithm

1 Introduction and Background

cP systems share the fundamental features of the traditional cell-like (tree-based) and tissue (graph-based) P systems: top-cells are organised in graph/digraph networks, top-cells contain nested (and labelled) sub-cells, the evolution is governed by multiset rewriting rules, possibly running in maximal parallel modes.

Although not strictly necessary – but also shared with other versions of the traditional P systems [10] – our typical rulesets are state based and run in a weak priority mode.

There are two main innovations in cP systems. First, unlike in traditional cell-like P systems, sub-cells do NOT have own rules. Basically, the sub-cells are just nested passive repositories of other sub-cells or atomic symbols; therefore, they can also be viewed as nested complex objects (or terms).

This seems a severe limitation. However, it is more than compensated by the provision of higher level rules, which extend the classical multiset rewriting rules with concepts borrowed from logic programming, namely Prolog unification. In other words, cP systems may be seen as adapting the classical Prolog unification from structured terms to multisets – which again is a novel feature.

However, unlike traditional Prolog, where rules are applied in a backward-chaining mode, with possible backtracks, cP rules work in a forward mode, like

© Springer International Publishing AG 2018
M. Gheorghe et al. (Eds.): CMC 2017, LNCS 10725, pp. 214–229, 2018.
https://doi.org/10.1007/978-3-319-73359-3_14

all known P system rules. This may perhaps allow better parallelism capabilities than the past and actual parallel versions of Prolog – but this topic will not be further followed here.

The net result is a powerful system which can crisply and efficiently solve complex problems, with small fixed-size alphabets and small, fast fixed-size rule-sets. In particular, cP systems enable a reasonably straightforward creation and manipulation of high-level data structures typical of high-level languages, such as: numbers, relations (graphs), associative arrays, lists, trees, strings.

In this sense, cP systems have been successfully used to develop parallel and distributed models in a large variety of domains, such as distributed algorithms, graph theory, image processing, NP complete problems.

In this paper, we further assess the "computer science" capabilities of our cP systems by solving a version of a famous *programming pearl*, initially posed by Jon Bentley (1984): printing the most common words in a text file, more precisely (but still a bit vague) [1]:

Given a text file and an integer k, print the k most common words in the file (and the number of their occurrences) in decreasing frequency.

Additionally, the integer N is typically used for the number of words, d is the number of distinct words, and f is the highest frequency count. Of course, one typically assumes that $N > d > k$ and $N - d + 1 \geq f \geq N/d$, but some solutions are optimised for the more special case $N \gg d \gg k$.

Several interesting solutions have been proposed by Knuth in 1986 – an exquisite model of literate programming [1], McIlroy in 1986 – an engineering example of combining a timeless set of tools [1], Hanson in 1987 – an alternate efficient solution [12]. All these three solutions can be considered as great literate programming sample models, if we take "literal programming" in a generic sense – not just Knuth's WEB/TANGLE implementation [2].

Here we propose a concise efficient solution, following Hanson's revised formulation [12] of the original problem specification, which clarifies the slight ambiguity of the original:

Given a text file and an integer k, you are to print the words (and their frequencies of occurrence) whose frequencies of occurrence are among the k largest in order of decreasing frequency.

A tiny but artificial example may clarify these specifications. Assume that $k = 2$ and the input text is:

```
ccc aa aa aa ccc bb d aa d
```

Note that, here, $N = 9, d = 4, f = 4$. Bentley's original formulation, used by Knuth and McIlroy [1], essentially requires – a bit ambiguously – one of the following two outputs:

```
4 aa
2 ccc
```

or

```
4 aa
2 d
```

In contrast, Hanson's revised formulation [12], requires the following output – which is unambiguous, if the order of word sublists is not relevant (i.e. ccc d ≡ d ccc):

```
4 aa
2 ccc d
```

Schematically, all these solutions follow *four main phases*: (I) reading and splitting the text file into words (parsing it); (II) computing the word frequencies; (III) sorting according to frequencies; and (IV) printing the required output.

Knuth and Hanson provide large *monolithic* solutions, which include all four phases. Moreover, they combine phases I and II, by using associative data structures: Knuth uses a custom hash-trie and Hanson a custom hashtable with splay (move to front) lists. For phase III, both authors try to use efficient sorting methods. Knuth uses a fast sorting method, assuming that $N \gg d \gg k$ and that most frequent words tend to appear from the beginning of the text – however, as McIlroy points out, this does not always hold. Hanson offers a more universal fast sorting method based on the *pigeonhole algorithm*, with f holes.

McIlroy's solution is a textbook example for the *separation-of-concerns* principle, via a pipeline of staple general-purpose utilities initially developed for UNIX. Each of the four phases is implemented via just one or two commands. Together, phases II and III take exactly three lines in the pipe [1]:

```
(3) sort |
(4) uniq -c |
(5) sort -rn |
```

Line (3) sorts the N input words (lexicographically). Line (4) counts then discards the duplicates, keeping d unique exemplars and their frequency counts (as count/word pairs). Line (5) sorts d count/word pairs, in reverse count order (numerically).

Intentionally not given here are pipe lines (1), (2) and (6), which deal with phases I and IV. Reading, splitting into words and printing can be defined in a seemingly endless multiplicity of ways, which may not be worth discussing here. In particular, the concept of "word" itself may be highly interpretable: does it include ASCII letters, UNICODE letters, digits, punctuation signs, does it have a length limit, etc. Here, we will stay away from this discussion.

McIlroy's solution is also reasonably fast – not as fast as the other two – but it is extremely crisp and clear, and can be flexibly adapted to other input and output formats. Such a solution can be developed and deployed in just a few minutes – this sounds amazing, but does not account for the many manmonths required to develop and tune the used building blocks (UNIX tools). McIlroy also notes that his solution could be sped up by replacing the more costlier lines (3) and (4) by a hypothetical tool based on associative arrays – in fact, this would bring his solution closer to Hanson's solution for phase II.

Our cP solution – which uses *one single top-level cell with data-only subcells* – follows the spirit of McIlroy's and Hanson's solutions. It is based on associative data types and a sorting idea close to Hanson's pigeonhole algorithm. It also uses a small fixed number of rules – close to McIlroy's pipeline size – but, in contrast, it is built from scratch (not on higher building block as the UNIX commands).

We offer two alternate solutions: (i) a solution which solves Hanson's version of the problem – where the result is a *sorted sequence of word multisets*; and (ii) a solution which solves the original problem, as posed by Bentley and used by Knuth and McIlroy – where the result is a *sorted sequence of words*.

In this process, we propose and use a *dynamic pigeonhole algorithm*, adaptable to other platforms with strong associative capabilities, where – metaphorically - pigeonholes are only opened one at at time, instantly attracting objects with matching keys.

In our case, we must first adapt the above problem formulation to typical P systems, where cells contain multisets of symbols, not ordered structures. What is a sorted multiset? Ordered structures must be constructed in terms of multisets – in cP systems, we can create the required high-level structures by deep nesting of complex symbols (subcells).

As above mentioned, we chose to skip over the reading phase (I) and we assume that all words are "magically" present at start-time in our single cell. Our focus is on phases II and III, where all operations are clearly defined and can be efficiently performed by cP systems.

Finally – as used in our first solution (i) – we simulate the printing phase IV, by *sequentially sending out the required results, in order, over a designated line.* Alternatively – as used in our second solution (ii) – we actually *build an ordered list containing the required results.*

For completeness, Sect. 2 introduces a few high-level data structures in cP systems and Appendix A offers a more complete definition of the cP systems – both these sections incrementally update the results and definitions given in our earlier paper [7]. The remaining sections discuss our solution.

2 Data Structures in cP Systems

We assume that the reader is familiar with the membrane extensions collectively known as *complex symbols*, proposed by Nicolescu et al. [6,8,9]. However, to ensure some degree of self-containment, our revised extensions, (still) called cP systems, are reproduced in Appendix A.

In this section we sketch the design of high-level data structures, similar to the data structures used in high-level pseudocode or high-level languages: numbers, relations, functions, associative arrays, lists, trees, strings, together with alternative more readable notations.

Natural numbers. Natural numbers can be represented via *multisets* containing repeated occurrences of the *same* atom. For example, considering that *1* represents an ad-hoc unary digit, the following complex symbols can be used to describe the contents of a virtual integer *variable* a: $a() = a(\lambda)$—the value of a is 0; $a(1^3)$—the value of a is 3. For concise expressions, we may alias these number representations by their corresponding numbers, e.g. $a() \equiv a(0), b(1^3) \equiv b(3)$. Nicolescu et al. [8,9] show how the basic arithmetic operations can be efficiently modelled by P systems with complex symbols.

Here follows a list of simple arithmetic expressions, assignments and comparisons:

$$
\begin{aligned}
x = 0 &\equiv x(\lambda) \\
x = 1 &\equiv x(1) \\
x = 2 &\equiv x(11) \\
x = n &\equiv x(1^n) \\
x \leftarrow y + z &\equiv y(Y)\, z(Z) \;\rightarrow\; x(YZ) \quad \text{destructive add} \\
x \leftarrow y + z &\equiv \;\rightarrow\; x(YZ) \mid y(Y)\, z(Z) \quad \text{preserving add} \\
x = y &\equiv x(X)\, y(X) \\
x \leq y &\equiv x(X)\, y(XY) \\
x < y &\equiv x(X)\, y(X1Y)
\end{aligned}
$$

Relations and functions. Consider the *binary relation* r, defined by: $r = \{(a,b), (b,c), (a,d), (d,c)\}$ (which has a diamond-shaped graph). Using complex symbols, relation r can be represented as a *multiset* with four r items, $\{r(\kappa(a)\, \upsilon(b)), r(\kappa(b)\, \upsilon(c)), r(\kappa(a)\, \upsilon(d)), r(\kappa(d)\, \upsilon(c))\}$, where ad-hoc atoms κ and υ introduce *domain* and *codomain* values (respectively). We may also alias the items of this multiset by a more expressive notation such as: $\{(a \overset{r}{\rightleftarrows} b), (b \overset{r}{\rightleftarrows} c), (a \overset{r}{\rightleftarrows} d), (d \overset{r}{\rightleftarrows} c)\}$.

If the relation is a *functional relation*, then we can emphasise this by using another operator, such as "mapsto". For example, the functional relation $f = \{(a,b), (b,c), (d,c)\}$ can be represented by multiset $\{f(\kappa(a)\, \upsilon(b)), f(\kappa(b)\, \upsilon(c)), f(\kappa(d)\, \upsilon(c))\}$ or by the more suggestive notation: $\{(a \overset{f}{\mapsto} b), (b \overset{f}{\mapsto} c), (d \overset{f}{\mapsto} c)\}$. To highlight the actual mapping value, instead of $a \overset{f}{\mapsto} b$, we may also use the succinct abbreviation $f[a] = b$.

In this context, the $\rightleftarrows$ and $\mapsto$ operators are considered to have a high associative priority, so the enclosing parentheses are mostly used for increasing the readability.

Associative arrays. Consider the *associative array* x, with the following key-value mappings (i.e. functional relation): $\{1 \mapsto a; 1^3 \mapsto c; 1^7 \mapsto g\}$. Using complex symbols, array x can be represented as a multiset with three items, $\{x(\kappa(1)\, \upsilon(a)), x(\kappa(1^3)\, \upsilon(c)), x(\kappa(1^7)\, \upsilon(g))\}$, where ad-hoc atoms κ and υ introduce keys and values (respectively). We may also alias the items of this multiset by the more expressive notation $\{1 \overset{x}{\mapsto} a, 1^3 \overset{x}{\mapsto} c, 1^7 \overset{x}{\mapsto} g\}$.

Lists. Consider the *list* y, containing the following sequence of values: $[u; v; w]$. List y can be represented as the complex symbol $y(\gamma(u\, \gamma(v\, \gamma(w\, \gamma()))))$, where the ad-hoc atom γ represents the list constructor *cons* and $\gamma()$ the empty list. We may also alias this list by the more expressive equivalent notation $y(u \,|\, v \,|\, w)$ – or by $y(u \,|\, y')$, $y'(v \,|\, w)$ – where operator $|$ separates the head and the tail of the list. The notation $z(|)$ is shorthand for $z(\gamma())$ and indicates an empty list, z.

Trees. Consider the *binary tree* z, described by the structured expression $(a, (b), (c, (d), (e)))$, i.e. z points to a root node which has: (i) the value a; (ii) a left node with value b; and (iii) a right node with value c, left leaf d, and right leaf e. Tree z can be represented as the complex symbol $z(a\ \phi(b)\ \psi(c\ \phi(d)\ \psi(e)))$, where ad-hoc atoms ϕ, ψ introduce left subtrees, right subtrees (respectively).

Strings. Consider the *string* $s = $ "*abc*", where a, b, and c are atoms. Obviously, string s can interpreted as the list $s = [a; b; c]$, i.e. string s can be represented as the complex symbol $s(\gamma(a\ \gamma(b\ \gamma(c\ \gamma()))))$, etc.

3   The Parallel cP Algorithm – Solution (i)

3.1   Initial State

We need *one single cell* with one designated output line. Required data structures are built as complex symbols (data-only subcells), using the interpretations and notations defined in Sect. 2. In particular, the N input words are strings built via functor w; these complex symbols are already extant when the systems starts. Figure 1 illustrates the initial cell contents for the sample given in Sect. 1.

"ccc" "aa" "aa" "aa" "ccc" "bb" "d" "aa" "d"

(a) High-level strings.

$w(c\,w(c\,w(c\,w())))$ $w(a\,w(a\,w()))$ $w(a\,w(a\,w()))$ $w(a\,w(a\,w()))$
$w(c\,w(c\,w(c\,w())))$ $w(b\,w(b\,w()))$ $w(d\,w())$ $w(a\,w(a\,w()))$ $w(d\,w())$

(b) Underlying complex symbols.

Fig. 1. Sample initial word multiset.

3.2   Phase II

Using an associative relation, α, each word is tagged with an initial "frequency" count of 1 and then we *merge all word duplicates* and *sum* their associated counts. In the end, we get d words, each one with its actual frequency count.

Figure 2 shows the three rules for phase II. This ruleset starts in state S_0. Rule (0) establishes relation α between extant strings given by $w(X)$ and the initial frequency count 1; it runs in `max` mode, so it completes its job in 1 cP step.

Rule (1) repeatedly merges word duplicates and sums their associated counts; it runs in `max` mode, so it completes its job in $\log(d)$ cP steps – this rule is non-deterministic but confluent.

After rule (1) completes, rule (2) moves to the final state of this ruleset, S_2. Table 1 illustrates the evolution of the cell contents for our initial sample.

$$
\begin{array}{llll}
S_0 & w(W) & \rightarrow_{\texttt{max}} S_1\ \alpha(w(W)\,f(1)) & (0) \\
S_1 & \alpha(w(W)\,f(F))\ \ \alpha(w(W)\,f(F')) \rightarrow_{\texttt{max}} S_1\ \alpha(w(W)\,f(FF')) & (1) \\
S_1 & & \rightarrow_{\texttt{min}} S_2 & (2)
\end{array}
$$

Fig. 2. Ruleset for phase II.

Table 1. Phase II evolution of the sample word multiset.

Apply	State	Cell contents
(0)	S_0	"ccc" "aa" "aa" "aa" "ccc" "bb" "d" "aa" "d"
(1)	S_1	$\alpha($"ccc" $f(1))\ \alpha($"aa" $f(1))\ \ \alpha($"aa" $f(1))\ \alpha($"aa" $f(1))$ ...
(1)	S_1	$\alpha($"ccc" $f(2))\ \alpha($"aa" $f(2))\ \alpha($"aa" $f(2))\ \alpha($"bb" $f(1))\ \alpha($"d" $f(2))$
(2)	S_1	$\alpha($"ccc" $f(2))\ \alpha($"aa" $f(4))\ \alpha($"bb" $f(1))\ \alpha($"d" $f(2))$
–	S_2	$\alpha($"ccc" $f(2))\ \alpha($"aa" $f(4))\ \alpha($"bb" $f(1))\ \alpha($"d" $f(2))$

3.3 Phase III

We create maximal word multisets by merging all words sharing the same *frequency counts*.

Figure 3 shows the two rules for phase III. This ruleset starts in state S_2, the final state for phase II (Sect. 3.2). Rule (3) merges word multisets sharing the same frequency counts; it runs in `max` mode, so it completes its job in $\log(f)$ cP steps – this rule is non-deterministic but confluent.

After rule (3) completes, rule (4) moves to the final state of this ruleset, S_3. Table 2 illustrates the evolution of the cell contents for the initial sample.

3.4 Phase IV

We send out all existing word multisets, sequentially, in decreasing order of their *frequency counts*. We propose and use a *dynamic* version of the classical

$$S_2 \quad \alpha(W \, f(F)) \quad \alpha(W' \, f(F)) \rightarrow_{\max} S_2 \, \alpha(W \, W' \, f(F)) \quad (3)$$

$$S_2 \qquad\qquad\qquad\qquad \rightarrow_{\min} S_3 \qquad\qquad (4)$$

Fig. 3. Ruleset for phase III.

Table 2. Phase III evolution of the sample word multiset.

Apply	State	Cell contents
(3)	S_2	$\alpha(\text{``ccc''} \, f(2)) \, \alpha(\text{``aa''} \, f(4)) \, \alpha(\text{``bb''} \, f(1)) \, \alpha(\text{``d''} \, f(2))$
(4)	S_2	$\alpha(\text{``ccc''} \, \text{``d''} \, f(2)) \, \alpha(\text{``aa''} \, f(4)) \, \alpha(\text{``bb''} \, f(1))$
–	S_3	$\alpha(\text{``ccc''} \, \text{``d''} \, f(2)) \, \alpha(\text{``aa''} \, f(4)) \, \alpha(\text{``bb''} \, f(1))$

pigeonhole algorithm (adaptable to other platforms with strong associative capabilities), where – metaphorically - pigeonholes are only opened one at time, instantly attracting objects with matching keys.

First, we determine the highest frequency count. Next, we repeatedly output the word multiset having the current highest frequency count – if any – and then decrement this count, until we reach 0. This current highest frequency count is the "enabled pigeonhole" which "attracts" the word multiset having the same frequency count. For simplicity, we do not consider the parameter k, but it is straightforward to include it in this ruleset.

Figure 4 shows the rules for phase IV. This ruleset starts in state S_3, the final state for phase III (Sect. 3.3). Rule (5) extracts frequency counts; it runs in max mode, so it completes its job in 1 cP steps.

Rule (6) determines the highest frequency count by taking pairwise maximums (note that all extant frequency counts are different); it runs in max mode, so it completes its job in $\log(f)$ cP steps – this rule is non-deterministic but confluent.

After rule (6) completes, rule (7) moves to the next state of this ruleset, S_5. Rule (8) outputs the word multiset having the current (highest) non-zero frequency count – if any – and then decrements this count; rule (9) just decrements this count, if there is no matching word multiset; this pair of rules complete their job in $\log(f)$ cP steps.

After all the word multisets are sent out, the cell remains idle in the final state, S_5 – alternatively, one more rule could clear the remaining $f(0)$ counter and transit to another state (e.g. S_6). Table 3 illustrates the evolution of the cell contents for the initial sample. Essentially, in this scenario we output the sequence [("aa", 4); ("ccc" "d", 2); ("bb", 1)].

$$S_3 \quad \alpha(W\, f(F)) \qquad\qquad \rightarrow_{\max} S_4\ \alpha(W\, f(F))\ f(F) \qquad (5)$$

$$S_4 \quad f(F)\ f(F1F') \qquad\quad \rightarrow_{\max} S_4\ f(F1F') \qquad\qquad\quad (6)$$

$$S_4 \qquad\qquad\qquad\qquad\quad \rightarrow_{\min} S_5 \qquad\qquad\qquad\qquad\quad (7)$$

$$S_5 \quad \alpha(W\, f(F1))\ f(F1) \rightarrow_{\min} S_5\ \alpha(W\, f(F1))\downarrow\ f(F)\ (8)$$

$$S_5 \quad f(F1) \qquad\qquad\qquad \rightarrow_{\min} S_5\ f(F) \qquad\qquad\qquad\ (9)$$

Fig. 4. Ruleset for phase IV.

Table 3. Phase IV evolution of the sample word multiset – each time it is applied, the highlighted rule (8) outputs one word multiset and its associated frequency count.

Apply	State	Cell contents
(5)	S_3	$\alpha(\text{“ccc” “d”}\ f(2))\ \alpha(\text{“aa”}\ f(4))\ \alpha(\text{“bb”}\ f(1))$
(6)	S_4	$\alpha(\text{“ccc” “d”}\ f(2))\ \alpha(\text{“aa”}\ f(4))\ \alpha(\text{“bb”}\ f(1))\ f(2)\ f(4)\ f(1)$
(6)	S_4	$\alpha(\text{“ccc” “d”}\ f(2))\ \alpha(\text{“aa”}\ f(4))\ \alpha(\text{“bb”}\ f(1))\ f(4)\ f(1)$
(7)	S_4	$\alpha(\text{“ccc” “d”}\ f(2))\ \alpha(\text{“aa”}\ f(4))\ \alpha(\text{“bb”}\ f(1))\ f(4)$
(8)	S_5	$\alpha(\text{“ccc” “d”}\ f(2))\ \alpha(\textbf{“aa”}\ \mathbf{f(4)})\ \alpha(\text{“bb”}\ f(1))\ f(4)$
(9)	S_5	$\alpha(\text{“ccc” “d”}\ f(2))\ \alpha(\text{“bb”}\ f(1))\ f(3)$
(8)	S_5	$\alpha(\textbf{“ccc” “d”}\ \mathbf{f(2)})\ \alpha(\text{“bb”}\ f(1))\ f(2)$
(8)	S_5	$\alpha(\textbf{“bb”}\ \mathbf{f(1)})\ f(1)$
–	S_5	$f(0)$

4 The Parallel cP Algorithm – Alternate Solution (ii)

Here we sketch an alternate implementation, which actually builds a *sorted list of words*, ordered on their frequency counts. This solution could be applied to get a sorted list of word multisets, but here we use it to get a *sorted list of words*, i.e. a result closer to the original problem formulation posed by Bentley and used by Knuth and McIlroy [1].

Conceptually, we start from the interim results of phase II of solution (i) (Sect. 3.2), but this time we give a complete solution (not explicitly split into phases).

We create a list of words, sorted in decreasing order of their *frequency counts*. As in the earlier phase II (Sect. 3.2) each word is tagged with an initial "frequency" count of 1 and then we *merge all word duplicates* and *sum* their associated counts. In the end, we get d words, each one with its actual frequency count.

Then, as in the earlier phase IV (Sect. 3.4), we use a *dynamic* version of the classical *pigeonhole algorithm*, but this time we stack the "attracted" words in a result list (instead of sending them out).

$$S_0 \quad w(W) \qquad\qquad\qquad\qquad\qquad \to_{max} S_1 \; \alpha(w(W)\,f(1)) \qquad\qquad (0)$$

$$S_1 \quad \alpha(w(W)\,f(F)) \; \alpha(w(W)\,f(F')) \to_{max} S_1 \; \alpha(w(W)\,f(FF')) \qquad (1)$$

$$S_1 \qquad\qquad\qquad\qquad\qquad\qquad \to_{min} S_2 \; f(1)\,\rho() \qquad\qquad\qquad (2)$$

$$S_2 \quad \alpha(w(W)\,f(F)) \; \rho(R) \qquad\qquad \to_{max} S_2 \; \rho(\alpha(w(W)\,f(F))\,\rho(R)) \;(3)$$
$$\mid f(F)$$

$$S_2 \quad f(F) \qquad\qquad\qquad\qquad\qquad \to_{min} S_2 \; f(F1) \qquad\qquad\qquad (4)$$
$$\mid \alpha(\_)$$

Fig. 5. Ruleset for alternate solution (ii).

First, we "enable a pigeonhole" for frequency 1 and create an empty result list. Next, we repeatedly stack all words having the current pigeonhole frequency count – if any – and then increment this count, until we exhaust all extant words. For simplicity, we again do not consider the parameter k, but it is straightforward to include it in this ruleset.

Figure 5 shows all rules for this alternate solution. Rules (0) and (1) are exactly as in the earlier phase II. Rule (2) is modified: to "enable a pigeonhole" for frequency 1 and to create an empty result list, ρ.

Table 4. Alternate solution (ii): possible evolution of the sample word multiset. Here the final result is the sorted list $[\alpha(\text{"}aa\text{"}\; f(4)); \; \alpha(\text{"}d\text{"}\; f(2)); \; \alpha(\text{"}ccc\text{"}\; f(2)); \; \alpha(\text{"}bb\text{"}\; f(1))]$.

Apply	State	Cell contents
(0)	S_0	"ccc" "aa" "aa" "aa" "ccc" "bb" "d" "aa" "d"
(1)	S_1	$\alpha(\text{"}ccc\text{"}\; f(1))\; \alpha(\text{"}aa\text{"}\; f(1))\; \alpha(\text{"}aa\text{"}\; f(1))\; \alpha(\text{"}aa\text{"}\; f(1))$ ...
(1)	S_1	$\alpha(\text{"}ccc\text{"}\; f(2))\; \alpha(\text{"}aa\text{"}\; f(2))\; \alpha(\text{"}aa\text{"}\; f(2))\; \alpha(\text{"}bb\text{"}\; f(1))\; \alpha(\text{"}d\text{"}\; f(2))$
(2)	S_1	$\alpha(\text{"}ccc\text{"}\; f(2))\; \alpha(\text{"}aa\text{"}\; f(4))\; \alpha(\text{"}bb\text{"}\; f(1))\; \alpha(\text{"}d\text{"}\; f(2))$
(3)	S_2	$f(1)\; \alpha(\text{"}ccc\text{"}\; f(2))\; \alpha(\text{"}aa\text{"}\; f(4))\; \alpha(\text{"}bb\text{"}\; f(1))\; \alpha(\text{"}d\text{"}\; f(2))\; \rho()$
(4)	S_2	$f(1)\; \alpha(\text{"}ccc\text{"}\; f(2))\; \alpha(\text{"}aa\text{"}\; f(4))\; \alpha(\text{"}d\text{"}\; f(2))\; \rho(\alpha(\text{"}bb\text{"}\; f(1))\; \rho())$
(3)	S_2	$f(2)\; \alpha(\text{"}ccc\text{"}\; f(2))\; \alpha(\text{"}aa\text{"}\; f(4))\; \alpha(\text{"}d\text{"}\; f(2))\; \rho(\alpha(\text{"}bb\text{"}\; f(1))\; \rho())$
(3)	S_2	$f(2)\; \alpha(\text{"}aa\text{"}\; f(4))\; \alpha(\text{"}d\text{"}\; f(2))\; \rho(\alpha(\text{"}ccc\text{"}\; f(2))\; \rho(\alpha(\text{"}bb\text{"}\; f(1))\; \rho()))$
(4)	S_2	$f(2)\; \alpha(\text{"}aa\text{"}\; f(4))\; \rho(\alpha(\text{"}d\text{"}\; f(2))\; \rho(\alpha(\text{"}ccc\text{"}\; f(2))\; \rho(\alpha(\text{"}bb\text{"}\; f(1))\; \rho())))$
(4)	S_2	$f(3)\; \alpha(\text{"}aa\text{"}\; f(4))\; \rho(\alpha(\text{"}d\text{"}\; f(2))\; \rho(\alpha(\text{"}ccc\text{"}\; f(2))\; \rho(\alpha(\text{"}bb\text{"}\; f(1))\; \rho())))$
(3)	S_2	$f(4)\; \alpha(\text{"}aa\text{"}\; f(4))\; \rho(\alpha(\text{"}d\text{"}\; f(2))\; \rho(\alpha(\text{"}ccc\text{"}\; f(2))\; \rho(\alpha(\text{"}bb\text{"}\; f(1))\; \rho())))$
–	S_2	$f(4)\; \rho(\alpha(\text{"}aa\text{"}\; f(4))\; \rho(\alpha(\text{"}d\text{"}\; f(2))\; \rho(\alpha(\text{"}ccc\text{"}\; f(2))\; \rho(\alpha(\text{"}bb\text{"}\; f(1))\; \rho()))))$

Rule (3) repeatedly stacks onto ρ all words having the current frequency count – if any; the standalone f acts as a promoter. Rule (4) increments this frequency count, if there are no (more) matching words for this count, but there are still other words to process; any extant $\alpha(...)$ acts as a promoter. The rules pair (3) and (4) complete their job in $\log(f)$ cP steps.

After all the words are stacked, the cell remains idle in the final state, S_2. The evolution is non-deterministic, which exactly corresponds to the slight vagueness of the original problem formulation. Table 4 illustrates a possible evolution of the cell contents for the initial sample. Essentially, in this scenario we obtain the list [("aa", 4); ("d" 2); ("ccc" 2); ("bb", 1)], but we could have also obtained the list [("aa", 4); ("ccc" 2); ("d" 2); ("bb", 1)].

5   Reflections and Open Problems

Both our solutions seem to have an optimal *runtime complexity*, or close to it, essentially $\mathcal{O}(\log(d) + \log(f))$ cP steps, which, in the worst case, is $\mathcal{O}(\log(N))$, but typically is much smaller. This optimality is not proven, but seems a believable hypothesis.

Also, our solutions seem to have a very decent *static complexity*, comparable to the best known solution in this regard, proposed by McIlroy: 10 or 5 rules – in our two solutions – vs. 4 lines – the combination of 4 powerful UNIX commands in McIlroy's excellent solution. Moreover, in contrast to this, our solutions are build from "scratch" (including the associative sorting!), not on other complex utilities. Also, as presented, McIlroy's solution runs in $\mathcal{O}(N \log(N))$ steps (because of the initial sorting), which makes it slower than ours. In all fairness, McIlroy mentions potential speed-ups, but these do not seem yet available.

In fact, these comparisons may be misleading, as our solution runs on a highly parallel engine – cP systems – while the other solutions are purely sequential. It may be interesting to evaluate other parallel solutions to this problem, including other P systems solutions, but we are not aware of any.

As earlier mentioned, cP systems rules generalise the traditional P systems rules by powerful Prolog-like unifications, but the classical Prolog unification algorithms do *not* work on multisets. More work is needed to design efficient unification algorithms which work on multisets and scale out well on parallel architectures.

It is also interesting to note that our solutions seem to struggle a bit when they are constrained to run in a purely sequential mode, as in phase IV of solution (i), but feel more comfortable when they can unleash the parallel associative potential of cP systems, as in solution (ii).

To the best of our knowledge, this paper proposes a novel sorting algorithm, with a remarkable crisp expression: a dynamic version of the classical pigeonhole algorithm, apparently suitable for any platform with strong associative features (such as many or most versions of P systems).

Finally, as an open problem, it might be worthwhile to invest more effort into developing a real literate model for P systems and to develop a set of tools corresponding to Knuth's WEB toolset – perhaps P-WEB or cP-WEB?

A   Appendix cP Systems: P Systems with Complex Symbols

We present the details of our cP framework, simplified from our earlier papers [5,6].

A.1   Complex Symbols as Subcells

Complex symbols or *subcells*, play the roles of cellular micro-compartments or substructures, such as organelles, vesicles or cytoophidium assemblies ("snakes"), which are embedded in cells or travel between cells, but without having the full processing power of a complete cell. In our proposal, *subcells* represent nested labelled data compartments which have no own processing power: they are acted upon by the rules of their enclosing cells.

Our basic vocabulary consists of *atoms* and *variables*, collectively known as *simple symbols*. *Complex symbols* are similar to Prolog-like *first-order terms*, recursively built from *multisets* of atoms and variables. Together, complex symbols and simple symbols (atoms, variables) are called *symbols* and can be defined by the following formal grammar:

```
<symbol> ::= <atom> | <variable> | <term>
<term> ::= <functor> '(' <argument> ')'
<functor> ::= <atom>
<argument> ::= λ | ( <symbol> )+
```

Atoms are typically denoted by lower case letters (or, occasionally, digits), such as a, b, c, 1. *Variables* are typically denoted by uppercase letters, such as X, Y, Z. *Functors* are term (subcell) labels; here functors can only be atoms, not variables.

For improved readability, we also consider *anonymous variables*, which are denoted by underscores ("_"). Each underscore occurrence represents a *new* unnamed variable and indicates that something, in which we are not interested, must fill that slot.

Symbols that do *not* contain variables are called *ground*, e.g.:

- Ground symbols: a, $a(\lambda)$, $a(b)$, $a(bc)$, $a(b^2c)$, $a(b(c))$, $a(bc(\lambda))$, $a(b(c)d(e))$, $a(b(c)d(e))$, $a(b(c)d(e(\lambda)))$, $a(bc^2d)$.
- Symbols which are not ground: X, $a(X)$, $a(bX)$, $a(b(X))$, $a(XY)$, $a(X^2)$, $a(XdY)$, $a(Xc())$, $a(b(X)d(e))$, $a(b(c)d(Y))$, $a(b(X^2)d(e(Xf^2)))$; also, using anonymous variables: $\_$, $a(b\_)$, $a(X\_)$, $a(b(X)d(e(\_)))$.
- This term-like construct which starts with a variable is not a symbol (this grammar defines first-order terms only): $X(aY)$.

Note that we may abbreviate the expression of complex symbols by removing inner λ's as explicit references to the empty multiset, e.g. $a(\lambda) = a()$.

In *concrete* models, *cells* may contain *ground* symbols only (no variables). Rules may however contain *any* kind of symbols, atoms, variables and terms (whether ground and not).

Unification. All symbols which appear in rules (ground or not) can be (asymmetrically) *matched* against *ground* terms, using an ad-hoc version of *pattern matching*, more precisely, a *one-way first-order syntactic unification* (one-way, because cells may not contain variables). An atom can only match another copy of itself, but a variable can match any multiset of ground terms (including λ). This may create a combinatorial *non-determinism*, when a combination of two or more variables are matched against the same multiset, in which case an arbitrary matching is chosen. For example:

- Matching $a(b(X)fY) = a(b(cd(e))f^2g)$ deterministically creates a single set of unifiers: $X, Y = cd(e), fg$.
- Matching $a(XY^2) = a(de^2f)$ deterministically creates a single set of unifiers: $X, Y = df, e$.
- Matching $a(b(X)c(1X)) = a(b(1^2)c(1^3))$ deterministically creates one single unifier: $X = 1^2$.
- Matching $a(b(X)c(1X)) = a(b(1^2)c(1^2))$ fails.
- Matching $a(XY) = a(df)$ non-deterministically creates one of the following four sets of unifiers: $X, Y = \lambda, df$; $X, Y = df, \lambda$; $X, Y = d, f$; $X, Y = f, d$.

A.2   High-Level or Generic Rules

Typically, our rules use *states* and are applied top-down, in the so-called *weak priority* order.

Pattern matching. Rules are matched against cell contents using the above discussed *pattern matching*, which involves the rule's left-hand side, promoters and inhibitors. Moreover, the matching is *valid* only if, after substituting variables by their values, the rule's right-hand side contains ground terms only (so *no* free variables are injected in the cell or sent to its neighbours), as illustrated by the following sample scenario:

- The cell's *current content* includes the *ground term*:
  $n(a\,\phi(b\,\phi(c)\,\psi(d))\,\psi(e))$.
- The following (state-less) *rewriting rule* is considered:
  $n(X\,\phi(Y\,\phi(Y_1)\,\psi(Y_2))\,\psi(Z)) \;\rightarrow\; v(X)\,n(Y\,\phi(Y_2)\,\psi(Y_1))\,v(Z)$.
- Our pattern matching determines the following *unifiers*:
  $X = a,\,Y = b,\,Y_1 = c,\,Y_2 = d,\,Z = e$.
- This is a *valid* matching and, after *substitutions*, the rule's *right-hand* side gives the *new content*:
  $v(a)\,n(b\,\phi(d)\,\psi(c))\,v(e)$.

Generic rules format. We consider rules of the following *generic* format (we call this format generic, because it actually defines templates involving variables):

> *current-state symbols*... $\rightarrow_\alpha$ *target-state* (*in-symbols*)...
> (*out-symbols*)$_\delta$...
> | *promoters*... $\neg$ *inhibitors*...

Where:

- *current-state* and *target-state* are atoms or terms;
- *symbols*, *in-symbols*, *promoters* and *inhibitors* are symbols;
- *in-symbols* become available after the end of the current step only, as in traditional P systems (we can imagine that these are sent via an ad-hoc fast *loopback* channel);
- subscript $\alpha \in \{\text{min}, \text{max}\}$, indicates the application mode, as further discussed in the example below;
- *out-symbols* are sent, at the end of the step, to the cell's structural neighbours. These symbols are enclosed in round parentheses which further indicate their destinations, above abbreviated as δ. The most usual scenarios include:
  - (*a*) $\downarrow_i$ indicates that *a* is sent over outgoing arc *i* (unicast);
  - (*a*) $\downarrow_{i,j}$ indicates that *a* is sent over outgoing arcs *i* and *j* (multicast);
  - (*a*) $\downarrow_\forall$ indicates that *a* is sent over all outgoing arcs (broadcast).

All symbols sent via one *generic rule* to the same destination form one single *message* and they travel together as one single block (even if the generic rule is applied in mode max).

Example. To explain our rule application mode, let us consider a cell, σ, containing three counter-like complex symbols, $c(1^2)$, $c(1^2)$, $c(1^3)$, and the two possible application modes of the following high-level "decrementing" rule:

> $(\rho_\alpha)\ S_1\ c(1\,X) \rightarrow_\alpha S_2\ c(X), \text{where } \alpha \in \{\text{min,max}\}.$

The left-hand side of rule ρ_α, $c(1\,X)$, can be unified in three different ways, to each one of the three c symbols extant in cell σ. Conceptually, we instantiate this rule in three different ways, each one tied and applicable to a distinct symbol:

$$(\rho_1)\ S_1\ c(1^2) \rightarrow S_2\ c(1),$$
$$(\rho_2)\ S_1\ c(1^2) \rightarrow S_2\ c(1),$$
$$(\rho_3)\ S_1\ c(1^3) \rightarrow S_2\ c(1^2).$$

1. If $\alpha = \text{min}$, rule ρ_{min} non-deterministically selects and applies one of these virtual rules ρ_1, ρ_2, ρ_3. Using ρ_1 or ρ_2, cell σ ends with counters $c(1)$, $c(1^2)$, $c(1^3)$. Using ρ_3, cell σ ends with counters $c(1^2)$, $c(1^2)$, $c(1^2)$.

2. If $\alpha = $ max, rule ρ_{max} applies in parallel all these virtual rules ρ_1, ρ_2, ρ_3. Cell σ ends with counters $c(1)$, $c(1)$, $c(1^2)$.

Special cases. Simple scenarios involving generic rules are sometimes semantically equivalent to loop-based sets of non-generic rules. For example, consider the rule

$$S_1 \; a(x(I) \; y(J)) \; \rightarrow_{\text{max}} \; S_2 \; b(I) \; c(J),$$

where the cell's contents guarantee that I and J only match integers in ranges $[1, n]$ and $[1, m]$, respectively. Under these assumptions, this rule is equivalent to the following set of non-generic rules:

$$S_1 \; a_{i,j} \; \rightarrow \; S_2 \; b_i \; c_j, \; \forall i \in [1, n], j \in [1, m].$$

However, unification is a much more powerful concept, which cannot be generally reduced to simple loops.

Benefits. This type of generic rules allow (i) a reasonably fast parsing and processing of subcomponents, and (ii) algorithm descriptions with *fixed-size alphabets* and *fixed-sized rulesets*, independent of the size of the problem and number of cells in the system (often *impossible* with only atomic symbols).

Synchronous vs asynchronous. In our models, we do not make any *syntactic* difference between the synchronous and asynchronous scenarios; this is strictly a *runtime* assumption [4]. Any model is able to run on both the synchronous and asynchronous runtime "engines", albeit the results may differ. Our asynchronous model matches closely the standard definition for asynchronicity used in distributed algorithms [3,11]; however, this is not needed in this paper so we don't follow this topic here.

References

1. Bentley, J., Knuth, D., McIlroy, D.: Programming pearls: a literate program. Commun. ACM **29**(6), 471–483 (1986). http://doi.acm.org/10.1145/5948.315654
2. Knuth, D.E.: Literate programming. Comput. J. **27**(2), 97–111 (1984). http://dx.doi.org/10.1093/comjnl/27.2.97
3. Lynch, N.A.: Distributed Algorithms. Morgan Kaufmann Publishers Inc., San Francisco (1996)
4. Nicolescu, R.: Parallel and distributed algorithms in P systems. In: Gheorghe, M., Păun, G., Rozenberg, G., Salomaa, A., Verlan, S. (eds.) CMC 2011. LNCS, vol. 7184, pp. 35–50. Springer, Heidelberg (2012). https://doi.org/10.1007/978-3-642-28024-5_4
5. Nicolescu, R.: Parallel thinning with complex objects and actors. In: Gheorghe, M., Rozenberg, G., Salomaa, A., Sosík, P., Zandron, C. (eds.) CMC 2014. LNCS, vol. 8961, pp. 330–354. Springer, Cham (2014). https://doi.org/10.1007/978-3-319-14370-5_21
6. Nicolescu, R.: Structured grid algorithms modelled with complex objects. In: Rozenberg, G., Salomaa, A., Sempere, J.M., Zandron, C. (eds.) CMC 2015. LNCS, vol. 9504, pp. 321–337. Springer, Cham (2015). https://doi.org/10.1007/978-3-319-28475-0_22

7. Nicolescu, R.: Revising the membrane computing model for byzantine agreement. In: Leporati, A., Rozenberg, G., Salomaa, A., Zandron, C. (eds.) CMC 2016. LNCS, vol. 10105, pp. 317–339. Springer, Cham (2017). https://doi.org/10.1007/978-3-319-54072-6_20

8. Nicolescu, R., Ipate, F., Wu, H.: Programming P systems with complex objects. In: Alhazov, A., Cojocaru, S., Gheorghe, M., Rogozhin, Y., Rozenberg, G., Salomaa, A. (eds.) CMC 2013. LNCS, vol. 8340, pp. 280–300. Springer, Heidelberg (2014). https://doi.org/10.1007/978-3-642-54239-8_20

9. Nicolescu, R., Wu, H.: Complex objects for complex applications. Rom. J. Inf. Sci. Technol. **17**(1), 46–62 (2014)

10. Păun, G., Rozenberg, G., Salomaa, A. (eds.): The Oxford Handbook of Membrane Computing. Oxford University Press Inc., New York (2010)

11. Tel, G.: Introduction to Distributed Algorithms. Cambridge University Press, Cambridge (2000)

12. Van Wyk, C.J.: Literate programming. Commun. ACM **30**(7), 583–599 (1987). http://doi.acm.org/10.1145/28569.315738

Tissue P Systems with Rule Production/Removal

Linqiang Pan[1,2], Bosheng Song[1(✉)], and Gexiang Zhang[3]

[1] Key Laboratory of Image Information Processing and Intelligent
Control of Education Ministry of China, School of Automation,
Huazhong University of Science and Technology, Wuhan 430074, Hubei, China
lqpan@mail.hust.edu.cn, boshengsong@hust.edu.cn
[2] School of Electric and Information Engineering,
Zhengzhou University of Light Industry, Zhengzhou 450002, Henan, China
[3] Robotics Research Center and Key Laboratory of Fluid and Power Machinery,
Xihua University, Chengdu 610039, China
zhgxdylan@126.com

Abstract. Tissue P systems are computational models inspired by the
way of biochemical substance movement/exchange between two cells or
between a cell and the environment, where all communication (sym-
port/antiport) rules used in a system are initially set up and keep
unchanged during any computation. In this work, a variant of tissue
P systems, called tissue P systems with rule production/removal (abbreviated as TRPR P systems) is considered, where rules in a system are
dynamically changed during a computation, that is, at any computation
step new rules can be produced and some existing rules can be removed.
The computation power of TRPR P systems is investigated. It is proved
that Turing universality is achieved for TRPR P systems with one cell,
and using symport rules of length at most 1, antiport rules of length at
most 2 or symport rules of length at most 2 and working in a maximally
parallel manner. We further show that TRPR P systems with two cells,
using symport rules of length at most 1, and working in a flat maximally
parallel manner, are Turing universal.

Keywords: Bio-inspired computing · Membrane computing
Tissue P system · Symport/antiport rule · Universality

1 Introduction

Cell is the basic unit of life, which can be viewed as an information processing device. Membrane computing is a computational paradigm inspired by the
structure and functioning of living cells, which was initiated in 1998 by Păun
[27] and the literature of this area has grown very fast in both theoretical and
practical aspects. Theoretical results include computation power [6,9], computation complexity [42,43], the variants of P systems [2,38,47], and the strategies

© Springer International Publishing AG 2018
M. Gheorghe et al. (Eds.): CMC 2017, LNCS 10725, pp. 230–244, 2018.
https://doi.org/10.1007/978-3-319-73359-3_15

of using rules in P systems [36,37]. In the practical aspect, P systems are used to solve real application problems, such as fault diagnosis [32,46], combinatorial optimization [48,49], image processing [11,13]. The computation devices in membrane computing are known as *P systems*, which have two main families: *cell-like P systems* [27], which have a hierarchical arrangement of membranes; and *tissue-like P systems* [21] or *neural-like P systems* [17], which have a net of cells or neurons. A comprehensive presentation of membrane computing can be found in [28,30], and the most up-to-date source of information is available on the P systems webpage http://ppage.psystems.eu. The present work deals with tissue-like P systems, introduced in [20].

A tissue-like P system consists of cells that are described by a directed graph, where cells are nodes of a graph, and the environment is considered as a distinguished node, an arc between two nodes corresponds to a communication channel between two regions (two cells or a cell and the environment). If a communication channel between two regions exists, then objects in these two regions can communicate by means of communication (symport/antiport) rules [25,26]. Symport rules move objects between two regions in one direction, whereas antiport rules move objects between two regions in opposite directions.

Since the seminal definition of tissue P systems, several research lines have been developed [1,7,18]. In [29], cell division was introduced into tissue P systems, and the SAT problem was solved in polynomial time by tissue P systems with cell division. In [10,44], generalized communicating P systems were proposed, where only pairs of objects synchronously move across components. Tissue P systems with evolutional symport/antiport rules were proposed in [41], where objects can evolve when moving from one region to another region. In [4], energy associated with each cell is introduced in tissue P systems, and Turing universality is reached when maximally parallel mode or sequential mode enforced with priorities are considered. Tissue P systems with channel states controlling the communication between two cells or between a cell and the environment were proposed in [15], several Turing universality results are achieved, where the systems work in a maximally parallel way with sequential behavior on channels. Cell/symbol complexity of tissue P systems with symport/antiport rules was investigated in [5], it was proved that tissue P systems with two channels between the cell and the environment are Turing universal when having six cells and one symbol, or two cells and three symbols, or three cells and two symbols.

In standard tissue P systems and the variants mentioned above, all symport/antiport rules used in a tissue P system are initially set up and keep unchanged during any computation. Actually, living cells, objects in cells are moving in order to achieve particular functioning and chemical reactions can be affected by both the contents in cells and the environmental conditions. Thus, it is a rather natural idea to consider rule production or removal during the process of a computation in a tissue P system.

Creating new evolution rules during a computation has been considered in Subsect. 3.6.4 in [28], where a rule in a P system is used, we say the rule is "consumed", that is, we take into consideration the multiplicity of rules, to work with multisets of rules in the same way as we have worked with multisets of objects. Specifically, when a rule $r : u \to v; z$ is applied, a copy of r is consumed, and all rules indicated by z are created.

In [3], sequential P systems with regular control were proposed, where all rules are initially set up and divided into different subsets, and the application of subsets of rules is controlled by a regular language.

In this work, we consider *tissue P systems with rule production/removal* (abbreviated as TRPR P systems), where rules in a system are dynamically changed during a computation, that is, at any computation step new rules can be produced and some existing rules can be removed. With this regulation mechanism, the computation power of tissue P systems working in a maximally parallel manner and in a flat maximally parallel manner is investigated. Specifically, it is proved Turing universality is achieved for TRPR P systems with one cell, and using symport rules of length at most 1, antiport rules of length at most 2 or symport rules of length at most 2 and working in a maximally parallel manner. We further show that the result holds true also for TRPR P systems with two cells, using symport rules of length at most 1 and working in a flat maximally parallel manner.

2   Tissue P Systems with Rule Production/Removal

It is necessary to recall some basic concepts of formal language theory used in this work, for further details of formal language theory, one can refer to the monographs [33].

For an alphabet Γ (a finite non-empty set of symbols), we denote by Γ^* the set of all strings over Γ, and by $\Gamma^+ = \Gamma^* \backslash \{\lambda\}$ we denote the set of non-empty strings. The number of symbols in a string u is the *length* of the string, and it is denoted by $|u|$. The number of occurrences of symbol a in a string u is denoted by $|u|_a$.

A *multiset* over an alphabet Γ is a function m from Γ to the set $\mathbb{N}$ of natural numbers, which gives a nonnegative *multiplicity* $m(x)$ for each $x \in \Gamma$. Let m_1, m_2 be multisets over Γ. The union of m_1 and m_2, denoted by $m_1 + m_2$, is the multiset over Γ defined as $(m_1 + m_2)(x) = m_1(x) + m_2(x)$ for each $x \in \Gamma$. The relative complement of m_2 in m_1, denoted by $m_1 \backslash m_2$, is the multiset defined as $(m_1 \backslash m_2)(x) = m_1(x) - m_2(x)$ if $m_1(x) \geq m_2(x)$, and $(m_1 \backslash m_2)(x) = 0$ otherwise.

Next we introduce the definition of tissue P systems with rules production/removal.

Definition 1. *A tissue P system with rule production/removal (abbreviated as TRPR P systems) of degree $q \geq 1$ is a tuple $\Pi = (\Gamma, \mathcal{E}, \mathcal{M}_1, \ldots, \mathcal{M}_q, \mathcal{R}_1, \mathcal{R}_2, i_{out})$, where*

- *Γ and $\mathcal{E}$ are finite alphabets such that $\mathcal{E} \subseteq \Gamma$;*
- *$\mathcal{M}_1, \ldots, \mathcal{M}_q$ are finite multisets over Γ;*
- *$\mathcal{R}_1$ is a finite set of rules of the following forms:*
    - *Symport rules: $(i, u/\lambda, j); \mathbf{r}$, for $0 \leq i \neq j \leq q, u \in \Gamma^+$;*

- *Antiport rules: $(i, u/v, j); \mathbf{r}$, for $0 \leq i \neq j \leq q, u, v \in \Gamma^+$;*
- $\mathcal{R}_2$ *is a finite set of rules of the following forms:*
  - *Symport rules with rules production/removal: $(i, u/\lambda, j); \mathbf{r}$, for $0 \leq i \neq j \leq q, u \in \Gamma^+$, and $\mathbf{r}$ is a finite set whose elements are of the type $r \in \mathcal{R}_1$ or $-r$ with $r \in \mathcal{R}_1$;*
  - *Antiport rules with rules production/removal: $(i, u/v, j); \mathbf{r}$, for $0 \leq i \neq j \leq q, u, v \in \Gamma^+$, and $\mathbf{r}$ is a finite set whose elements are of the type $r \in \mathcal{R}_1$ or $-r$ with $r \in \mathcal{R}_1$;*
- $i_{out} \in \{0, 1, \ldots, q\}$.

A TRPR P system of degree $q \geq 1$ can be viewed as a set of q cells labelled by $1, \ldots, q$ such that: (a) $\mathcal{M}_1, \ldots, \mathcal{M}_q$ represent the finite multisets of objects initially placed in the q cells of the system; (b) $\mathcal{E}$ is the set of objects initially located in the environment of the system, all of them available in an arbitrary number of copies; (c) $\mathcal{R}_2$ is a finite set of rules initially present in the system; (d) i_{out} is the label of a distinguished region which will encode the output of the system. The term region i ($0 \leq i \leq q$) refers to cell i in case $1 \leq i \leq q$ and refers to the environment in case $i = 0$. The length of a symport rule with rules production/removal $(i, u/\lambda, j); \mathbf{r}$ (an antiport rule with rules production/removal $(i, u/v, j); \mathbf{r}$, respectively) is defined as $|u|$ ($|u| + |v|$, respectively).

Note that if set $\mathbf{r}$ contains both a creation rule r and a removal rule $-r$, then it is assumed that first a creation rule r is produced and then this rule r is removed immediately, this process takes one step. If set $\mathbf{r}$ contains a non-existing removal rule $-r$, then this removal rule $-r$ will not work in the following computation steps, that is, this removal rule $-r$ works only if there exists a rule r in the system.

A *configuration* of a TRPR P system at any instant is described by all multisets of objects over Γ associated with all cells in the system, and the multiset of objects over $\Gamma \backslash \mathcal{E}$ associated with the environment at that moment. Note that the objects from $\mathcal{E}$ have an arbitrary number of copies, hence they are not properly changed along the computation. The *initial configuration* is $(\mathcal{M}_1, \ldots, \mathcal{M}_q; \emptyset)$.

A symport rule with rules production/removal $(i, u/\lambda, j); \mathbf{r}$ is applicable to a configuration at a moment if there is a region i which contains multiset u. When such a rule is applied, the objects specified by u in region i are sent to region j, simultaneously, if $r_i \in \mathbf{r}$ then rule r_i is produced in the system; if $-r_i \in \mathbf{r}$ then rule r_i is removed from the system. An antiport rule with rules production/removal $(i, u/v, j); \mathbf{r}$ is applicable to a configuration at a moment if there is a region i which contains multiset u and a region j which contains multiset v. When such a rule is applied: (a) the objects specified by u in region i are sent to region j; (b) the objects specified by v in region j are sent to region i; and (c) if $r_i \in \mathbf{r}$ then rule r_i is produced in the system; if $-r_i \in \mathbf{r}$ then rule r_i is removed from the system.

The rules of a TRPR P system in this work are applied in two manners: (1) maximally parallel manner: at each step, we apply a multiset of rules which is maximal, no further rule can be added being applicable; (2) flat maximally parallel manner: in each step, in each cell, a maximal set of concurrently applicable rules is chosen and each rule in the set is applied exactly once.

Starting from the initial configuration and applying rules as described above, a sequence of consecutive configurations is obtained. Each passage from a configuration to a successor configuration is called a *transition*. A configuration is a *halting configuration* if no rule of the system is applicable to it. A sequence of transitions starting in the initial configuration is a *computation*. Only a computation reaching a halting configuration gives a result, encoded by the number of copies of objects present in the output region i_{out}.

We denote by $NOtP_m^{pr}(sym_{t_1}, anti_{t_2}, max)$ and $NOtP_m^{pr}(sym_{t_1}, anti_{t_2}, fmax)$ (resp., $NOtP_m(sym_{t_1}, anti_{t_2}, max)$) the family of sets of numbers computed by tissue P systems with at most m cells, and using symport rules with rules production/removal (resp., symport rules) of length at most t_1, antiport rules with rules production/removal (resp., antiport rules) of length at most t_2 working in a maximally parallel manner and in a flat maximally parallel manner. If one of the parameters m, t_1, t_2 is not bounded, then it is replaced with $*$.

The following fundamental result is known from Theorem 5.9 in Chap. 5 (Freund, Alhazov, Rogozhin, Verlan, Communication P systems) in [30].

Theorem 1. $NOtP_1(sym_1, anti_2, max) \cup NOtP_1(sym_2, max) \subseteq NFIN$ *(the family of finite sets of non-negative integers).*

3 Universality of Tissue P Systems with Rules Production/Removal

A very useful characterization of NRE (the family of sets of numbers which are Turing computable) is obtained by means of *register machines*, we here introduce the notion of register machines.

A register machine is a construct $M = (m, H, l_0, l_h, I)$, where m is the number of registers, H is a set of labels, l_0 is the label of the initial instruction and l_h is the label of the halting instruction, and I is a set of instructions of the form $l_i: (op(i), l_j, l_k)$ such that $op(i)$ is an operation on register i of M, l_i, l_j, l_k are labels from I, $l_i \neq l_h$. Give an instruction $l_i: (op(i), l_j, l_k)$, if operation $op(i)$ can be applied to register i, then one continues with the instruction with label l_j, otherwise one continues with the instruction with label l_k.

The instructions $l_i: (op(i), l_j, l_k)$ are of the following forms:

- $l_i: (\text{ADD}(r), l_j, l_k)$ (add 1 to register r and then go to one of the instructions with labels l_j, l_k, non-deterministically chosen);
- $l_i: (\text{SUB}(r), l_j, l_k)$ (if the contents of register r are greater than zero, then subtract 1 from register i, and go to the instruction with label l_j; otherwise, do not change the contents of register i, and go to the instruction with label l_k);
- $l_h: \text{HALT}$ (the halt instruction).

A register machine M recognizers the set $N(M)$ of all natural numbers such that M starts with the initial instruction l_0 and halts in halting instruction. It is known that register machines are equivalent to Turing machines in the sense that they recognize the same family of sets of numbers, hence they characterize NRE [22].

3.1   Tissue P Systems with Rules Production/Removal Working in the Maximally Parallel Manner

In this subsection, we prove that tissue P systems with one cell and using symport rules with rules production/removal of length at most 2 or using symport rules with rules production/removal of length at most 1, antiport rules with rules production/removal of length at most 2, and working in the maximally parallel manner can generate all recursively enumerable sets of numbers, i.e., they characterize NRE. However, in the case of standard tissue P systems with symport/antiport rules, these Turing universality results cannot be obtained by such P systems (see Theorem 1).

Theorem 2. $NOtP_1^{pr}(sym_1, anti_2, max) = NRE$.

Proof. We only need to prove the inclusion $NOtP_1^{pr}(sym_1, anti_2, max) \supseteq NRE$, and the reverse inclusion follows from the Church-Turing thesis.

We use the characterization of NRE by means of register machines. Let $M = (m, H, l_0, l_h, I)$ be a register machine, which generates the set of numbers $N(M)$. We construct the TRPR P system of degree 1 to simulate register machine M.

$$\Pi = (\Gamma, \mathcal{E}, \mathcal{M}_1, \mathcal{R}, 1),$$

where

- $\Gamma = \{a_i \mid 1 \le i \le m\} \cup \{b, l, l', l'', l''' \mid b, l \in H\}$,
- $\mathcal{E} = \{l', l'', l''' \mid l \in H\}$,
- $\mathcal{M}_1 = \{b \mid b \in H\} \cup \{l_0\}$,

and the set of symport/antiport rules with rules production/removal is as follows:

- For each ADD instruction l_i: $(\text{ADD}(r), l_j, l_k)$ of M, the following rules are produced in cell 1:
    $r_{i,1}$: $(1, l_i/l'_i, 0); r_{i,2}$,
    $r_{i,2}$: $(1, b_i/a_r, 0); -r_{i,2}, r_{i,3}$,
    $r_{i,3}$: $(1, \lambda/b_i, 0); r_{i,4}, r_{i,5}$,
    $r_{i,4}$: $(1, l'_i/l_j, 0); -r_{i,4}, r_{j,1}, -r_{h,1}$,
    $r_{i,5}$: $(1, l'_i/l_k, 0); -r_{i,5}, r_{k,1}, -r_{h,1}$.

An ADD instruction l_i is simulated in four steps. At step 1, rule $r_{i,1}$ is applied, object l_i in cell 1 is exchanged with object l'_i in the environment, simultaneously, rule $r_{i,2}$ is produced. At the next step, rule $r_{i,2}$ is used, one copy of object a_r is sent into cell 1, object b_i is sent to the environment and this object will be sent back into cell 1 by using the created rule $r_{i,3}$, moreover, rule $r_{i,2}$ is removed. At step 3, by using rule $r_{i,3}$, rules $r_{i,4}, r_{i,5}$ are produced. At the next step, rules $r_{i,4}$ and $r_{i,5}$ are used non-deterministically. By applying rule $r_{i,4}$ (resp., $r_{i,5}$), object l'_i in cell 1 is exchanged with object l_j (resp., l_k) in the environment; simultaneously, rule $r_{j,1}$ (resp., $r_{k,1}$) is produced, rules $r_{i,4}$ and $r_{h,1}$ (if appeared) (resp., $r_{i,5}$ and $r_{h,1}$ (if appeared)) are removed. Hence, one copy of object a_r is introduced into cell 1 (simulating that the number stored in register r is increased by one), the system starts to simulate an instruction with label l_j or l_k. So the instruction l_i of M is correctly simulated by Π.

- For each SUB instruction l_i: $(\text{SUB}(r), l_j, l_k)$ of M, the following rules are produced in cell 1:

$r_{i,1}$: $(1, l_i/l'_i, 0); r_{i,2}$,
$r_{i,2}$: $(1, b_i/l''_i, 0); -r_{i,2}, r_{i,3}, r_{i,4}$,
$r_{i,3}$: $(1, a_r/b_i, 0); r_{i,5}, r_{i,6}$,
$r_{i,4}$: $(1, l'_i/l'''_i, 0); -r_{i,4}, r_{i,7}$,
$r_{i,5}$: $(1, l''_i/\lambda, 0); -r_{i,5}, -r_{i,7}$,
$r_{i,6}$: $(1, l'''_i/l_j, 0); -r_{i,6}, r_{j,1}, -r_{h,1}$,
$r_{i,7}$: $(1, l'''_i/b_i, 0); -r_{i,7}, r_{i,8}$,
$r_{i,8}$: $(1, l''_i/l_k, 0); -r_{i,8}, r_{k,1}, -r_{h,1}$.

A SUB instruction l_i is simulated in the following way. At step 1, rule $r_{i,1}$ is used, object l'_i is sent into cell 1, simultaneously, rule $r_{i,2}$ is produced. At step 2, by using rule $r_{i,2}$, object b_i is sent to the environment, object l''_i is sent into cell 1, simultaneously, rule $r_{i,2}$ is removed, and rules $r_{i,3}, r_{i,4}$ are produced. In what follows, there are two cases.

- There is at least one copy of object a_r in cell 1 (corresponding to that the number stored in register r is grater than 0). In this case, at step 3, rules $r_{i,3}$ and $r_{i,4}$ are enabled. By using rule $r_{i,3}$, object a_r in cell 1 is exchanged with object b_i in the environment, and rules $r_{i,5}, r_{i,6}$ are produced. By applying rule $r_{i,4}$, object l'_i in cell 1 is exchanged with l'''_i in the environment, simultaneously, rule $r_{i,4}$ is removed, and rule $r_{i,7}$ is produced. At the next step, rules $r_{i,5}$ and $r_{i,6}$ are enabled. By using rule $r_{i,5}$, object l''_i is sent to the environment, and rules $r_{i,5}, r_{i,7}$ are removed. By applying rule $r_{i,6}$, object l'''_i in cell 1 is exchanged with object l_j in the environment, rules $r_{i,6}$ and $r_{h,1}$ (if appeared) are removed, and rule $r_{j,1}$ is produced. In this case, one copy of object a_r in cell 1 is consumed (simulating that the number stored in register r is decreased by one), and the system starts to simulate the instruction l_j.
- There is no object a_r in cell 1 (corresponding to that the number stored in register r is 0). In this case, at step 3, only rule $r_{i,4}$ can be used, object l'''_i is sent into cell 1, rule $r_{i,4}$ is removed, and rule $r_{i,7}$ is produced. At the next step, rule $r_{i,7}$ is enabled and applied, object l'''_i in cell 1 is exchanged with object b_i in the environment, simultaneously, rule $r_{i,7}$ is removed, rule $r_{i,8}$ is produced. At step 5, by using rule $r_{i,8}$, object l_k is sent into cell 1, rules $r_{i,8}$ and $r_{h,1}$ (if appeared) are removed, and rule $r_{k,1}$ is produced. Hence, the system starts to simulate the instruction l_k.

Hence, the SUB instruction of M is correctly simulated by system Π.

When object l_h appears in cell 1, rule $r_{h,1}$ is produced, simultaneously, this rule is removed at the same step, no rule can be used in the system, and the computation halts. The number of the copies of object a_1 in cell 1 corresponds to the result of the computation, hence $N(M) = N(\Pi)$.

Theorem 3. $NOtP_1^{pr}(sym_2, max) = NRE$.

Proof. We only need to prove the inclusion $NOtP_1^{pr}(sym_2, max) \supseteq NRE$, and the reverse inclusion follows from the Church-Turing thesis.

We use the characterization of NRE by means of register machines. Let $M = (m, H, l_0, l_h, I)$ be a register machine, which generates the set of numbers $N(M)$. We construct the TRPR P system of degree 1 to simulate register machine M.

$$\Pi = (\Gamma, \mathcal{E}, \mathcal{M}_1, \mathcal{R}, 1),$$

where

- $\Gamma = \{a_i \mid 1 \le i \le m\} \cup \{b, b', l, l', l'', l''' \mid b, l \in H\}$,
- $\mathcal{E} = \{l', l'', l''' \mid l \in H\}$,
- $\mathcal{M}_1 = \{b, b' \mid b \in H\} \cup \{l_0\}$,

and the set of symport rules with rules production/removal is as follows:

- For each ADD instruction l_i: $(\text{ADD}(r), l_j, l_k)$ of M, the following rules are produced in cell 1:

  $r_{i,1}$: $(1, b_i l_i / \lambda, 0); r_{i,2}$,
  $r_{i,2}$: $(1, \lambda / a_r b_i, 0); -r_{i,2}, r_{i,3}$,
  $r_{i,3}$: $(1, b_i / \lambda, 0); -r_{i,3}, r_{i,4}, r_{i,5}$,
  $r_{i,4}$: $(1, \lambda / b_i l_j, 0); -r_{i,4}, r_{j,1}, -r_{h,1}$,
  $r_{i,5}$: $(1, \lambda / b_i l_k, 0); -r_{i,5}, r_{k,1}, -r_{h,1}$.

An ADD instruction l_i is simulated in four steps. At step 1, rule $r_{i,1}$ is used, objects $b_i l_i$ in cell 1 are sent to the environment, and rule $r_{i,2}$ is produced. At the next step, rule $r_{i,2}$ is applied, objects $a_r b_i$ are sent into cell 1, simultaneously, rule $r_{i,2}$ is removed and rule $r_{i,3}$ is produced. At step 3, object b_i is sent to the environment, rule $r_{i,3}$ is removed, and rules $r_{i,4}$ and $r_{i,5}$ are produced. At step 4, rules $r_{i,4}$ and $r_{i,5}$ are used non-deterministically. By applying rule $r_{i,4}$ (resp., $r_{i,5}$), objects $b_i l_j$ (resp., $b_i l_k$) are sent into cell 1; simultaneously, rules $r_{i,4}$ and $r_{h,1}$ (if appeared) (resp., $r_{i,5}$ and $r_{h,1}$ (if appeared)) are removed, rule $r_{j,1}$ (resp., $r_{k,1}$) is produced. Hence, one copy of object a_r is introduced into cell 1 (simulating that the number stored in register r is increased by one), the system starts to simulate an instruction with label l_j or l_k. So the instruction l_i of M is correctly simulated by Π.

- For each SUB instruction l_i: $(\text{SUB}(r), l_j, l_k)$ of M, the following rules are produced in cell 1:

  $r_{i,1}$: $(1, b_i l_i / \lambda, 0); r_{i,2}$,
  $r_{i,2}$: $(1, \lambda / b_i l_i', 0); -r_{i,2}, r_{i,3}, r_{i,4}$,
  $r_{i,3}$: $(1, a_r b_i / \lambda, 0); -r_{i,3}, r_{i,6}, r_{i,8}$,
  $r_{i,4}$: $(1, b_i' l_i'' / \lambda, 0); r_{i,5}, r_{i,10}$,
  $r_{i,5}$: $(1, \lambda / b_i' l_i''', 0)$,
  $r_{i,6}$: $(1, \lambda / b_i l_i''', 0); r_{i,7}, -r_{i,10}$,
  $r_{i,7}$: $(1, b_i' l_i''' / \lambda, 0); r_{i,9}$,
  $r_{i,8}$: $(1, l_i'' / \lambda, 0); -r_{i,8}$,
  $r_{i,9}$: $(1, \lambda / b_i' l_j, 0); -r_{i,9}, r_{j,1}, -r_{h,1}$,

$r_{i,10}$: $(1, b_i l_i''' / \lambda, 0); -r_{i,3}, r_{i,11},$
$r_{i,11}$: $(1, \lambda / b_i l_k, 0); -r_{i,11}, r_{k,1}, -r_{h,1}.$

A SUB instruction l_i is simulated in the following way. At step 1, rule $r_{i,1}$ is used, objects $b_i l_i$ are sent to the environment, simultaneously, rule $r_{i,2}$ is produced. At step 2, by using rule $r_{i,2}$, objects $b_i l_i'$ are sent into cell 1, rule $r_{i,2}$ is removed, and rules $r_{i,3}, r_{i,4}$ are produced. In what follows, there are two cases.

- There is at least one copy of object a_r in cell 1 (corresponding to that the number stored in register r is grater than 0). In this case, at step 3, rules $r_{i,3}$ and $r_{i,4}$ are enabled. By using rule $r_{i,3}$, objects $a_r b_i$ in cell 1 are sent to the environment, rule $r_{i,3}$ is removed, and rules $r_{i,6}, r_{i,8}$ are produced. By applying rule $r_{i,4}$, objects $b_i' l_i'$ in cell 1 are sent to the environment, simultaneously, rules $r_{i,5}, r_{i,10}$ are produced. At the next step, rules $r_{i,5}$ and $r_{i,6}$ are enabled. By using rule $r_{i,5}$, objects $b_i' l_i''$ are sent into cell 1. By applying rule $r_{i,6}$, objects $b_i l_i'''$ are sent into cell 1, rule $r_{i,10}$ is removed, and rule $r_{i,7}$ is produced. At step 5, rules $r_{i,7}$ and $r_{i,8}$ are enabled. By using rule $r_{i,7}$, objects $b_i' l_i'''$ are sent to the environment, rule $r_{i,9}$ is produced. By applying rule $r_{i,8}$, object l_i'' is sent to the environment, and this rule is removed. At step 6, objects $b_i' l_j$ are sent into cell 1 by using rule $r_{i,9}$, where rule $r_{j,1}$ is produced, and rules $r_{i,9}$ and $r_{h,1}$ (if appeared) are removed. In this case, one copy of object a_r in cell 1 is consumed (simulating that the number stored in register r is decreased by one), and the system starts to simulate the instruction l_j.
- There is no object a_r in cell 1 (corresponding to that the number stored in register r is 0). In this case, at step 3, only rule $r_{i,4}$ can be used, objects $b_i' l_i'''$ are sent to the environment, rules $r_{i,5}$ and $r_{i,10}$ are produced. At the next step, rule $r_{i,5}$ is enabled and applied, objects $b_i' l_i'''$ are sent into cell 1. At step 5, by using rule $r_{i,10}$, objects $b_i l_i''$ are sent to the environment, rule $r_{i,3}$ is removed, and rule $r_{i,11}$ is produced. At step 6, by using rule $r_{i,11}$, objects $b_i l_k$ are sent into cell 1, $r_{i,11}$ and $r_{h,1}$ (if appeared) are removed, and rule $r_{k,1}$ is produced. Hence, the system starts to simulate the instruction l_k.

Hence, the SUB instruction of M is correctly simulated by system Π.

When object l_h appears in cell 1, rule $r_{h,1}$ is produced, simultaneously, this rule is removed at the same ste p, no rule can be used in the system, and the computation halts. The number of the copies of object a_1 in cell 1 corresponds to the result of the computation, hence $N(M) = N(\Pi)$.

3.2   Tissue P Systems with Rules Production/Removal Working in the Flat Maximally Parallel Manner

Flat maximal parallelism of using rules was first considered in [16,45] and then further investigated in [23,39], where in each step, in each membrane, a maximal set of applicable rules is chosen and each rule in the set is applied exactly once. In this subsection, we prove that TRPR P system with two cells and using symport rules with rules production/removal of length at most 1 working in the flat maximally parallel manner can generate all recursively enumerable sets of numbers.

Theorem 4. $NOtP_2^{pr}(sym_1, fmax) = NRE$.

Proof. We only need to prove the inclusion $NOtP_1^{pr}(sym_1, fmax) \supseteq NRE$, and the reverse inclusion follows from the Church-Turing thesis.

We use the characterization of NRE by means of register machines. Let $M = (m, H, l_0, l_h, I)$ be a register machine, which generates the set of numbers $N(M)$. We construct the tissue P system of degree 1 to simulate register machine M.

$$\Pi = (\Gamma, \mathcal{E}, \mathcal{M}_1, \mathcal{M}_2, \mathcal{R}, 1),$$

where

- $\Gamma = \{a_i \mid 1 \leq i \leq m\} \cup \{b, l, l', l'' \mid b, l \in H\}$,
- $\mathcal{E} = \{l', l'' \mid l \in H\}$,
- $\mathcal{M}_1 = \{b \mid b \in H\} \cup \{l_0\}$, $\mathcal{M}_2 = \emptyset$,

and the set of producing/removing rules is as follows:

- For each ADD instruction l_i: $(\text{ADD}(r), l_j, l_k)$ of M, the following rules are produced in cell 1 and in cell 2:
    $r_{i,1}$: $(1, l_i/\lambda, 0); r_{i,2}, r_{i,3}$,
    $r_{i,2}$: $(1, \lambda/a_r, 0); -r_{i,2}$,
    $r_{i,3}$: $(1, b_i/\lambda, 0); -r_{i,3}, r_{i,4}, r_{i,5}$,
    $r_{i,4}$: $(1, \lambda/b_i, 0); r_{i,6}$,
    $r_{i,5}$: $(2, \lambda/b_i, 0); r_{i,7}, r_{i,8}$,
    $r_{i,6}$: $(1, \lambda/l_j, 0); -r_{i,6}, r_{j,1}, -r_{h,1}$,
    $r_{i,7}$: $(1, \lambda/b_i, 2)$,
    $r_{i,8}$: $(1, \lambda/l_k, 0); -r_{i,8}, r_{k,1}, -r_{h,1}$.

An ADD instruction l_i is simulated in the following way. At step 1, rule $r_{i,1}$ is used, object l_i in cell 1 is sent to the environment, and rules $r_{i,2}, r_{i,3}$ are produced. At the next step, rules $r_{i,2}$ and $r_{i,3}$ are enabled. By using rule $r_{i,2}$, one copy of object a_r is sent into cell 1 (due to the flat maximal parallelism), simultaneously, rule $r_{i,2}$ is removed. At step 3, object b_i is sent to the environment, rule $r_{i,3}$ is removed, and rules $r_{i,4}$ and $r_{i,5}$ are produced. At step 4, rules $r_{i,4}$ and $r_{i,5}$ are used non-deterministically. By applying rule $r_{i,4}$ (resp., $r_{i,5}$), object b_i is sent into cell 1 (resp., cell 2); simultaneously, rule $r_{i,6}$ (resp., $r_{i,7}, r_{i,8}$) is produced. At step 4, by applying rule $r_{i,6}$, only one copy of object l_j is sent into cell 1 due to the flat maximal parallelism, simultaneously, rules $r_{i,6}$ and $r_{h,1}$ (if appeared) are removed, and rule $r_{j,1}$ is produced. By using rules $r_{i,7}, r_{i,8}$, object b_i in cell 2 is sent to cell 1, one copy of object l_k in the environment is sent into cell 1 due to the flat maximal parallelism, rules $r_{i,8}$ and $r_{h,1}$ (if appeared) are removed, and rule $r_{k,1}$ is produced. Hence, one copy of object a_r is introduced into cell 1 (simulating that the number stored in register r is increased by one), the system starts to simulate an instruction with label l_j or l_k. So the instruction l_i of M is correctly simulated by Π.

- For each SUB instruction l_i: $(\text{SUB}(r), l_j, l_k)$ of M, the following rules are produced in cell 1:

$r_{i,1}$: $(1, l_i/\lambda, 0); r_{i,2}, r_{i,3},$

$r_{i,2}$: $(1, a_r/\lambda, 0); -r_{i,2}, r_{i,4},$

$r_{i,3}$: $(1, b_i/\lambda, 0); -r_{i,2}, -r_{i,3}, r_{i,5}, r_{i,6},$

$r_{i,4}$: $(1, \lambda/l_i', 0); -r_{i,4}, r_{i,7},$

$r_{i,5}$: $(1, \lambda/l_i'', 0), -r_{i,5}, r_{i,8},$

$r_{i,6}$: $(1, \lambda/b_i, 0); -r_{i,6},$

$r_{i,7}$: $(1, l_i'/\lambda, 0); -r_{i,7}, r_{i,9}, -r_{i,10},$

$r_{i,8}$: $(1, l_i'''/\lambda, 0); -r_{i,8}, r_{i,10},$

$r_{i,9}$: $(1, \lambda/l_j, 0); -r_{i,9}, r_{j,1}, -r_{h,1},$

$r_{i,10}$: $(1, \lambda/l_k, 0); -r_{i,10}, r_{k,1}, -r_{h,1}.$

A SUB instruction l_i is simulated in the following way. At step 1, rule $r_{i,1}$ is used, object l_i is sent to the environment, simultaneously, rules $r_{i,2}, r_{i,3}$ are produced. In what follows, there are two cases.

- There is at least one copy of object a_r in cell 1 (corresponding to that the number stored in register r is grater than 0). In this case, at step 2, rules $r_{i,2}$ and $r_{i,3}$ are enabled. By using rule $r_{i,2}$, object a_r in cell 1 is sent to the environment, rule $r_{i,2}$ is removed, and rule $r_{i,4}$ is produced. By applying rule $r_{i,3}$, object b_i in cell 1 is sent to the environment, simultaneously, rules $r_{i,2}, r_{i,3}$ are removed, rules $r_{i,5}, r_{i,6}$ are produced. At the next step, rules $r_{i,4}, r_{i,5}, r_{i,6}$ are enabled. By using rule $r_{i,4}$, one copy of object l_i' is sent into cell 1 due to the flat maximal parallelism, simultaneously, rule $r_{i,4}$ is removed and rule $r_{i,7}$ is produced. By applying rule $r_{i,5}$, one copy of object l_i'' is sent into cell 1 (flat maximal parallelism), rule $r_{i,5}$ is removed, and rule $r_{i,8}$ is produced. By using rule $r_{i,6}$, object b_i is sent back to cell 1, and this rule is removed. At step 4, rules $r_{i,7}$ and $r_{i,8}$ are enabled. By using rule $r_{i,7}$, object l_i' is sent to the environment, rules $r_{i,7}, r_{i,10}$ are removed, rule $r_{i,9}$ is produced. By applying rule $r_{i,8}$, object l_i'' is sent to the environment, and this rule is removed, rule $r_{i,10}$ is produced. Note that at step 4, rule $r_{i,10}$ is produced by using rule $r_{i,8}$ and this rule is removed by using rule $r_{i,7}$, hence after step 4, there is no rule $r_{i,10}$ in the system. At step 5, only rule $r_{i,9}$ is enabled and applied, only one copy of object l_j is sent into cell 1 due to the flat maximal parallelism, simultaneously, rule $r_{j,1}$ is produced, and rules $r_{i,9}$ and $r_{h,1}$ (if appeared) are removed. In this case, one copy of object a_r in cell 1 is consumed (simulating that the number stored in register r is decreased by one), and the system starts to simulate the instruction l_j.
- There is no object a_r in cell 1 (corresponding to that the number stored in register r is 0). In this case, at step 2, only rule $r_{i,3}$ can be used, objects b_i is sent to the environment, rules $r_{i,2}$ and $r_{i,3}$ are removed, rules $r_{i,5}$ and $r_{i,6}$ are produced. At the next step, rules $r_{i,5}$ and $r_{i,6}$ are enabled and applied, and rule $r_{i,8}$ is produced. At step 4, by using rule $r_{i,8}$, object l_i'' is sent to the environment, rule $r_{i,10}$ is produced. At step 5, by using rule $r_{i,10}$, only one copy of object l_k is sent into cell 1 due to the flat maximal parallelism, $r_{i,10}$ and $r_{h,1}$ (if appeared) are removed, and rule $r_{k,1}$ is produced. Hence, the system starts to simulate the instruction l_k.

Hence, the SUB instruction of M is correctly simulated by system Π.

When object l_h appears in cell 1, rule $r_{h,1}$ is produced, simultaneously, this rule is removed at the same step, no rule can be used in the system, and the computation halts. The number of the copies of object a_1 in cell 1 corresponds to the result of the computation, hence $N(M) = N(\Pi)$.

4   Conclusions and Discussions

In this work, tissue P systems with rules production/removal have been investigated. With the regulation mechanism of producing or removing rules, we have shown that Turing universality is achieved for tissue P systems with one cell, and using symport rules with rules production/removal of length at most 1, antiport rules with rules production/removal of length at most 2 or symport rules with rules production/removal of length at most 2 and working in a maximally parallel manner. Moreover, the result holds true also for tissue P systems with two cells, using symport rules with rules production/removal of length at most 1 and working in a flat maximally parallel manner.

Cell division [12,14] or cell separation [24,31], which can generate an exponential workspace in polynomial time, has been introduced into tissue P systems to solve **NP**-complete problems. It remains open how we construct tissue P systems with rules production/removal and cell division or cell separation to solve **NP**-complete problems with the condition that the number of initial rules is as small as possible.

Time-free manner of using rules was considered to solve **NP**-complete problems in membrane computing [34,35,40], where the correctness of the solution does not depend on the precise timing of the involved rules. It is of interest to construct tissue P systems with rules production/removal and cell division to solve **NP**-complete problems in a time-free manner.

Tissue P systems with cell division or with cell separation and without environment were considered in [8,19], where the alphabet of the environment of such P systems is empty. It would be interesting to consider the computational efficiency of tissue P systems with rules production/removal and cell division or cell separation without environment.

Acknowledgements. The work was supported by National Natural Science Foundation of China (61602192, 61772214, 61320106005 and 61033003), China Postdoctoral Science Foundation (2016M600592, 2017T100554), and the Innovation Scientists and Technicians Troop Construction Projects of Henan Province (154200510012).

References

1. Alhazov, A., Fernau, H., Freund, R., Ivanov, S., Siromoney, R., Subramanian, K.G.: Contextual array grammars with matrix control, regular control languages, and tissue P systems control. Theoret. Comput. Sci. **682**, 5–21 (2017)
2. Alhazov, A., Freund, R.: Variants of small universal P systems with catalysts. Fund. Informa. **138**(1–2), 227–250 (2015)

3. Alhazov, A., Freund, R., Heikenwälder, H., Oswald, M., Rogozhin, Y., Verlan, S.: Sequential P systems with regular control. In: Csuhaj-Varjú, E., Gheorghe, M., Rozenberg, G., Salomaa, A., Vaszil, G. (eds.) CMC 2012. LNCS, vol. 7762, pp. 112–127. Springer, Heidelberg (2013). https://doi.org/10.1007/978-3-642-36751-9_9

4. Alhazov, A., Freund, R., Leporati, A., Oswald, M., Zandron, C.: (Tissue) P systems with unit rules and energy assigned to membranes. Fund. Informa. **74**(4), 391–408 (2006)

5. Alhazov, A., Freund, R., Oswald, M.: Cell/symbol complexity of tissue P Systems with symport/antiport. Int. J. Found. Comput. Sci. **17**, 3–26 (2006)

6. Aman, B., Ciobanu, G.: Efficiently solving the bin packing problem through bio-inspired mobility. Acta Inform. **54**(4), 435–445 (2017)

7. Besozzi, D., Busi, N., Cazzaniga, P., Ferretti, C., Leporati, A., Mauri, G., Pescini, D., Zandron, C.: (Tissue) P systems with cell polarity. Math. Struct. Comput. Sci. **19**(6), 1141–1160 (2009)

8. Christinal, H.A., Díaz-Pernil, D., Gutiérrez-Naranjo, M.A., Pérez-Jiménez, M.J.: Tissue-like P systems without environment. In: Proceedings of the Eight Brainstorming Week on Membrane Computing, Sevilla, Spain, pp. 53–64 (2010)

9. Cienciala, L., Ciencialová, L.: Some new results of p colonies with bounded parameters. Nat. Comput. (2016). https://doi.org/10.1007/s11047-016-9591-0

10. Csuhaj-Varjú, E., Verlan, S.: On generalized communicating P systems with minimal interaction rules. Theoret. Comput. Sci. **412**, 124–135 (2011)

11. Díaz-Pernil, D., Berciano, A., Peña-Cantillana, F., Gutiérrez-Naranjo, M.A.: Segmenting images with gradient-based edge detection using membrane computing. Pattern Recogn. Let. **34**(8), 846–855 (2013)

12. Díaz-Pernil, D., Gutiérrez-Naranjo, M.A., Pérez-Jiménez, M.J., Riscos-Núñez, A.: A uniform family of tissue P system with cell division solving 3-Col in a linear time. Theoret. Comput. Sci. **404**, 76–87 (2008)

13. Díaz-Pernil, D., Peña-Cantillana, F., Gutiérrez-Naranjo, M.A.: A parallel algorithm for skeletonizing images by using spiking neural P systems. Neurocomputing **115**, 81–91 (2013)

14. Díaz-Pernil, D., Pérez-Jiménez, M.J., Riscos-Núñez, A., Romero-Jiménez, Á.: Computational efficiency of cellular division in tissue-like membrane systems. Rom. J. Inf. Sci. Tech. **11**(3), 229–241 (2008)

15. Freund, R., Păun, G., Pérez-Jiménez, M.J.: Tissue P systems with channel states. Theoret. Comput. Sci. **330**, 101–116 (2005)

16. Freund, R., Verlan, S.: (Tissue) P systems working in the k-restricted minimally or maximally parallel transition mode. Nat. Comput. **10**(2), 821–833 (2011)

17. Ionescu, M., Păun, G., Yokomori, T.: Spiking neural P systems. Fund. Informa. **71**(2–3), 279–308 (2006)

18. Krishna, S.N., Lakshmanan, K., Rama, R.: Tissue P systems with contextual and rewriting rules. In: Păun, G., Rozenberg, G., Salomaa, A., Zandron, C. (eds.) WMC 2002. LNCS, vol. 2597, pp. 339–351. Springer, Heidelberg (2003). https://doi.org/10.1007/3-540-36490-0_22

19. Macías-Ramos, L.F., Pérez-Jiménez, M.J., Riscos-Núñez, A., Rius-Font, M., Valencia-Cabrera, L.: The efficiency of tissue P systems with cell separation relies on the environment. In: Csuhaj-Varjú, E., Gheorghe, M., Rozenberg, G., Salomaa, A., Vaszil, G. (eds.) CMC 2012. LNCS, vol. 7762, pp. 243–256. Springer, Heidelberg (2013). https://doi.org/10.1007/978-3-642-36751-9_17

20. Martín-Vide, C., Pazos, J., Păun, G., Rodríguez-Patón, A.: A new class of symbolic abstract neural nets: tissue P systems. In: Ibarra, O.H., Zhang, L. (eds.) COCOON 2002. LNCS, vol. 2387, pp. 290–299. Springer, Heidelberg (2002). https://doi.org/10.1007/3-540-45655-4_32

21. Martín-Vide, C., Pazos, J., Păun, G., Rodríguez-Patón, A.: Tissue P systems. Theoret. Comput. Sci. **296**(2), 295–326 (2003)

22. Minsky, M.L.: Computation: Finite and Infinite Machines. Prentice-Hall Inc., Englewood Cliffs (1967)

23. Pan, L., Păun, G., Song, B.: Flat maximal parallelism in P systems with promoters. Theoret. Comput. Sci. **623**, 83–91 (2016)

24. Pan, L., Pérez-Jiménez, M.J.: Computational complexity of tissue-like P systems. J. Complexity **26**(3), 296–315 (2010)

25. Păun, A., Păun, G.: The power of communication: P systems with symport/antiport. New Generat. Comput. **20**(3), 295–305 (2002)

26. Păun, A., Păun, G., Rozenberg, G.: Computing by communication in networks of membranes. Int. J. Found. Comput. Sci. **13**, 779–798 (2002)

27. Păun, G.: Computing with membranes. J. Comput. Syst. Sci. **61**(1), 108–143 (2000)

28. Păun, G.: Membrane computing. In: Lingas, A., Nilsson, B.J. (eds.) FCT 2003. LNCS, vol. 2751, pp. 284–295. Springer, Heidelberg (2003). https://doi.org/10.1007/978-3-540-45077-1_26

29. Păun, G., Pérez-Jiménez, M.J., Riscos-Núñez, A.: Tissue P systems with cell division. Int. J. Comput. Commun. **3**(3), 295–303 (2008)

30. Păun, G., Rozenberg, G., Salomaa, A. (eds.): The Oxford Handbook of Membrane Computing. Oxford University Press, New York (2010)

31. Pérez-Jiménez, M.J., Sosík, P.: An optimal frontier of the efficiency of tissue P systems with cell separation. Fund. Informa. **138**, 45–60 (2015)

32. Peng, H., Wang, J., Pérez-Jiménez, M.J., Wang, H., Shao, J., Wang, T.: Fuzzy reasoning spiking neural P system for fault diagnosis. Inf. Sci. **235**, 106–116 (2013)

33. Rozenberg, G., Salomaa, A. (eds.): Handbook of Formal Languages, vol. 3. Springer, Berlin (1997). https://doi.org/10.1007/978-3-642-59136-5

34. Song, T., Macías-Ramos, L.F., Pérez-Jiménez, M.J.: Time-free solution to SAT problem using P systems with active membranes. Theoret. Comput. Sci. **529**, 61–68 (2014)

35. Song, B., Pan, L.: Computational efficiency and universality of timed P systems with active membranes. Theoret. Comput. Sci. **567**, 74–86 (2015)

36. Song, T., Pan, L.: Spiking neural P systems with rules on synapses working in maximum spiking strategy. IEEE Trans. Nanobiosci. **14**, 465–477 (2015)

37. Song, T., Pan, L.: Spiking neural P systems with rules on synapses working in maximum spikes consumption strategy. IEEE Trans. Nanobiosci. **14**, 38–44 (2015)

38. Song, T., Pan, L.: Spiking neural P systems with request rules. Neurocomputing **193**, 193–200 (2016)

39. Song, B., Pérez-Jiménez, M.J., Păun, G., Pan, L.: Tissue P systems with channel states working in the flat maximally parallel way. IEEE Trans. Nanobiosci. **15**(7), 645–656 (2016)

40. Song, B., Song, T., Pan, L.: A time-free uniform solution to subset sum problem by tissue P systems with cell division. Math. Struct. Comput. Sci. **27**(1), 17–32 (2017)

41. Song, B., Zhang, C., Pan, L.: Tissue-like P systems with evolutional symport/antiport rules. Inf. Sci. **378**, 177–193 (2017)

42. Sosík, P., Cienciala, L.: A limitation of cell division in tissue P systems by PSPACE. J. Comput. Syst. Sci. **81**, 473–484 (2015)

43. Sosík, P., Păun, A., Rodríguez-Patón, A.: P systems with proteins on membranes characterize PSPACE. Theoret. Comput. Sci. **488**, 78–95 (2013)
44. Verlan, S., Bernardini, F., Gheorghe, M., Margenstern, M.: Generalized communicating P systems. Theoret. Comput. Sci. **404**, 170–184 (2008)
45. Verlan, S., Quiros, J.: Fast hardware implementations of P systems. In: Csuhaj-Varjú, E., Gheorghe, M., Rozenberg, G., Salomaa, A., Vaszil, G. (eds.) CMC 2012. LNCS, vol. 7762, pp. 404–423. Springer, Heidelberg (2013). https://doi.org/10.1007/978-3-642-36751-9_27
46. Wang, J., Shi, P., Peng, H., Pérez-Jiménez, M.J., Wang, T.: Weighted fuzzy spiking neural P systems. IEEE Trans. Fuzzy Syst. **21**(2), 209–220 (2013)
47. Wu, T., Zhang, Z., Păun, G., Pan, L.: Cell-like spiking neural P systems. Theoret. Comput. Sci. **623**, 180–189 (2016)
48. Zhang, G., Gheorghe, M., Pan, L., Pérez-Jiménez, M.J.: Evolutionary membrane computing: a comprehensive survey and new results. Inf. Sci. **279**, 528–551 (2014)
49. Zhang, G., Rong, H., Neri, F., Pérez-Jiménez, M.J.: An optimization spiking neural P system for approximately solving combinatorial optimization problems. Int. J. Neural Syst. **24**(5), 1–16 (2014)

Reversing Steps in Membrane Systems Computations

G. Michele Pinna[(✉)]

Dipartimento di Matematica e Informatica, Università di Cagliari, Cagliari, Italy
gmpinna@unica.it

Abstract. The issue of reversibility in computational paradigms has gained interest in recent years. In this paper we investigate how to *reverse* steps in membrane systems computations. The problem is that computation steps in membrane systems do not preserve all the information that has to be used when reversing them. We try to formalize the relevant information needed, and we show that the proposed approach enjoy the so called *loop lemma*, which basically assures that the undoing obtained by reversely applying rules is correct.

1 Introduction

Membrane systems, introduced by Păun (see [22,23] for a first account on membrane systems), are nowadays a popular and extensively studied computational paradigm inspired by how computations in the living cells take place.

The ingredients of this computational paradigm are a *membrane structure* (which is a tree-like structure), a multiset of *objects* associated to each membrane (spatial distribution of resources) and a set of *evolution rules* for each membrane (acting at local states). A computation step is performed by the application of a bunch of rules which consume objects from a membrane and produce objects in this membrane and possibly in the neighbouring membranes as well. All the possible instances of applicable rules are used, as it happens usually in nature, but this is not actually always needed to make the computational paradigm Turing equivalent (for instance, in [21] membrane systems where the rules have a special format are considered, and maximality is not required; similarly in [5] or [9] where, respectively, minimal parallelism or the presence of special objects called *catalysts* is considered). The computational paradigm has also been compared with many other paradigms (see [23] and the chapters therein for a fairly detailed account), and the relative expressivity has been studied (see, for instance, [6,7] or [4]).

Reversibility in computation paradigms is an issue that recently has received great attention[1]. Reversibility in nature has a quite precise meaning: once

---

Work partially supported by RAS, Sardinia Regional Government, Convenzione triennale tra la Fondazione di Sardegna e gli Atenei Sardi Regione Sardegna, (CUP: F72F16003030002), and P.I.A. 2013 "NOMAD".

[1] This is testified by the series of workshops and conferences entitled *Reversible Computation* (RC) organized since 2009, which is a conference since 2013.

© Springer International Publishing AG 2018
M. Gheorghe et al. (Eds.): CMC 2017, LNCS 10725, pp. 245–261, 2018.
https://doi.org/10.1007/978-3-319-73359-3_16

reached a certain state (say F) from a starting one (say I) with a sequence of steps, there is the capability of reaching again the state I, possibly applying the various steps in reverse order. Furthermore in nature also energy is considered, and the final balance after reversing steps should be zero. When focussing on computational devices, reversibility in general accounts on understanding how certain rules are applicable in reverse order and in particular the amount of information to be preserved. We do not discuss here further why reversibility is worth to be considered, and we refer to [16] for more motivations.

As already pointed out in [16], when reversibility is *backtracking* (the feature that certain *non deterministic* computations enjoy, which allows to *explore* all the possible alternatives), then reversibility is well understood. Just a suitable coding of the choices and of the applied rules is enough. It is much less clear in the case of *distributed* or *concurrent* systems, where the applications of the rules is done in a local fashion. Membrane systems have to be considered computing devices of this kind.

The aim of this paper is to investigate on how to *reverse* computation steps in membrane systems in such a way that if a configuration is reached from another one, there is a way to reverse this step.

Reversing computations can be achieved in various manners. One is to add suitable rules having the *reverse* effect of other rules, another approach is orthogonal to this one and it is based on devising on how to apply the same rule *reversely*. In the first way the fact that a computation is reversed is just a matter of observation on the results achieved by the computation itself, making the approach a sort of *simulation* of reversibility. Still some information about the computations may have to be considered (for instance, in the approach presented in [1] some information should be kept, as rules having as effect the dissolution of membranes are considered). In the case it is necessary to keep track of the previous existence of some membranes.

Another way focusses on how a rule is *reversely* applied to a given stage of the computation, and to apply a rule reversely it is often necessary to keep some information about the previous stages of the computation. The conditions to be established are such that a *loop lemma* can be proven. The loop lemma simply states that if one goes from a stage of the computation to another one by applying a bunch of rules together, then from the reached stage it is possible to *go back* by reversely applying the same bunch of rules. Though this seems to be an easy and minimal requirement, it is not obvious that it generally holds for concurrent and distributed systems. In fact, as discussed in [8] (see also [16]), further information have to be given in order to be able to reverse computations steps consistently. The added information have to guarantee that the previous stage of the computation can be *reconstructed* properly.

We achieve this result by enriching the notion of configuration of a membrane system with a *memory* which records the (minimal) information to be considered in reversing steps. The notion of memory we adopt is similar to the one of event structure associated to a membrane system developed in [2,20]. We are able to prove the loop lemma, though we get a weaker version which we will discuss.

The choice of adding a memory is not the unique solution to the problems posed when reversing steps, as objects may be enriched with the full history. However the amount of information the memory may have is able to cover this other approach, hence we believe that what we propose is general enough.

Though reversibility often means to *fully* undo some steps, it is important to observe that this is not actually needed. In fact it seems more reasonable to allow to undo part of the steps rather than the whole one and this is feasible in our approach.

The paper in organized as follows. In the remaining part of this introduction we briefly recall how the issue of reversibility in membrane systems has been considered in literature.

In the next section we give some background and in Sect. 3 we review the notion of membrane systems and formalize the notion of membrane systems computation. In Sect. 4 we first state in general what reversing computations in membrane systems may be, discussing briefly its limitation, and then develop our approach: in Subsect. 4.1 we discuss how the information is added to configurations. Few ideas for future developments conclude the paper.

Reversibility in membrane systems: other approaches. Reversibility has been previously considered in membrane systems. In [1] Agrigoroaiei and Ciobanu present a first attempt to study reversibility in membrane systems. They develop a way to consider new *reversed* rules, called *dual* rules. Dual rules replace the original rules of the membrane system and reversed computations are studied with the aim at easing the search of appropriate solutions to problems *backward* rather than *forward* (and indeed the membrane systems introduced and studied in [1] are also called *dual* membrane systems). Thus computations are reversed as the whole system is actually reversed, which is different from undoing something.

Other papers consider when computations can be reversed, and they usually require that the membrane systems looked at are deterministic. For instance, [3] considers membrane systems where reversibility (or strong reversibility) means that every reachable configuration of the system can be *obtained* by a single configuration (and in the stronger version the reachability request is dropped), and the determinism issue is considered as well, meaning that every reachable configuration has just one successor configuration (again the strong version is the one requiring that the reachability request is dropped). In this paper conditions to achieve reversibility, strong reversibility, determinism and strong determinism are studied, and the expressivity of the associated systems is made precise. In [11] the problem of strong reversibility is further studied, and it is shown that it is decidable if a membrane system is strongly reversible. It is also worth to stress that the membrane systems considered have just one membrane.

In [18] the author considers membrane systems with *symport/antiport* rules, and it is shown that every reversible register machine can be simulated by a *deterministic* membrane system with *symport/antiport* rules. In [24] spiking neural systems are taken into account, and the investigations focus on the expressivity issue. Indeed it is shown that these systems are reversible because they are equivalent to reversible computing machines, and in all the above mentioned approaches the focus is on deterministic systems, whereas we consider reversibility without constraining it to special cases.

In [17] reversibility is considered as it is shown how to simulate Fredkin circuits with membrane systems, focussing on energy. Being Fredkin gates the base for achieving reversibility at circuit level, hence allowing to restore not only the state but also the energy, the fact that suitable membrane systems can simulate these circuits is quite relevant.

2 Background

We first fix some notation. With $\mathbb{N}$ we denote the set of *natural numbers* including zero, and with $\mathbb{N}^+$ the set of positive natural numbers. Given a set X, with 2^X we indicate the set of subsets of X and with 2^X_{fin} the set of *finite* subsets of X.

Given a set X, a partial order $\sqsubseteq$ on X is a reflexive, transitive and anti-symmetric relation. Let $(X, \sqsubseteq)$ be a partially ordered set and $Y \subseteq X$, we say that Y has a *minimum* iff there exists $x \in X$ such that $\forall y \in Y$ it holds that $x \sqsubseteq y$. Dually it has a *maximum* iff there exists $x \in X$ such that $\forall y \in Y$ it holds that $y \sqsubseteq x$. The elements of $Y \subseteq X$ are referred to as *incomparable* iff $\forall y, y' \in Y$. $y \neq y'$ implies that $y \not\sqsubseteq y'$ and $y' \not\sqsubseteq y$. Given a partial order $(X, \sqsubseteq)$, with $max(X, \sqsubseteq)$ we denote the set of elements $Y \subseteq X$ such that (a) for each $y \in Y$ and for each $x \in X$ if $y \sqsubseteq x$ then $y = x$ (the element y is not dominated by any other element of X), and (b) for each $x \in X$ such that there is no $x' \in X$ with $x' \neq x$ and $x \sqsubseteq x'$, then $x \in Y$ (the set is the greatest subset of incomparable and maximal elements of X), and similarly with $min(X, \sqsubseteq)$ we denote the greatest subset of elements $Y \subseteq X$ that are minimal with respect to the partial order relation. Given two elements $x, y \in X$ such that $x \sqsubseteq y$, we say that x is an *immediate* predecessor of y iff $x \neq y$ and $\forall z \in X$. $x \sqsubseteq z \sqsubseteq y$ either implies $x = z$ or $z = y$. If x is the immediate predecessor of y, we indicate this with $x \hat{\sqsubseteq} y$.

A partial order $(X, \sqsubseteq)$ is a *tree* if $\sqsubseteq$ is such that each subset $Y \subseteq X$ of incomparable elements has no maximum, and each subset $Y \subseteq X$ has a minimum. The minimum of X is called the *root* of the tree. We define some auxiliary partial functions over trees. Given a tree $(X, \sqsubseteq)$, we define the partial function father $: X \rightarrow X$ by father$(x) = y$ whenever $y \hat{\sqsubseteq} x$. Clearly, the root of a tree has no father. The function children $: X \rightarrow 2^X$ is defined by children$(x) = \{y \in X \mid x \hat{\sqsubseteq} y\}$. If x is a leaf, then children$(x) = \emptyset$. We assume that the trees have a finite degree, namely for each node x we assume that children$(x) \in 2^X_{fin}$.

Multisets. Given a set S, a *multiset* over S is a function $m : S \rightarrow \mathbb{N}$; we denote by ∂S the set of multisets of S. The *multiplicity* of an element s in m is given by $m(s)$. A multiset m over S is *finite* iff the set $\text{dom}(m) = \{s \in S \mid m(s) \neq 0\}$ is finite and we always consider finite multisets. A multiset m such that $\text{dom}(m) = \emptyset$ is called *empty*, and it is denoted by $\mathbf{0}$. The cardinality of a multiset is defined as $\#(m) = \sum_{s \in S} m(s)$. Given a multiset in ∂S and a subset $S' \subseteq S$, by $m|_{S'}$

we denote the multiset over S' such that $m|_{S'}(s) = m(s)$. We write $m \subseteq m'$ if $m(s) \leq m'(s)$ for all $s \in S$, and $m \subset m'$ if $m \subseteq m'$ and $m \neq m'$. The operator $\oplus$ denotes *multiset union*: $(m \oplus m')(s) = m(s) + m'(s)$. The operator $\ominus$ denotes *multiset difference*: $(m \ominus m')(s) =$ if $m(s) > m'(s)$ then $m(s) - m'(s)$ else 0. The *scalar product* of a number j with a multiset m is $(j \cdot m)(s) = j \cdot (m(s))$. We sometimes write a multiset $m \in \partial S$ as the sum $\oplus_{s \in S} m(s) \cdot s$, where we omit the summands whenever $m(s)$ is equal to 0. Finally we assume that all the operations defined so far extend (with overloading of notation) to vectors of multisets, applying the operations component-wise.

Membranes structure. The language of *membrane structure*, which we will denote with MS, is a language over the alphabet $\{[,]\}$, and it is defined inductively as follows:

- $[\,] \in$ MS, and
- if $\mu_1, \ldots, \mu_n \in$ MS then also $[\mu_1 \ldots \mu_n] \in$ MS.

Two words in MS are *equivalent* whenever they represent the same tree up to isomorphisms, and a *membrane* μ is the equivalence class of all the words with respect to this equivalence. Observe that, given a membrane μ, a *matching pair* of parentheses is any substring of μ which is again a membrane. The number of membranes appearing in a membrane μ is calculated as follows:

$$\#_{\mathsf{MS}}(\mu) = \begin{cases} 1 & \text{if } \mu = [\,] \\ 1 + \sum_{i=1}^{k} \#_{\mathsf{MS}}(\mu_i) & \text{if } \mu = [\mu_1 \ldots \mu_k] \end{cases}$$

and to each membrane μ' appearing in a membrane μ, including μ itself, it is possible to associate an unique index i ranging from 1 to $\#_{\mathsf{MS}}(\mu)$, and we denote this index with $\mathsf{index}(\mu')$. If $\mu_i = [\mu_{i_1} \ldots \mu_{i_k}]$ then $\mathsf{father}(i_j) = i$ for $1 \leq j \leq k$, and $\mathsf{children}(i) = \{i_1, \ldots, i_k\}$. We assume that the index 1 is given to the root. Obviously the set $(\{1, \ldots, \#_{\mathsf{MS}}(\mu)\}, \sqsubseteq^*)$ is a tree, where $\mathsf{index}(\mu') \sqsubset \mathsf{index}(\mu_i)$ whenever $\mu' = [\mu_1 \ldots \mu_k]$, with $1 \leq i \leq k$, and $\sqsubseteq^*$ is the reflexive and transitive closure of $\sqsubset$.

3 Membrane Systems

We are now ready to recall the notion of *membrane system*. The main ingredients of a membrane system are three: a membrane structure, a multiset of objects associated to each membrane and a set of *evolution rules* associated to each membrane. The membrane structure represents the various compartments where the computations take place (in general simultaneously), and the conditions under which certain evolution rules can be applied is checked *locally*, *i.e.* in the same membrane to which the rules are associated. The result of the application of a rule has a more global effect, as it will be clear in the following.

We fix a finite alphabet of (names of) objects (sometimes called molecules), that we denote with $\mathcal{O}$ and we fix an alphabet of *rule names*, that will be denoted with Name, and it will be ranged over by $\mathfrak{n}$.

Definition 1. *A membrane system* over a set of objects $\mathcal{O}$ *is a construct* $\Pi = (\mathcal{O}, \mu, w_1^0, \ldots, w_n^0, R_1, \ldots, R_n)$ *where:*

- μ *is a* membrane structure *with n membranes indexed from 1 to n, where* $n = \#_{\mathsf{MS}}(\mu)$,
- *each w_i^0 is a multiset over $\mathcal{O}$ associated with membrane i, and*
- *each R_i is a finite set of* reaction (or evolution) rules *r associated with the membrane i, each rule having the format $r : u \to v$, where u is a non empty finite multiset in $\partial\mathcal{O}$, v is a finite multiset over $\mathcal{O} \times (\{\mathsf{here}, \mathsf{out}\} \cup \{\mathsf{in}_j \mid \mathsf{father}(j) = i\})$, and $\mathsf{name}(r) \in \mathsf{Name}$ is the name of the rule r.*

The definition is almost standard, the difference is that we omitted the output membrane which is usually considered when one wishes to focus on what is calculated by a membrane system, and we focus on a rule format where a multiset of objects of a membrane are possibly *transformed* in multisets of objects in the same membrane and in the neighbouring ones (*i.e.* the father and the children). Two rules r, r' belonging to different sets of reaction rules (thus associated to different membranes) may be equal, where equal means that if $r : u \to v$ and $r' : u' \to v'$ then $u = u'$ and $v = v'$. We however assume that all the rules in a membrane system have distinct names, *i.e.* for each $r, r' \in \bigcup_{1 \le i \le n} R_i$, if $r \ne r'$ then $\mathsf{name}(r) \ne \mathsf{name}(r')$ and if $r = r'$ then there exists $k, j \in \{1, \ldots, n\}$ such that $r \in R_k, r' \in R_j, k \ne j$ and $\mathsf{name}(r) \ne \mathsf{name}(r')$. Given a rule $r \in \bigcup_{1 \le i \le n} R_i$, with $\mathsf{index}(r)$ we denote the index of the membrane this rule is associated to, thus if $r \in R_i$ then $\mathsf{index}(r) = i$.

The application of a rule $r : u \to v$ in a membrane i will *consume* the multiset u that must be in the membrane i and may cause the *production* of multisets not only in the same membrane i but also in the neighbouring membranes, if there are, namely those that are children of i and the $\mathsf{father}(i)$ membrane, if this exists. With $\mathcal{I}(r)$ we denote the set with the indices of the membranes where a rule r actually produces an object. Given a rule r, u is the *left hand side* of r and v is the *right hand side* of r, and they are denoted with $\mathsf{lhs}(r)$ and $\mathsf{rhs}(r)$, respectively. To simplify the notation, given a multiset z over $\mathcal{O} \times (\{\mathsf{here}, \mathsf{out}\} \cup \{\mathsf{in}_j \mid \mathsf{father}(j) = i\})$, with $z|_\alpha$ we denote the multiset on $\mathcal{O}$ obtained from z by considering all the elements with the second component equal to α, where $\alpha \in \{\mathsf{here}, \mathsf{out}, \mathsf{in}_1, \ldots, \mathsf{in}_n\}$. Given a rule r, its $\mathsf{rhs}(r) = v$ may be represented as $(v|_{\mathsf{here}}, \mathsf{here}) \oplus (v|_{\mathsf{out}}, \mathsf{out}) \oplus (v|_{\mathsf{in}_{j_1}}, \mathsf{in}_{j_1}) \oplus \cdots \oplus (v|_{\mathsf{in}_{j_k}}, \mathsf{in}_{j_k})$ where $\{j_1, \ldots, j_k\} = \mathsf{children}(\mathsf{index}(r))$. Observe that it may be that some of the $v|_\alpha$ are equal to $\mathbf{0}$. Given a rule r, the indices involved in the effect of this rule are $\{\mathsf{index}(r) \mid \mathsf{rhs}(r)|_{\mathsf{here}} \ne \mathbf{0}\} \cup \{\mathsf{father}(\mathsf{index}(r)) \mid \mathsf{rhs}(r)|_{\mathsf{out}} \ne \mathbf{0}\} \cup \{i \mid i \in \mathsf{children}(\mathsf{index}(r)) \wedge \mathsf{rhs}(r)|_{\mathsf{in}_i} \ne \mathbf{0}\}$. We assume that, for each rule r, it holds that $\mathcal{I}(r) \ne \emptyset$, hence each rule has an effect different from the *annihilation* of all the objects involved[2].

---

[2] This requirement is reasonable when one imagine that reversing means undoing the effects of a rule, thus if a rule just serves to annihilate all the objects to be rewritten then one can imagine that such a rule can be always reversed, in any multiplicity.

Membrane Systems Evolution. A membrane system Π evolves from a configuration to another configuration as a consequence of the application of (multisets of) rules in each region. The rules are applied *simultaneously*. We start formalizing the notion of configuration of a membrane system.

Definition 2. *Let* $\Pi = (\mathcal{O}, \mu, w_1^0, \ldots, w_n^0, R_1, \ldots, R_n)$ *be a membrane system, then a* configuration *is a tuple* $C = (w_1, \ldots, w_n)$ *where each* w_i *is a multiset over* $\mathcal{O}$. $C_0 = (w_1^0, \ldots, w_n^0)$ *is the* initial *configuration of* Π.

A computation step of a membrane system is *triggered* by the application of multisets of rules in each membrane. These multisets of rules are collected in a vector.

Definition 3. *Let* $\Pi = (\mathcal{O}, \mu, w_1^0, \ldots, w_n^0, R_1, \ldots, R_n)$ *be a membrane system, then a* multi-rule vector $\overrightarrow{R}$ *is the tuple* $(\widehat{R}_1, \ldots, \widehat{R}_n)$, *where* $\widehat{R}_i$ *is a multiset over* R_i.

The multi-rule vector $\overrightarrow{R}$ contains all the rules that have to be applied simultaneously to a configuration of a membrane system, with their proper multiplicities.

A multi-rule vector $\overrightarrow{R}$ is *enabled* at a configuration C whenever each multiset of objects in each region is greater than or equal to what all the rules to be applied in that region consume. Given a multi-rule vector $\overrightarrow{R}$, for each i between 1 and n we denote with $\mathsf{Lhs}(\overrightarrow{R})_i$ the multiset over $\mathcal{O}$ defined as follows: $\bigoplus_{r \in R_i} \widehat{R}_i(r) \cdot \mathsf{lhs}(r)$. The tuple of these multisets is denoted with $\mathsf{Lhs}(\overrightarrow{R})$.

Definition 4. *Let* $\Pi = (\mathcal{O}, \mu, w_1^0, \ldots, w_n^0, R_1, \ldots, R_n)$ *be a membrane system,* $\overrightarrow{R}$ *a multi-rule vector and* C *a configuration. Then* $\overrightarrow{R}$ *is* enabled *at* $C = (w_1, \ldots, w_n)$ *if* $\forall i \in \{1, \ldots, n\}$. $\mathsf{Lhs}(\overrightarrow{R})_i \subseteq w_i$. *We denote the enabling of a multi-rule vector* $\overrightarrow{R}$ *at a configuration* C *with* $C[\overrightarrow{R}\rangle$.

The effects of the *application* of a multi-rule vector $\overrightarrow{R}$ (which acts in all membranes concurrently) in the membrane i are the following: the multiset of objects $\bigoplus_{r \in R_i} \widehat{R}_i(r) \cdot \mathsf{rhs}(r)|_{\mathsf{here}}$ is the effect of the rules in the same membrane, $(\bigoplus_{r \in R_{\mathsf{father}(i)}} \widehat{R}_{\mathsf{father}(i)}(r) \cdot \mathsf{rhs}(r)|_{\mathsf{in}_i})$ those of the rules in the father membrane, and finally $(\bigoplus_{j \in \mathsf{children}(i)} (\bigoplus_{r \in R_j} \widehat{R}_i(r) \cdot \mathsf{rhs}(r)|_{\mathsf{out}}))$ those from the children membranes. Like previously, these three parts are combined by using $\oplus$. For each membrane, we denote the effects by $\mathsf{Rhs}(\overrightarrow{R})_i$. The tuple of these effects is written as $\mathsf{Rhs}(\overrightarrow{R})$.

The following definition captures the notion of evolution of a membrane system with the application of a multi-rule vector $\overrightarrow{R}$.

Definition 5. *Let* $\Pi = (\mathcal{O}, \mu, w_1^0, \ldots, w_n^0, R_1, \ldots, R_n)$ *be a membrane system,* $C = (w_1, \ldots, w_n)$ *be a configuration and* $\overrightarrow{R} = (\widehat{R}_1, \ldots, \widehat{R}_n)$ *be a multi-rule vector such that* $C[\overrightarrow{R}\rangle$. *Then* $\overrightarrow{R}$ *can be executed and its execution leads to a configuration* $C' = (w_1', \ldots, w_n')$ *where* $w_i' = w_i \ominus \mathsf{Lhs}(\overrightarrow{R})_i \oplus \mathsf{Rhs}(\overrightarrow{R})_i$. *The execution of a multi-rule vector* $\overrightarrow{R}$ *at a configuration* C *is denoted with* $C[\overrightarrow{R}\rangle C'$.

For the enabling and the execution of a multi-rule vector we adopt a notation resembling the one usually adopted for Petri nets, also because of the tight connections among these two formalisms (see [6,7,12,13,20] among others, or the chapter in [23]). Sometimes we will call an evolution step of a membrane system as a *reaction step*.

We now formalize the *chain* of "reactions" for a given membrane system: C_0 is a reaction sequence, and if $C_0 [\vec{R}_1\rangle C_1 \ldots C_{n-1} [\vec{R}_n\rangle C_n$ is a reaction sequence, and $C_n [\vec{R}\rangle C$, then $C_0 [\vec{R}_1\rangle C_1 \ldots C_n [\vec{R}\rangle C$ is also a reaction sequence. A configuration C is said to be *reachable* if there is a reaction sequence starting from the initial configuration and leading to C, *i.e.* $C_0 [\vec{R}_1\rangle C_1 \ldots C_{n-1} [\vec{R}_n\rangle C_n$ with $C = C_n$.

The evolution of membrane systems may have several strategies, and usually it is assumed that in each membrane all the applicable rules are actually applied in a *maximally parallel* way. Thus if $\vec{R}$ is enabled at the configuration C ($C [\vec{R}\rangle$) it is implicitly assumed that there is no rule r in any of the rules sets R_i such that $C [\vec{R'}\rangle$ where $\vec{R'}$ is obtained from $\vec{R}$ adding an instance of the rule r to the proper multiset. However, other strategies may be used, for instance maximality with respect to a specific membrane index (no rule associated to that membrane can be added to the multi-rule vector), or the rules to be applied are those involving the presence of a specific object called catalyst, or to each rule a readiness index can be associated and the criteria is to maximize the sum of these indices, or simply a priority can be attached to each rule and those enabled with highest priorities have to be applied. The various strategies that can be adopted have an influence on the expressiveness of the paradigm, that is not our concern, as we already mentioned in the introduction.

4   Reversing Membrane System Computations

Reversibility in membrane systems is strongly connected to the idea that computations are *deterministic*. Here we consider an approach which is more similar to the one taken when reversibility is considered in the realm of distributed and concurrent computations.

Rather than introducing new rules (reversed, like in dual membrane systems where the effect of *undoing* is obtained applying reversed rules) we formalize what the reverse application of a multi-rule vector is.

Definition 6. *Let* $\Pi = (\mathcal{O}, \mu, w_1^0, \ldots, w_n^0, R_1, \ldots, R_n)$ *be a membrane system,* $C = (w_1, \ldots, w_n)$ *a configuration and* $\vec{R}$ *be a multi-rule vector. Then* $\vec{R}$ *is reversely enabled at* C *whenever, for all* $i \in \{1, \ldots, n\}$*, it holds that* $\mathsf{Rhs}(\vec{R})_i \subseteq w_i$*, and it is denoted with* $C \langle \vec{R}]$*.*

The intuition is almost trivial: the enabling is done by checking on the effects of the application of rules. Observe that this fits easily when rule formats like symport/antiport are considered, or like in [7] where a more general format for rules is considered.

Definition 7. *Let* $\Pi = (\mathcal{O}, \mu, w_1^0, \ldots, w_n^0, R_1, \ldots, R_n)$ *be a membrane system,* $C = (w_1, \ldots, w_n)$ *a configuration and* $\overrightarrow{R}$ *be a multi-rule vector such that* $C \langle \overrightarrow{R}]$. *Then* $\overrightarrow{R}$ *can be* reversed *and the effects of reversing this multi-rule vector are, for all* $i \in \{1, \ldots, n\}$, $w_i' = w_i \ominus \mathsf{Rhs}(\overrightarrow{R})_i \oplus \mathsf{Lhs}(\overrightarrow{R})_i$. *We write* $C \langle \overrightarrow{R}] C'$ *to state that the configuration* C' *is the effect of reversing the multi-rule vector* $\overrightarrow{R}$. *In this case we say that* $\overrightarrow{R}$ *is* reversely executed.

Once we have established what reversely enabling and reverse execution might be, we start to connect these notion with the usual *forward* executions.

Proposition 1. *Let* $\Pi = (\mathcal{O}, \mu, w_1^0, \ldots, w_n^0, R_1, \ldots, R_n)$ *be a membrane system,* $C = (w_1, \ldots, w_n)$ *a configuration and* $\overrightarrow{R}$ *be a multi-rule vector such that* $C [\overrightarrow{R}\rangle$, *and let* C' *be the configuration reached executing* $\overrightarrow{R}$, *i.e.* $C [\overrightarrow{R}\rangle C'$. *Then* $C' \langle \overrightarrow{R}]$.

The loop lemma can be easily proven also in this setting:

Lemma 1 (Loop lemma). *Let* $\Pi = (\mathcal{O}, \mu, w_1^0, \ldots, w_n^0, R_1, \ldots, R_n)$ *be a membrane system,* $C = (w_1, \ldots, w_n)$ *a configuration and* $\overrightarrow{R}$ *be a multi-rule vector such that* $C [\overrightarrow{R}\rangle$, *and let* C' *be the configuration reached executing* $\overrightarrow{R}$, *i.e.* $C [\overrightarrow{R}\rangle C'$. *Then* $C' \langle \overrightarrow{R}] C$.

The proof of the following theorem is obvious.

Theorem 1. *Let* Π *be a membrane system,* C *a configuration and* $\overrightarrow{R}$ *be a multi-rule vector such that* $C [\overrightarrow{R}\rangle C'$. *Then there exists a multi-rule vector* $\overrightarrow{R}'$ *such that* $C' \langle \overrightarrow{R}'] C$.

Observe that not necessarily $\overrightarrow{R}'$ should be equal to $\overrightarrow{R}$. In fact they may differ.

Example 1. Consider the membrane system with just one membrane, the unique rule associated to the membrane are $r^1 = a \rightarrow (b, \mathsf{here})$ and $r^2 = a \oplus b \rightarrow (2b, \mathsf{here})$, and the initial configuration is $a \oplus b$. The rule r^1 is enabled at the initial configuration and its application leads to the configuration $2b$. Now also r^2 can be reversely applied at this configuration and the initial configuration can be obtained again.

The main problem is that membrane systems do not keep any information about the past, thus at a certain configuration it could be that a multi-rule vector $\overrightarrow{R}$ can be reversely executed even when no $\overrightarrow{R}'$ such that $\overrightarrow{R} \subseteq \overrightarrow{R}'$ has been "forwardly" executed. This contrasts the idea that reversibility is like undoing something that has been done previously.

Example 2. Consider the membrane system with 2 membranes $[\, [\,]_2 \,]_1$, where the indices are the ones associated to the membranes, and with the following sets of rules: $\{r_1^1 : 2a \rightarrow (a \oplus b, \mathsf{here}) \oplus (b, \mathsf{in}_2), r_2^1 : b \rightarrow (a, \mathsf{here}) \oplus (c, \mathsf{in}_2), r_3^1 : a \oplus b \rightarrow$

$(2a, \mathsf{here}) \oplus (b, \mathsf{in}_2), r_4^1 : a \to (b, \mathsf{here}) \oplus (c, \mathsf{in}_2), r_5^1 : 2a \to (b \oplus c, \mathsf{in}_2)\}$ are the rules associated to the first membrane, and $\{r_1^2 : b \to (2a, \mathsf{out}), r_2^2 : c \to (b, \mathsf{out}), r_3^2 : b \to (a, \mathsf{out}), r_4^2 : c \to (c, \mathsf{out})\}$ are those associated to the second membrane. The initial configuration is (w_1^0, w_2^0) where $w_1^0 = 2a \oplus b$ and $w_2^0 = \mathbf{0}$. The configuration $(2a \oplus b, b \oplus c)$ can be reached either executing the multi-rule vector $(r_1^1 \oplus r_2^1, \mathbf{0})$ or the one $(r_3^1 \oplus r_4^1, \mathbf{0})$. At this configuration these two multi-rule vectors are reversely enabled, but also the multi-rule vector $(r_5^1, \mathbf{0})$, and reversely executing it we would obtain the configuration $(2a, \mathbf{0})$ which is not reachable using the rules in the membrane system.

A similar problem is present in all the algebraic process calculi for which reversibility has been studied (see [8,10,14,15] among others). The solution is usually to add a *memory* which helps to keep track of the evolution of the processes. Here we pursue a similar idea by adding information to configurations (membranes). We assume that Name contains $\perp$ as a name which is not associated to any rule.

4.1 Membranes with Memory

Objects of a membrane system may be enriched by adding the name of the rule producing them. Thus objects would be $\mathcal{O} \times \mathsf{Name}$, and reversing a step would be to find out whether there are enough objects with specific rules names. The *forward* enabling would ignore the information on which rule produced the object, and the execution of the step would simply add the proper name of each object produced. This solution allow to undo just one step, as the information on the name of the rule of the *consumed* object are lost.

To be able to undo more steps we have to figure out a different structure, which we call memory and we will add it to configurations.

We briefly discuss what the *memory* in this case could be. The idea is rather simple: the memory is a labeled partial order, where the labeling gives a triple composed by an object, the index of a membrane and a rules name, thus $\langle o, i, \mathfrak{n} \rangle$ conveys the idea that the object o has been produced in the membrane i using the rule $\mathfrak{n}$.

Definition 8. *Let* Name *be a set of rules names such that* $\perp \in \mathsf{Name}$*, let* $\mathcal{O}$ *be a set of objects and let* $\mathcal{I}$ *be a set of indices. Then a* memory m *is the labeled partial order* $(X, \preceq, l)$ *where* $(X, \preceq)$ *is a partial order and* $l: X \to \mathcal{O} \times \mathcal{I} \times \mathsf{Name}$ *is a labeling mapping With* Mem *we denote the set of memories.*

Given an element of $(o, i, \mathfrak{n}) \in \mathcal{O} \times \mathcal{I} \times \mathsf{Name}$, we define some obvious projections operators, that carry over on multistes of $\mathcal{O} \times \mathcal{I} \times \mathsf{Name}$. $\mathsf{obj}_m : \mathcal{O} \times \mathcal{I} \times \mathsf{Name} \to \mathcal{O}$ is defined as $\mathsf{obj}_m(o, i, \mathfrak{n}) = o$, $\mathsf{i}_m : \mathcal{O} \times \mathcal{I} \times \mathsf{Name} \to \mathcal{I}$ as $\mathsf{i}_m(o, i, \mathfrak{n}) = i$, and finally $\mathsf{rule}_m : \mathcal{O} \times \mathcal{I} \times \mathsf{Name} \to \mathsf{Name}$ as $\mathsf{rule}_m(o, i, \mathfrak{n}) = \mathfrak{n}$. Given $\mathsf{m} = (X, \preceq, l)$, with $\mathsf{max}(\mathsf{m})$ we denote the (multi)set $\oplus_{x \in max(X, \preceq)} l(x)$.

On memories we define two operations: one to add a vertex and another one to remove a vertex. These operations are obviously extended to sets of vertices. Given an element $\mathsf{a} \in \mathcal{O} \times \mathcal{I} \times \mathsf{Name}$ and a set of vertices $Y \subseteq X$, with add we denote the operation that takes a memory $m = (X, \preceq, l)$, the set of vertices Y and the element a and add a new vertex, labeled with a, which is greater than all the vertex in Y. Formally $\text{add}(m, Y, a)$ is the memory $m' = (X \cup \{y\}, \preceq', l')$ where $y \notin X$, $l'(y) = a$ and $l'(x) = l(x)$ if $x \in X$, and $\preceq'$ is obtained closing transitively and reflexively the relation $\preceq \cup \{(y', y) \mid y' \in Y\}$ (though not explicitly stated here, we imagine that the set Y is not empty and is a subset of $max(X, \preceq)$). With remove we denote the operation of removing a vertex x from a memory, thus given a memory $m = (X, \preceq, l)$, and $x \in X$, with $\text{remove}(m, x)$ we denote the memory $m' = (X \backslash \{x\}, \preceq', l')$ where $\preceq'$ and l' are the restriction of $\preceq$ and l respectively to $X \backslash \{x\}$ (though not explicitly stated here, we imagine that only maximal elements are removed). We do need some further notation. Consider a multiset z over $\mathcal{O} \times \{1, \ldots, n\} \times \mathsf{Name}$, and an index $i \in \{1, \ldots, n\}$, with $\lfloor z \rfloor_i$ we denote the multiset defined as follows: $\lfloor z \rfloor_i(a) = z(a)$ if $i_m(a) = i$ and $\lfloor z \rfloor_i(a) = 0$ otherwise.

The notion of membrane system does not change, it changes however the one of configuration (than now has a memory).

Definition 9. *Let $\Pi_m = (\mathcal{O}, \mu, w_1^0, \ldots, w_n^0, R_1, \ldots, R_n)$ be a membrane system. Then a configuration with memory is the pair $C = (C, m)$ where $C = (w_1, \ldots, w_n)$ is the tuple of multisets over $\mathcal{O}$ and $m = (X, \preceq, l)$ is a memory such that for each $i \in \{1, \ldots, n\}$ it holds that $w_i = \text{obj}_m(\lfloor \max(m) \rfloor_i)$.*

The initial configuration C_0 is the pair (C_0, m_0), where $C_0 = (w_1^0, \ldots, w_n^0)$ and $m_0 = (X, \preceq, l)$ is a memory such that $\forall x \in X$, $\text{rule}_m(l(x)) = \perp$ and $\forall x, y \in X$. $x \preceq y$ implies $x = y$.

Given a configuration with memory $C = (C, m)$, then $\eta(C)$ is C and $\gamma(C)$ is m.

A configuration has now a memory and the requirement is that for each maximal element of the memory corresponds an object in the membrane configuration. The initial memory is such that the maximal elements carry the information on the rule stating that they have not been produced by any rule, and the partial ordering is the discrete one.

Example 3. Consider the membrane system with just one membrane with the set of rules: $\{r_1^1 : a \to (a, \mathsf{here}), r_2^1 : a \to (2a, \mathsf{here}), r_3^1 : b \to (a \oplus b, \mathsf{here}), r_4^1 : a \oplus b \to (a, \mathsf{here})\}$ and the following initial configuration: $(a \oplus b, (\{v_1, v_2\}, id, l))$, where id is the identity relation on $\{v_1, v_2\}$, $l(v_1) = (a, 1, \perp)$ and $l(v_2) = (b, 1, \perp)$.

The definition of enabling of a multi-rule vector is the same as for membrane systems: it should be checked on the object part of a configuration (which is closely related to the memory).

Definition 10. *Let $\Pi_m = (\mathcal{O}, \mu, w_1^0, \ldots, w_n^0, R_1, \ldots, R_n)$ be a membrane system with memory, $C = (C, m)$ a configuration with memory, and $\overrightarrow{R}$ a multi-rule vector. Then $\overrightarrow{R}$ is enabled at C whenever $\eta(C)[\overrightarrow{R}\rangle$, We denote the enabling of $\overrightarrow{R}$ at C with $C\{[\overrightarrow{R}\rangle$.*

Consider a memory $\mathsf{m} = (X, \preceq, l)$ and a subset of vertex $Y \subseteq max(X, \preceq)$ with $\widetilde{max}(Y)$ we denote the multiset $\oplus_{y \in Y} l(y)$.

Given a configuration with memory $\mathcal{C} = ((w_1, \ldots, w_n), \mathsf{m})$ and a multi-rule vector $\overrightarrow{R}$, for each rule r such that $\widehat{R}_{\mathsf{index}(r)}(r) > 0$, with $\mathsf{LHS}_m(r)$ we denote the pair $(u_{\mathsf{index}(r)}, Y)$ where $u_{\mathsf{index}(r)} \subseteq w_{\mathsf{index}(r)}$ is such that $\mathsf{lhs}(r) = u_{\mathsf{index}(r)}$, with $w_{\mathsf{index}(r)}$ in $\eta(\mathcal{C})$, and Y is a subset of the maximal elements in $\gamma(\mathcal{C}) = (X, \preceq, l)$ such that $\lfloor \widetilde{max}(Y) \rfloor_{\mathsf{index}(r)} = u_{\mathsf{index}(r)}$.

Once a multi-rule vector $\overrightarrow{R}$ is enabled at a configuration with memory we have to state the effects of the application of a rule r. The idea is now the following: for each object of the multiset *produced* by a rule we add to the memory a new vertex labeled with the object, the membrane index it belongs to, and the name of rule r.

Consider a rule r enabled at a configuration $\mathcal{C}$, and consider $\mathsf{LHS}_m(r) = (u_{\mathsf{index}(r)}, \{Y\})$. Consider now $\mathsf{rhs}(r)$, and take $\mathsf{rhs}(r)|_\alpha$ with $\alpha \in \{\mathsf{here}, \mathsf{out}\} \cup \{\mathsf{in}_i \mid \mathsf{father}(i) = \mathsf{index}(r)\}$. Then $\mathsf{RHS}_m(r)_i$ is the multiset in $\mathcal{O}$ defined as usual as $\mathsf{Rhs}(r)_i$, and the new memory is obtained from $\gamma(\mathcal{C}) = (X, \preceq, l)$ by adding for each object o in $\mathsf{RHS}_m(r)_i$ a new vertex y greater than any vertex in Y and labeled with $(o, i, \mathsf{name}(r))$. We denote this operation as $\mathsf{Add}(\gamma(\mathcal{C}), \mathsf{RHS}_m(r)_i, Y)$ and it is the extension of the operation add defined previously. Given a multi-rule vector $\overrightarrow{R}$, for each i between 1 and n, with overloading of notation, we denote with $\mathsf{LHS}_m(\overrightarrow{R})_i$ the multiset of pairs over $\mathcal{O}$ and set of subsets of indices, defined as $\bigoplus_{r \in R_i} \widehat{R}_i(r) \cdot \mathsf{LHS}_m(r)$ (where the sum for pairs acts as the sum on the multiset part and union on the other), and the tuple of these pairs is denoted with $\mathsf{LHS}_m(\overrightarrow{R})$, $\widetilde{\mathsf{LHS}_m}(\overrightarrow{R})$ is the tuple obtained considering only the first components of $\mathsf{LHS}_m(\overrightarrow{R})$ (thus $\mathsf{Lhs}(\overrightarrow{R})$), and $\widehat{\mathsf{LHS}_m}(\overrightarrow{R})$ is the set of subsets of vertices and it is such that $\forall Y, Y' \in \widehat{\mathsf{LHS}_m}(\overrightarrow{R})$, $Y \neq Y'$ implies that $Y\mathcal{Y}' = \emptyset$ (all the involved vertices are distinct). Similarly, for each membrane, we denote the effects by $\mathsf{RHS}_m(\overrightarrow{R})_i$ and $\mathsf{RHS}_m(\overrightarrow{R})$ denotes the tuple of these effects and on memory is $\mathsf{Add}(\gamma(\mathcal{C}), \mathsf{RHS}_m(\overrightarrow{R}), \widehat{\mathsf{LHS}_m}(\overrightarrow{R}))$ where $\widehat{\mathsf{LHS}_m}(\overrightarrow{R})$ is a *set* of subset of the maximal elements in $\gamma(\mathcal{C})$ that have to be followed by the new objects (thus there is a set of maximal elements for each applied rule).

Definition 11. *Let $\Pi_m = (\mathcal{O}, \mu, w_1^0, \ldots, w_n^0, R_1, \ldots, R_n)$ be a membrane system with memory, $\mathcal{C}$ a configuration with memory, and $\overrightarrow{R}$ a multi-rule vector such that $\mathcal{C} \{\!\{\overrightarrow{R}\rangle$, and assume that $\widehat{\mathsf{LHS}_m}(\overrightarrow{R})$ is the list of maximal elements of $\gamma(\mathcal{C})$ as described above. Then $\mathcal{C} \{\!\{\overrightarrow{R}\rangle \mathcal{C}'$ where $\mathcal{C}'$ is obtained by $\mathcal{C}$ as follows: for each membrane index i, $w_i' = w_i \ominus \mathsf{Lhs}(\overrightarrow{R})_i \oplus \mathsf{Rhs}(\overrightarrow{R})_i$ and the memory is $\mathsf{Add}(\gamma(\mathcal{C}), \mathsf{RHS}_m(\overrightarrow{R}), \widehat{\mathsf{LHS}_m}(\overrightarrow{R}))$.*

The definition is rather obvious: for each object o produced in a membrane i by the rule n a new vertex is added in the memory which is greater than the elements *consumed* by the rule.

Observe that the elements added to the configuration are precisely among the maximal elements in the memory.

Proposition 2. *Let $\Pi_m = (\mathcal{O}, \mu, w_1^0, \ldots, w_n^0, R_1, \ldots, R_n)$ be a membrane system with memory, $\mathcal{C}$ a configuration with memory, and $\overrightarrow{R}$ a multi-rule vector such that $\mathcal{C} \{\!\lfloor \overrightarrow{R} \rangle \mathcal{C}'$. Take $Y = \max(\gamma(\mathcal{C}'))$ and consider $l(Y)$ which can be seen as a multiset over $\mathcal{O} \times \{1, \ldots, n\} \times$ Name. Then for each $i \in \{1, \ldots, n\}$. $\mathsf{obj}_m(\lfloor l(Y) \rfloor_i) = w_i'$ where $\eta(\mathcal{C}') = (w_1', \ldots, w_n')$.*

Example 4. Consider the membrane system of Example 3. At the initial configuration the following sets of rules are enabled: $\{r_1^1 \oplus r_3^1\}, \{r_2^1 \oplus r_3^1\}, \{r_4^1\}$. Consider the last one. The execution of it gives the configuration $((a, r_4^1), (\{v_1, v_2, v_3\}, id \cup \{(v_1, v_3), (v_2, v_3)\}, l'))$ where $l'(v_1) = l(v_1), l'(v_2) = l(v_2)$ and $l'(v_3) = (b, 1, r_4^1)$.

Performing another one, for instance $\{r_1^1 \oplus r_3^1\}$, would give a different memory.

We show that this is a conservative extension of membrane systems, as to each step in a membrane system with memory, a step corresponds in the membrane system where all the added information is forgotten.

Proposition 3. *Let $\Pi_m = (\mathcal{O}, \mu, w_1^0, \ldots, w_n^0, R_1, \ldots, R_n)$ be a membrane system, $\mathcal{C}$ a configuration with memory, $\overrightarrow{R}$ a multi-rule vector such that $\mathcal{C} \{\overrightarrow{R}\rangle$, and let $\mathcal{C} \{\!\lfloor \overrightarrow{R} \rangle \mathcal{C}'$. Then $\eta(\mathcal{C}) [\overrightarrow{R}\rangle$ and $\eta(\mathcal{C}) [\overrightarrow{R}\rangle \eta(\mathcal{C}')$.*

We discuss now when a rule r can be *reversely* applied in this setting. Again the intuition is rather simple, just check if there are enough objects bearing the name of the rule r among the maximal elements of the memory. Let m be a memory, n be a rule name, and i a membrane index, then with $\blacktriangleleft_{\mathsf{name}(r)}^i (\mathsf{m})$ we denote the multiset on $\mathcal{O}$ defined as

$$\blacktriangleleft_{\mathsf{name}(r)}^i (\mathsf{m}) = \bigoplus_{x \in \mathsf{max}(\mathsf{m})} \{\mathsf{obj}_m(l(x)) \mid \mathsf{rule}_m(l(x)) = \mathsf{name}(r) \wedge \mathsf{i}_m(l(x)) = i\}$$

Let r be a rule and $\mathcal{C}$ be a configuration of a membrane system with memory Π_m. Then r is reversely enabled at $\mathcal{C} = ((w_1, \ldots, w_n), \mathsf{m})$ whenever, for all $k \in \mathcal{I}(r), \mathsf{rhs}(r)_k \subseteq \blacktriangleleft_{\mathsf{name}(r)}^k (\mathsf{m})$. The reverse enabling is summarized in the following definition.

Definition 12. *Let $\Pi_m = (\mathcal{O}, \mu, w_1^0, \ldots, w_n^0, R_1, \ldots, R_n)$ be a membrane system with memory, $\mathcal{C}$ a configuration, and $\overrightarrow{R}$ a multi-rule vector. Then $\overrightarrow{R}$ is reversely enabled at $\mathcal{C}$ if for rule r in $\overrightarrow{R}$ $\widehat{R}_{\mathsf{index}(r)} \cdot \mathsf{rhs}(r)_k \subseteq \blacktriangleleft_{\mathsf{name}(r)}^{w_k} (\gamma(\mathcal{C}))$. The reverse enabling of a multi-rule vector is denoted with $\mathcal{C} \langle\!\lfloor \overrightarrow{R} \rfloor\!\rangle$.*

In this case we have to find, for each each instance of a given rule, enough objects produced by an instance of the same rule at the same (local) configuration.

Once a multi-rule vector is reversely enabled, it may be applied. We start showing what it means to undo a single rule r. Given a configuration $\mathcal{C}$, with the memory $\gamma(\mathcal{C}) = (X, \preceq, l)$, for each index $k \in \mathcal{I}(r)$ we have that $\mathsf{rhs}(r)_k$

is contained in $\blacktriangleleft_{\mathsf{name}(r)}^{k}$ $(\gamma(\mathcal{C}))$. Consider a subset $Y \subseteq max(X, \preceq)$ such that $\mathsf{obj}_m(\lfloor \oplus_{y \in Y} l(y) \rfloor_k) = \mathsf{rhs}(r)_k$, then what we have to do on the memory is just to remove the set Y from the memory. The set of these vertices are denoted with $\widetilde{\mathsf{RHS}_m}(r)$ and it extends obviously to $\overrightarrow{R}$. Clearly we require that these sets of vertices are disjoint.

Definition 13. *Let* $\Pi_m = (\mathcal{O}, \mu, w_1^0, \ldots, w_n^0, R_1, \ldots, R_n)$ *be a membrane system with memory,* $\mathcal{C} = ((w_1, \ldots, w_n), \mathsf{m})$ *be a configuration, and* $\overrightarrow{R}$ *a multirule vector such that* $C \langle\!\langle \overrightarrow{R} \rbrace\!\rbrace$. *Then* $\mathcal{C}' = ((w_1', \ldots, w_n'), \mathsf{m}')$, *where* $w_i' = w_i \ominus \mathsf{Rhs}(\overrightarrow{R})_i \oplus \mathsf{Lhs}(\overrightarrow{R})_i$ *and* m' *is obtained from* m *by removing all the vertex in* m *corresponding to the object in* $\mathsf{RHS}_m(\overrightarrow{R})$, *thus* $\mathsf{m}' = \mathsf{remove}(\mathsf{m}, \widetilde{\mathsf{RHS}_m}(\overrightarrow{R}))$, *is the configuration reached by reversely executing* $\overrightarrow{R}$ *at* C. *As before it is denoted with* $C \langle\!\langle \overrightarrow{R} \rbrace\!\rbrace C'$.

Example 5. Consider the membrane system of Example 3 and the computation step done in Example 4. The set $\{r_4^1\}$ is reversely enabled and

$$(b, (\{v_1, v_2, v_3\}, id \cup \{(v_1, v_3), (v_2, v_3)\}, l')) \ \langle\!\langle \{r_4^1\} \rbrace\!\rbrace \ (a \oplus b, (\{v_1, v_2\}, id, l))$$

where the labeling are those in Examples 3 and 4.

Consider another membrane system with just one membrane with the set of rules: $\{r_1^1 : b \rightarrow (a \oplus b, \mathsf{here})\}$ and the initial configuration (b, m_0). Applying to this configuration $\{r_1^1\}$ we have

$$(b, \mathsf{m}_0) \ \{\!\{\{r_1^1\}\rangle \ (a \oplus b, \mathsf{m}_1)$$

where $\mathsf{m}_1 = (\{v_1, v_2, v_3\}, \preceq, l)$ where $v_1 \preceq v_2, v_1 \preceq v_3$ and l is the following: $l(v_1) = (b, 1, \bot), l(v_2) = (a, 1, r_1^1)$ and $l(v_3) = (b, 1, r_1^1)$. To this configuration we can apply again the same rule:

$$(a \oplus b, \mathsf{m}_1) \ \{\!\{\{r_1^1\}\rangle \ (a \oplus a \oplus b, \mathsf{m}_2)$$

where now m_2 is $(\{v_1, v_2, v_3, v_4, v_5\}, \preceq', l')$ with $v_3 \preceq' v_4, v_3 \preceq' v_5$ and the new vertices are labelled as $l(v_4) = (a, 1, r_1^1)$ and $l(v_5) = (b, 1, r_1^1)$. Reversely applying the unique rule we could have now a choice: either consider the vertices $\{v_4, v_5\}$ or $\{v_2, v_5\}$. In the latter case we have

$$((a \oplus a \oplus b, \mathsf{m}_2) \ \langle\!\langle \{r_1^1\}\} \ (a \oplus b, \mathsf{m}_3)$$

where m_3 is obtained from m_2 by removing the vertices v_2 and v_5. This choice (which is investigated in a different setting in [19]) has as consequence that we cannot further undo going back to the initial configuration.

If the vertices $\{v_4, v_5\}$ are taken into accont, then the configuration $(a \oplus b, \mathsf{m}_1)$ is obtained again.

Again the loop lemma can be proved also in this setting but, as the previous example points out, it is a weaker version with respect to the one we introduced previously.

Lemma 2 (Loop lemma for membrane system with memory). *Let Π_m = $(\mathcal{O}, \mu, w_1^0, \ldots, w_n^0, R_1, \ldots, R_n)$ be a membrane system with memory, $\mathcal{C}$ a configuration, and $\overrightarrow{R}$ be a multi-rule vector such that $\mathcal{C} \{\!\!\{\overrightarrow{R}\rangle$, and let $\mathcal{C}'$ be the configuration reached by executing $\overrightarrow{R}$, i.e. $\mathcal{C} \{\!\!\{\overrightarrow{R}\rangle \mathcal{C}'$. Then there exists a set of vertices in $\gamma(\mathcal{C}')$ associated to the object to be removed by the reverse application of $\overrightarrow{R}$, such that $\mathcal{C}' \langle\overrightarrow{R}\}\!\!\}\mathcal{C}''$ and $\mathcal{C} = \mathcal{C}''$.*

Observe that not necessarily the objects consumed by the application of a multi-rule vector are those used in the reverse application of it. Hence we not necessarily obtain again the same memory. However, if the memory is the same, then the vector multi-rule reversely applied is the same we started with.

Theorem 2. *Let Π_m be a membrane system with memory, $\mathcal{C}$ a configuration, and $\overrightarrow{R}$ be a multi-rule vector such that $\mathcal{C} \{\!\!\{\overrightarrow{R}\rangle \mathcal{C}'$. Then for all multi-rule vector $\overrightarrow{R'}$ such that $\mathcal{C}' \langle\overrightarrow{R'}\}\!\!\} \mathcal{C}$ it holds that $\overrightarrow{R'} = \overrightarrow{R}$.*

Obviously, the reversing in a membrane system with memory and the reversing in the membrane system where the additional information are forgotten, are related in a precise way.

Proposition 4. *Let Π_m = $(\mathcal{O}, \mu, w_1^0, \ldots, w_n^0, R_1, \ldots, R_n)$ be a membrane system with memory, $\mathcal{C}$ a configuration, and $\overrightarrow{R}$ be a multi-rule vector such that $\mathcal{C} \{\!\!\{\overrightarrow{R}\rangle$, and let $\mathcal{C}' \langle\overrightarrow{R}\}\!\!\} \mathcal{C}$. Then $\eta(\mathcal{C}') \langle\overrightarrow{R}] \eta(\mathcal{C})$.*

5   Future Works

Reversibility in membrane systems has several facets. One is connected with determinism and the fact that each configuration has just a single predecessor, another is related to the amount of information needed to *reconstruct* past configurations. Concerning this view of reversibility, we have proposed a way to add all the relevant informations to *undo* steps properly. It must be said that many other solutions are conceivable, depending on the amount of information needed, for instance objects may be enriched to carry the history. The approach we presented here has the characteristic that the memory not only allow to reverse steps properly but also keep tracks of the dependencies among steps and objects.

Beside continuing to investigate on how reversibility can be achieved in membrane systems, we put two possible research issues. Here we have considered that all the rules are reversible, but this assumption is a maybe too strong when computations that are inspired by nature are considered. We may imagine that some rules produce *irreversible* effects, that cannot be undone. This may be modelled simply forgetting the rules names in both approaches. However this opens many questions on how to actually reverse computations and also on the notions of causality as investigated in [20] or [2]. Various situations may be devised in this setting, similarly to what is done in [19]. Here some events are undone but still some of their effects may remain. This idea can be possibly implemented also in membrane systems, opening new interesting feature.

Another issue is the possibility of combining the two ways: a part of the multi-rule vector is used to compute forward, another part is used to undo some effects. Again this has to be fully investigated.

Acknowledgement. The author acknowledge the useful remarks and suggestions by the anonymous reviewers.

References

1. Agrigoroaiei, O., Ciobanu, G.: Reversing computation in membrane systems. J. Logic Algebraic Program. **79**(3–5), 278–288 (2010)
2. Agrigoroaiei, O., Ciobanu, G.: Rule-based and object-based event structures for membrane systems. J. Logic Algebraic Program. **79**(6), 295–303 (2010)
3. Alhazov, A., Freund, R., Morita, K.: Sequential and maximally parallel multiset rewriting: reversibility and determinism. Nat. Comput. **11**(1), 95–106 (2012)
4. Aman, B., Ciobanu, G.: Computational power of protein interaction networks. In: Mauri, G., Dennunzio, A., Manzoni, L., Porreca, A.E. (eds.) UCNC 2013. LNCS, vol. 7956, pp. 248–249. Springer, Heidelberg (2013). https://doi.org/10.1007/978-3-642-39074-6_25
5. Ciobanu, G., Pan, L., Păun, G., Pérez-Jiménez, M.J.: P systems with minimal parallelism. Theoret. Comput. Sci. **378**(1), 117–130 (2007)
6. Ciobanu, G., Pinna, G.M.: Catalytic Petri nets are turing complete. In: Dediu, A.-H., Martín-Vide, C. (eds.) LATA 2012. LNCS, vol. 7183, pp. 192–203. Springer, Heidelberg (2012). https://doi.org/10.1007/978-3-642-28332-1_17
7. Ciobanu, G., Pinna, G.M.: Catalytic and communicating Petri nets are Turing complete. Inf. Comput. **239**, 55–70 (2014)
8. Danos, V., Krivine, J.: Reversible communicating systems. In: Gardner, P., Yoshida, N. (eds.) CONCUR 2004. LNCS, vol. 3170, pp. 292–307. Springer, Heidelberg (2004). https://doi.org/10.1007/978-3-540-28644-8_19
9. Freund, R., Kari, L., Oswald, M., Sosík, P.: Computationally universal P systems without priorities: two catalysts are sufficient. Theoret. Comput. Sci. **330**(2), 251–266 (2005)
10. Giachino, E., Lanese, I., Mezzina, C.A., Tiezzi, F.: Causal-consistent reversibility in a tuple-based language. In: Daneshtalab, M., Aldinucci, M., Leppänen, V., Lilius, J., Brorsson, M. (eds.) PDP 2015, pp. 467–475. IEEE Computer Society (2015)
11. Ibarra, O.H.: On strong reversibility in P systems and related problems. Int. J. Found. Comput. Sci. **22**(1), 7–14 (2011)
12. Kleijn, J., Koutny, M.: A Petri net model for membrane systems with dynamic structure. Nat. Comput. **8**(4), 781–796 (2009)
13. Kleijn, J.H.C.M., Koutny, M., Rozenberg, G.: Towards a Petri net semantics for membrane systems. In: Freund, R., Păun, G., Rozenberg, G., Salomaa, A. (eds.) WMC 2005. LNCS, vol. 3850, pp. 292–309. Springer, Heidelberg (2006). https://doi.org/10.1007/11603047_20
14. Lanese, I., Mezzina, C.A., Stefani, J.-B.: Reversing higher-order Pi. In: Gastin, P., Laroussinie, F. (eds.) CONCUR 2010. LNCS, vol. 6269, pp. 478–493. Springer, Heidelberg (2010). https://doi.org/10.1007/978-3-642-15375-4_33

15. Lanese, I., Mezzina, C.A., Stefani, J.: Reversibility in the higher-order π-calculus. Theoret. Comput. Sci. **625**, 25–84 (2016)
16. Lanese, I., Mezzina, C.A., Tiezzi, F.: Causal-consistent reversibility. Bull. EATCS (114) (2014)
17. Leporati, A., Zandron, C., Mauri, G.: Reversible P systems to simulate Fredkin circuits. Fundamenta Informaticae **74**(4), 529–548 (2006)
18. Nishida, T.Y.: Reversible P systems with symport/antiport rules. In: Paun, G., Pérez-Jiménez, M.J., Riscos-Núñez, A. (eds.) WMC 2010, pp. 452–460 (2010)
19. Phillips, I., Ulidowski, I.: Reversibility and asymmetric conflict in event structures. J. Logic Algebraic Methods Program. **84**(6), 781–805 (2015)
20. Pinna, G.M., Saba, A.: Modeling dependencies and simultaneity in membrane system computations. Theoret. Comput. Sci. **431**, 13–39 (2012)
21. Păun, A., Păun, G.: The power of communication: P systems with Symport/Antiport. New Gener. Comput. **20**(3), 295–306 (2002)
22. Păun, G.: Computing with membranes: an introduction. Bull. EATCS **67**, 139–152 (1999)
23. Păun, G., Rozenberg, G., Salomaa, A.: The Oxford Handbook of Membrane Computing. Oxford University Press, Oxford (2010)
24. Song, T., Shi, X., Xu, J.: Reversible spiking neural P systems. Front. Comput. Sci. **7**(3), 350–358 (2013)

Families of Languages Encoded by SN P Systems

José M. Sempere$^{(\boxtimes)}$

Departamento de Sistemas Informáticos y Computación,
Universitat Politècnica de València, Valencia, Spain
jsempere@dsic.upv.es

Abstract. In this work, we propose the study of SN P systems as classical information encoders. By taking the spike train of an SN P system as a (binary) source of information, we can obtain different languages according to a previously defined encoding alphabet. We provide a characterization of the language families generated by the SN P systems in this way. This characterization depends on the way we define the encoding scheme: bounded or not bounded and, in the first case, with one-to-one or non injective encodings. Finally, we propose a network topology in order to define a cascading encoder.

Keywords: SN P systems · Formal languages · Codes
Word enumerations

1 Introduction

Spiking Neural P systems (SN P systems) were proposed as a model that combines some aspects of neural networks and some others from P systems. Basically, they have been proposed as acceptor systems, language generators or (encoded) word transducers. We focus our attention on the generative capacity of this model. Typically, the language generated by the system is taken as the set of binary words defined by the spike train that the system outputs. This approach was first formulated in [5], and later developed in [1].

In this work, we consider a SN P system as a classical information source that can generate encoded strings as outputs. The binary codes can be established in an exogenous predefined way and, for a fixed encoding alphabet, the system generates a (possibly) infinite language. So, any SN P system can generate different languages depending on the encoding that has been defined. We will overview different situations within this approach: First, for a fixed integer value we will distinguish between one-to-one and non-injective cases. Then, different encoding schemes where the integer value tends to infinity will be overviewed and, finally, a network topology that connect different SN P systems to produce a cascading encoder will be proposed.

© Springer International Publishing AG 2018
M. Gheorghe et al. (Eds.): CMC 2017, LNCS 10725, pp. 262–269, 2018.
https://doi.org/10.1007/978-3-319-73359-3_17

2 Basic Concepts

We consider that the reader knows basic concepts and results from formal language theory, otherwise we refer to [10]. In the same way, we consider that the reader is familiar with the basic concepts and results about P systems and membrane computing, otherwise we refer to [4,8].

In what follows, we provide some basic definitions related to Spiking Neural P systems from [4].

Definition 1. *A spiking neural P system (SN P system, for short) of degree $m \geq 1$ is defined by the tuple $\Pi = (O, \sigma_1, \sigma_2, \cdots, \sigma_m, syn, in, out)$ where*

1. $O = \{a\}$ is the singleton alphabet of spikes
2. $\sigma_1, \sigma_2, \cdots, \sigma_m$ are neurons *of the form $\sigma_i = (n_i, R_i)$, $1 \leq i \leq m$, where*
   (a) $n_i \geq 0$ is the initial number of spikes contained in σ_i
   (b) R_i is a finite set of rules of the following two forms
      i. firing or spiking rules $E/a^c \rightarrow a; d$ where E is a regular expression over a, and $c \geq 1$, $d \geq 0$ are integer numbers. We will omit E whenever it be equal to a^c, and we will omit d if it is equal to 0.
      ii. forgetting rules $a^s \rightarrow \lambda$, for $s \geq 1$, with the restriction that for each spiking rule $E/a^c \rightarrow a; d$ then $a^s \notin L(E)$ ($L(E)$ is the regular language defined by E)
3. $syn \subseteq \{1, 2, \cdots, m\} \times \{1, 2, \cdots, m\}$ with $(i, i) \notin syn$, for $1 \leq i \leq m$, is the directed graph of synapses between neurons;
4. $in, out \in \{1 \cdots m\}$ indicate the input *and the* output *neurons of Π.*

At neuron σ_i, the firing rules $E/a^c \rightarrow a; d$ are applied as follows: if the neuron contains $k \geq c$ spikes and $a^k \in E$ then c spikes are removed from σ_i and one spike is delivered to all the neurons σ_j connected to σ_i with $(i, j) \in syn$. If $d = 0$ the spike is immediately emitted, otherwise it is emitted after d computation steps (during these computation steps, the neuron is closed, so it cannot receive spikes, it cannot apply the rules and, subsequently it cannot send new spikes). At neuron σ_i, the forgetting rule $a^s \rightarrow \lambda$ is applied as follows: if the neuron σ_i contains exactly s spikes and no firing rule can be applied then all the spikes of the neuron are removed.

A configuration of the system at an instant t during a computation is defined by the tuple $(i_1/t_1, \cdots, i_m/t_m)$ that denotes the number of spikes that are at every neuron together with the computation time needed to open the neuron. The initial configuration of the SN P system is $(n_1/0, \cdots, n_m/0)$. A computation of Π is a (finite or infinite) sequence of configurations such that: (a) the first term of the sequence is the initial configuration of the system and each of the remaining configurations are obtained from the previous one by applying rules of the system in a maximally parallel manner with the restrictions previously mentioned; and (b) if the sequence is finite (called halting computation) then the last term of the sequence is a halting configuration, that is a configuration where all neurons are open and no rule can be applied to it.

During a computation, the moments of time when a spike is emitted by the output neuron will be marked by '1' while the other moments are marked by '0'. The binary sequence that is obtained in such a way during the computation is called the *spike train* of the system. In the sequel, we will omit the input neuron, and we will work with SN P systems as *language generators*.

The language generated by any SN P system depends on the interpretation given to the spike train that it outputs. For any halting computation, we can take the finite spike train as a string over the binary alphabet $B = \{0,1\}$, or we can take the intervals between output spikes with different approaches such as those described in [9]. In what follows, we will consider the spike train as a generator of binary strings.

For any SN P system Π, the language generated by Π as described before will be denoted by $L_1(\Pi)$.

3   Languages Encoded by SN P Systems

Our approach to the languages generated by SN P systems is different from the previously referred ones. Actually, the present research idea occurred in a framework related to classical communication channels with encoded information, where, for every SN P system, different languages can be associated to the system depending on a parameter that fixes a time window to analyze the spike train.

For any SN P system Π, we take the binary language $L_1(\Pi)$ and we encode blocks of k digits, for all the positive integer values k, in such a way that languages $L_k(\Pi)$ are obtained. Of course, we have to take care of the case when the spike train is not of a length which is a multiple of the considered k. In this case, we add symbols 0 so that the obtained binary string is of a length divisible by k.

More formally, let $B = \{0,1\}$ be the binary alphabet, let $k \geq 1$ be a natural number, let B^k be the set of all strings from B whose length is k, and V_k be an alphabet. In general, any alphabet can be considered but we will associate a different symbol for every word in B^k. Consider a mapping $\varphi_k : B^k \longrightarrow V_k$. For each string $w \in B^*$ we consider the string $_kw = w0^t$, where $t = \min\{n \geq 0 \mid |w0^n|$ is a multiple of $k\}$.

The string $_kw$ can be written in the form $_kw = x_1x_2\ldots x_s$, such that $|x_j| = k$ for all $j = 1, 2, \ldots, s$. Then, φ_k can be extended to $(B^k)^*$ in the natural way: $\varphi_k(y_1y_2\ldots y_t) = \varphi_k(y_1)\varphi_k(y_2)\ldots\varphi_k(y_t)$ for all $y_i \in B^k, 1 \leq i \leq t, t \geq 0$. We can see the encoding approach that we have just described in Fig. 1.

Thus, for an SN P system Π and an encoding φ_k as above, we can define the language

$$L_{\varphi_k}(\Pi) = \{\varphi_k(_kw) \mid w \in L_1(\Pi)\}.$$

In what follows, we write $L_k(\Pi)$ instead of $L_{\varphi_k}(\Pi)$. The language $L_k(\Pi)$ depends on the encoding φ_k, hence a family of languages can be associated with Π by varying k and the mapping φ_k. Observe, that the language $L_1(\Pi)$, as defined at the end of Sect. 2, is a particular case of $L_k(\Pi)$ when $k = 1$, given

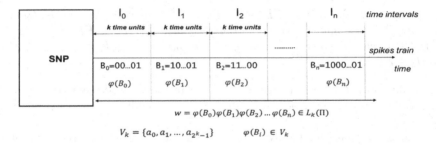

Fig. 1. SN P systems as language encoders: the case of intervals of lenght k.

that φ_1 can be trivially defined as the identity mapping. We define the family of languages $F(\Pi) = \{L_k(\Pi)|k \geq 1\}$.

Already at this very general level there appear several research issues. In what follows, we consider two classes of mappings φ_k and investigate the closure properties of the corresponding families of languages generated by SN P systems.

3.1 The One-to-One Case

A natural possibility is to order in a precise way, e.g., lexicographically, the strings in B^k, and to associate with each of them a distinct symbol from an alphabet V_k with 2^k elements, that is, assuming that φ_k is injective.

We can establish the following properties depending on whether $L_1(\Pi)$ is finite or not.

Property 1. *Let Π be an SN P system. Then, if $L_1(\Pi)$ is finite the so are each $L_k(\Pi)$ for $k > 1$.*

From the Property 1, we can deduce that if $L_1(\Pi)$ is finite, then the family $F(\Pi)$ is finite, up to a renaming of symbols of alphabets V_k.

Property 2. *Let Π be an SN P system. Then, if $L_1(\Pi)$ is infinite, then so are each $L_k(\Pi)$ for $k > 1$.*

If $L_1(\Pi)$ is infinite, then $F(\Pi)$ can be an infinite family, because the alphabet of $L_{k+1}(\Pi)$ might be larger than the alphabet of $L_k(\Pi)$. This is the case, for instance, for the SN P system Π generating $L_1(\Pi) = \{1^n 0 1^m \mid n, m \geq 1\}$ (which is an infinite regular language).

The fact that the encoding is one-to-one is rather restrictive: the passing from the binary language $L_1(\Pi)$ to a given $L_k(\Pi)$ can be done by means of a sequential transducer (a gsm, in the usual terminology, [10]). Conversely, the passage from $L_k(\Pi)$ to $L_1(\Pi)$ is done by an one-to-one (non-erasing) morphism, which implies that the converse passage is done by an inverse morphism. This observation can be formally formulated as follows.

Proposition 1. *If $L_1(\Pi) \in FL$, where FL is a family of languages closed under gsm mappings or under inverse morphisms, then $L_k(\Pi) \in FL$, for all $k \geq 1$. If FL is closed under non-erasing morphisms and $L_k(\Pi) \in FL$, then also $L_1(\Pi) \in FL$.*

Families as FL above are REG, LIN, CF in the Chomsky hierarchy, hence if $L_1(\Pi)$ is regular, linear or context-free, then so are all languages $L_k(\Pi)$, and conversely.

This means that each family $F(\Pi)$ contains only languages of the same type in the Chomsky hierarchy (for instance, it is not possible to have a context-free non-regular language $L_k(\Pi)$ together with a regular language $L_j(\Pi)$, for some $k \neq j$.

3.2   The Non-injective Case

The previous type-preserving Proposition 1 does not hold in the case of using encodings which are not one-to-one.

Here is an example: Consider Π such that $L_1(\Pi) = \{1^n 0 1^n \mid n \geq 1\}$ (SN P systems are universal, [5], hence any language can be taken as the starting language). Of course, $L_1(\Pi)$ is context-free non-regular.

Consider the encoding $\varphi_k : B^k \longrightarrow \{a, b\}$ defined by $\varphi_k(w) = a$ if $|w|_0 \leq 1$, and $\varphi_k(w) = b$ if $|w|_0 \geq 2$. We get

$$L_k(\Pi) = a^+ \cup a^* b, \text{ for } k \geq 4,$$

$L_3(\Pi) = a^+ \cup (aa)^+ b$, and $L_2(\Pi) = aa^+$.

Clearly, the languages $L_k(\Pi), k \geq 2$, are regular, in spite of the fact that $L_1(\Pi)$ is (context-free) non-regular.

The properties of the encoding is crucial for the properties of the obtained language families (this is true also in other frameworks, see, e.g., [3] and its references), hence this issue deserves further research efforts.

4   The Unbounded Case

In the previous section, an encoding of the languages based on blocks of length k has been considered. Now, we consider the limit case, when every string from $L_1(\Pi)$ encodes a different string while k tends to ∞.

Formally, we consider an alphabet $\Sigma = \{a_0, a_1, \cdots, a_p\}$, and the ordered set of strings $\Sigma^* = \{w_0, w_1, \cdots w_i, \cdots\}$. We define the encoding $\varphi_{int} : B^* \longrightarrow \Sigma^*$ such that for every binary string x, $\varphi_{int}(x) = w_{int(x)}$ where $int(x)$ is the integer value of x by taking x as a binary number. The encoding scheme over the SN P system is shown at Fig. 2.

For a given alphabet Σ and an application $\varphi_{int} : B^* \longrightarrow \Sigma^*$, we can define the encoded language of any SN P system, as we have described before, as follows

$$L_\infty(\Pi) = \{w \in \Sigma^* \mid \exists x \in L_1(\Pi) \text{ such that } w = z_{int(x)}\}$$

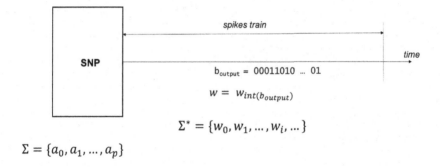

Fig. 2. SN P systems as language encoders: the unbounded case.

Observe, that Σ^* must be ordered within a precise enumeration of all its words. In this case, the enumeration of the strings in Σ^* (actually, its order) is decisive to preserve the language class from $L_1(\Pi)$ to $L_\infty(\Pi)$.

For example, let us take $L_1(\Pi) = \{(01)^n \mid n \geq 0\}$ that is a regular language that can be generated by an SN P system given that they have been proved to be universal.

Let $\Sigma = \{a, b\}$ and the languages $L_1 = \{a^n b^n \mid n \geq 0\}$ and $L_2 = \Sigma^* - L_1$. We consider that $L_1 = \{x_1, x_2, x_3, \cdots\}$ and $L_2 = \{y_1, y_2, y_3, \cdots\}$ are lexicographically ordered.

We can define the following enumeration over $\Sigma^* = \{z_1, z_2, \cdots, z_i, \cdots\}$, where

1. If $i \mod 2 = 0$ then $z_i = y_{\frac{i}{2}} \in L_2$ (*even indexes*)
2. If $i \mod 2 = 1$ then $z_i = x_{\lceil \frac{i}{2} \rceil} \in L_1$ (*odd indexes*)

Observe that every string $x \in L_1(\Pi) = \{(01)^n : n \geq 0\}$ encodes an odd integer number given that the binary string ends with '1'. Hence, $L_\infty(\Pi)$ is an infinite subset of L_1 given that, for every string x in $L_1(\Pi)$, the string $z_{int(x)}$ occupies an odd position and, subsequently, it belongs to L_1. Hence. $L_1(\Pi)$ is regular while L_∞ is not.

5   Networks of SN P Systems as Cascading Encoders

Finally, we propose a new way of encoding languages by composing a finite number of SN P systems. In this case we propose a topology based on SN P systems with a tissue-like configuration within a bus connection. Our proposal is shown in Fig. 3.

We have a finite set of n SN P systems defined in the usual way. We connect them in the following way: every time that the SN P system i halts, its spike train encodes an integer value k_i that is the parameter to encode the language in the SN P system $i + 1$. Hence, a network of SN P systems can be viewed as a cascading encoder for languages. If we connect the SN P systems in a bus topology then, for the iterated case, the last system is connected to the first one.

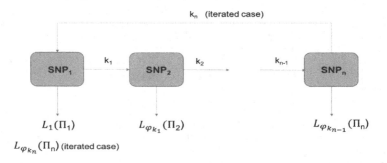

Fig. 3. A network of SN P systems generates a family of languages.

This opens a new framework which is related to previous works on DNA computing and formal languages [6, 7], where iterated transductions were proved to characterize the entire class of recursively enumerable languages.

6   Final Comments and Future Research

The idea of associating a family of languages with a given P system is rather natural. We have illustrated it here with the case of SN P systems, but the same strategy can be applied for any type of P systems producing a language (such that cell-like P systems with external output, SN P systems generating trace languages [2], etc.).

A more systematic study of this idea is of interest, starting with relevant examples, continuing with "standard" formal language theory questions, and ending with possible applications of this approach (as languages generated by the same P system are "genetically" related, maybe in this way one can capture biological connections/dependencies or other types of relationships).

More precisely, we enumerate the following questions related to our proposal:

1. We have described a way to encode languages within SN P systems. Now, the reverse problem arises i.e., to decode languages from the spike train. Here, from a spike train we should obtain the set of binary spike trains that encode it. This issue should be studied in order to complete a classical communication framework.
2. With respect to the encoding properties, we have overviewed only the aspects related to the (non) injective property. Different properties from code theory should produce new results that connect formal language theory, SN P systems and communications systems.
3. The last issue that we have proposed opens different problems related to it. If a network of SN P systems is proposed then we should study the effects of the network topology and the number of SN P systems over the families of languages. In this sense, the number of SN P system could be considered a descriptional complexity measure.

These aspects and new ones will be reported in future works.

Acknowledgements. Part of this work appeared as *Families of Languages Associated with SN P Systems: Preliminary Ideas, Open Problems.* Gh. Păun, J.M. Sempere. *Bulletin of the Membrane Computing Society,* Issue 2, December 2016, pp. 161–164. http://membranecomputing.net/IMCSBulletin/. The author is indebted to Gh. Păun for his original contribution to this work.

References

1. Chen, H., Freund, R., Ionescu, M., Păun, G., Pérez-Jiménez, M.J.: On string languages generated by spiking neural P systems. Fundam. Inf. **75**(1–4), 141–162 (2007)
2. Chen, H., Ionescu, M., Păun, A., Păun, G., Popa, B.: On trace languages generated by spiking neural P systems. In: Eighth International Workshop on Descriptional Complexity of Formal Systems (DCFS 2006), Las Cruces, New Mexico, USA, pp. 94–105, 21–23 June 2006
3. Csuhaj-Varjú, E., Vaszil, G.: On counter machines versus dP automata. In: Alhazov, A., Cojocaru, S., Gheorghe, M., Rogozhin, Y., Rozenberg, G., Salomaa, A. (eds.) CMC 2013. LNCS, vol. 8340, pp. 138–150. Springer, Heidelberg (2014). https://doi.org/10.1007/978-3-642-54239-8_11
4. Ibarra, O.H., Leporati, A., Păun, A., Woodworth, S.: Spiking neural P systems. In: Păun, G., Rozenberg, G., Salomaa, A. (eds.) The Oxford Handbook of Membrane Computing, Oxford University Press (2010)
5. Ionescu, M., Păun, G., Yokomori, T.: Spiking neural P systems. Fundam. Inf. **71**(2–3), 279–308 (2006)
6. Manca, V.: On the generative power of iterated transduction. In: Ito, M., Păun, G., Yu, S. (eds.) Words, Semigroups, and Transductions, pp. 315–327. World Scientific (2001)
7. Manca, V., Martín-Vide, C., Păun, G.: New computing paradigms suggested by DNA computing: computing by carving. BioSystems **52**, 47–54 (1999)
8. Păun, G.: Membrane Computing. An Introduction. Springer, Heidelberg (2002). https://doi.org/10.1007/978-3-642-56196-2
9. Păun, G., Pérez-Jiménez, M.J., Rozenberg, G.: Spike trains in spiking neural P systems. Int. J. Found. Comput. Sci. **17**(4), 975–1002 (2006)
10. Rozenberg, G., Salomaa, A. (eds.): Handbook of Formal Languages, vol. 3. Springer, Heidelberg (1997). https://doi.org/10.1007/978-3-642-59136-5

On the Robust Power of Morphogenetic Systems for Time Bounded Computation

Petr Sosík[2(✉)], Vladimír Smolka[2], Jan Drastík[2], Jaroslav Bradík[2], and Max Garzon[1]

[1] Computer Science, The University of Memphis, Memphis, TN, USA
[2] Research Institute of the IT4Innovations Centre of Excellence,
Faculty of Philosophy and Science, Silesian University, Opava, Czech Republic
petr.sosik@fpf.slu.cz

Abstract. The time appears ripe to enrich the original idea of membrane computing with principles of self-assembly in space. To this effect, a first step was taken with the introduction of a new such family of models **M systems** (for *morphogenetic system*) that own a number of basic macro-properties exhibited by higher living organisms (such as self-assembly, cell division akin to mitosis and self-healing), while still only leveraging local interactions of simple atomic components and explicit geometric constraints of their constituting elements. Here we further demonstrate that, experimentally *in silico*, M systems are in general also capable of demonstrating these properties robustly after being assembled from scratch from some atomic components and entering a homeostatic regime. The results are obtained through a series of experiments carried out with an M system simulator designed to implement this kind of model by researchers interested in exploring new capabilities. We further define probabilistic complexity classes for M systems and we show that the model is theoretically capable of solving **NP**-complete problems in **P**-time, despite apparent problems of an implementation, such as kinetic and concentration bottlenecks.

1 Introduction

The relationship between the macrosciences (such as biology) and the microsciences (such as quantum mechanics and physics) has been a topic of increasing interest for decades. In a pioneering work, Schrödinger [20] explored this connection and pointed to the future developments of a molecular basis for biology, later fully validated by the discovery of the structure of DNA [25] in the 1950s, the development of biotechnology in the 1980s and the genome projects (HGPs, www.ornl.gov) of the 1990s. Subsequently, the informatics of biology has been pushed to the forefront by extensive work in ∗-omics in the field of bioinformatics in the 21st century. Bioinformatics can be broadly characterized by the application of computer science methods to address biological problems, primarily from the point of view of the science and management of large amounts of data by efficient algorithms. This approach does not address the alternative and

© Springer International Publishing AG 2018
M. Gheorghe et al. (Eds.): CMC 2017, LNCS 10725, pp. 270–292, 2018.
https://doi.org/10.1007/978-3-319-73359-3_18

more fundamental question of whether biological processes are in essence, at some level, fundamentally information processors, or at least can be understood from that perspective. Turing's paper [24] is perhaps the original most famous attempt at a positive answer, by suggesting a model that would explain why the patterns in a leopard skin exhibit the morphogenesis and resilience to injuries typical in biological organisms.

The primary unit in biological sciences is an *organism* and its fundamental characteristic is *reproduction*. A fundamental distinction between biology and the other natural sciences can be formulated as follows: while physics and chemistry, for example, are governed by interactions that appear immutable and perennial over time, a biological organism is conceived by the physics and chemistry of the world, undergoes a growth process that turns it into an idiosyncratic adult, but eventually dies back into the material world. In the process, the organism produces offspring that inherit some of its uniqueness and perpetuate it over time, but in a very mutable way that creates some sort of living memory and gives rise to evolution. Understandably, the significance of the answers and the complexity of evolution have led computer scientists, and perhaps even biologists, to focus their work on the latter (primarily, natural selection and ∗-omics), which has resulted in relatively poor attention devoted to the organisms themselves, e.g., the morphogenetic growth processes, which may nonetheless play an equally important role in the adult organism itself. A major aim of this work is to focus on models of morphogenesis and the transition into what we term *homeostasis*, i.e., a sustainable, balanced functioning state as a "productive" organism.

There have been two major avenues to address this question, namely membrane computing and virtual cells [23]. The original inspiring idea of *membrane computing*, now usually referred to as P systems [17], was to develop models that could begin to shed light on the role of membranes in the process of morphogenesis of the living cell, while obtaining new insights and approaches to solving difficult problems in computer science. A survey of membrane computing (see [18]) shows a number of works hinting at this kind of model. [11] studies synchronized colonies of membrane-inspired agents, including their behavioral robustness in cases of agent loss or rule failure. A *Spatial P system* embedded in a 2D lattice, partly resembling cellular automata, appeared in [4]. The model was later applied to simulate the collective formation and movement of herring schools [3]. The same authors introduced the *Spatial Calculus of Looping Sequences* (Spatial CLS) [2], assigning to membranes exclusive positions in 2D/3D space. Membrane systems allowing self-assembly of graphs were studied in [5-7]. A model of morphogenesis of a multicellular body based on abstract membranes displacement and attachment in 3D space was presented in [13] and applied to simulate the growth of colonies of *Dictyostelium discoideu*. Finally, [1] relates membrane systems to 2D *finite interactive systems* representing 2D regular languages. However, all these models assumed an abstract cell as an atomic assembly unit of an abstract nature. Here, we are interested in exploring the developmental process from scratch, i.e., through self-assembly of 1D or 2D primitives allowing for self-assembly of 3D cell-like forms. To be sure, we are not interested in cloning biological organisms (an exercise that sheds little understanding of the key mechanisms at play), but in a deeper examination of potential mechanisms or strategies whereby they may be achieved through a complexification process distributed in space and time, emerging from the bottom-up through local interactions among atomic components naturally available in an environment. Specifically, the objective is to explore higher functions such as internal dynamical homeostasis, self-reproduction, self-healing, for example, and their relationships. (We must point out that, to the best of our knowledge, the actual etiology of these process in biology is not fully known, but even if it were, knowledge of such mechanisms or strategies may prove useful both within biology and other fields such as artificial or extraterrestrial life.)

Perhaps the most appealing feature of membranes is that they bring into the picture an obvious but most fundamental ingredient in the formation of a biological cell, namely the walls that separate it from the external world or the various parts of it. Less known is the more general and primary role of other spatial relationships and constraints in the organization of biological systems, let alone the role of *geometric shape*. An attempt at a general approach to formalization of spatial and geometrical interaction in complex (biological) systems is the 3π calculus [10] based on process algebra.

Recent research points to an increasingly important role in biological morphogenesis of topological and geometric features such as crevices and wrinkles (see e.g., [22]). Another example of current interest is the formation of the mammalian brain cortex. Mechanical and biochemical models have been used. Mechanical models hypothesize that gyris (foldings) in the brain are the results of anisotropic differential growth, while numerical solutions to chemically reaction-diffusion (RD) systems have produced qualitatively approximate patterns in cortex formation, both in 2D and 3D models. Genetic factors, particularly the protein β-catenin recently, are also implicated in the process. These models can be used for prognosis of brain malformations during development in terms of coefficients in the RD model (e.g., polymicrogyria and lissencephaly). Biologists are also now beginning to discover the importance of the role of even more elementary physical phenomena, such as electric fields and chemical gradients, including their role in chemical signaling in the living cell [19], e.g. in critical mechano-sensitive channels [8].

Simultaneously and from a separate direction, computational ideas from the field of DNA Computing have developed models and theories of DNA self-assembly that capture more directly a "morphogenetic" process of sorts in the form of models of self-assembly of patterns and families of patterns and afford clues as to the nature of and capabilities of morphogenesis [12]. However, once again, these models do not directly afford new knowledge on the fundamental biological problem of morphogenesis and homeostasis that would bring them anywhere near the kind of contribution that other models in natural sciences like physics and chemistry provide us about motion and matter transformation.

Inspired by these developments, the time appears ripe to hybridize P systems and geometric self-assembly in order to explore models of morphogenesis and homeostasis, balancing three somewhat conflicting properties to the best degree possible: biological realism, physical-chemical realism and computational realism. To achieve physical-chemical realism, very critical components and the corresponding dynamic process occurring in a living cell will be specifically represented in the model by appropriate data structures and algorithmic interactions. To achieve computational realism, all components and processes must be modeled at the appropriate level of granularity in both time and resources in order to maintain the computational feasibility of the model. To achieve biological realism, the aggregate observables accumulated over time and space in the model must reflect, to some degree, the corresponding macroscopic observables, e.g., must reflect to some scale or level of granularity known properties of biological organisms at the observable (nano, micro or macro) level, independently of whether they faithfully describe factual processes in biological organisms.

Therefore, the desirable features of the model are self-assembly, self-controlled growth and emerging global behavior that is consistent with observable properties of biological organisms, but which arise from nondeterministic local interactions of elementary components, also consistent with self-assembly and P systems. Towards this goal, we introduced a new such model, **M** systems, in [21], where we also showed its computational universality in the Turing sense. The model is summarized in Sect. 2 to make this paper self-contained. In Sect. 3, we discuss arguments that show how these properties may be guaranteed or to what extent, including a theoretical result and experimental evidence that these properties actually do emerge with very high probability, and provide a characterization of their behavior probabilistically. Sections 4 and 5 complete the view by first defining families of Monte Carlo M systems, and then demonstrating their computational power under a set of restrictions from the perspective of traditional complexity theory. Finally, in Sect. 6, we present some discussion on the significance of the model, some of its implications, and some interesting further problems that could be addressed with plausible extensions of it or experimentation with a simulator.

2   M Systems

In this section we briefly introduce morphogenetic (M) systems, basically following the more detailed description in [21]. The reader is referred to [21] or to web sources sosik.zam.slu.cz/msystem or bmc.memphis.edu/cytos for further information.

As mentioned above, introducing geometric features in P systems is a natural and interesting idea of its own. First, it is an intriguing question that may help realize the potential of the original idea of membrane computing, as spatial arrangement is critical for information processing in living cells, colonies, tissues and organisms. Second, it may also further our understanding of computation beyond the scope of traditional computer science, where shape and geometry are not native concepts, but rather that require enormous amounts of effort to build back in, while on the other hand, our understanding of the world is inherently dependent on it. Besides being able to compute in the Turing sense, a model should be able to interact with and "sense" its physical environment, so as to be capable of self-modification and unenthropical evolution, i.e., to increase its fitness (however defined) in its embedding environment.

A primary biological carrier of shape is a protein. This feature is explicitly used in P systems with proteins on membranes [15, 16]. The **M system** extends this concept with explicit geometric features and self-assembly capabilities. The whole system is embedded in an nD Euclidean space $\mathbb{R}^n$ There are three types of objects present in the system: *proteins*, *tiles* and *floating objects*.

Floating objects are small shapeless atomic objects floating freely within the environment, but having at each moment their specified position in space. They can pass through protein channels and participate in mutual reactions with other types of objects, in *discrete time steps*.

Tiles have their pre-defined size and shape, together with specified position and orientation in space at each moment. Tiles can stick together along their edges or at selected points. These edges/points are called *connectors* and they are covered with *glues*. Their connection is controlled by a pre-defined *glue relation*. Thus the tiles can self-assemble into interconnected structures.

Proteins are placed on tiles and, apart from acting as protein channels letting floating objects pass through, they also catalyze their reactions.

Unlike current models of membrane systems, *membranes* are not present even implicitly, but they can only be formed of tiles during the evolution of the M system. Therefore, at the beginning of the evolution, typically *no membranes* are present and they must be subsequently self-assembled. The connected tiles can be also disconnected and/or destroyed under certain conditions. The following definitions provide the elements to capture these properties in a formal model (they can be skipped without hindering understanding of Sect. 3).

2.1 Polytopic Tiling

The cornerstone of our concept of morphogenetic self-assembly is an nD tile shaped as a bounded convex polytope (n-polytope) [29], with faces of dimension $n - 1$ called *facets*. Hence, a 1D tile is a segment/rod whose facets are its endpoints, a 2D tile is a convex polygon with its edges as facets, a 3D tile is a convex polyhedron with polygons as facets, and so forth. We usually describe a polytope by an ordered list of its vertices.

Furthermore, tile may contain connectors defining its connection to other tiles. Let G be a finite set of *glues*. A *connector* of a tile based on an n-polytope Δ is a triple (Δ_c, g, φ), where

$\Delta_c \subset \Delta$ is a bounded convex k-polytope where $0 \leq k < n$,
$g \in G$ is a glue,
$\varphi \in (-\pi, \pi)$ is the connecting angle.

We distinguish

- *facet connectors* with $k = n - 1$ where Δ_c is a facet of the polytope Δ;
- *non-facet connectors* with $k \leq n - 1$ placed anywhere on the surface of the tile.

Two or more connectors can share the same position on a tile. Formally, an *n-dimensional tile* is defined as

$$t = (\Delta, \{c_1, \ldots, c_k\}, g_s), \text{ for } k \geq 0,$$

where Δ is a bounded convex n-polytope, $c_1, \ldots, c_k$ are connectors and $g_s \in G$ is the *surface glue* covering the entire surface of the tile except where connectors are placed.

If an $(n - 1)$-dimensional tile embedded in $\mathbb{R}^n$ we denote its two sides by *in* and *out*. By convention, a 2D tile seen from the side *in* has its vertices ordered *clockwise*. A *non-facet* connector with positive connecting angle is placed on side *in*, one with negative angle is placed on side *out*, and one with zero angle can only be located on some facet of the tile.

Definition 1. *A polytopic tile system in $\mathbb{R}^n$ is a construct $T = (Q, G, \gamma, d_g, S)$, where*

Q *is the set of tiles of dimensions $\leq n$;*
G *is the set of glues;*
$\gamma \subseteq G \times G$ *is the glue relation;*
$d_g \in \mathbb{R}_0^+$ *is the gluing distance (assumed to be small compared to the size of tiles);*
S *is the finite multiset of seed tiles from Q randomly distributed in space.*

Note that we generalized definitions in the previous paper [21] so that (a) tiles in $\mathbb{R}^n$ can now have dimension from 1 to n, (b) non-facet connectors can now have dimensions from 1 to $n - 1$.

Definition 2. *Consider tiles*

t_1 *with a connector $c_1 = (\Delta_1, g_1, \varphi_1)$, where $\Delta_1 = (u_1, \ldots, u_k)$,*
t_2 *with a connector $c_2 = (\Delta_2, g_2, \varphi_2)$, where $\Delta_2 = (v_1, \ldots, v_k)$,*

for some $k \geq 1$. Connector c_2 can connect to c_1 if the following conditions are met:

1. *both c_1 and c_2 are both unconnected;*
2. *$(g_1, g_2) \in \gamma$;*
3. *t_2 can be positioned so that $u_1, \ldots, u_k$ match $v_k, \ldots, v_1$, in this order;*
4. *at least one of c_1, c_2 is a facet connector.*

Note that for two 2D tiles connecting with their edges, condition (3) implies the matching of sides *in–in* and *out–out*. As the relation γ is generally non-symmetric, "c_2 can connect to c_1" does not imply that also c_1 can connect to c_2. This is in accordance with natural morphogenetic processes which are often irreversible [9].

Tile t_2 connects to t_1 at angle φ_1, if the connector is $(n-2)$-dimensional. The connecting angle provides a degree of freedom (chosen randomly) to t_2 in the case of k-dimensional connectors, where $k \leq n - 3$, on one hand. On the other hand, the connecting angle is not applicable in the case of $(n-1)$D connectors.

If t_2, after its connection, still has a free connector(s) c_2' now positioned within the distance d_g from a free connector c_1' on another tile already in place, and either c_1' can connect to c_2' or conversely, then they immediately connect together. Similarly, if a free connector of t_2 with a glue g lies within the distance d_g from an existing tile t_3 with surface glue g_s such that $(g, g_s) \in \gamma$, then t_2 connects to the surface of t_3.

Example 1. Consider a polytopic tile system in $\mathbb{R}^3$ with a single glue g and the glue relation $\gamma = \{(g, g)\}$. Let Q contain a 2D tile q shaped as a regular pentagon, with five facet connectors on its edges, each with the glue g and with the connecting angle $\varphi = 2.0345$ rad, which is the inner angle between two faces in a dodecahedron. Let finally $S = \{q\}$ be the only seed tile, see the leftmost image. Then, provided that q is available in enough copies, the system assembles as follows.

1. Five tiles q would connect to the five connectors of the seed tile in the first phase, connecting also their five edges starting at vertices of the seed tile as they stick together. The connecting angle determines them to shape as a cup with zig-zag rim with 10 edges (central-left image).
2. Another five tiles would connect to these edges, determined by the connecting angle to form an almost-closed shape (central-right image).
3. Finally, the last attached tile encloses the dodecahedral "soccer-ball". All connectors on the tiles match and connect together, hence no further assembly is possible (rightmost image).

2.2   Morphogenetic Systems

An M system naturally merges principles of both self assembly and membrane computing. Geometrical structure and growth of each M system is determined by its underlying polytopic tile system. Unlike usual tiling systems, the M system does not assume availability of an unlimited number of copies of each tile. The M system life cycle starts in an initial configuration where only seed tiles are present. Further structures can only be created by the application of rules of the M system.

Formally, for a multiset M we denote by $|M|_a$ the multiplicity of elements a in M. A multiset M with the underlying set O can be represented by a string $x \in O^*$ (by O^* we denote the free monoid generated by O with respect to the concatenation and the identity λ) such that the number of occurrences of $a \in O$ in x represents the value $|M|_a$.

Definition 3. *A morphogenetic system (M system) in $\mathbb{R}^n$ (unless stated otherwise, we assume $\mathbb{R}^3$) is a tuple*

$$\mathcal{M} = (F, P, T, \mu, R, r, \sigma),$$

where

$F = (O, m, \epsilon)$ *is the catalogue of floating objects, where:*
  O is the set of floating objects;
  $m : O \longrightarrow \mathbb{R}^+$ is the mean mobility of each floating object in the environment;
  $\epsilon : O \longrightarrow \mathbb{R}_0^+$ is the concentration of each floating object in the environment: $\epsilon(o)$ copies of object o per spatial unit 1^n;
P *is the set of proteins;*
$T = (Q, G, \gamma, d_g, S)$ *is a polytopic tile system in $\mathbb{R}^n$, with O, P, Q, G all pairwise disjoint;*
μ *is the mapping assigning to each tile $t \in Q$ a multiset of proteins placed on t together with their positions: $\mu(t) \subset P \times \Delta$ where Δ is the underlying polytope of t;*
R *is a finite set of reaction rules;*
$r \in \mathbb{R}_0^+$ *is the reaction radius; a reaction rule can be applied when all objects entering the reaction are positioned within this radius;*
$\sigma : \gamma \longrightarrow O^*$ *is the mapping assigning to each glue pair $(g_1, g_2) \in \gamma$ a multiset of floating objects which are released to the environment within the reaction radius from a new connection with (g_1, g_2), when the connection is established.*

A *reaction rule* from the set R has the form $u \to v$, where u and v are strings containing floating objects, proteins, glues and tiles due to types of rules specified bellow. The necessary condition to apply the rule is that all objects in u are present in the environment within radius r, while certain rules may specify further conditions on the location of objects.

Metabolic Rules

Let $u, v \in O^+$ be non-empty multisets of floating objects and $p \in P$ be a protein. The rules containing the symbol [are applicable only when p is placed on an $(n-1)$-dimensional tile, where object to the left of [in the string correspond to the side "out" and those to the right correspond to the side "in" of the tile.

Note that these rules are rather powerful and we will mostly consider some restrictions when studying M systems from the computational power point of view.

Type	Rule	Effect
Simple	$u \to v$	Objects in multiset u react to produce v
Catalytic	$pu \to pv$	Objects in u react in presence of p to produce v
	$u[p \to v[p$	Eventually, u, v must both appear on the side "out"
	$[pu \to [pv$	Or on the side "in" of the tile on which p is placed
Symport	$u[p \to [pu$	Passing of u through protein channel p
	$[pu \to u[p$	To the other side of the tile
Antiport	$u[pv \to v[pu$	Interchange of u and v through protein channel p

Creation Rules. $ut \to v$,

where $t \in Q$ and $u \in O^+$. The rule creates tile t while consuming the floating objects in u. It can be applied if the following holds:

(i) there already exists a tile (say s) in the environment with a free connector c_s such that t can connect to c_s by some of its connectors, and
(ii) floating objects in u exist in the environment within the distance r from c_s.

Then an attempt is made to create tile t and connect it to c_s as specified in Sect. 2.1. If t would intersect another existing tile, say s', then s' is pushed away to make room for t. This may cause a chain reaction of mutual pushing of tiles in the way. If it is impossible to make enough room for t and t is a polygon, the rule is not applied, otherwise t is shortened so that it just touches s'. Its connector(s) at the shortened end (if any) are preserved.

Destruction Rules. $ut \to v$,

where $t \in Q$, $u, v \in O^+$. Tile t is destroyed in the presence of the "destructor" multiset of floating objects u. All connectors on other tiles connected to t are released. The objects in u are consumed and the multiset v of "waste" objects is produced.

Division Rules. $g \overset{u}{\longrightarrow} h \to g, h$,

where g—h is a pair of glues on connectors of two connected tiles, and $u \in O^+$. The rule can be applied when all objects in u are located within reaction distance of the pair of connectors. As a result of application, the two connectors disconnect, while the multiset u is consumed. The connectors remain in their position but they do not reconnect again automatically.

Configuration of the M system is determined by

- list all tiles in the environment and their relative positions;
- interconnection graph of connectors on these tiles;
- positions of all floating objects modulo the reaction radius.

Hence, two configurations are equivalent if the tiles form the same structures and floating objects in their respective reaction radii form the same multisets, even if their exact positions can be different. Configurations where any two objects (tiles or floating objects) occupy the same position in space or overlap are not allowed. The initial configuration contains only (unconnected) seed tiles in S and a random distribution of floating objects given by their concentration ϵ.

Computation of the M System

The system transits between configurations by application of rules in the set R. At each step, each floating object can be subject to at most one rule, each connector can be subject to at most one creation or division rule, and each tile can be subject to at most one destruction rule.

The rules within each group are chosen nondeterministically until their maximum applicable multiset is obtained, subject to possible trade-offs between rules. Then all the selected rules are applied in parallel to the actual configuration. Finally, each floating object o with mean mobility $m(o)$ changes randomly its position at each step due to the Maxwell-Boltzmann distribution [28] with parameter $a = \sqrt{\pi/8}\, m(o)$ corresponding to Brownian motion of particles in liquid media.

A sequence of transitions of an M system between configurations is called a *computation*. The computation can be finite (if an M system cannot apply any rule, it halts) or infinite, and it is, by definition, nondeterministic. The reader is referred to [21] or to supplementary material available at sosik.zam.slu.cz/msystem or bmc.memphis.edu/cytos for examples.

3   Robust Computational Morphogenesis and Homeostasis

In [21] we have described an demonstrated that M systems are indeed capable of self-assembling from scratch from some atomic components, undergo a process of morphogenesis by the unfolding of the self-assembly rules defined by their local interactions as given by the catalytic, creation and destruction rules, and eventually enter a stable dynamical equilibrium of adulthood in which they will continue to function as long as certain conditions in their environment remain. The system $\mathcal{M}_0$ builds a geometrical structure on two sets of 2D pentagonal tiles: larger tiles self-assembling in a cell-like membrane, and smaller tiles assembling a nuclear membrane. These tiles are much alike those in Example 1 but with different glues on their edges. Some of the larger tiles also contain point connectors on their inner surface, connecting to rod-shaped 1D tiles. Endpoints of rods bear one (straight-oriented) or two (fork-oriented) connectors allowing the rods to assemble a tree-like structure of cytoskeleton. Specifically, we established that

Proposition 1. *Assuming discrete time and bounded finite resources in the environment, an arbitrary run of the M system $\mathcal{M}_0$ crosses a critical time at which it stops growing and enters a period of homeostasis, where it will remain in functional equilibrium despite certain fluctuations in the environment and/or damage to its internal structure.*

We summarize the essential part below to make this paper self-contained. (Full description of the M system and more proof details are provided as a supplementary material at sosik.zam.slu.cz/msystem or at bmc.memphis.edu/cytos.)

As pointed out above, discrete time interactions guarantee that at any given time, only a finite number of membranes and objects are contained therein throughout the life of the model, (although they could potentially contain an uncountable number of objects as a continuum.) In the terminology of self-assembly systems, $\mathcal{M}_0$ is locally deterministic and attachment of tiles proceeds as in the aTAM model [26, 27]. As illustrated by Example 1, the geometric structure of the tiles forces them to curve as they are attached and to close upon themselves to eventually form a dodecahedron and present plain geometric blocking for further growth, which thus finishes the membrane building phase when the last keystone tile is attached. Simultaneously an analogous process creates a much smaller nuclear membrane. The attached tiles bear proteins triggering the formation of cytoskeleton by rods, which can grow nondeterministically in various directions from both "poles" of the membrane. Eventually, addition of rods is no longer possible, again for excluded volume reasons, so the cytoskeleton, and hence morphogenesis, is now complete and $\mathcal{M}_0$ enters the "adult" homeostatic phase. Even before this phase is fully completed, the contact of growing rods with the nuclear membrane triggers the process of mitosis which proceeds to create two copies of the cells and separate it into two identical parts, which will then begin the entire process anew and continue while enough supplies and room for growth remain. All this is fully controlled only by local interactions of tiles and floating objects. These properties illustrate how geometry can perform a great deal of work to control the shape of products in self-assembly that could only be performed through other means with great effort, e.g. by hard coding it into the seed, as in the binary counters in the aTAM model [27].

At any point in the morphogenetic process, any "damage" to a configuration of the system $\mathcal{M}_0$ such as knocking off tile that has just been attached, or punching a hole in a membrane) will either simply revert to a previous configuration, or detach a piece of the systems altogether, which will reset it back to a previous state, from which it may further develop as it did before, *perhaps through a different run as it is a nondeterministic system*. Because the stable equilibrium is achieved again with similar characteristics, perhaps the same original individual will not be formed again, but the new individual will bear the characteristic features of the original one. Therefore, the original organism is capable of sustaining certain injuries to some degree of severity to its internal structure, without changing the overall characteristics of the adult organism.

To verify this property quantitatively, we have built an M system simulator (see the link in the previous proof) for arbitrary M systems and run it on $\mathcal{M}_0$ 100 times for 40 iterations causing various injuries to it as described in Fig. 1.

As pointed out in the introduction, computational study of characteristic biological properties has been an intriguing but poorly addressed subject. Most work has been in the material sciences for simple polymers, gels and even metals, despite the fact that early experimentation in self-assembly made such properties

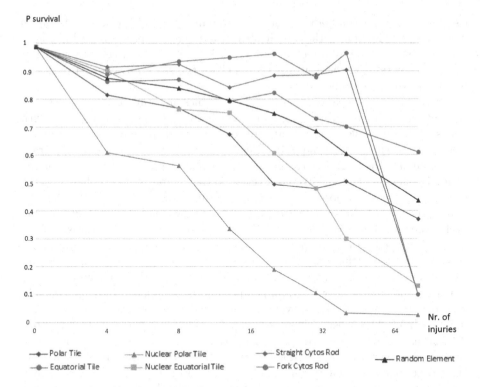

Fig. 1. Self-healing properties of the morphogenetic system $\mathcal{M}_0$ to a number of simultaneous injuries (x-axis) as given by the probability of survival, i.e., to remain in the same and only homeostatic cycle that would have been obtained before the injuries. The estimates have been obtained by 100 runs of the system with injuries inflicted randomly in seven (7) possible ways with up to 80 injuries, as described. The most damaging harm are injuries to nucleus which drop the probability of survival (y-axis) most rapidly. The system is self-healing even when inflicted removal of as many as 40 tiles of any kind, except at nuclear tiles, which reflects the few vulnerabilities of the system. Interestingly, the probability of survival increase with certain number of injuries to cytoskeleton elements with up to 40 rods!

as self-healing evident [27], with the notable exception of a procedure to re-factor tiles [27] in aTAM systems to build binary counters and the Sierpinski triangle that enable self-healing [27] of holes in partial assemblies in linear time. Here, we generalize the results in Fig. 1 by providing a general definition of morphogenetic and homeostatic phases in M systems, that enables a general definition of self-healing in M systems, and demonstrate that a subfamily of M systems simultaneously exhibits an additional robustness property characteristic of biological organisms, i.e. a degree of *self-healing*.

We first define more precisely the concepts of "morphogenesis" and "homeostasis", as follows, assuming that the definition of an M system includes a bounded amount of resources in the environment throughout the course of its development. A *configuration* of an M system is the full list of objects (*up to displacement*), including their multiplicity and relative position within membranes, that could be obtained at any point in a valid run of the system. Thus two configurations are identical if they include the same objects and positions relative to the membranes.

From the seed as a root, the system defines its *configuration space* – a computation-directed graph (digraph) (which we continue to denote M) with nodes *all* the possible system configurations obtained from *any* valid computations/runs of the system and with directed arcs all the possible one-step transitions among them. A *homeostatic component* is defined as the union of the transitive closure $C!$ of a (directed) cycle C in the computation graph and all the configuration nodes whose transitive closure fully includes $C!$, plus all the arcs joining them to $C!$. Note that such a component may contain several intersecting cycles and/or nonintersecting cycles. The *homeostatic phase* M_H consists of the union of all homeostatic components and their joining arcs. The subdigraph consisting of the complementary nodes and arcs is the *morphogenetic phase* M_M of the M system. Because the amount of resources available in the environment is bounded, the computation digraph is finite and is partitioned into the two subdigraphs M_M and M_H. Thus, every morphogenetic configuration x belongs to a unique maximal homeostatic component (or simply h-component.) For example, $\mathcal{M}_0$ has as many homeostatic components as there are copies of the invidividual cells it grows. Every mitosis produces one more such component disjoint from the mother one. The morphogenetic phase consists of the formation of the external membrane and some of the cytoskeleton (afforded by the external resources available and not destroyed during mitosis.)

Thus, we can now define more precisely the concept of "damage", as follows.

Definition 4. *An* injury *to a morphogenetic system M is a transition of the system given by a pair of configurations (x, y) such that y cannot be obtained from x by a valid application of any one rule of the system M. The* degree *of the injury is the graph-theoretic distance between x and y. An injury is* sustainable *if both x and y belong to the same h-component. The system is* self-healing *(of degree m, respectively) if and only it can sustain any injury to any homeostatic node x (of degree m, respectively) with probability at least 50%.*

An injury could be caused by an agent in the environment external to M or by a malfunction of (the implementation of) the rules of M, and may not necessarily destroy any objects in the system, e.g. if y is successor of x in a computation of M. Note that although injuries could cause a transition to a state z that is a not a node in configuration space, the definition implies that the new configuration will not lead to the same homeostatic regime as if no injury had occurred, so that type of injury is never sustainable. Therefore we will only consider injuries as described in Definition 4. An M system is called *locally deterministic* if it leads to a unique terminal assembly (one with no successors by further tile attachments) that is never destroyed by the M system. The construction of the terminal assembly is thus the morphogenetic phase, which is followed by the homeostatic phase. Locally deterministic M systems may have a degree of nondeterminism in the paths leading the terminal configuration in the assembly. They are systems with only one possible overall "future".

Proposition 2. *Assuming discrete time and bounded finite resources in the environment, every locally deterministic M system is self-healing. In particular, $\mathcal{M}_0$ is self-healing.*

Proof. It is easy to verify that every deterministic system is self-healing, as an injury only amounts to time travel to the past or future along a run of the system. More generally, a locally deterministic system has a unique h-component.   □

Conjecture 1. Assuming discrete time and arbitrary bounded finite resources in the environment as initial conditions, there exist self-healing systems that are also computationally universal.

4 Families of Monte Carlo M Systems

Let us denote a *decision problem* X as a pair (I_X, θ_X) where I_X is a language over a finite alphabet (whose elements are called *instances*) and θ_X is a total boolean function over I_X. In order to study the computational efficiency of membrane systems, a concept of *recognizer P systems* [14] was introduced. These P systems always halt, and they use specific objects *yes* and *no* such that *exactly one* kind of these objects is produced at the end of each computation. However, halting contradicts the nature of morphogenetic systems whose computation is probabilistic and often reaches a homeostasis where the system stays alive forever (or until external conditions change).

Therefore, we define a *Monte Carlo M system* as follows: it has a distinguished floating object yes $\in O$ such that $\epsilon(\text{yes}) = 0$ (its concentration in the environment is zero). Its computation is called *accepting* if the object yes is eventually released to the environment, otherwise it is *rejecting*. Furthermore, either at least $1/2$ of computations are accepting, or all computations are rejecting. We say that a Monte Carlo M system *accepts in time* t if the object yes is released in first t steps of its arbitrary computation with probability at least $1/2$.

Definition 5. *We say that a decision problem $X = (I_X, \theta_X)$ is solvable in a semi-uniform way and randomized polynomial time by a family $\boldsymbol{M} = \{\mathcal{M}(w) \mid w \in I_X\}$ of Monte Carlo M systems if the following holds:*

1. *The family $\boldsymbol{M}$ is polynomially uniform by Turing machines, that is, there exists a deterministic Turing machine working in polynomial time which constructs the system $\mathcal{M}(w)$ from w.*
2. *There exists a polynomial function p, such that for each $u \in I_X$:*
   (a) if $\theta_X(u) = 0$, then every computation of $\mathcal{M}(u)$ is rejecting;
   (b) if $\theta_X(u) = 1$, then $\mathcal{M}(u)$ accepts in time $p(|u|)$.

Let $\mathcal{T}$ be a specific class of morphogenetic systems. We denote by $\mathbf{MRP}^*_{\mathcal{T}}$ the set of all decision problems which can be solved in a semi-uniform way and randomized polynomial time by means of families of M systems from $\mathcal{T}$. Symbol $\mathcal{T}$ can be omitted when general M systems are considered.

5   Computational Efficiency

In this section we present a semi-uniform family of Monte Carlo M systems which can probabilistically solve, in a polynomial time, the standard NP-complete problem 3-SAT. The construction and computation of the family is based on the classical strategy of trading space for time, often used in the framework of membrane computing.

Consider a formula $\Phi = C_1 \wedge \cdots \wedge C_m$ in CNF, using the set of variables $\{x_1, \ldots, x_n\}$, for $m, n \geq 1$. We define a polytopic tile system $T_n = (Q, G, \gamma, d_g, S)$ in $\mathbb{R}^2$, where

$Q = \{u_i, \overline{u}_1, v_i \mid 1 \leq i \leq n\} \cup \{w, s_1, s_2, t_b, t_{t1}, t_{t2}, r\}$, where
  $u_i, \overline{u}_i$ $1 \leq i \leq n$, are rods of length 2;
  v_i $1 \leq i \leq n$, are rectangular 2D tiles of size 2×1;
  w is a rod of length 1;
  s_1, s_2 are rods of length $2n$;
  t_b is a rod of length 2;
  t_{t1}, t_{t2} are rods of length 1;
  r is a rod of length 5;
$G = \{g_{ib}, \overline{g}_{ib}, g_{it}, g_i, \overline{g}_i, g_{iv}, \overline{g}_{iv} \mid 1 \leq i \leq n\} \cup$
  $\{g_p, g_w, g_{1sb}, g_{1st}, g_{2sb}, g_{2st}, g_{1tb}, g_{2tb}, g_{1t1}, g_{1t2}, g_{2t1}, g_{2t1}\}$;
$\gamma = \{(g_p, g_p), (g_{nt}, g_{1t1}), (g_{1t2}, g_{1st}), (g_{1sb}, g_{2tb}), (g_{1tb}, g_{2sb}), (g_{2tb}, g_{2t1})\} \cup$
  $\{(g_{it}, g_{(i+1)b}), (\overline{g}_{it}, g_{(i+1)b}) \mid 1 \leq i \leq n-1\} \cup$
  $\{(g_{it}, g_w), (g_i, g_{iv}), (\overline{g}_i, \overline{g}_{iv}), (g_{iv}, g_i), (\overline{g}_{iv}, \overline{g}_i) \mid 1 \leq i \leq n\}$;
$d_g = 0.1$;
$S = \{u_1\}$.

Let us adopt the convention that a rod of length x has its vertices $(0, x)$, and a rectangular tile of size $x \times y$ has vertices $((0, 0), (0, y), (x, y), (x, 0))$. Tiles in the set Q have the following connectors:

$u_i, 1 \leq i \leq n$, have
  – two facet connectors $c_{ib} = (0, g_{ib}, 0)$ and $c_{it} = (2, g_{it}, \varphi_{it})$ (b stands for "bottom" and t for "top"), where $\varphi_{it} = 0$ for $i < n$ and $\varphi_{nt} = \pi/2$;
  – two non-facet connectors $c_{i,in} = (1, g_p, \pi/2)$, $c_{i,out} = (1, g_p, -\pi/2)$;
  – non-facet 1D connector $c_{i1} = (\langle \frac{3}{2}, \frac{1}{2} \rangle, g_i, \pi/2)$;
$\overline{u}_i, 1 \leq i \leq n$, have
  – two facet connectors $\overline{c}_{ib} = (0, \overline{g}_{ib}, 0)$ and $c_{it} = (2, g_{it}, \varphi_{it})$;
  – two non-facet connectors $c_{in} = (1, g_p, \pi/2)$, $c_{out} = (1, g_p, -\pi/2)$;
  – non-facet 1D connector $\overline{c}_{i1} = (\langle \frac{1}{2}, \frac{3}{2} \rangle, \overline{g}_i, \pi/2)$;
$v_i, 1 \leq i \leq n$, have two facet connectors on their short edges: $c_i = (\langle (0, 0), (0, 1) \rangle, g_{iv}, 0)$ and $\overline{c}_i = (\langle (1, 1), (1, 0) \rangle, \overline{g}_{iv}, 0)$;
w has single facet connector $c_w = (0, g_w, 0)$;
$s_i, 1 \leq i \leq 2$, have two facet connectors $c_{ist} = (2n, g_{ist}, \pi/2)$ (top) and $c_{isb} = (0, g_{isb}, \pi/2)$ (bottom);
t_b has two facet connectors $c_{tb1} = (0, g_{1tb}, \pi/2)$, $c_{tb2} = (2, g_{2tb}, \pi/2)$;
$t_{ti}, 1 \leq i \leq 2$, have two facet connectors $c_{ti1} = (0, g_{it1}, \pi/2)$, $c_{ti2} = (1, g_{it2}, \pi/2)$;
r has a single facet connector $(0, g_p, 0)$.

The set of tiles $\{u_1, \overline{u}_1 \mid 1 \le i \le n\}$ represents possible interpretations of variables $x_1, \ldots, x_n$: u_i stands for x_i =true, $\overline{u}_i$ for x_i = false. To simplify the description, let us denote by U_i a tile which is either u_i or $\overline{u}_i$, $1 \le i \le n$.

Consider furthermore an M system $\mathcal{M}_\Phi = (F, P, T, \mu, R, r, \sigma)$ in $\mathbb{R}^2$, where:

$F = (O, m, \epsilon)$, where:

$\quad O = \{a_1, \ldots, a_6, b_1, \ldots, b_{m+1}, yes\}$, are floating objects;

$\quad m(o) = 2$ for each $o \in O$;

$\quad \epsilon(a_4) > 0$ (see proof of Lemma 4 in the following) and $\epsilon(o) = 0$ for all other $o \in O$;

$P = C$;

T is the polytopic tile system described above;

$\mu(t_{t2}) = \{p_t\}$, $\mu(s_2) = \{p_y\}$, and $\mu(u_i) = \{p_i\}$, $\mu(\overline{u}_i) = \{\overline{p}_i\}$, $1 \le i \le n$, all proteins placed in centres of their respective tiles;

R contains several kinds of rules described below.

Metabolic rules:

$\quad \{a_i \to a_{i+1}, 1 \le i \le 5\} \cup$

$\quad \{a_6 \to a_1, [p_t a_1 \to [p_t b_1, b_{m+1} \to yes, [p_y yes \to yes[p_y] \cup$

$\quad \{b_j[p_i \to b_{j+1}[p_i \mid C_j \text{ contains } x_i, 1 \le j \le m, 1 \le i \le n\} \cup$

$\quad \{b_j[\overline{p}_i \to b_{j+1}[\overline{p}_i \mid C_j \text{ contains } \overline{x}_i, 1 \le j \le m, 1 \le i \le n\}$.

Creation rules:

$\quad \{a_1 \to r, \ a_1 \to t_{t1}, \ a_3 \to w, \ a_3 \to s_1, \ a_4 \to t_b, \ a_5 \to s_2, \ a_6 \to t_{t2}\} \cup$

$\quad \{a_1 \to u_i \mid 2 \le i \le n\} \cup \{a_4 \to v_i, \ a_5 \to u_i, \ a5 \to \overline{u}_i \mid 1 \le i \le n\}$.

Destruction rules:

$\quad \{a_2 r \to a_3, \ a_6 w \to a_1\} \cup \{a_6 v_i \to a_1 \mid 1 \le i \le n\}$.

$r = 2$;

$\sigma(g_i, g_j) = \emptyset$ for all $(g_i, g_j) \in \gamma$.

The initial configuration of the M system $\mathcal{M}$ contains the seed tile (rod) t_1 and a high concentration of objects a in the environment. The computation of the M system $\mathcal{M}_\Phi$ consist of a *generating phase* when all possible interpretations of the logical variables $x_1, \ldots, x_n$ are generated, and a *checking phase* during which the interpretations are checked in parallel whether they satisfy the formula.

5.1   Generating Phase

During a computation of the M system the tiles U_i assemble to sequences $U_1, \ldots, U_n$. This process completes in n cycles, each consisting of six steps.

Lemma 1. *Let the space $\mathbb{R}^2$ where the M system $\mathcal{M}_\Phi$ is placed contains 2^k connected sequences of tiles $U_1, \ldots, U_k$, $1 \le k \le n-1$, covering all possible truth assignments to variables $x_1, \ldots, x_k$. Assume that all applicable creation/destruction rules of $\mathcal{M}_\Phi$ are always applied. Then, after 6 steps, there will be 2^{k+1} connected sequences $U_1, \ldots, U_{k+1}$, covering all possible truth assignments to variables $x_1, \ldots, x_{k+1}$.*

Proof. The six steps of computation proceed as follows:

1. All tiles U_i, $1 \leq i \leq k$, create and attach perpendicular rods r to connectors c_{in} and c_{out} (rule $a_1 \to r$) resulting in pushing of tiles in the direction of rods so that mutual distances between sequences are set to 5. Furthermore, each tile U_k attaches a new tile u_{k+1} to its connector c_{kt} (resp. $\bar{c}_{kt}$), lengthening the sequences $\{U_i\}$ to $k+1$ elements (rules $a_1 \to u_i$, $2 \leq i \leq n$).
2. Rods r are destroyed (rule $a_2 r \to a_3$).
3. Tiles w are attached to connectors $c_{(k+1)t}$ of tiles u_{k+1}, blocking further vertical growth in the next two steps (rule $a_3 \to w$).
4. Each U_i, $1 \leq i \leq k$, attaches to its connector c_{i1} (resp. $\bar{c}_{i1}$) tile v_i such that its longer edge is perpendicular to U_i (rules $a_4 \to v_i$, $1 \leq i \leq n$).
5. Each v_i, $1 \leq i \leq k$, attaches to its free connector a new tile $\bar{u}_i$ or u_i (rule $a_5 \to u_i$, $a_5 \to \bar{u}_i$, $1 \leq i \leq n$) such that compositions $u_i - v_i - \bar{u}_i$ or $\bar{u}_i - v_i - u_i$ are produced. Therefore, a "ladder" containing two complementary sequence $U_1, \ldots, U_k$ with v_i's as rungs is produce. The new tiles U_i also connect together by their facet connectors.
6. Tiles w and v_i, $1 \leq i \leq k$, are destroyed, disconnecting old sequences of tiles and new complementary sequences (rules $a_6 w \to a_1$, $a_6 v_i \to a_1$, $1 \leq i \leq n$).

□

Lemma 2. *Assume that all applicable creation/destruction rules of $\mathcal{M}_\Phi$ are always applied. Then $\mathcal{M}_\Phi$ produces in $6n + 3$ initial steps of its computation a set of 2^n interconnected sequences of tiles $U_1 - \cdots - U_n$ covering all possible assignments to propositional variables $x_1, \ldots, x_n$. The sequences are enclosed in separate closed subspaces ("cells") composed of tiles $t_{t1}, s_1, t_b, s_2, t_{t2}$.*

Proof. The system $\mathcal{M}_\Phi$ starts with a single seed tile u_1 and with the environment containing many objects a_4. By Lemma 1, steps 4, 5, 6, also tile $\bar{u}_1$ is produced. Then, again by Lemma 1 and by the induction argument, sequences $U_1 - \cdots - U_n$ covering all possible assignments to $x_1, \ldots, x_n$ are produced in $6(n - 1)$ steps. The computation proceeds as follows:

1. Perpendicular tiles t_{t1} are attached to by their connectors c_{t11} to tiles U_n ending the sequences (rules $a_1 \to t_{t1}$) so that t_{t1} are oriented towards the side *in* of U_n. Meantime, rods r are attached to all tiles U_i as in step 1 of Lemma 1, creating mutual space between sequences.
2. Rods r are destroyed.
3. Vertical tiles s_1 are attached to connectors c_{t11} of tiles t_{t1} (rules $a_3 \to s_1$) so that they are parallel to sides *in* of all tiles U_i in their associated sequence.
4. Horizontal tiles t_b are attached to connectors c_{1sb} of tiles s_1 (rules $a_4 \to t_b$), forming bottom of a future rectangular cell. Note that tiles v_i cannot be attached to $U_i's$ as in step 4 of Lemma 1 since their growth is blocked by s_1.
5. Vertical tiles s_2 are attached to connectors c_{tb1} of tiles t_b (rules $a_5 \to s_2$) so that they are parallel to sides *out* of all tiles U_i in their associated sequence.
6. Finally, tiles t_{t2} are attached to connectors c_{2st} of tiles s_2 (rules $a_6 \to t_{t2}$), enclosing the sequence $U_1, \ldots, U_n$ in a rectangular cell.

Observe that, after assembling the cells, no creation/destruction rules can be used anymore to alter their structure.   □

5.2   Checking Phase

In this phase the M system $\mathcal{M}_\Phi$ checks in parallel, whether any of the cells formed in the generating phase represent a model of the formula Φ.

Lemma 3. *The M system $\mathcal{M}_\Phi$ can release the object* yes *to the environment if and only if there is a sequence of tiles $U_1 - \cdots - U_n$ representing a model of Φ, enclosed in a "cell" composed of tiles $t_{t1}, s_1, t_b, s_2, t_{t2}$. In the affirmative case, the object* yes *appears in the environment in $\mathcal{O}(n.m^2)$ steps after forming the cell with probability $p > 3/4$.*

Proof. Note first that a sequence of rules leading eventually to production of the object *yes* must start with the rule $[p_t a_1 \rightarrow [p_t b_1$ using protein p_t. This protein appears only on tile t_{t2} which is assembled to the remaining tiles only as the last tile enclosing a cell composed of $t_{t1}, s_1, t_b, s_2, t_{t2}$. Hence, without forming a completed cell in the generating phase, no object yes can be produced.

If the cell is formed, the rule is applied with a probability close to 1 due to a high concentration of objects a_1 inside the cell, releasing objects b_1 inside. Then for each clause C_j, $1 \leq j \leq m$, with k literals, there are k rules of the form

$b_j[p_i \rightarrow b_{j+1}[p_i$ if C_j contains x_i,

$b_j[\overline{p}_i \rightarrow b_{j+1}[\overline{p}_i$ if C_j contains $\overline{x}_i$,

where proteins p_i are placed on tile u_i and $\overline{p}_i$ are placed on $\overline{u}_i$. Hence, object b_{j+1} can be produced if an only if the interpretation represented by tiles $U_1 - \cdots - U_n$ in the cell is a model of C_j. By induction, object b_{m+1} can be produced if and only if this interpretation is a model of all clauses $C_1, \ldots, C_m$, i.e., model of the whole formula Φ. Finally, by using the rules $b_{m+1} \rightarrow yes$ and $[p_y yes \rightarrow yes[p_y$, where protein p_y is placed on the tile s_2, object *yes* is eventually sent to the environment.

Assume now that the rules producing object *yes* can be applied, and calculate the probability of this event. Let us divide the "cell" into n vertically arranged rectangles, each containing tile U_i, $1 \leq i \leq n$. Each tile u_i ($\overline{u}_i$) has a protein p_i ($\overline{p}_i$) placed inj its center, so that the whole volume of i-th rectangle lies within its reaction radius $r = 2$. Therefore, whenever an object b_j enters i-th rectangle, a rule $b_j[P_i \rightarrow b_{j+1}[P_i$, where $P_i \in \{p_i, \overline{p}\}$, is applicable.

Let us calculate first the probability that a randomly moving object b_j visits i-th rectangle, for an arbitrary but fixed $1 \leq i \leq n$, in at least one of n consecutive steps:

$$P_1 = 1 - \left(\frac{n-1}{n}\right)^n > 1 - e^{-1} \text{ for each } n \geq 1,$$

since the value of the fraction converges from 0 to e^{-1} as $n \longrightarrow \infty$. Consequently, the probability that the object b_j visits the rectangle during $m \cdot n$ consecutive steps is greater than $1 - e^{-m}$. Hence, provided that the sequence $U_1 - \cdots - U_n$ represents a model of Φ, each of the rules $b_j[P_i \rightarrow b_{j+1}[P_i, 1 \leq j \leq m$, is applied in the cell in $m \cdot n$ steps with probability $> 1 - e^{-m}$. The resulting probability of application of all these rules in nm^2 steps is $(1 - e^{-m})^m$. The rule $b_{m+1} \to yes$ is applied with certainty whenever the object b_{m+1} is produced, and the last rule $[p_y yes \to yes[p_y$ is again applied in $m \cdot n$ steps with probability $> 1 - e^{-m}$. Hence the final probability that the checking phase for a formula Φ with m clauses releases object yes to the environment in $nm(m + 1)$ steps is

$$P_{\text{check}}(m) = (1 - e^{-m})^{m+1}.$$

Observe that $P_{\text{check}}(3) \approx 0.81 > 3/4$ and the value converges quickly to 1 with growing m. This concludes the proof. $\square$

Lemma 4. *The M system $\mathcal{M}_\Phi$ can send the object yes to the environment if and only if the formula Φ is satisfiable. Furthermore, in the affirmative case, the object yes appears in the environment in $\mathcal{O}(n.m^2)$ steps with probability $p > 1/2$.*

Proof. By Lemma 3, the object yes is never produced in the M system $\mathcal{M}_\Phi$ if the formula Φ is unsatisfiable.

Consider now the case when Φ has a model corresponding to a connected sequence of tiles $U_1, \ldots, U_n$. The "cell" satisfying the assumption of Lemma 3 is assembled if none of the rules participating in construction of the sequence (creating or destroying tiles) failed due to absence of floating objects involved in the rule.

By definition, a rule is applied when all the objects at its left-hand side are present within the reaction radius r. Note that each rule of $\mathcal{M}_\Phi$ has a single floating object a_i at its left-hand side, $1 \le i \le 6$. by definition, the rule is applied when the floating object is located within a certain "reaction ball" of radius r with volume $v = \frac{4}{3}\pi r^3$. The ball is located in a (large) environment of a volume V, containing on average $V\epsilon(a_i)$ objects. Assuming their uniform random distribution, the probability that the ball contains no object a_i is

$$P(\emptyset) = \left(\frac{V - v}{V}\right)^{V\epsilon(a_i)} = \left(\frac{zv - v}{zv}\right)^{zv\epsilon(a_i)} = \left[\left(\frac{z-1}{z}\right)^z\right]^{v\epsilon(a_i)}$$

where we used substitution $z = V/v$. As the environment is large (unbounded), the expression in square brackets converges from bellow to e^{-1} with growing V. Observe furthermore that some of objects a_i in the ball can participate simple rules, too, hence only their fraction $\alpha \approx 1/2$ will be available for the chosen creation/destruction rule r_i. Therefore, the probability of application of a single instance of rule r_i using object a_i is

$$P(r) = 1 - P(\emptyset)^\alpha > 1 - e^{-v\alpha\epsilon(a_i)}.$$

To produce a randomly chosen sequence of tiles $U_1, \ldots, U_n$ enclosed in its "cell" by construction in the proof of Lemma 2 requires three rules applied in three initial steps, then cycles from $i = 1$ to $n-1$ such that $3i+4$ rules creating/destroying tiles $U_i/v_i/w$ are applied in each of them, and finally five steps to assemble the "cell." (We do not count rules creating/destroying perpendicular auxiliary rods as their failure is repaired in the next cycle.) Hence we get the total number

$$R(n) = 3 + 5 + \sum_{i=1}^{n-1}(3i + 4) = \frac{3}{2}n(n - 1) + 4(n - 1) + 8 = \mathcal{O}(n^2)$$

of applications of creation/destruction rules. Therefore, it is enough to choose the concentration $\epsilon(a_1)$ such that

$$P(r)^{R(n)} > (1 - e^{-v\alpha\epsilon(a_i)})^{R(n)} \geq \frac{3}{4}$$

to guarantee that a "cell" satisfying the assumption of Lemma 3 is assembled. Given the values of the constants $v\alpha \approx \frac{16}{3}\pi \approx 17$, it is easy to verify that a reasonable concentration satisfies this condition.

Therefore, if the formula Φ is satisfiable, then a cell representing its model is assembled with probability $> \frac{3}{4}$ and by Lemma 3 the object *yes* is released to the environment with probability at least $\frac{3}{4} \cdot \frac{3}{4} > \frac{1}{2}$ which concludes the proof.

$\square$

Corollary 1. NP $\subseteq$ MRP$^*_{MR_1}$, *where MR_1 is the class of M systems with rules contains a single floating object at their left-hand side.*

Proof. It is easy to verify that the family of M systems $\{\mathcal{M}_\Phi \mid \Phi$ is a formula in 3CNF$\}$ defined above is polynomially uniform by Turing machines. Then the statement follows by Lemma 4.

$\square$

6   Conclusions

We have further developed a recent new hybrid model, *M systems*, that leverages properties of self-assembly and P systems exhibit controlled growth and robustness akin to those observed in cell biology. The model is inspired by P systems and self-assembly and the new properties are obtained by introducing geometric concepts of shape and arrangement of atomic objects at specific locations. Basic abstract operations in the model include reactions among objects, their transport through protein channels, and their mutual interconnection, leading to construction and destruction of complex geometric structures, which are cell-inspired in the examples we have provided, but which can adopt virtually any geometric forms.

M systems has been proven to be computationally universal in the Turing sense [21], and in this paper we have studied their computational efficiency, showing that despite restrictions imposed by its geometry, the model is still capable, in a probabilistic way, to solve NP complete problems in polynomial time. As an added value, geometrical properties allow to identify some bottlenecks appearing in the simulated processes, as the concentration or kinetic bottlenecks. Note, e.g., that we define the result of computation by presence of a specific object(s) in the environment, but their concentration decreases rapidly as the size of the occupied part of the environment grows exponentially.

As some known models of P systems allow to solve even PSPACE-complete problems in polynomial time, a natural open question arises whether an analogous result can be obtained in the framework of M system, too.

We have further shown that M systems are universal in a perhaps more restricted but more biological sense, i.e., they exhibit a morphogenetic and homeostatic structure in their life cycle and can live forever by replication, unless environmental resources are consumed. We have also demonstrated their capability to grow complex cell-inspired information processing structures, providing a model of the cytoskeleton growth which in turn controls a process akin to biological mitosis.

We have also developed a software simulator of M systems to continue research on this models that is available at url sosik.zam.slu.cz/msystem or bmc.memphis.edu/cytos. Finally, we have begun to address several questions poised in by providing natural definitions of "injuries" and "self-repair." Many problems of interest arise. What kind of "injuries" will harm the model beyond repair? How exactly can injury be properly defined to establish more specific properties and limitations of self-healing? Third, adding evolutionary properties to the model is an intriguing possibility – the capability to evolve unenthropically towards more efficient behavior related to its specific goals, which can be of many kinds. To this end, the model should be equipped with a kind of abstract genetic code defining shapes of tiles and placement of connectors and other proteins on them. Perhaps the evolution of new floating objects and proteins and their mutual reactions should be allowed, too, reflecting the evolution of new "organic" molecules. This evolution may produce new development of models *in silico*, a kind of artificial life closer to biological life as we know it.

Acknowledgements. This work was supported by The Ministry of Education, Youth and Sports Of the Czech Republic from the National Programme of Sustainability (NPU II) project IT4Innovations Excellence in Science - LQ1602, and by the Silesian University in Opava under the Student Funding Scheme, project SGS/13/2016.

References

1. Banu-Demergian, I., Stefanescu, G.: The geometric membrane structure of finite interactive systems scenarios. In: Alhazov, A., Cojocaru, S., Gheorghe, M., Rogozhin, Y. (eds.) 14th International Conference on Membrane Computing, pp. 63–80. Institute of Mathematics and Computer Science, Academy of Sciences of Moldova, Chisinau (2013)
2. Barbuti, R., Maggiolo-Schettini, A., Milazzo, P., Pardini, G.: Spatial calculus of looping sequences. Theor. Comput. Sci. **412**(43), 5976–6001 (2011)
3. Barbuti, R., Maggiolo-Schettini, A., Milazzo, P., Pardini, G.: Simulation of spatial P system models. Theor. Comput. Sci. **529**, 11–45 (2014)
4. Barbuti, R., Maggiolo-Schettini, A., Milazzo, P., Pardini, G., Tesei, L.: Spatial P systems. Nat. Comput. **10**(1), 3–16 (2011)

5. Bernardini, F., Brijder, R., Cavaliere, M., Franco, G., Hoogeboom, H.J., Rozenberg, G.: On aggregation in multiset-based self-assembly of graphs. Nat. Comput. **10**(1), 17–38 (2011)
6. Bernardini, F., Brijder, R., Rozenberg, G., Zandron, C.: Multiset-based self-assembly of graphs. Fundamenta Informaticae **75**(1–4), 49–75 (2007)
7. Bernardini, F., Gheorghe, M., Krasnogor, N., Giavitto, J.-L.: On self-assembly in population P systems. In: Calude, C.S., Dinneen, M.J., Păun, G., Pérez-Jímenez, M.J., Rozenberg, G. (eds.) UC 2005. LNCS, vol. 3699, pp. 46–57. Springer, Heidelberg (2005). https://doi.org/10.1007/11560319_6
8. Blount, P., Sukharev, S.I., Moe, P.C., Schroeder, M.J., Guy, H., Kung, C.: Membrane topology and multimeric structure of a mechanosensitive channel protein of escherichia coli. EMBO J. **15**(18), 4798–4805 (1996)
9. Bourgine, P., Lesne, A.: Morphogenesis: Origins of Patterns and Shapes. Springer complexity. Springer, Heidelberg (2010)
10. Cardelli, L., Gardner, P.: Processes in space. In: Ferreira, F., Löwe, B., Mayordomo, E., Mendes Gomes, L. (eds.) CiE 2010. LNCS, vol. 6158, pp. 78–87. Springer, Heidelberg (2010). https://doi.org/10.1007/978-3-642-13962-8_9
11. Cavaliere, M., Mardare, R., Sedwards, S.: A multiset-based model of synchronizing agents: computability and robustness. Theor. Comput. Sci. **391**(3), 216–238 (2008)
12. Krasnogor, N., Gustafson, S., Pelta, D., Verdegay, J.: Systems Self-Assembly: Multidisciplinary Snapshots. Studies in Multidisciplinarity. Elsevier Science, Amsterdam (2011)
13. Manca, V., Pardini, G.: Morphogenesis through moving membranes. Nat. Comput. **13**(3), 403–419 (2014)
14. Pérez-Jiménez, M., Romero-Jiménez, A., Sancho-Caparrini, F.: Complexity classes in models of cellular computing with membranes. Nat. Comput. **2**, 265–285 (2003)
15. Păun, A., Popa, B.: P systems with proteins on membranes. Fundamenta Informaticae **72**(4), 467–483 (2006)
16. Păun, A., Popa, B.: P systems with proteins on membranes and membrane division. In: Ibarra, O.H., Dang, Z. (eds.) DLT 2006. LNCS, vol. 4036, pp. 292–303. Springer, Heidelberg (2006). https://doi.org/10.1007/11779148_27
17. Păun, G.: Membrane Computing - An Introduction. Springer, Berlin (2002)
18. Păun, G., Rozenberg, G., Salomaa, A. (eds.): The Oxford Handbook of Membrane Computing. Oxford University Press, Oxford (2010)
19. Robinson, K., Messerli, M.: Left/right, up/down: the role of endogenous electrical fields as directional signals in development, repair and invasion. Bioessays **25**, 759766 (2003)
20. Schrödinger, E.: What is Life? The Physical Aspect of the Living Cell. Trinity College, Dublin (1944)
21. Sosík, P., Smolka, V., Drastík, J., Moore, T., Garzon, M.: Morphogenetic and homeostatic self-assembled systems. In: Patitz, M.J., Stannett, M. (eds.) UCNC 2017. LNCS, vol. 10240, pp. 144–159. Springer, Cham (2017). https://doi.org/10.1007/978-3-319-58187-3_11
22. Tangirala, K., Caragea, D.: Generating features using burrows wheeler transformation for biological sequence classification. In: Pastor, O., et al. (eds.) Proceedings of the International Conference on Bioinformatics Models, Methods and Algorithms, pp. 196–203. SciTePress (2014)
23. Tomita, M.: Whole-cell simulation: a grand challenge of the 21st century. Trends Biotechnol. **19**(6), 205–210 (2001)
24. Turing, A.: The chemical basis of morphogenesis. Philos. Trans. R. Soc. Lond. B **237**, 7–72 (1950)

25. Watson, J., Crick, F.: A structure for deoxyribose nucleic acid. Nature **171**, 737–738 (1953)
26. Winfree, E.: Models of experimental self-assembly. Ph.D. thesis, Caltech (1998)
27. Winfree, E.: Self-healing tile sets. In: Chen, J., Jonoska, N., Rozenberg, G. (eds.) Nanotechnology: Science and Computation. Natural Computing Series, pp. 55–66. Springer, Heidelberg (2006). https://doi.org/10.1007/3-540-30296-4_4
28. Maxwell-Boltzmann distribution, Wikipedia (cit 2017-1-29). https://en.wikipedia.org/wiki/Maxwell-Boltzmann_distribution
29. Ziegler, G.: Lectures on Polytopes. Graduate Texts in Mathematics. Springer, New York (1995)

Author Index

Adorna, Henry N.   1, 151
Alhazov, Artiom   1, 15
Aman, Bogdan   40

Bakir, Mehmet Emin   183
Barbuti, Roberto   54
Bradík, Jaroslav   270
Buño, Kelvin C.   151

Cabarle, Francis George C.   151
Cienciala, Luděk   88
Ciencialová, Lucie   88
Ciobanu, Gabriel   40
Csuhaj-Varjú, Erzsébet   88, 105, 118

Drastík, Jan   270

Förster, Benjamin   129
Freund, Rudolf   15

Garzon, Max   270
Gori, Roberta   54

Hernandez, Nestine Hope S.   151
Hinze, Thomas   129

Ipate, Florentin   183
Ivanov, Sergiu   15

Juayong, Richelle Ann B.   151

Kántor, Kristóf   167
Konur, Savas   183

Lefticaru, Raluca   183
Leporati, Alberto   196

Manzoni, Luca   196
Mauri, Giancarlo   196
Michele Pinna, G.   245
Milazzo, Paolo   54

Nicolescu, Radu   214

Orellana-Martín, David   74

Pan, Linqiang   1, 230
Pérez-Jiménez, Mario J.   74
Porreca, Antonio E.   196

Riscos-Núñez, Agustín   74

Sempere, José M.   262
Smolka, Vladimír   270
Song, Bosheng   1, 230
Sosík, Petr   270
Stannett, Mike   183

Valencia-Cabrera, Luis   74
Vaszil, György   167
Verlan, Sergey   105, 118

Zandron, Claudio   196
Zhang, Gexiang   230

Printed in the United States
By Bookmasters